ROUTLEDGE HANDBOOK ON VICTIMS' ISSUES IN CRIMINAL JUSTICE

The *Routledge Handbook on Victims' Issues in Criminal Justice* is a comprehensive and authoritative handbook on current issues, with a distinctive emphasis on the delivery of suitable and effective services. The editor provides an introduction and conclusion to the handbook, synthesizing original contributions from current leaders in the field, surveying victims' rights in the United States, victim participation in the criminal justice system, victims' welfare and needs, and most notably the services that have been developed in response. A section on special populations in the United States brings focus to current and emerging issues faced within the country, while a section covering international and transnational victimization explores globalization and the implications of other legal traditions and systems.

This handbook addresses the crucial and complex topic of victims' issues, examining both societal and governmental reactions to victims' concerns and acquainting readers with the issues that discord may cause.

Cliff Roberson, LL.M., Ph.D., is an Emeritus Professor of Criminal Justice at Washburn University, Topeka, Kansas, and a retired Professor of Criminology at California State University, Fresno, California. His educational background includes a Ph.D. in Human Behavior from U.S. International University; an LL.M., in Criminal Law, Criminology, and Psychiatry from George Washington University; a J.D. from American University; a B.A. in Political Science from the University of Missouri; and one year of post-graduate study at the University of Virginia School of Law.

His previous academic experiences include Associate Vice-President for Academic Affairs, Arkansas Tech University; Dean of Arts and Sciences, University of Houston, Victoria; Director of Programs, National College of District Attorneys; Professor of Criminology and Director of Justice Center, California State University, Fresno; and Assistant Professor of Criminal Justice, St. Edwards University. His non-academic experience includes services as a U.S. Marine Corps infantry officer, as well as service as a military judge and marine judge advocate. Other legal experience includes time as a Trial Supervisor, Office State Counsel for Offenders, Texas Board of Criminal Justice, and judge pro tempore in the California Courts. He has authored or co-authored over 60 books and texts on legal subjects.

"Within victimology, in addition to journal articles, textbooks, and research reports, there is a continuing need to fill in the gaps. This *Handbook on Victims' Issues*, edited by Cliff Roberson, will stand out as such a document. This scholarly text offers a variety of information, and could serve as an excellent companion anthology for an advanced course."— **John P. Dussich**, *Ph.D., Emeritus Professor, California State University*

"Roberson's *Handbook on Victims' Issues in Criminal Justice* is an indispensable resource for any criminal justice professional who deals with crime victims. The major topics are thoroughly covered, as well as cutting-edge topics, including restorative justice and LGBT victims."—**Robert Winters,** *J.D., Professor, Kaplan University*

ROUTLEDGE HANDBOOK ON VICTIMS' ISSUES IN CRIMINAL JUSTICE

Edited by Cliff Roberson

Routledge
Taylor & Francis Group
LONDON AND NEW YORK

First published 2017 by Routledge

2 Park Square, Milton Park, Abingdon, Oxfordshire OX14 4RN
52 Vanderbilt Avenue, New York, NY 10017

Routledge is an imprint of the Taylor & Francis Group, an informa business

First issued in paperback 2019

Library of Congress Cataloging in Publication Data
A catalog record for this book has been requested

ISBN: 978-1-138-18471-8 (hbk)
ISBN: 978-0-367-20491-4 (pbk)

Typeset in Bembo
by Swales & Willis Ltd, Exeter, Devon, UK

CONTENTS

TABLES

PREFACE

The idea of a handbook on victimology and victim services originated while attending a World Society of Victimology Congress in Perth, Australia. As I listened to the inspiring presentations by individuals who are dedicated to providing the best services possible to victims of crime, I wondered if presentations could be included in a handbook that would be available to both current and future students and professionals in victims' services. After obtaining the support of Routledge publisher professionals, I requested chapter contributions from the leaders in the fields of victims' services and victimology. I was surprised at how many professionals responded and submitted chapters in their areas of expertise.

The handbook is divided into four parts. Part I is an overall introduction to victim services. Part II discusses victim issues regarding specific types of victimization. Part III discusses victim services and Part IV discusses various victimology and victim services' organization. Also included in Part IV is the final chapter, which deals with the issues involving victims and the media. While I am listed as the sole editor of the handbook, numerous others have helped bring this project to life including the Routledge professionals: Ellen Boyne, Mickey Braswell, and Eve Strillacci. In addition, I appreciate the work of the production editor Adam Bell and the copy-editor, Ting Baker, in correcting all the mistakes in the manuscript and producing a professional-quality publication.

Cliff Roberson

FOREWORD

Elena Azaola

For many years, the victim has been a forgotten party in the world's criminal justice systems. The victims' rights movement has helped change that and now in most countries the victim is an integral part of any criminal case. The victims' movement has also helped victims and reduced their pain of victimization.

Having spent the majority of my professional life advocating for human rights and the rights of crime victims, this movement is seen as a welcomed and much needed reform to the justice systems. There are a few countries that still need to join the movement and in all countries there is still a lot more that needs to be done to assist victims and to alleviate their suffering.

While the victims' rights movement has accomplished many goals and reforms in most of the world's justice systems, it is not enough. We need to continue and stress that our goals are to ensure that each and every victim receives help, counseling, and, if needed, compensation. Instead of being a silent party in a criminal case, the victim's status has been elevated and his or her rights should continue to be one of the primary considerations of law enforcement, courts, and corrections systems. The professionals in each country's criminal justice system should work on ensuring that never again will the victim be the forgotten party in any criminal case.

A review of the chapters presented in this handbook indicates that the subjects cover critical issues in victimology and victims' services. I also note that the list of contributors and their achievements are very impressive. This handbook should increase the base of knowledge in the field. While the victims' movement started late in comparison with the other criminal justice professions, it appears that with texts such as the handbook that the dedicated individuals in the victim's rights movement are working overtime to catch up.

PART I

Introduction to Victims' Rights

The first four chapters of this handbook are designed to introduce the reader to the rights of a victim in the criminal justice system. Generally, victims have eight categories of rights. The categories are:

- right to be treated with dignity, respect, and sensitivity;
- right to be informed as to the proceeding in the case;
- right of protection for the victim and his or her family;
- right to apply for compensation;
- right to restitution;
- right to prompt return of personal property;
- right to a speedy trial;
- the enforcement of his or her rights as a victim.

The first chapter in the handbook, Issues in Victim Services, provides a general overview of the treatment and assistance programs for crime victims. Chapter 2 discusses federal legislations on victims' rights and services. Also included in Chapter 2 is an overview of the victims' movement in the United States. Chapter 3 discusses victims' assistance programs and provides suggested reforms that are needed to improve their effectiveness.

Chapter 4 explains the victim–offender overlap, situational and social interactionist theories, as well as social and structural processes. In addition, the chapter looks at the role of life course perspective in the understanding of victimization.

Chapter 5 explains the historical development of victims' rights from a comparative perspective and identifies and discusses specific issues hindering the implementation of victims' rights legislation across cultures. The chapter also develops a conceptual framework of the role of victims in the criminal justice system.

1
ISSUES IN VICTIM SERVICES

Heather Zaykowski

Keywords

victim services; service utilization; eligibility; service barriers; service delivery; victim blame; service access; victims with special needs

Objectives

After studying this chapter, the reader should understand:

- What are victim services.
- Who is most likely to access and receive victim services.
- Barriers to service utilization.
- Issues with service delivery and victim satisfaction.
- Considerations for victims with special needs.

Introduction

Victim services are a broad scope of assistance programs for victims of crime such as helping victims with filing compensation claims, hotlines, legal aid, counseling, support groups, and financial assistance. Some service agencies specialize in one specific form of support, while others provide more extensive wrap-around services. Although receiving support from policymakers, practitioners, and victims alike, there are a number of important issues regarding victim services. First, despite the scope and nature of services available to victims, very few victims actually seek help from such support agencies. Research has identified a number of reasons why victim service utilization is low including lack of awareness that services exist, an inability to access services, and perceived or actual ineligibility for services offered.

Another key issue is whether victims are satisfied with the services they receive. Although research finds that victims who receive services are generally satisfied, there are some differences in terms of victim expectations and what they actually get, as well as what service providers are capable of providing. For example, although a great deal of funding has been allocated to support victim services, individual providers may lack training and resources to meet victim needs. This chapter will examine the origin of victim services and examine these key issues and more.

Overview of Victim Services

The Victim's Rights Movement inspired the creation and growth of victim service agencies. It was inspired by the Civil Rights Movements of the mid-to late twentieth century and converging interests between liberal activists and the conservative "tough on crime" movement during the 1970s and 1980s (Simon 2007). The first victim services were established in St. Louis Missouri, San Francisco, California and Washington DC in 1972. These initial programs emphasized assistance for victims of rape and domestic violence (National Center for Victims of Crime 2016). However, support for services was arguably most widely supported after President Reagan commissioned a task force to document the problems faced by crime victims in 1982. This report provided dozens of recommendations for enhancing support for victims of crime including giving victims greater voice and participation in the criminal justice process and additional funding for victim services (Mastrocinque 2010).

Today, every state has programs available to victims for general or specific types of victimization. Public and private victim services programs receive federal, state, and tribal funding from a variety of sources, but most notably the Crime Victims Fund ("the Fund"), established by the Victims of Crime Act of 1984 (VOCA). The Fund is supported by criminal fines, forfeitures, and donations. However, nearly all funds come from criminal fines. According to a study in 2005, 98 percent of funding was attributed to offender fines. Between 2009 and 2010, $4.1 billion was deposited into the Fund (U.S. Department of Justice 2012).

According to the Office for Victims of Crime Online Directory, more than 10,000 victim service programs had been identified through their directory in the United States and abroad.[1] Similarly, the National Center for Victims of Crime Resource Center provides a searchable database with over 13,000 service providers.[2] Other sources indicate that over 3,000 organizations provide services specifically for domestic violence across the United States and Canada.[3] Victim services cover a wide variety of assistance including but not limited to advocacy/guidance, counseling/therapy, financial assistance, housing/shelter, legal services and medical assistance. Table 1.1 provides an overview of the types of services that exist for victims.

Table 1.1 Types of Victim Services

Service type	*Description*
Advocacy/guidance	Victims' services may include a victim advocate, hotline, or other method of information delivery and assistance dealing with the process of navigating victim services and the criminal justice system. For example, an advocate may help victims understand how to file a victim compensation claim, where to seek counseling, or accompany a victim to the hospital.
Counseling/therapy	Victimization is often a traumatic event that may require immediate, short- or long-term counseling and therapy. Treatment may include mental health services, group and/or family counseling, or individual sessions with a professional.
Financial assistance	Financial assistance may be crucial to victims to cover lost wages, transportation, housing, medical, and counseling/therapy. Although laws and programs vary, every state offers some kind of victim compensation program. However, there are limitations as to which victims may be eligible and the time frame in which victims can apply. In addition to compensation, which is often a funding source of last resort, victims may file claims through their insurance or receive assistance through restitution, in which the perpetrator is required to make payments to the victim.
Housing/shelter	Housing is an important need for victims, particularly those who leave domestic violence situations. Shelters provide victims with a temporary space to live for themselves and their children. Shelters may provide short or longer term safe spaces for victims to live and may also provide other types of victims' services or referrals to services. Some compensation programs help victims with relocation costs.

Legal services	The criminal justice system is difficult to navigate for victims. Legal services can also help victims understand their options and rights with regard the criminal justice process, civil suits, or child custody disputes. Victims may also need legal services quickly such as emergency restraining orders.
Medical assistance	Although not always considered under the umbrella of victim services, medical assistance is obviously crucial for injured victims. Victim service agencies may also provide some medical services such as forensic examinations for victims of sexual assault. In addition, hospitals may hire medical staff with specific expertise for treating crime victims.

Barriers to Service Utilization

Few victims actually seek help from victim services despite increasing growth and support for crime victim remedies. In an analysis of data from the National Crime Victimization Survey (NCVS), the largest ongoing collection of data on crime victimization in the United States, between 1993 and 2009 only 9 percent of victims of serious violent crime (rape or sexual assault, robbery and aggravated assault) aged 12 and older sought help from services (Langton 2011). Further, only 12 percent of victims who experienced socio-emotional problems sought help from services between 2009 and 2012 (Langton & Truman 2015).

Evidence from state and local studies indicate similarly low contact with service agencies (Campbell et al. 2001; Fugate et al. 2005; Henning & Klesges 2002; Keilitz et al. 1997; Sims et al. 2005; Ullman & Filipas 2001). In a telephone survey of Pennsylvania residents who had experienced victimization in the past 12 months, Sims et al. (2005) found that only 3 percent of crime victims reported using victim service programs. Keilitz and colleagues (1997) found that among women seeking protection orders, one third received assistance from community services, with fewer receiving services from counseling (12.6 percent), private legal services (11.2 percent) and government services (6.3 percent). Among women who were victims of domestic violence, findings by Henning and Klesges (2002) showed that only 14.9 percent of victims sought assistance. While estimates in general remain low, victim services use appears to be higher for rape/sexual assault victims compared with other offenses. For example, research by Campbell et al. (2001) indicated that nearly 40 percent of rape victims received mental health services and 21 percent had contact with rape crisis centers. Ullman and Filipas (2001) found that just over half of victims had contacted mental health counselors and approximately 14 percent sought help from rape crisis centers.

Contact with victim services also varies by demographic characteristics of the victim and the circumstances of the crime incident. A greater proportion of females report that they had assistance from victim services compared to males. Victim services utilization is also greater for those who are older (35 and over) compared with those who are 18 to 24. Victims who are of more than one race, American Indian/Alaskan Native and White (non-Hispanic) received assistance more than other racial and ethnic groups (Langton 2011). Data also indicate that the primary seekers of services are victims of known perpetrators and victims of rape and sexual assault (Langton 2011; Zaykowski 2014).

Low service utilization has led to a growing body of research examining barriers to victim services. Of some of the most prominent limitations, issues include:

- Victims lack of knowledge about services;
- Victims do not want or think they need services;
- Victims lack access to services;
- Victims fear re-victimization and blame by service providers;
- Victims are not eligible to receive services.

Victims Lack Knowledge about Services or Do Not Want Them

A key reason why victims do not seek services is because they are not clear that such services exist or think that they wouldn't be eligible for services (Fugate et al. 2005; Logan et al. 2005; Sims et al. 2005). For example, Sims et al. (2005) found that 40 percent of victims stated that they did not know what victim services offered. In another study, one-quarter of women who were victims of domestic violence and sexual assault did not think there were any services available in their community (Zweig et al. 2002). Logan et al. 2005 found that many rural victims lacked knowledge that services existed. This lack of knowledge was propelled by the reality that rape just wasn't a topic that was discussed in the community. In the same study, urban participants had a misunderstanding about the services available to them. Urban participants noted that the name of services as "trauma" or "crisis" meant that only urgent needs would be addressed (Logan et al. 2005).

Victim awareness of services is shaped by resources available to providers to advertise and referrals. An important link between victims and services are agents of criminal justice. If these individuals do not inform victims that they are eligible for services or that such services exist, victims may never know. Police officers are one of the first contacts a victim has with the criminal justice system and maybe the only one. Therefore, police referrals make them gatekeepers to victim services (Kendall et al. 2009; Zaykowski 2014). Police reporting is also important to obtain specific services. Many victim compensation programs require filing a police report. In one study using data from the NCVS, victims reporting to the police were *three times* more likely to seek help from victim services. Reporting had the greatest increase in the likelihood of receiving services for victims of intimate partner and family violence (Zaykowski 2014).

Of course, there are also issues and limitations with reporting to the police. Only half or fewer of victimizations of nonfatal violent crimes are reported to the police according to the National Crime Victimization Survey. Reporting rates do vary by type of crime. In 2014 about 60 percent of robbery victimizations and 58 percent of aggravated assault victimizations were reported compared with one-third of rape/sexual assault victimizations and 40 percent of simple assaults (Truman & Langton 2015). Victimizations are more likely to be reported to police when the victim is female, married and older, when the victim is injured, when a weapon is used by the offender, multiple offenders are involved, and the incident takes place in a private location (Baumer & Lauritsen 2010). Relying on police as a service link is particularly problematic for victims of sexual assault who are less likely to report compared with other violent crimes, yet are more likely to cause socio-emotional problems (Langton & Truman 2014). When asked what is the most important reason why they did not report to the police, victims of violence stated that they dealt with it in another way or considered it a personal matter (Langton et al. 2012).

It's possible that the reasons why victims do not report to the police are the same as why they do not seek help from services (Stohr 2005). Victims may simply not be interested in services (Stohr 2005; Sims et al. 2005; 2006). Victims who previously sought help from victim services or other social service systems may have had negative experiences and therefore are reluctant to reach out to victim services (Sims et al. 2006). In a study of Pennsylvania services, the two most often reported reasons for not seeking help from services were that victims received the help they needed from friends and family (49 percent) and that they did not need any help (48 percent). Other prominent reasons for not seeking help included preference to solve their own problems, did not have time to get involved, and that victim service programs could not help someone like them (Sims et al. 2005).

Victim Fear of Re-victimization and Self-blame

Another issue that affects service assistance is the feeling of self-blame (Logan et al. 2004; Logan et al. 2005; Zweig et al. 2002). Women indicate that they are embarrassed to seek victim assistance (Logan et al. 2004). In addition, victims feel that they don't deserve service assistance, that it was their fault, that they feel guilty, or that no one would believe them (Logan et al. 2005). Research has indicated that women who are victimized often feel responsible for the harms they experience, particularly if they were under the influence of alcohol or other substances. Nearly half of the women in a study by Zweig and colleagues indicated that victims feared being blamed by service providers and that they would not be taken seriously (Zweig et al. 2002). Victims fears are also propelled by stigmatization in their own communities in which family and friends encourage victims to keep quiet (Logan et al. 2005).

Access to Services

Access to services is another critical barrier for many victims of crime. While victims in urban, suburban and resource rich areas may have numerous services and outreach support, victims in rural and more disadvantaged communities are unlikely to have the same opportunities. Location, in particular, plays a large role in limiting victims from seeking assistance. Research finds that many victims in rural communities lack access to Internet/telephone services, transportation, or simply are too far from resources in which travel would pose a great burden (Logan et al. 2015). This is particularly complex for situations where victims are harmed by a domestic abuser and are continuously prohibited from access to communication and transportation, and separated from friends and family (Dekeseredy & Schwartz 2009).

Access may also be limited by cost. Victims who lack financial resources often face difficulty in accessing services (Logan, et al. 2004; Zweig et al. 2002). Logan et al. (2004) found that many women reported that the cost of services was too high and would not be covered by their insurance. In a study of rural rape survivors, victims indicated that cost of services was a big issue. Victims said that if they didn't have insurance they couldn't get the service they needed. Participants also felt that this was the dominant belief among victims even if it wasn't true (Logan et al. 2005). Although many victim services are supported through the Victim Fund and other resources and therefore are low or no cost to victims, some services and victims who do not meet eligibility criteria will not be compensated (Newmark et al. 2003).

Victim Eligibility and Compatibility for Services

Another challenge with victim services is that although a wide variety of services exist, they may not be suitable for a large portion of victims. As Trulson (2005) argues, "although the victims' rights movement was meant to be inclusive of crime victims, a closer examination shows that *exclusion is everywhere*" (p. 399, emphasis original). A prominent exclusion criterion is victims who contribute to the crime. In other words, victims need to be "innocent" to meet legal definitions and eligibility for series (Trulson 2005). Although commonly presented images and discourse on victimization emphasize stark differences between who is the victim and who is the offender, in reality, these lines are frequently less clear (Christie 1986). Victimization is also often linked to prior offending or may lead to future offending (Lauritsen & Laub 2007).

Many victim compensation funds require that victims do not "contribute" to the crime, while some also prevent victims from receiving benefits if they have prior offenses. This may also extend to family members for funeral and burial cost supports (Newmark et al. 2003; Zaykowski 2015).

Definitions of "who is a victim" vary widely across states, shaping which types of victims are viewed as more worthy than others (Trulson 2005). There are also limitations for victims who are otherwise misbehaving at the time of the incident. In a study by Hatten and Moore (2010), one quarter of police officers said they would not be likely to request a victim advocate if the victim was under the influence of a controlled substance.

In addition to victim worthiness, few services are directed to males or the types of victimization that males are more likely to experience. While female victims have higher victimization in intimate partner settings, males have higher victimization rates across other forms of serious victimization including aggravated assault, robbery and homicide, and tend to be harmed by their peers, acquaintances and strangers (Catalano 2013; Truman & Langton 2015). Therefore, traditional victim services may not be appropriate for many male victims. Designing services for male victims may be challenging. Research has shown that males are less likely to seek help than females across multiple help-seeking domains including for health problems and reporting to the police (Galdas et al. 2005; Zaykowski 2014). Male help-seeking is shaped by hegemonic masculinity. It is counter to a masculine identity to indicate need or support. Instead, men learn to demonstrate strength and self-reliance (Galdas et al. 2005). Furthermore, adopting an identity as a "victim" contradicts the notion of "what it means to be a man" (Sered 2014).

Issues with Service Delivery

Despite the barriers and reasons for not seeking services, several issues exist with regard to service delivery. Research on victim satisfaction and challenges from perspectives of service providers indicate the following issues:

- Victims feel re-victimized by service providers;
- Services available are not the types of services victims need;
- Victim service providers need additional resources and training.

A primary concern with victim services is that victims may be unsatisfied by the services they receive. In a study of rape survivors, researchers examined victim satisfaction with legal, medical, mental health, rape crisis and religious/community services and systems. The latter three types of services were viewed as "healing" by at least 70 percent of victims. However, less than half of victims said the same for medical services and only one-third viewed experiences with the legal system as healing (Campbell et al. 2001). In another study, service providers reported that some victims were dually traumatized both by their original victimization, then by victim services. In addition, participants noted that victims with substance use and mental health problems were more likely to be questioned by the system when it comes to credibility. These victims were more likely to be blamed or not taken seriously (Zweig et al. 2002).

Victims who access services have certain expectations of the types of help they will receive and the nature of these services. Although victims overall were fairly satisfied with services, Skogan and colleagues (1990) found that victims would have wanted to talk to someone about their feelings, learn how to avoid becoming a victim, protect themselves, improve home security, and repair damaged property. A needs assessment conducted in Denver suggested that victims would have liked services at the crime scene, protection, and were interested in receiving updates about the status of their case (Stark 2000). In addition to not receiving the types of services of interest, victims also experience issues with navigating bureaucracy, dealing with staff incompetence and lack of training, and believe that providers need to be more sensitive (Glenn & Goodman 2015; Logan et al. 2005). Victims feel that it is harmful to keep telling the story of the victimization over and over again and the ongoing chain of referrals (Logan et al. 2005). Victims also desire greater staff sensitivity and knowledge to promote recovery (Glenn & Goodman 2015). In one study, victims were angered that hospital staff did not know the procedure for conducting a rape exam. Victims were also concerned about confidentiality. Service providers known to the victim and more tight-knit communities have led to private information becoming public (Logan et al. 2005).

Despite extensive growth in funding for victim services, many remain understaffed or ill equipped to achieve their desired goals and outreach to victims. Staff may not have proper training to deal with victims or to meet their needs (Glenn & Goodman 2015). One-quarter of service providers in one study indicated that a key barrier for victims is that they lacked services in their community (Zweig et al. 2002). However, it is also important to note that although few victims seek assistance, this doesn't mean that some service agencies are not overwhelmed by clients in need (Stohr 2005). For example, victim advocates met victims at the hospital, but due to distance it took a long time. The time spent with one counselor was then limited because the same counselor served so many people across a large geography (Logan et al. 2005). Services are also often not equipped to address longer term needs of victims, which may be recognized much after the crime incident or continue for a long period of time (Monroe et al. 2005; Sims et al. 2006).

Finally, an important component of service delivery is that victim outcomes show positive change. Although the goals will vary across different types of services, some key objectives include preventing future victimization, improving feelings of self-worth, reducing trauma symptoms, and increasing awareness of resources. In an analysis of victim services funded by the STOP Formula Grants Program, researchers found that women benefited from victim services and that services were most effective when coordinated with the legal system and other local agencies. However, this study did not find that victims in funded communities had greater levels of knowledge about services (Zweig et al. 2003). An evaluation of a law-based advocacy intervention found that women who received assistance from law students reported lower rates of re-victimization compared with women without advocacy from a sample of women seeking temporary restraining orders, but were not significantly different with regard to depressive symptoms (Bell & Goodman 2001). In a last example, an analysis of services to rape survivors indicated that both hotline and advocacy contacts improved knowledge and feelings of support, as well as improvements in mental health for counseling clients. However, it is important to note that about one-quarter of survivors and other seekers of knowledge such as their friends/family did not participate in the study due to elevated distress (Wasco et al. 2004).

Services for Victims with Special Needs

Existing victim services are often limited in handling populations with unique needs and circumstances. Although there are extensive forms of needs for victims, the following examples are highlighted below:

- legal challenges with undocumented, refugee and immigrant populations;
- cultural and linguistic differences;
- victims with disabilities;
- LGBT victims.

Research on immigrant and refugee populations cites concern over deportation and language issues as barriers to seeking assistance (Clawson & Dutch 2008; Reina & Lohman 2015; Salcido & Adelman 2004). Abuse pertaining to citizenship status has also further prevented victims from seeking help. Abusers may threaten "outing" victims if they tell the authorities (Hass et al. 2000). Many immigrant groups may also be unaware of laws that may protect them (Raj & Silverman 2002). Victims who are undocumented are further disadvantaged by lack of income and access to education (Orloff & Garcia 2013).

In addition to linguistic and cultural issues, victims of human trafficking also remain an underserved population for a number of reasons. Human traffickers detach victims from the outside world through psychosocial coercion, restricting communication, confiscating legal documents, or threatening to report victims to the police. By the nature of their victimization, these victims are often detached from the outside world and lack knowledges about services that exist. It is also difficult to identify human trafficking victims because of these circumstances (Hodge 2014).

Human trafficking victim services are supported through the Trafficking Victims Protection Act of 2000 (TVPA), which designated the Department of Health and Human Services responsible for handling these victim services. One of their key roles is to certify international victims who are adults to be eligible for services. Without this certification, undocumented victims could be considered criminals and face deportation. This status is similar to that of a certified refugee (Clawson & Dutch 2008; Peters 2013). International victims under 18 are given a letter of eligibility but do not need certification. Domestically trafficked victims do not require such certification. However, domestic victims also do not receive the protections and services provided under the TVPA (Peters 2013). Several challenges exist with TVPA protections. A requirement of the certification is that human trafficking victims must comply with law enforcement with their ongoing investigations. Further, even though victims may be determined eligible for services, it is often the case that such services may not be available or accessible. With the broader population of human trafficking victims, little literature exists on domestically trafficked adults as agencies do not report on this population (Clawson & Dutch 2008).

Another group identified with unique circumstances are American Indian and Alaska Native (AIAN) women and children who are believed to be particularly high risk populations for domestic trafficking (Pierce & Koepplinger 2011) and violent victimization generally (Bachman et al. 2008). Violence against native populations extends from a long history of violence at the hands of the United States government and colonists (Smith 1999). Current responses to victims is further complicated by the complex jurisdictional oversight, which may include federal, state, local, and tribal police (Bachman et al. 2008). AIAN women today have higher rates of rape and sexual assault relative to Black and White women (Bachman et al. 2010). In addition to barriers already mentioned including geographic access to services, and language barriers, Native victim needs may conflict with services available. AIAN populations may favor Native Healers or other local culturally sensitive interventions (Hamby 1998).

Another underserved population is persons with disabilities. Some estimates suggest that people with disabilities are victimized at higher rates relative to persons without disabilities. Research has found that many victim services do not have the necessary accommodations for victims with disabilities (Frantz et al. 2006; Mansell et al. 1992). In a study of Pennsylvania domestic violence and rape crisis centers, no provider was in full compliance with Americans with Disabilities Act guidelines. Although most programs had accidental disability features such as ramps, handicap bathrooms and space for mobility around the building, fewer services incorporated disability needs into their program structure such as asking clients if they needed accommodations or providing materials in a variety of formats such as audio or Braille (Frantz et al. 2006). Persons with disabilities and other dependent populations such as the elderly are further inhibited due to reliance on caretakers, who may be the source of abuse (Lachs & Pillemer 2004).

In a final example, although findings vary across studies, it is generally found that rates of victimization among LGBT populations are higher than their heterosexual counterparts. Data from the National Intimate Partner and Sexual Violence Survey estimate that lifetime prevalence of violence by an intimate partner (including rape, physical violence and/or stalking) was experienced by nearly half of lesbian and just over 60 percent of bisexual women, and among one in four gay men and almost 40 of bisexual men—compared with 35 percent of heterosexual women and 29 percent of heterosexual men (Walters et al. 2013). LGBT victims have difficulty locating services and often find them harmful (Edwards et al. 2015). Research finds that service providers are unlikely to help battered men (Glenn & Goodman 2015; Merrill & Wolfe 2000). In many cases, victims of same-sex relationships are not eligible for services such as shelter protection. Renzetti (1992) found that shelter providers perceived their services to be available for heterosexual women. Shelter policy and procedures in place to protect female victims from male abusers would not shield lesbian victims against female abusers. Among those able to receive services, victims are more satisfied when treatment is tailored to LBGT victim populations (Edwards et al. 2015; St. Pierre & Senn 2010).

Summary

In summary, this chapter examined issues with victim services including (1) victim underutilization of services; (2) issues with service delivery; and (3) challenges for populations with special needs. One of the most consistent issues illustrated across the literature is that most victims do not seek help from services. Research examining why suggests that victims do not know that services exist, do not want services, believe services won't be helpful, cannot access services, fear re-victimization by service-providers, or are not eligible. Among victims who receive services, some reasons why victims do not feel satisfied are because the specific services they need are not available, they feel re-victimized by service providers, or feel that staff require additional training and greater sensitivity to victim needs. Although funding for victim services has increased over time, many service providers feel limited in their ability to adequately serve victim needs and promote their services to victims. Finally, some victim populations have additional needs that are not always able to be addressed by service providers. These needs may include barriers such as legal knowledge, citizenship status, cultural and/or linguistic differences, victim disability, and sexual orientation.

In light of these issues, there are several directions that may improve victim services. First, it must be recognized that many victims do not seek services because they do not want them (Stohr 2005). However, it should be determined if the reasons victims don't want services are because they haven't yet felt trauma associated with victimization, because they do not trust service providers, or because they may not see themselves as "victims." If any of these reasons are the case, then services should aim reach out to victims beyond the immediate aftermath of the incident (Sims et al. 2006) and to be tailored to the local and cultural context in which victimization occurs. This may include non-traditional sources and forms of services (Sered 2014).

Second, one of the most common responses from victims was that they were unaware services existed or were misinformed about their eligibility for services (Sims et al. 2005; Logan et al. 2005). Given limited resources available to providers for outreach, researchers have suggested that the police play a key role in referring victims to services (Kendall et al. 2009; Zaykowski 2014). However, victim distrust of the police may preclude them from reporting and therefore miss a key referral source. There are also limitations to police knowledge of services, victim eligibility, and assessments of victim worthiness (Farrell & Pfeffer 2014; Sims et al. 2005; Trulson 2005). Police training and knowledge are essential to linking victims to services, but also in general, identifying policing practices that promote legitimacy and trust (Tyler 2004).

Remaining issues may be addressed through conducting thorough needs assessments to understand the complexity of barriers facing victims across different communities. A needs assessment is an evaluation method that systematically documents the gaps between what exists and what is needed through collecting and analyzing existing data and collecting new data via interviews, focus groups, or surveys of target populations and service providers. In addition, interventions should be assessed through rigorous evaluation methods documenting program implementation, process and fidelity, and program outcomes and effects (Rossi et al. 2004).

Discussion Questions

1. If you were a victim of crime, would you seek help from victim services? Why or why not? What type of services would be most important to you?
2. What are the pros and cons of victim service utilization?
3. Should victim services be available to victims who contributed to the crime or victims who have previously committed crimes?
4. In addition to the ideas presented in the chapter, what are some ways in which access to victim services could be improved?

Notes

1 Office for Victims of Crime, Director of Crime Victim Services: An Online Resource. Available at: http://ovc.ncjrs.gov/findvictimservices/

2 The National Center for Victims of Crime, Connect Directory. Available at: http://victimsofcrime.org/help-for-crime-victims/find-local-assistance---connect-directory

3 Domestic Shelters, State Summaries. Available at: https://www.domesticshelters.org/state-city-domestic-violence-statistics#.V2GXX-YrLBI

References

Bachman, R., Zaykowski, H., Kallmyer, R., Poteyeva, M., & Lanier, C. (2008). *Violence against American Indian and Alaska Native women and the criminal justice response: What is known*. Washington, DC: National Institute of Justice.

Bachman, R., Zaykowski, H., Lanier, C., Poteyeva, M., & Kallmyer, R. (2010). Estimating the magnitude of rape and sexual assault against American Indian and Alaska Native (AIAN) women. *Australian & New Zealand Journal of Criminology, 43*(2), 199–222.

Baumer, E. P., & Lauritsen, J. L. (2010). Reporting crime to the police, 1973–2005: a multivariate analysis of long-term trends in the National Crime Survey (NCS) and National Crime Victimization Survey (NCVS). *Criminology, 48*(1), 131–185.

Bell, M. E., & Goodman, L. A. (2001). Supporting battered women involved with the court system an evaluation of a law school-based advocacy intervention. *Violence Against Women*, 7(12), 1377–1404.

Campbell, R., Wasco, S. M., Ahrens, C. E., Sefl, T., & Barnes, H. E. (2001). Preventing the "second rape" rape survivors' experiences with community service providers. *Journal of Interpersonal Violence, 16*(12), 1239–1259.

Catalano, S. (2013). *Intimate partner violence: Attributes of victimization, 1993–2011*. Washington, DC: US Department of Justice, Office of Justice Programs, Bureau of Justice Statistics. Available at: http://www.bjs.gov/content/pub/pdf/ipvav9311.pdf

Christie, N. (1986) The ideal victim. In E. A. Fattah (ed.) *From crime policy to victim policy* (pp. 17–30). London: Macmillan.

Clawson, H. J., & Dutch, N. (2008). *Addressing the needs of victims of human trafficking: Challenges, barriers, and promising practices*. Department of Health and Human Services, Office of the Assistant Secretary for Planning and Evaluation. Available at: https://aspe.hhs.gov/basic-report/addressing-needs-victims-human-trafficking-challenges-barriers-and-promising-practices

DeKeseredy, W., & Schwartz, M. (2009). *Dangerous exits: Escaping abusive relationships in rural America*. Piscataway, NJ: Rutgers University Press.

Edwards, K. M., Sylaska, K. M., & Neal, A. M. (2015). Intimate partner violence among sexual minority populations: a critical review of the literature and agenda for future research. *Psychology of Violence, 5*(2), 112.

Farrell, A. & Pfeffer, R. (2014). Policing human trafficking cultural blinders and organizational barriers. *The Annals of the American Academy of Political and Social Science, 653*(1), 46–64.

Frantz, B. L., Carey, A. C., & Bryen, D. N. (2006). Accessibility of Pennsylvania's victim assistance programs. *Journal of Disability Policy Studies, 16*(4), 209–219.

Fugate, M., Landis, L., Riordan, K., Naureckas, S., & Engel, B. (2005). Barriers to domestic violence help seeking implications for intervention. *Violence Against Women, 11*(3), 290–310.

Galdas, P. M., Cheater, F., & Marshall, P. (2005). Men and health help-seeking behaviour: literature review. *Journal of Advanced Nursing, 49*(6), 616–623.

Glenn, C., & Goodman, L. (2015). Living with and within the rules of domestic violence shelters a qualitative exploration of residents' experiences. *Violence Against Women, 21*(12), 1481–1506.

Hamby, S. L. (1998). Cultural relativity or cultural imperialism? Ethical dilemmas in extending the domestic violence movement worldwide. *Register Report, 24*(3), 10–11.

Hass, G. A., Dutton, M. A., & Orloff, L. E. (2000). Lifetime prevalence of violence against Latina immigrants: Legal and policy implications. *International Review of Victimology*, 7(1–3), 93–113.

Hatten, P., & Moore, M. (2010). Police officer perceptions of a victim-services program. *Journal of Applied Social Science*, *4*(2), 17–24.

Henning, K. R., & Klesges, L. M. (2002). Utilization of counseling and supportive services by female victims of domestic abuse. *Violence and Victims*, *17*(5), 623–636.

Hodge, D. R. (2014). Assisting victims of human trafficking: strategies to facilitate identification, exit from trafficking, and the restoration of wellness. *Social Work*, *59*(2): 111–118.

Keilitz, S. L., Hannaford, P. L., & Efkeman, H. S. (1997). *Civil protection orders: The benefits and limitations for victims of domestic violence: Executive summary*. Washington, DC: Department of Justice. Available at: https://www.ncjrs.gov/pdffiles1/pr/172223.pdf

Kendall, J., Pelucio, M. T., Casaletto, J., Thompson, K. P., Barnes, S., Petit, E., & Aldrich, M. (2009). Impact of emergency department intimate partner violence intervention. *Journal of Interpersonal Violence*, *24*, 280–306.

Lachs, M. S., & Pillemer, K. (2004). Elder abuse. *The Lancet*, *364*(9441), 1263–1272.

Langton, L. (2011). *Use of victim service agencies by victims of serious violent crime, 1993–2009*. Washington, DC: US Department of Justice, Office of Justice Programs, Bureau of Justice Statistics. Available at: http://www.bjs.gov/content/pub/pdf/uvsavsvc9309.pdf

Langton, L., & Truman, J. (2014). *Socio-emotional impact of violent crime*. Washington, DC: US Department of Justice, Office of Justice Programs, Bureau of Justice Statistics. Available at: http://www.bjs.gov/content/pub/pdf/sivc.pdf

Langton, L., Berzofsky, M., Krebs, C. P., & Smiley-McDonald, H. (2012). *Victimizations not reported to the police, 2006–2010*. Washington, DC: US Department of Justice, Office of Justice Programs, Bureau of Justice Statistics. Available at: http://www.bjs.gov/content/pub/pdf/vnrp0610.pdf

Lauritsen, J. L., & Laub, J. H. (2007). Understanding the link between victimization and offending: new reflections on an old idea. *Crime Prevention Studies*, *22*, 55.

Logan, T. K., Evans, L., Stevenson, E., & Jordan, C. E. (2005). Barriers to services for rural and urban survivors of rape. *Journal of Interpersonal Violence*, *20*(5), 591–616.

Logan, T. K., Stevenson, E., Evans, L., & Leukefeld, C. (2004). Rural and urban women's perceptions of barriers to health, mental health, and criminal justice services: implications for victim services. *Violence and Victims*, *19*(1), 37–62.

Mansell, S., Sobsey, D., & Calder, P. (1992). Sexual abuse treatment for persons with developmental disabilities. *Professional Psychology: Research and Practice*, *23*(5), 404.

Mastrocinque, J. M. (2010). An overview of the victims' rights movement: historical, legislative, and research developments. *Sociology Compass*, *4*(2), 95–110.

Merrill, G. S., & Wolfe, V. A. (2000). Battered gay men: an exploration of abuse, help seeking, and why they stay. *Journal of Homosexuality*, *39*(2), 1–30.

Monroe, L. M., Kinney, L. M., Weist, M. D., Spriggs Dafeamekpor, D., Dantzler, J., & Reynolds, M. W. (2005). The experience of sexual assault: findings from a statewide victim needs assessment. *Journal of Interpersonal Violence*, *20*(7), 767–776.

National Center for Victims of Crime (2016) *Crime victims' rights in America: An historical overview*. Available at: https://ovc.ncjrs.gov/ncvrw2016/pdf/2016NCVRW_5_Landmarks_FINAL-508.pdf

Newmark, L., Bonderman, J., Smith, B., & Liner, B. (2003). The national evaluation of state Victims of Crime Act assistance and compensation programs: trends and strategies for the future. *Report to the National Institute of Justice. Washington, DC: The Urban Institute*. Available at: https://www.ncjrs.gov/pdffiles1/nij/grants/203198.pdf

Orloff, L., & Garcia, O. (2013). Dynamics of domestic violence experienced by immigrant victims. In L. Orloff & K. Sullivan (eds.), Breaking barriers: A complete guide to legal rights and resources for battered immigrants (pp. 1–21). Washington, DC: Legal Momentum.[note style] Available at: http://iwp.legalmomentum.org/reference/manuals/domestic-violence-family-violence

Pierce, A. & Koepplinger, S. (2011). New language, old problem: sex trafficking of American Indian women and children. *Harrisburg, PA: VAWnet, a project of the National Resource Center on Domestic Violence*. Available at: http://www.vawnet.org/Assoc_Files_VAWnet/AR_NativeSexTrafficking.pdf

Peters, A. J. (2013). Disparate protections for American human trafficking victims. *Cleveland State Law Review*, *61*(1), 1–45.

Reina, A. S., & Lohman, B. J. (2015). Barriers preventing Latina immigrants from seeking advocacy services for domestic violence victims: a qualitative analysis. *Journal of Family Violence*, *30*(4), 479–488.

Raj, A., & Silverman, J. (2002). Violence against immigrant women the roles of culture, context, and legal immigrant status on intimate partner violence. *Violence Against Wwomen*, *8*(3), 367–398.

Renzetti, C. M. (1992). *Violent betrayal: Partner abuse in lesbian relationships*. Newbury Park, CA: Sage Publications.

Rossi, P., Lipsey, M. and Freeman, H. (2004) *Evaluation: A systematic approach*. 7th edition. SAGE: Thousand Oaks, California.

St. Pierre, M., & Senn, C. Y. (2010). External barriers to help-seeking encountered by Canadian gay and lesbian victims of intimate partner abuse: An application of the barriers model. *Violence and Victims*, *25*(4), 536–552.

Salcido, O., & Adelman, M. (2004). "He has me tied with the blessed and damned papers": undocumented-immigrant battered women in Phoenix, Arizona. *Human Organization*, *63*(2), 162–172.

Sered, D. (2014). Young men of color and the other side of harm: addressing disparities in our responses to violence. Vera Institute of Justice. Retrieved from http:// www.vera.org/sites/default/files/resources/downloads/men-of-color-as-victimsof-violence-v3.pdf

Skogan, W. G., Davis, R. C., & Lurigio, A. J. (1990). *Victims' needs and victim services: Final report to the National Institute of Justice*. US Department of Justice, National Institute of Justice. Available at: https://www.ncjrs.gov/pdffiles1/Digitization/132415NCJRS.pdf

Simon, J. (2007). *Governing through crime: How the war on crime transformed American democracy and created a culture of fear*. New York, NY: Oxford University Press.

Sims, B., Yost, B., & Abbott, C. (2005). Use and nonuse of victim services programs: implications from a state-wide survey of crime victims. *Criminology & Public Policy*, *4*(2), 361–384.

Sims, B., Yost, B., & Abbott, C. (2006). The efficacy of victim services programs alleviating the psychological suffering of crime victims? *Criminal Justice Policy Review*, *17*(4), 387–406.

Smith, A. (1999). Sexual violence and American Indian genocide. *Journal of Religion & Abuse*, *1*(2), 31–52.

Stark, E. (2000) *Denver victim services 2000 needs assessment*. Washington DC, Crime Victims Institute. Available at: https://www.ncjrs.gov/ovc_archives/bulletins/dv_10_2000_1/files/NCJ183397.pdf

Stohr, M. K. (2005). Victim services programming: if it is efficacious, they will come. *Criminology & Public Policy*, *4*, 391.

Trulson, C. R. (2005). Victims' rights and services: eligibility, exclusion, and victim worth. *Criminology & Public Policy*, *4*, 399.

Truman, J. L. & Langton, L. (2015). *Criminal victimization in the United States, 2014*. Washington, DC: US Department of Justice, Office of Justice Programs, Bureau of Justice Statistics. Available at: http://www.bjs.gov/content/pub/pdf/cv14.pdf

Tyler, T. R. (2004). Enhancing police legitimacy. *The annals of the American Academy of Political and Social Science*, *593*(1), 84–99.

Ullman, S. E., & Filipas, H. H. (2001). Correlates of formal and informal support seeking in sexual assault victims. *Journal of Interpersonal Violence*, *16*(10), 1028–1047.

U.S. Department of Justice. Office for Victims of Crime (2012). *Rising to the challenge: A new era in victim services*. Available at: http://www.ovc.gov/pubs/reporttonation2011/ReporttoNation2011.pdf

Walters, M. L., Chen, J., & Breiding, M. J. (2013). The National Intimate Partner and Sexual Violence Survey (NISVS): 2010 findings on victimization by sexual orientation. *Atlanta, GA: National Center for Injury Prevention and Control, Centers for Disease Control and Prevention*, *648*(73), 6. Available at: http://www.cdc.gov/ViolencePrevention/pdf/NISVS_SOfindings.pdf

Wasco, S. M., Campbell, R., Howard, A., Mason, G. E., Staggs, S. L., Schewe, P. A., & Riger, S. (2004). A statewide evaluation of services provided to rape survivors. *Journal of Interpersonal Violence*, *19*(2), 252–263.

Zaykowski, H. (2014). Mobilizing victim services: the role of reporting to the police. *Journal of Traumatic Stress*, *27*(3), 365–369.

Zaykowski, H. (2015). "The penal couple": an examination of the relationship between victimization and offending and its implications for criminal justice. *Sociology Compass*, *9*(5), 336–347.

Zweig, J. M., Burt, M. R., & Van Ness, A. (2003). The effects on victims of victim service programs funded by the STOP formula grants program. *Washington, DC: The Urban Institute. Prepared for the National Institute of Justice*. Available at: http://www.urban.org/sites/default/files/alfresco/publication-pdfs/410645-The-Effects-on-Victims-of-Victim-Service-Programs-Funded-by-the-STOP-Formula-Grants-Program.PDF

Zweig, J. M., Schlichter, K. A., & Burt, M. R. (2002). Assisting women victims of violence who experience multiple barriers to services. *Violence Against Women*, *8*(2), 162–180.

2
FEDERAL VICTIMS' LEGISLATION

Maren Trochmann, Angela R. Gover, and Maria J. Patterson

Keywords

federal legislation; statutes; constitutional amendments; social movements; restitution; victims' protections

Objectives

This chapter allows the reader to:

- Understand the historical context, including social movements, grassroots coalitions, and lobbying efforts that led to increased awareness of victims' rights and the passage of crime victims' rights legislation.
- Identify and describe major federal crime victim statutes and legislation.
- Recognize the future path federal victims' legislation may take in the United States.

Victims' Rights Movement

The U.S. criminal justice system has traditionally concentrated on offenders in terms of prevention, punishment, and rehabilitation. The U.S. Constitution has long provided rights and protections to accused offenders in the criminal justice system through the Sixth Amendment. More recently, however, advocates and legislators have called for increased protections and rights for victims of crime. While victims come from all walks of life, they share the commonalities of being harmed by offenders, benefitting from public and private agencies that provide social and systemic support, and benefitting from opportunities to participate in the trial process. The victims' rights movement is one systemic response to wider-spread recognition of the ways the criminal justice system can work to respond to victims' needs, in addition to rehabilitating and punishing perpetrators.

First arising in the early 1970s, the crime victims' movement was heavily influenced by several earlier social movements including the civil rights, law-and-order, and women's rights movements, as well as later social justice movements. The civil rights movement emphasized the importance of fair treatment and access for all victims of crime. The call for equality and justice for all, regardless of race or other protected class, extended as well to victims of crime and emphasized widespread dissatisfaction with the criminal justice system.

Around the same time, law-and-order advocates of the 1960s sought to tip the balance in favor of crime victims through swift and sure punishment of offenders. The law-and-order movement was sparked by public fear of rising crime rates and a perception that the scales of justice were unfairly weighted in favor of the offender. As a result, hardliners called for a strengthened law enforcement response to crime in the form of enhanced powers for government actors including police, the courts, and the prison system. Accordingly, advocates managed to foster significant changes in the forms of harsher sentencing and stricter guidelines for granting bail, probation, and parole to offenders, despite dissenting concerns about potential false convictions and excessive punishments.

The women's rights movement of the 1970s shone a spotlight on female crime victims, particularly victims of male perpetrators. Women victims, especially those of color and those suffering economically, were in dire need of support when it came to navigating a criminal justice system largely controlled by white, privileged males. As a result, women turned to one another for empowerment. Feminists began instituting important resources for victims in the form of rape crisis centers and domestic violence shelters, giving voice to those who would otherwise have suffered in silence and isolation. Often spearheaded by former victims intent on combatting the types of societal misogyny that leads to violence against women, these resources fostered empowerment for victims by exposing sexism, providing support to victims, and bringing together a like-minded community of women to campaign against rape, domestic violence, and sexual harassment.

Activists from the more recent civil liberties, children's rights, seniors' rights, and LGBTQ rights movements have also positively impacted the victims' rights movement. For example, civil liberties advocates have promoted professionalism within law enforcement in terms of interacting with the public, as well as reinforced the doctrine of equal protection under the law. Children's rights advocates positively impact victims by campaigning against child sexual abuse, child battering, child neglect, and other forms of maltreatment. That movement also led to stricter reporting guidelines for child abuse, the expedient arrest and prosecution of perpetrators, social services for the youngest victims, and increased efforts towards child protection.

In 1972, the first National Crime Survey (now called the National Crime Victimization Survey) found large discrepancies between the number of crimes reported to law enforcement and the number of crimes that survey respondents were willing to report (Boland and Butler, 2009). These discrepancies led to a focus, consideration, and treatment of crime victims within the criminal justice system. As a result of these data and the advocacy of the social movements noted above, over the last two decades, both state and federal governments have expanded victims' rights through a number of acts designed to increase victim participation through providing information, support, and restitution to crime victims. This chapter focuses on those groundbreaking federal laws and statutes passed to protect victims of crime.

Victim and Witness Protection Act of 1982

The Victim and Witness Protection Act of 1982 (hereafter referred to as VWPA) was passed in reaction to the alienation victims experience at the hands of the criminal justice system. Although the criminal justice system depends on victim and witness cooperation to run smoothly, victims often find themselves subjected to psychological and financial strains not only as a result of the initial crime but also due to their participation in the criminal proceedings. With fewer crimes being reported to police and dwindling cooperation with and confidence in the criminal justice system on the part of the public, it became apparent that crime victims and witnesses needed more protection in order to foster their participation in criminal cases.

Prior to the VWPA, victims and witnesses were not given the same information and assistance afforded to defendants; nor were victims and witnesses given sufficient protection from the legal system against intimidation or threats received as a result of participating in criminal proceedings.

While defendants were presented with counsel to explain their rights and the criminal justice process, victims were not entitled to a similar assistance. As a result, victims were often not informed of significant changes in case proceedings, such as a changed court date, the release of a defendant, or even the dismissal of a case.

According to the VWPA, the federal government has a responsibility to ensure that crime victims and witnesses are assisted and protected as much as possible, given the available resources, as long as such protections do not infringe upon the defendant's constitutional rights. Though the main goal of the VWPA was to protect victims and witnesses of federal crimes, the hope was that this change would be copied and implemented at state and local levels. This imperative was essential because most critical crimes fall under the jurisdiction of local or state law enforcement agencies (Sever, 1985).

On the whole, the VWPA extends protections to victims and witnesses by adding a victim impact statement in pre-sentence reports, penalizing acts of tampering with victims and witnesses, and allowing courts to order that defendants make restitution to victims. In this way, the Act allows for the victims and witnesses to be protected throughout court proceedings. First, the VWPA supports the victim by amending rule 32(c) of the Federal Rules of Criminal Procedure to require certain details about the defendant and the victim be presented in the pre-sentence trial. As amended, the pre-sentence report is required to contain the defendant's prior criminal record, circumstances related to how the offense was committed, and any circumstances influencing the defendant's behavior. Notably, with the VWPA the pre-sentence report is also required to include information about any harm or loss—be it physical, social, psychological, or financial—victims of the offense face. The report must also include information on the victims' needs for restitution and related information that would assist the court in sentencing.

Victims are further protected by penalties for tampering with a witness, victim, or informant; by prohibiting retaliation against a victim or witness; and by clarifying how civil action may be used to restrain harassment of witnesses and victims. More specifically, §1512 prohibits the tampering with or retaliation against a victim, witness, or informant through intimidation, verbal or physical threats, or deceptive behavior. If any person uses these means with the intent of influencing a person's testimony; causes a person to withhold or alter a testimony, document, or artifact from an official proceeding; prevents a person from appearing when summoned; or stalls communication to a law enforcement officer or judge regarding the commission of a federal offense, this person faces a fine of up to $250,000, imprisonment, or both. Similarly, §1513 prohibits retaliation against victims, witnesses, or informants. Any person who intentionally injures a person or damages their property (or threatens or attempts to do so) as an act of retaliation against someone due to their participation in an official proceeding is subject to the same penalty.

As a final act of protection, §1514 states that temporary restraining orders may be issued in order to prohibit the harassment of a witness or victim in federal criminal cases. Given sufficient reason to believe that a victim or witness is being harassed, the court may issue a 10-day restraining order. This temporary restraining order can be ordered against a person without notice only if the prosecuting attorney finds that such a notice is not required. Additionally, these protection orders can be dissolved or expanded to any length of time the court finds requisite for the prevention of victim or witness harassment, so long as that period of time does not exceed three years.

One important aspect of the VWPA revolves around the issue of restitution. As written, the court may order restitution from the defendant during the sentencing of said defendant. Additionally, if the court chooses not to do so, the court must state its reasons for not ordering restitution on the record. For example, the court may order the defendant to return property, pay restitution equal to the value of damaged or lost property, or pay a sum equivalent to costs a victim faces as a result of bodily injury. Notably, this restitution should be equitable and fair to the victim but not draw out or complicate the sentencing process. Finally, restitution amounts are to be determined with regard both to the defendant's available financial resources and the losses suffered by victim(s) due to the offense.

Lastly, section 6 outlines the Federal guidelines for victim and witness treatment within the criminal justice system. The VWPA states that law enforcement should provide victims with regular access to social and medical services as well as information about possible compensation, treatment programs, what the victim can expect from the criminal justice process and the victim's role within that process, and information about crucial stages of the criminal justice process. Additionally, victims should be notified of available protections from intimidation and harassment. Victims and witnesses should also be notified of scheduling changes in a timely manner. In the case of serious crimes, victims and witnesses—and even minors or family members of homicide victims—are entitled to prompt information related to their case's judicial proceedings, especially with regard to arrest, sentencing, imprisonment, and release from imprisonment. Victims are also entitled to a consultation by a government attorney about their views on dismissals, releases of accused persons, and plea negotiations. Finally, victims and witnesses are to have separate waiting areas, receive their property once it is no longer deemed necessary for the case, receive notification to be given to their employers, and have access to other general assistance (including transportation and translation services).

Though the act was regarded as being a tremendous step forward, some found aspects of the VWPA to be lacking. The most criticized section of the VWPA is the restitution portion. For example, in *United States v. Welden*, the court found the restitution guidelines of VWPA to be unconstitutional, suggesting that such legislation violates due process requirements as well as the defendant's right to a fair trial. The VWPA has also been criticized for its failure to provide specific definitions for terms such as "victim" and "offense," allowing for wide interpretations of which individuals would be eligible to receive restitution (Sever, 1985). These and similar restitution-related criticisms are part of what prompted the creation of the Victims of Crime Act of 1984.

Victims of Crime Act of 1984 (VOCA)

President Ronald Reagan established the Presidential Task Force on Victims of Crime in the early 1980s to study the trends of crime and the criminal justice system's treatment of crime victims. In 1982, this task force released a report that outlined methods to aid victims and encourage victim participation in the criminal justice system without compromising the rights of defendants. The report showed that most victims were not receiving fair or timely compensation; rather, existing victim compensation programs were under-resourced, under-staffed, and slow to process and satisfy victim claims. One remedy the report suggested was the expansion of monetary victim compensation. The Victims of Crime Act was passed in 1984 as a result of this report and those recommendations.

The Victims of Crime Act of 1984 (VOCA) established a federal account for victim compensation, the Crime Victims Fund, to provide a means to aid state programs in imparting compensation for victims at 42 U.S.C. § 10601. Though there had been attempts to secure compensation for state and federal crime victims since 1965, passing state and federal legislation for victim compensation proved to be a slow process. In 1965, California became the first state to pass legislation to adopt a state compensation program; by 1982, over half of U.S. states had developed state victim compensation programs. On a federal level, however, attempts were made to pass legislation for victim compensation starting in 1965 but were unsuccessful until Congress enacted VOCA. Support for victim compensation on a state level continued to grow significantly throughout the 1980s, especially after the passage of VOCA, and by 1992 all 50 states had passed legislation to adopt state victim compensation programs.

VOCA revolutionized the way that victims were compensated for their crimes. Rather than using tax dollars, the Crime Victims Fund is generated by fines from federal crimes, money a court has designated to be paid into the Fund, bail forfeitures, and, since 2002, private gifts and donations through the USA Patriot Act of 2001. For the first eight years there was an annual cap on allowed Fund deposits, which fluctuated between $100 and $150 million per year. The cap was lifted in 1993, allowing all types of criminal fines to be deposited into the Fund. Today, the Crime Victims Fund remains a stable source of aid for federal and state assistance and compensation programs for victims.

The money in the Crime Victims Fund is disbursed between four separate categories. The first $10 million (plus a varying amount, depending on the year's deposits) are allocated to programs for the investigation and prevention of child abuse. More specifically, $8.5 million is allocated to the U.S. Department of Health and Human Services, while the rest goes to the Office for Victims of Crime (OVC), which is used to aid Native Americans in the investigation and prosecution of cases involving child abuse. After the initial $10 million, 48.5 percent of the funds are given to state compensation programs while another 48.5 percent go to state assistance programs. Finally, the last 3 percent constitute discretionary funds that the OVC uses to improve support for victims. These funds are used in a variety of ways including trainings on victims' issues, creating materials to aid victims in understanding their rights and services that may be available to them, supporting and expanding programs that assist federal crime victims, and sustaining other initiatives such as curricula development, trainings, and program evaluations.

VOCA's establishment of the Crime Victims Fund has been highly instrumental in expanding compensation for crime victims. Victims of crime are often met with a variety of expenses such as medical or counseling costs, loss of wages or financial support, funeral costs, and crime scene cleaning. Using money from the Crime Victims Fund, filtered through state victim compensation programs, crime victims are compensated directly—or someone is compensated on the victim's behalf—in relation to expenses incurred as a result of the crime. As a result of the Crime Victims Fund, victims have a much better chance of receiving the amount of compensation they seek.

Not all victims receive crime compensation, however. In order to receive compensation from state compensation programs, victims are usually required to report crimes to an officer of the law within three days of the crime and file a claim within two years. States can, however, extend these periods of time given reason to do so. Additionally, compensation will only cover that which is not covered by resources such as private insurance. Nonetheless, the compensation programs sometimes award as much as $10,000 to $25,000 to victims of federal crimes (Office for Victims of Crime, 1999).

In addition to financial compensation, some funds from the Crime Victim Fund are distributed to victim assistance grants. Every U.S. state in addition to the District of Columbia, Puerto Rico, and the U.S. Virgin Islands receives $500,000 as a baseline. Approximately 3,300 organizations that provide assistance to victims receive some funds from VOCA. However, VOCA funds for victim assistance can only be used in services that directly help crime victims. Some common examples of allowed victim assistance include counseling, crisis intervention, criminal justice advocacy, emergency shelter, and emergency transportation (OVC, 1999). Less direct forms of assistance, including criminal justice improvements, crime prevention, and offender rehabilitation, cannot be supported by VOCA victim assistance funds.

Victims' Rights and Restitution Act of 1990 (VRRA)

The 1990 passage of the Victims' Rights and Restitution Act (VRRA) was another groundbreaking piece of legislation in that it codified specific victims' rights and services into law. Passed on November 29, 1990, the Public Law 101-647, title V, § 503 is enshrined in the U.S. Code at 42 U.S.C. § 10607. Requirements of the VRRA extend to all federal law enforcement agencies.

The primary and overarching goal enshrined in VRRA is to treat victims with fairness and give respect to the victim's dignity and privacy. Moreover, the VRRA enumerated various new victim services.

In response to the shortcomings of VWPA noted above, the VRRA explicitly defines victims as any person who has suffered direct physical, emotional, or financial hardship as the result of a crime. This includes an authorized representative of an institution if the victim is an institutional entity or organization. For instance, this may include a business, university, or other organization. When a victim is not a legal adult or is incapacitated, deceased, or incompetent, the law outlines that one of the following designees, in order of preference, will be given the rights typically granted to the victim: a spouse, a legal guardian, a parent, a child, a sibling, another family member, or a person designated by the court.

The law requires that the head of each federal department or agency prosecuting crimes shall designate responsible official(s) to identify victims of crime and provide services to them as outlined in the law. The VRRA requires prompt identification and outreach to crime victims, as defined above, notifying each victim of his or her right to receive outreach and referral services and the contact information for the responsible official. Once identified, the responsible official must provide referral services and information to the victim(s).

Victims are also given the right to be informed of: (1) any places where the victim may access emergency medical and social services, (2) any restitution or relief to which the victim may be entitled under this and other laws as well as the manner the victim may obtain such relief, and (3) the public and private programs that are available for counseling, treatment, and support. Additionally, the VRRA provides protection to the victim's person and property by requiring the victim be protected from their offender and others who may act on behalf of the offender. As such, the responsible official is required to arrange for this protection to the greatest extent possible. Moreover, the responsible official must ensure that any property of the victim collected in evidence be kept in good condition and returned to the victim as soon as possible, when and if it is no longer required for evidence.

The VRRA enshrines seven rights related to timely notices to be provided to the victim related to the investigation and prosecution of the crime. Specifically, the responsible official must provide the earliest possible notification to the victim of the following: (1) the status of the investigation of the crime, to the extent that it does not interfere with any investigations; (2) the arrest of a suspected offender; (3) the filing of charges against a suspect; (4) the scheduling of each court proceeding that the victim is entitled to attend; (5) the release or detention status of a suspected offender; (6) the acceptance of any pleas or no contest (nolo contendere) and the rendering of the verdict; and (7) the sentence imposed, including the date the offender would be eligible for parole.

The VRRA also provides rights to the victim during court proceedings and after the trial. For example, during the proceedings the responsible official must provide the victim a waiting area away from the defendant and defense witnesses. After the trial, the victim must continue to be notified regarding the scheduling of any parole hearings, any release of custody of the offender (including escape, work release, or furlough), and the death of the offender if it occurs while the offender is in custody. In sum, the victim must be provided with general information regarding the corrections process and the custody of the offender, as noted above, including any aspect of the offender's eligibility for release or probation.

The VRRA requires specific restitution in the case of sexual assault victims. For instance, the Attorney General (AG) or agency head of the department conducting any sexual assault investigation shall directly pay or reimburse a victim for the cost of any physical examination that was necessary or useful for evidentiary purposes. Additionally, the AG must pay for the cost of up to two anonymous and confidential sexually transmitted diseases (STD) screenings, including those for HIV, gonorrhea, herpes, chlamydia, and syphilis, during the year following the sexual assault in which there is risk of transmission. The AG must also pay for the cost of any counseling session by a medical professional on the accuracy of the tests and the risk of transmission. The victim has the right to waive the anonymity and confidentiality of the tests paid for under this law.

In the implementation of the VRRA, the U.S. Attorneys' Offices in the Department of Justice (DOJ) developed the Attorney General Guidelines for Victim and Witness Assistance to direct how, when, and in what ways the AG's office assists crime victims throughout the investigation, prosecution, and corrections of a federal case. The U.S. Attorneys' Offices have specific victim-witness personnel who are highly trained to evaluate victims' needs and make appropriate service referrals in accordance with the VRRA and other legislation specific to certain victim populations.

In terms of restitution, the DOJ and AG have established a Federal Crime Victim Assistance Fund (FCVAF) to assist federal crime victims with services. The FCVAF is funded by criminal fines and assessments paid by criminal defendants. These funds are to be used when no other sources of funding for victims' services are available. The FCVAF has been used for transportation costs, emergency shelters, crisis intervention, and other necessary and immediate services. The DOJ's website provides several examples of FCVAF's uses including translation services, transportation costs for victims to attend hearings, and mental health counseling for PTSD associated with crimes.

International Parental Kidnapping Crime Act of 1991

In 1991, the International Parental Kidnapping Crime Act (the Act) was introduced in Congress to amend the federal criminal code to penalize a person for the international kidnapping of a child. This legislation was not enacted until 1993, when it was reintroduced and passed by Congress as H.R. 3378, in response to some of the Children's Rights Movement advocacy previously noted. The Act was signed by the president, codified as Public Law 114-38, Title XVIII, § 1, and is enshrined in the U.S. Code at 18 U.S.C. § 1204. This legislation imposes penalties in the form of fines and/or imprisonment of up to three years for any person who removes a child from the United States, attempts to do so, or retains a child outside of the country with the intent to obstruct the lawful exercise of parental rights.

The International Parental Kidnapping Crime Act defines a child as a person under the age of 16, and defines "parental rights" as the right to the physical custody of the child, including joint or sole custody, visitation rights, and those rights obtained from any law, court order, or legally binding agreement. The Act is intended to protect children in the case that one parent takes a child outside of the U.S. to block the rights of another person who has parental custodial rights to the child. The U.S. Department of Justice (DOJ) provides one example of such an instance: A married couple with a son has a marital dispute, and the father moves with the son to another country to keep him away from the mother with no intent to return. Under this law, such an example would be considered a federal crime of international parental kidnapping.

Several caveats and exceptions are included in this law. If the fleeing party meets any one of three exceptions, they may not be prosecuted under federal criminal statutes. First, an exception is made if the defendant has a valid court order, effective during the time of the alleged kidnapping, granting legal custody or visitation. Moreover, the order must have been obtained under the Uniform Child Custody Jurisdiction Act or the Uniform Child Custody Jurisdiction and Enforcement Act. Second, if the defendant is fleeing a pattern or incidence of domestic violence, they are not culpable or punishable under this law. Finally, if the defendant has physical custody of the child under a court order granting legal custody or visitation rights and fails to return the child due to circumstances beyond the defendant's control, they are excluded from the Act. In this instance, the defendant must notify or make reasonable attempts to notify the other parent or legal guardian of the child within 24 hours after the visitation period expires, and return the child as soon as possible.

The Act also states that it, in no way, detracts from *The Hague Convention on the Civil Aspects of International Parental Child Abduction*, enacted in 1980. This international convention, to which the U.S. is a signatory, facilitates international cooperation to return kidnapped children via negotiation. The U.S. State Department handles this coordination with foreign officials, but the Convention only applies if both countries involved are signatories. The U.S. DOJ emphasizes that working through the Department of State is the safest and best way to facilitate the return of a child internationally. The International Parental Kidnapping Crime Act may enhance the enforcement of this act, as it allows for formal criminal charges to be brought against a parent. The law allows for extradition, or legal surrender of an alleged criminal to the jurisdiction of the United States, as they are culpable of a criminal act under this law. However, the DOJ warns that this extradition would only apply to the parent and not the child. Therefore, negotiation with the Department of State under the Convention is critical to safe return of the child.

To implement the International Parental Kidnapping Crime Act, the DOJ has established the Child Exploitation and Obscenity Section (CEOS) to provide advice and litigation support to the U.S. Attorney's Office. The CEOS coordinates with the Department of State and the National Center for Missing and Exploited Children (NCMEC) to monitor active cases and provide legal assistance. This law is crucial in providing penalties and deterrence for parents acting against the best interests of children. As the NCMEC reports in its book *Family Abduction: Prevention and Response* (2009):

> Children who are victims of family abduction are uprooted from their homes and deprived of their other parent. Often they are told the other parent no longer loves them or is dead. Too often abducted children live a life of deception, sometimes under a false name, moving frequently and lacking the stability needed for healthy emotional development.

The DOJ reports that these child victims are often isolated from their community support, family, and friends. Child victims of parental kidnapping may miss years of education and suffer long-term psychological effects of traumatic events, such as anxiety, aggressive behavior, identity and relationship issues. The International Parental Kidnapping Crime Act of 1993 is one way that child victims are supported through federal legislation in a way that also recognizes victims of domestic violence.

Violence Against Women Act of 1994

The Women's Rights Movement also garnered a great victory in federal victims' rights legislation with the passage of the Violence Against Women Act (VAWA). VAWA was passed in 1994, as Title IV of the Violent Crime Control and Law Enforcement Act. A previous effort to introduce the bill in 1990 was unsuccessful. Incremental changes occurred in the legislation prior to 1994, although nothing was as far-reaching and comprehensive as VAWA in terms of protections of women and in line with the goals of the Women's Movement noted previously. Prior legislation that addressed portions of VAWA included the Family Violence Prevention Services Act of 1984, which was the first time that Congress designated federal funds to serve battered women and children victims of abuse. In 1988, the Victims of Crime Act was amended to require that state victims' compensation programs also provide moneys to domestic violence victims. However, it was not until after the Senate Judiciary Committee issued its 1993 report *Violence against Women – The Response to Rape: Detours on the Road to Justice*, the culmination of a three-year investigation, that enough bipartisan support was garnered for the passage of VAWA.

VAWA was passed into law on September 13, 1994 as Public Law 103-322, incorporating several broad federal requirements and providing grant money for federal programs related to ending and addressing violence against women. In broad terms, VAWA enhanced investigations and prosecutions of sex offenses and crimes of violence against women and also funded grant programs to address violence against women from various lenses (Sacco, 2015). VAWA requires a coordinated community response to domestic violence, sexual assault, and stalking by encouraging jurisdictions to improve community-wide responses. It made federal penalties for repeat sex offenders harsher and included a provision to protect victims of sexual crimes in trial by preventing offenders from using their past sexual conduct against them under the "Rape Shield Law." VAWA implements full faith and credit provisions requiring states, territories, and tribal governments to enforce any protection order issued by another state. Finally, it also provides legal relief for battered immigrants, making it easier for abused immigrant women to call police and seek safety without concern for repercussions under immigration law.

Under VAWA – and subsequent reauthorization acts in 2000, 2005, 2013—the Department of Justice's Office on Violence against Women (OVW) administers 24 grant programs. These programs include four formula grant awards: (1) STOP Violence Against Women Formula Grant Program to encourage arrest policies and train police and prosecutors; (2) Sexual Assault Services Formula Grant Program to provide direct intervention and assistance to victims of sexual assault; (3) State and Territorial Sexual Assault and Domestic Violence Coalitions Program to help state domestic violence coalitions and sexual assault coalitions to coordinate victim services; and (4) Grants to Tribal Domestic Violence and Sexual Assault Coalitions Program to support tribal coalitions in their coordinated response. Formula grants are awarded and allocated to all eligible recipients based on statutory requirements.

Unlike formula grants, discretionary grant awards are typically awarded through a competitive process in which the administering agency creates program parameters, qualifications and eligibility requirements, and deliverables in line with authorizing legislation. Under VAWA and subsequent reauthorizations, OVW administers 14 discretionary grant programs. These programs include grants to: address children and youth experiencing domestic and sexual assault; enhance training to end elder abuse; encourage arrest policies and protection order enforcement; enhance culturally specific services for victims; provide outreach and services to underserved populations; reduce sexual assault on campuses; support families in the justice system; provide legal assistance for victims; address rural sexual assault, domestic violence, dating violence, and stalking; provide culturally specific sexual assault services; end violence against women with disabilities; provide transitional housing assistance for victims; and assist tribal governments and tribal sexual assault services. Additionally, OVW continues to administer open grants under six discretionary grant programs, including: Court Training and Improvements Program; Engaging Men in Preventing Sexual Assault, Domestic Violence, and Dating Violence; Grants to Assist Children and Youth Exposed to Violence Program; Safe Havens: Supervised Visitation and Safe Exchange Grant Program; Services to Advocate for and Respond to Youth Grant Programs; and Services, Training, Education and Policies to Reduce Sexual Assault, Domestic Violence, Dating Violence, and Stalking in Secondary Schools Grant Program.

In addition to the grant funding awarded and administered under the DOJ, VAWA also provides funding and directives to other federal agencies. For instance, VAWA authorized the Department of Health and Human Services (HHS) to establish the National Domestic Violence Hotline, which began operation in 1996. Additionally, HHS is required to support women's shelters, rape prevention education, and coordinated community responses. VAWA also mandates the Department of Housing and Urban Development (HUD) to provide protections for participants in HUD-funded affordable housing programs who are victims of domestic violence, sexual assault, and stalking.

Subsequent reauthorizations of VAWA extended grant programs and funding, as well as expanded and strengthened protections. Such reauthorizations highlighted assisting specific victim populations, including immigrants, the elderly, the disabled, and those experiencing dating violence. Moreover, the 2000 VAWA reauthorization added "dating violence" to the previous language of "domestic violence, sexual assault, and stalking," thus extending protections. It also funded new grant programs, as specified above, including grants to tribal governments and coalitions. Finally, VAWA of 2000 expanded interstate stalking laws to include cyberstalking and tribal lands. The 2005 VAWA reauthorization continued this trend of increasing emphasis on addressing violence against Native American women. The 2005 reauthorization also emphasized victims of sexual assault and youth victims, funding numerous new programs for special populations.

The VAWA 2013 reauthorization further extends powers to sovereign tribal governments, recognizing their rights to exercise special domestic violence criminal jurisdiction (SDVCJ) over defendants, regardless of Native or non-Native status, when they commit acts of violence against women on tribal lands. This law took effect in March 2015; tribal governments were free to choose to participate, with some tribes participating sooner under a pilot program. While this VAWA reauthorization authorized up to $25 million for tribal grants, Congress has not appropriated any of these funds (Sacco, 2015). This reauthorization further extends protections to Native American victims who may not have been protected under previous VAWA legislation and reauthorization acts. The VAWA 2013 also extends provisions of the Trafficking Victims Protection Act of 2000, which includes protections for victims of human and sex trafficking.

Future Directions in Federal Crime Victims' Legislation

Although there is no constitutional amendment protecting victims' rights in the United States, the Crime Victims' Rights Act (CVRA)—enacted as part of the Justice for All Act of 2004 – serves as a sort of statutory Bill of Rights for victims. CVRA establishes the rights of crime victims in federal criminal justice proceedings, provides mechanisms for victims to enforce those rights, and gives victims and prosecutors standing to assert victims' rights (Davis and Mulford, 2008). Despite its strengthened protections for victims, this Act does not go so far as creating a constitutional amendment to permanently enshrine those rights and protections. Constitutional amendments have firmer footing to guarantee specific rights than do statutes, and they are generally more intractable and permanent than statutes which may be changed based on the legislative will at any given time.

Advocates for a constitutional change believe that such an amendment would increase the strength, permanence, and enforceability of victims' rights (The National Center for Victims of Crime [NCVC], 2012). An amendment would ensure the protection of crime victims' rights in the same way that defendants' rights are currently constitutionally protected and an amendment to the Constitution would ensure that no state or federal legislative action could violate such a protected provision. Thus, a constitutional amendment would strengthen current protections to victims provided under a patchwork of laws currently in place. Secondly, an amendment would assure that crime victims' rights would be permanently enshrined and protected in the criminal justice system. Finally, any constitutional amendment would allow for enforcement power in the courts should crime victims' rights be violated. Thus, it is important to understand the ongoing fight and efforts for a constitutional amendment at the federal level to fully grasp the potential future of crime victims' rights and the ongoing legislative dialogue and crime victims' advocacy climate in the United States in order to fully understand potential future directions of crime victims' rights.

Efforts for a Federal Constitutional Amendment

The Task Force on Victims of Crime in 1982 under President Ronald Reagan presented the first proposal for a constitutional amendment for crime victims' rights (Herrington et al., 1982). The task force report reads:

> We do not make this recommendation lightly. . . The combined experience brought to this inquiry and everything learned during its process affirmed that an essential change must be undertaken. The fundamental rights of innocent citizens cannot adequately be preserved by any less decisive action.
>
> *(Herrington et al., 1982: 114–115)*

This task force found that the criminal justice system had lost an essential balance of protecting all citizens, not just those accused of crime. The simple amendment proposed by the task force over two decades ago would augment the sixth amendment of the Constitution, which protects the accused in criminal prosecutions. The amendment language proposed by the task force would tack on one sentence to the existing amendment: "Likewise, the victim, in every criminal prosecution shall have the right to be present and to be heard at all critical stages of judicial proceedings" (Herrington et al., 1982: p. 114). Thus, this task force recommended that only action as strong as a constitutional amendment could fully protect innocent, victimized individuals. The politically conservative task force ended this section of the report by quoting the words of Thomas Jefferson and appealing to even the most fiercely conservative and federalist members of the political system.

Upon issuance of this report, advocacy members formed a Victims' Constitutional Amendment Network (Victims CAN) and began to study the feasibility of such reform (National Center for Victims of Crime [NCVC], 1999). Victims CAN decided to begin lobbying for such changes first at the state level through legislative hearing testimony, a strong organized network of advocates, and development of a media campaign (NCVC, 1999). Since that time, over 30 states of passed some form of a constitutional amendment to date.

Nevertheless, a federal change to the Constitution has not yet been implemented and lobbying efforts continue. Constitutional amendments incorporating protections for crime victims have been proposed and heard in Congress numerous times over the last decades. While the momentum for change at the state level continues, no federal amendment to the constitution has yet gained enough support to ensure its passage in Congress. The most recent constitutional amendment proposed was via a hearing on May 1, 2015. That amendment—House Joint Resolution (H.J. Res.) 45—sought to pass a more comprehensive amendment to the constitution than that proposed in 1982.

In the opening statement for a hearing on a similar proposed Victims Rights Amendment (VRA) in 2013, Representative Trent Franks of Arizona noted the VRA's broad and bipartisan support at both the state and federal levels. Representative Franks called the patchwork of victims' rights legislation inadequate and insufficient, citing findings of the Justice Department. The most recent iterations of this proposed amendment enumerate various victims' rights: to respect and dignity, to reasonable notice of proceedings and escape or release of the accused, to consideration of the victim's safety, privacy, and restitution, and to lawful representation. Moreover, the proposed VRA asserts the crime victim, defined as any person against whom the criminal offense is committed or who is directly or indirectly harmed by the crime, has a right to fully enforce those enumerated rights in court.

Lobbying groups for crime victims' rights continue to support these efforts. The recent amendment proposal was offered with letters of support from many of the lobbying groups mentioned previously, including Mothers Against Drunk Driving (MADD), National Center for Victims of Crime (NCVC), National Crime Victims Law Institute (NCVLI), National Organization of Parents of Murdered Children (POMC), National Organization for Victim Assistance (NOVA), and We Save Lives (National Victims' Constitutional Amendment Passage, 2012). Moreover, high profile figures such as governors, local mayors, and professors have testified in support of such an amendment.

A major point of contention in the various versions of proposed constitutional amendments is that of scope and applicability. Several versions of the proposed constitutional amendment apply only to crimes and cases prosecuted at the federal level, whereas other versions—such as the more recent one proposed by Representative Franks—would also apply to crimes and the victims of those crimes perpetrated and prosecuted under state law. Advocates for federalism and States' rights argue that such a constitutional amendment would be a violation of a founding principle of our country, which allows state discretion.

Summary

Over the last several decades, social movements and advocates have brought a growing awareness to the needs, rights, and protections of victims of crime. Beginning in the 1960s and 1970s, social movements brought increased attention to the victims of crime and their rights, often overlooked by a legal and constitutional system focused on protecting the due process of accused offenders. State governments and the federal legislature have responded in kind through the passage of various Acts and statutes offering new and strengthened protections. However, the future of crime victims' rights may be fought on the battlefield of a constitutional amendment as advocates and elected officials alike continue to recognize the importance of the strength, perdurability, and enforceability of such rights.

Discussion Questions

1. Why were victims of crime not always the focal point of the criminal justice system and the courts in the United States?
2. What factors and events led to an increased attention to victims' rights?
3. What are some major federal statutes in the United States that address crime victims' rights?
4. Which pieces of legislation do you believe provided the most important advances for victims? Why?
5. What would a constitutional amendment for victims' rights entail? Do you believe such an amendment is important and/or necessary? Why or why not?

Bibliography

Boland, M. L. & Butler, R. (2009). Crime victims' rights: From illusion to reality. *Criminal Justice 24*(1): 1–7.

Child Exploitation and Obscenity Section (CEOS). (2015a). *International Parental Kidnapping*. U.S. Department of Justice. Retrieved from: https://www.justice.gov/criminal-ceos/international-parental-kidnapping.

Child Exploitation and Obscenity Section (CEOS). (2015b). *Citizen's Guide to U.S. Federal Law on International Parental Kidnapping*. U.S. Department of Justice. Retrieved from: https://www.justice.gov/criminal-ceos/international-parental-kidnapping.

Congressional Research Services. (2016a). *H.R. 3378 – International Parental Kidnapping Crime Act*. Retrieved from: www.congress.gov/bill/103rd-congress/house-bill/3378.

Congressional Research Services. (2016b). *H.R. 5368 – Victims' Rights and Restitution Act*. Retrieved from: https://www.congress.gov/bill/101st-congress/house-bill/5368.

Davis, R. C., & Mulford, C. (2008). Victim rights and new remedies: Finally getting victims their due. *Journal of Contemporary Criminal Justice*.

Herrington, L. H., Bobo, G., Carrington, F., Damos, J. P., Donal, D. L., Eikenberry, K. O., Miller, R. J., Robertson, P., Rev., & Samenow, S. E. (1982). President's Task Force on Victims of Crime. *The Office of the President*. Retrieved from: http://www.ovc.gov/publications/presdntstskforcrprt/welcome.html.

Indexed legislative history of the Victims of Crime Act of 1984. (1985). Washington, D.C.: U.S. Dept. of Justice, Office of Justice Programs, Office of General Counsel, 1985.

International Parental Kidnapping Crime Act of 1993, 18 U.S.C. 1204 (1993). Retrieved from: https://www.law.cornell.edu/uscode/text/18/1204.

Issues: Constitutional Amendments. (2012). *The National Center for Victims of Crime [NCVC]*. Retrieved from: https://victimsofcrime.org/our-programs/public-policy/amendments.

National Center for Missing and Exploited Children. (2009). *Family abduction: Prevention and response, 6th Ed.* Retrieved from: http://www.missingkids.org/en_US/publications/NC75.pdf.

National Center for Victims of Crime [NCVC]. (1999). Factsheets: Constitutional Rights for Crime Victims. Retrieved from: http://www.svfreenyc.org/survivors_factsheet_72.html.

Office for Victims of Crime. (1999, July). Victims of Crime Act Crime Victims Fund. Retrieved June 10, 2016, from: https://www.ncjrs.gov/ovc_archives/factsheets/cvfvca.htm.

Office for Victims of Crime. (2013). Crime Victims Fund. Retrieved June 9, 2016, from http://www.ovc.gov/pubs/crimevictimsfundfs/index.html.

Offices of the United States Attorneys. (2014). *Services to Crime Victims*. U.S. Department of Justice. Retrieved from: https://www.justice.gov/usao/priority-areas/victims-rights-services/services-crime-victims.

Sacco, Lisa N. (2015). The Violence Against Women Act: Overview, legislation, and federal funding. *Congressional Research Services*. 1–39. Retrieved from: http://digital.library.unt.edu/ark:/67531/metadc689371/m1/1/high_res_d/R42499_2015May26.pdf.

Senate Committee on the Judiciary, Senate, 103rd Cong. (1993). The responses to rape: Detours on the road to equal justice. Retrieved from: http://library.niwap.org/wp-content/uploads/2015/VAWA-Lghist-SenateJudiciary-6.93.pdf.

Sever, Laura Munster. (1985). The Victim and Witness Protection Act of 1982: Who are the victims of which offenses? *Valparaiso University Law Review, 20*(1): 109–144.

Tucker Davis, J. (2005). The grassroots beginnings of the crime victims' rights movement. *National Crime Victim Law Institute*. Retrieved from: http://law.lclark.edu/live/files/6453-the-grassroots-beginnings-of-the-victims-rights.

Victim and Witness Protection Act of 1982. (1982). [Washington, D.C.: U.S. G.P.O.: Supt. of Docs., U.S. G.P.O., distributor, 1982].

Victims of Crime Act of 1984. (1984). [Washington, D.C.: U.S. G.P.O.: Supt Docs.]

VictimLaw Database. (2012). *About Victims' Rights. VictimLaw Database*. Retrieved from: https://www.victimlaw.org/victimlaw/pages/victimsRight.jsp.

Victims' Rights Amendment: Hearings before the Committee on Judiciary, House of Representatives, 106th Cong. 2000. Retrieved from: http://commdocs.house.gov/committees/judiciary/hju64735.000/hju64735_0f.htm.

Victims' Rights Amendment: Hearings before the Committee on Judiciary, House of Representatives, 113th Cong. (2013). (Testimony of Trent Franks). Retrieved from: https://judiciary.house.gov/wp-content/uploads/2016/02/113-18_80543.pdf.

Victims' Rights and Restitution Act of 1990, 42 U.S.C. 10607. (1990). Retrieved from: https://www.law.cornell.edu/uscode/text/42/10607.

3

VICTIMS' ASSISTANCE PROGRAMS' REFORMS

Bethany A. Poff and Catherine D. Marcum

Keywords

victims' assistance programs; protection services; formal sources of support; informal sources of support; domestic violence; cycle of abuse; Bard and Berkowitz's intervention model; student right-to-know; Campus Security Act of 1990

Objectives

After studying this chapter, the reader should understand:

- The history of victims' assistance programs in the United States.
- How victims' assistance programs have been utilized.
- Common types of victims' assistance programs.
- Reasons victims' assistance programs have been underutilized.
- How victims' assistance programs have adapted and changed.
- What future improvements could be made to victims' assistance programs to make them more effective.

Introduction

The idea of victims' assistance programs developed as a result of societal demand and the criminal justice system recognized the need to address victims' rights. However, when compared with the rights upheld for offenders, the idea and implementation of victims' rights is a challenge the criminal justice system is continuously facing (Eckman & Seng, 2009). These programs have been implemented worldwide since the 1970s (Sims, Yost, & Abbott, 2005). However, literature exists that suggests there are still struggles to overcome in this arena both in the training necessary to adequately provide resources to victims and in determining how to effectively meet the needs of these victims (Maguire, 1991; Sims et al., 2005). The purpose of this chapter is to provide an overview of the development of victims' assistance programs, their evolving applications, and suggested methods of improving the ways we can improve the lives of victims with these programs once the criminal justice process is complete.

Victims' Assistance Programs

In 1967, the President's Commission on Crime stated that crime victims should have a "systematic method" for alleviating any negative effects they may be experiencing due to their victimization. As early as the late 1960s, states were implementing victim compensation programs and in 1984, the federal government passed legislation stating that victims could be compensated for federal crimes (Doerner & Lab, 2002). Today, a large number of programs exist, including but not limited to: victim compensation programs, victim-witness programs, various forms of counseling, shelters for victims of domestic violence, and job training and placement programs (Sims et al., 2005).

Historically, research has suggested that a small number of victims utilize the services available to them. Knudten, Meade, Knudten, and Doerner (1976) found that a small number of victims sought out assistance from victim assistance programs. A later study found that only 15 percent of individuals reported using any type of government services and only 1 percent of those had used victim assistance programs (Friedman, Bischoff, Davis, & Person, 1982). In 1990, Davis and Henley found that in New York City, between 2 and 10 percent of victims notified about assistance programs ever utilized them.

It is perhaps not too surprising to hear these numbers when it is considered who actually makes use of these services—individuals who do not have access to resources anywhere else (Sims et al., 2005). Friedman and colleagues (1982) supported this idea with their findings that users of these services tend to be concentrated in lower socioeconomic status. Davis (1987) suggested that these users also tend to be affected more greatly by other social problems such as poor health and unemployment. Not much is known about why victims do not take advantage of these services. While one study found that even after a strong effort was made to contact victims and inform them of services available (Davis & Henley, 1990), another suggested that perhaps they do not know about the services (Knudten et al., 1976).

It could be suggested that the reasons for not utilizing these services are strongly related to reasons why crimes go unreported. These reasons include thinking their experience was not important enough to contact the police, it is not worth the effort (Skogan, 1977), doing so will not make a difference, their experience was a private matter (Bachman & Saltzman, 1995), or because of a general lack of trust in the police (Feldman-Summers & Ashworth, 1981). By not reporting a crime, the victim has thus eliminated the most common source of information about victim assistance programs, especially in the case of sexual assault, arguably the most heavily underreported crime.

Needs of Victims

In order to better understand the needs of victims, several studies have been conducted over the years. One of the most recent, the Denver Victim Services Assessment, took place in 2000 to determine what victims' needs were and to understand how these needs were being met (U.S. Department of Justice, 2000). The survey administered asked specific questions about services that had been utilized, satisfaction with these services, and services that could have been helpful in their situation but were not available. The surveys were distributed to Denver victim services agencies and each agency was to distribute five to ten surveys to clients who had used their services. Overall, victims were satisfied with the services received and the ease of accessing these services. However, there was an indication that some of their needs went unmet, including crisis intervention at the scene of the crime, victim assistance at the scene of the crime, victims' rights information, protection services, and updates on the status of the case they were involved with (U.S. Department of Justice, 2000).

Another survey conducted by Skogan, Davis, and Lurigio (1990) sought to interview both users and non-users of victim services provided by the state. They inquired about the needs of victims, where they sought assistance, the kind of assistance they received, and problems they felt did not get solved. These individuals had fallen victim to robbery, assault, and burglary. The results of the survey identified four primary needs among this sample of victims: 1) someone to talk to; 2) information about how to avoid repeat victimization; 3) how to protect themselves from offenders; and 4) repairing broken doors or locks or improving overall security. It was concluded that most of these victims received the help they needed from sources outside of the formal victim services structure, such as family or friends (Skogan et al., 1990).

A study conducted by Sims et al. (2005) found support for previous findings that victim services are rarely utilized. However, they also found potential correlates for use and non-use of services. In the bivariate model, they found that age, gender, race, income, marital status, receiving government assistance, and employment status all significantly correlated with the use or non-use of services. The multivariate analysis, on the other hand, found that the strongest predictors of using these services were age and type of crime. The authors suggested that, from a policy standpoint, the bivariate results should not be discarded and that programming specifically for men, whites, and higher income categories would be beneficial (Sims et al., 2005).

In addition, Sims et al. (2005) found that older victims sought the aid of services more so than younger victims, even though younger individuals have a higher chance of being the victim of a crime. Victims of violent crime were generally the most likely to seek assistance. Sims and colleagues suggested this could be caused by the traumatizing aspect of violent crime, which tends to be much stronger than that of property crime and the fact that police and other victim compensation program staff are more likely to inform a victim of a violent crime about services available (Sims et al., 2005).

The largest problem the previous study encountered was that victims were simply not aware that these services were available or lacked the knowledge needed to utilize them properly. In their statewide study, they found that 40 percent of crime victims reported not knowing what kinds of services were offered by victim services programs (Sims et al., 2005). This could be due to understaffing of these programs affecting the low rate of information dissemination and the low level of training and experience of the staff. In general, the authors argue that not much has changed from the findings of victim surveys in the early 1980s and crime victims are simply choosing to not seek out victim services just as they choose to not report a crime (Sims et al., 2005).

Victims of Domestic Violence

Perhaps the most common and most utilized types of victims' assistance programs are those for victims (individuals or families) of domestic violence. In the United States, rates of domestic violence, or family violence, against women range from 4 to 23 percent, depending on the population studied, the setting of the study, and how the study defined this type of violence (Moracco, Runyan, Bowling, & Earp, 2007; Wilt & Olson, 1996). The cost of this violence can range from five to ten billion dollars annually in court costs, medical treatment, shelters and foster care, sick leave, absenteeism, and nonproductivity (Teske, 1995). If the effects on children are taken into account, the cost could increase to around 164 billion dollars. Because of the serious effects this type of violence has on children, if effective intervention and services are not offered, the cycle of abuse could continue to play out from generation to generation (Jolin & Moose, 1997).

There are a number of factors that affect the ultimate outcome of a domestic violence situation and a lot of them involve the police since they are the first point of contact and play a crucial role in how the situation is resolved (Hendricks, 1991). These calls are a challenge to law enforcement for several reasons. First, they are timely matters to handle because they are so frequently complicated, so it takes a lot of time to sort them out. Victims will often have questions and the responding officer is not always able to answer these questions completely (Oppenlander, 1982). Second, these cases typically have very low prosecution rates and a high number of them are dismissed, leading officers to view them as a waste of time and effort. Lastly, victims may contact the police simply because they want the violence to stop, they do not necessarily want the perpetrator arrested or prosecuted, further leading officers to view these calls as unworthy of the time and effort needed to respond to them (Davis & Smith, 1995).

Responses to these calls have changed in big ways over the decades. In the early 1950s and 1960s, families were encouraged to work out their problems together and come to a conclusion on their own (Stalans & Lurigio, 1995). In fact, prior to 1966, not a single police department in the United States offered training on domestic disturbances and only a few had written policies or procedures on the subject (Hendricks, 1991). Changes have come due to three factors: 1) the women's movement, which greatly increased awareness of the struggles of abused women (Stalans & Lurigio, 1995); 2) an increasing number of lawsuits filed against police departments for not protecting victims of domestic violence (Roberts, 1996); and 3) a national study on the deterrent effects of arrest strongly influenced police departments to change their arrest policies in instances of domestic violence (Sherman, 1992).

The first step toward reform in the traditional law enforcement approach to domestic violence calls occurred in 1967 when Bard and Berkowitz designed a program to train officers in mediation and crisis intervention as well as instructing them to use arrest only as a last resort, but instead to mediate the dispute and make referrals to clinical psychologists (Buzawa & Buzawa, 1996). By 1971, 14 other police departments had adopted this intervention model and had created specialized officers who served primarily to mediate disputes (Liebman & Schwartz, 1973). Unfortunately, studies of this approach found that officers were often more concerned with the abuser in these situations than the victim and only 4 percent of officers were making referrals to social service agencies in the area (Oppenlander, 1982). Because of these difficulties, trained victim assistance workers were brought in to assist police at the scenes of these disputes. A crisis team composed of a victim assistance team member and an armed police officer was established by the Pawtucket, Rhode Island Police Department in 1974 to back-up uniformed officers on domestic disturbance calls. A survey taken the following year revealed that 79 percent of families who received services from this team believed the services to be helpful (Carr, 1982). In 1975, a similar team was established in Tuscon, Arizona, through the District Attorney's office (Robers, 1990). This team was on patrol every night and arrived at the scene to relive police officers once their duties had been finished with the goal of providing immediate crisis counseling, advocacy, transportation to shelters, and referrals to community resources (Horton & Williamson, 1988).

Victims of Sexual Assault

Another common type of victims' assistance comes in the form of programs and resources for victims of sexual assault. In some cases, these individuals are also victims of domestic violence—the two are not mutually exclusive. In a meta-analysis of 34 studies of college students, Spitzberg (1999) found that, on average, the prevalence of female rape victimization was 12 percent. Survivors of this type of assault often experience a wide range of debilitating effects, including both physical and emotional distress (Kimerling & Calhoun, 1994). The strongest predictor of sexual assault is previous history of sexual abuse (Himelein, 1995), though studies have shown there are other predictors as well (Kearns & Calhoun, 2010).

Because of the attention and increased public awareness female sexual assault victimization has received, public policy and legislative changes have taken place (Maxwell, Robinson, & Post, 2003).

In the late 1980s, most universities were offering educational programs for students and federal funding of more than $8 million was provided to colleges and universities to continue efforts to combat domestic violence, sexual assault, and stalking on their campuses. In 1990, Congress passed the Student Right-to-Know and Campus Security Act of 1990, which required colleges and universities to make their crime statistics and public policies public. In 1992, the Campus Sexual Assault Victims' Bill of Rights was added and in 1998, it was amended again to expand reporting obligations and security provisions on college campuses (Fisher & Cullen, 2000).

While a great deal of attention has been paid to female college students and their experiences with and exposure to sexual assault, little focus has been placed on sexual assault of and between adolescents. A study by Maxwell et al. (2003) found that a majority of female adolescents studied had experienced at least one act of sexual coercion, about one in four experienced sexual assault at a criminal level, and more than one in ten had been raped. In the same study, fewer males reported committing a sexually aggressive act than females reported being victimized, which could be due to a small percentage of males victimizing a larger number of females or it could point to victimization of females at an earlier age, not by a peer. They also found that the probability of sexual aggression perpetration and victimization increased with the number of dating partners an individual had (Maxwell et al., 2003).

Studies have shown that there is a strong association between sexual assault and significant mental health problems. There exists, however, a very small percentage of victims studied who have sought out mental health services after an assault (George, Winfield, & Blazer, 1992). Frazier, Rosenberger, and Moore (2000) found that only 9 percent of 533 sexual assault victims seen in a given emergency room returned to follow up with counseling. Koss, Koss, and Woodruff (1991) went so far as to conclude that victims were more likely to contact physicians than mental health professionals. Although individuals who are assaulted by a known perpetrator suffer similar levels of psychological distress than those assaulted by a stranger (Ullman & Siegel, 1993), individuals who know their attacker are less likely to label their experience as rape and are therefore less likely to seek assistance after the fact (Stewart, Hughes, Frank, Anderson, Kendall, & West, 1987).

After an event, most assault victims do not tell anyone about their assaults immediately, but about two-thirds of survivors do tell someone at some point. This support typically comes from informal sources such as family and friends, not formal assistance (Golding, Siegel, Sorenson, Burnam, & Stein, 1989). Norris, Kaniasty, and Scheer (1990) found that those victims who have high levels of informal social support are more likely to use mental health services. In some instances, formal support providers such as police and physicians have been rated as being less supportive than informal support providers (Ullman, 1999). Some of this could possibly be attributed to less than adequate training for health professionals about how to respond to and treat sexual assault victims (Campbell, Raja, & Grining, 1999). Because of this potentially negative response, many face a dilemma over whether or not to disclose their assault. Those who choose not to disclose avoid the negative reactions, but do not get the support they need and miss the opportunity to process the trauma and the positive effects on psychological and physical health that can come from disclosing traumas (Pennebaker, Kiecolt-Glaser, & Glaser, 1988).

Even though few victims (5 to 10 percent) seek help from rape crisis centers (Golding, et al., 1989), data suggests this type of assistance is perceived to be helpful, possibly because of the training these agencies provide in how to handle these situations (Ullman, 1996). Evidence shows that the effects of negative social reactions can have serious consequences on a victim's psychological and physical well-being. For instance, a study of 102 rape survivors found that victims of nonstranger rape who received little assistance from the legal or medical system but received victim-blaming behaviors from system personnel exhibited more symptoms of posttraumatic stress (Campbell, Sefl, Barnes, Ahrens, Wasco, & Zaragoza-Diesfeld, 1999).

Suggested Reforms

While some reforms have been made to victims' assistance programs over the past decades, there are still some crucial changes that need to be made to these programs in general, and to programs dealing with specific victims' needs. According to Sims et al. (2005), if providers want to increase the chances of victims seeking out their services, they need to make greater investments into educating the public about the services they provide. They must also better address the needs of victims by providing programs that are broader in scope, making the effort of the victim worthwhile. Staffing issues with these programs need to be addressed as well. Staffing needs to be increased, but these individuals need to be well trained and qualified if they are to come in contact with victims (Sims et al., 2005).

On a broader level, Sims et al. (2005) suggest that the criminal justice system get behind these types of reform and funnel resources from other areas that are emphasized under the "get tough" approach of the modern system. With the help and support of the broader system, while still difficult, these changes in education, staffing, and resources would be a much more realistic outcome. It should, however, be considered that the lack of utilization of these services could be a function of where an individual is situated within a socioeconomic class and not entirely a function of a lack of knowledge or education. It could be that no amount of public awareness or notification will entice an individual from a higher economic and education status to utilize victim services when they have a wider range of personal resources available.

Specific to sexual assault programs, authors Maxwell et al. (2003) have some recommendations. They believe that it is important to design an effective prevention program for adolescents that begins in junior high school and continues through high school and college. Research on adolescent sexual assault is also something they are passionate about to continue increasing the depth of knowledge and understanding of these assaults. Likewise, Ullman and Filipas (2001) suggest that schools and the media can play a part in this reform by adding programming on sexual assault issues to raise public awareness about acquaintance rape. They suggest that education and training specific to sexual assault and treatment of victims is needed for the fields of medicine, mental health, education, and criminal justice and legal professions.

Conclusion

In short, the United States has come a long way in the journey to provide better services and programs to victims of various crimes, especially sexual assault and domestic violence. While this is a good start, there is still a long way to go before victims can truly feel comfortable seeking help and, when they do, feeling like the help that they received was adequate and effective. Reforms have been suggested by those in the field who have put in the time and effort to study victim populations. While in some instances more studies are needed and more knowledge needs to be gathered, there is sufficient groundwork laid to begin the discussion of reform; the next step comes in appealing to legislators and other professionals in the field to get these reforms implemented so they can begin to provide victims with the assistance and services they truly need.

Summary

Victims' assistance programs have been in existence in the United States for many decades. However, they remain underutilized as many victims seek assistance from informal sources such as family and friends. It is also highly likely that victims are not aware of the programs and assistance available to them. The most common types of victims' assistance programs are for victims of sexual assault and domestic violence. These programs have shifted and adapted over the years but are still in need of some change, including increasing staffing, training for staff, and educating the public on what programs are available.

Discussion Questions

1. What are some logical ways to increase awareness of the programs available to victims?
2. Do you think the rise of technology has affected the means by which victims seek out support?
3. Should it be the job of the justice system to inform victims about services available or should it be the responsibility of the victim to seek out these services themselves?

References

Bachman, R. & Saltzman, L. E. (1995). *Violence against women*. Washington, D.C.: Bureau of Justice Statistics.

Buzawa, E., & Buzawa, C. (1996). *Domestic violence: The criminal justice response*. Thousand Oaks, CA: Sage.

Campbell, R., Raja, S., & Grining, P. L. (1999). Training mental health professionals on violence against women. *Journal of Interpersonal Violence, 14*, 1003–1013.

Campbell, R., Sefl, T., Barnes, H. E., Ahrens, C. E., Wasco, S. M., & Zaragoza-Diesfeld, Y. (1999). Community services for rape survivors: Enhancing psychological well-being or increasing trauma? *Journal of Consulting and Clinical Psychology, 67*, 847–858.

Carr, J. (1982). *The abusive partner: An analysis of domestic battering*. New York: Van Nostrand Reinhold Company, Inc.

Davis, R. C. (1987). *Providing help to victims: A study of psychological and material outcomes*. Report to the Victim Services Agency. New York.

Davis, R. C. & Henley, M. (1990). Victim service programs. In A. J. Lurigio, W. G. Skogan, & R. C. Davis (Eds.), *Victims of crime: Problems, policies, and programs*. Newbury Park, CA: Sage, pp. 116–250.

Davis, R., & Smith, B. (1995). Domestic violence reforms: Empty promises or fulfilled expectations? *Crime Delinquency, 41*(4), 541–552.

Doerner, W. G., & Lab, S. P. (2002). *Victimology*. (3rd ed.). Cincinnati: Anderson.

Eckman, M. S., & Seng, M. J. (2009). On-scene victim assistance units within law enforcement agencies. *Policing, 32*(4), 719–738. doi: http://0-dx.doi.org.wncln.wncln.org/10.1108/13639510911000786

Feldman-Summers, S. & Ashworth, C. D. (1981). The victim-offender relationship and call the police in assaults. *Criminology, 37*, 931–947.

Fisher, B. S., & Cullen, F. T. (2000). Measuring the sexual victimization of women: Evolution, current controversies, and future research. In D. Duffee (Ed.), *Measurement and analysis of crime and justice* (NCJ 182411, Vol. 4). Criminal Justice 2000, Office of Justice Programs, National Institute of Justice, U.S. Department of Justice, Washington, D.C.

Frazier, P., Rosenberger, S., & Moore, N. (2000). *Correlates of service utilization among sexual assault survivors*. Poster session presented at the annual meeting of the American Psychological Association, Washington, D.C.

Friedman, K., Bischoff, H., Davis, R.C., & Person, A. (1982). *Victims and helpers: Reactions to crime*. Washington, D.C.: U.S. Government Printing Office.

George, L. K., Winfield, I., & Blazer, D. G. (1992). Sociocultural factors in sexual assault: Comparison of two representative samples of women. *Journal of Social Issues, 48*, 105–125.

Golding, J. M., Siegel, J. M., Sorenson, S. B., Burnam, M. A., & Stein, J. A. (1989). Social support sources following sexual assault, *Journal of Community Psychology, 17*, 92–107.

Hendricks, J. (ed.). (1991). *Crisis intervention in criminal justice and social service*. Springfield, IL: Charles C. Thomas Publishers.

Himelein, M. J. (1995). Risk factors for sexual victimization in dating: A longitudinal study of college women. *Psychology of Women Quarterly, 19*, 31–48.

Horton, A., and Williamson, J. (Eds.). (1988). *Abuse and religion*. Lexington, MA: D.C. Heath and Company.

Jolin, A., & Moose, C. (1997). Evaluating a domestic violence program in a community policing environment: Research implementation issues. *Crime Delinquency, 43*(3), 279–297.

Kearns, M. C., & Calhoun, K. S. (2010). Sexual revictimization and interpersonal effectiveness. *Violence and Victims, 25*(4), 504–17. Retrieved from http://0-search.proquest.com.wncln.wncln.org/docview/650829192?accountid=8337

Kimerling, R., & Calhoun, K. S. (1994). Somatic symptoms, social support, and treatment seeking among sexual assault victims. *Journal of Consulting and Clinical Psychology, 62*, 333–340.

Knudten, R. D., Meade, A., Knudten, M., & Doerner, W. (1976). *Victims and witnesses: The impact of crime and their experience with the criminal justice system*. Washington, D.C.: U.S. Government Printing Office.

Koss, M. P., Koss, P. G., & Woodruff, W. J. (1991). Deleterious effects of criminal victimization on women's health and medical utilization. *Archives of Internal Medicine, 151*, 342–347.

Liebman, D. A., & Schwartz, J. A. (1973). Police programs in domestic crisis intervention: A review. In J. R. Snibbe & H. M. Snibbe (Eds.), *The urban policeman in transition*. Springfield, IL: Charles C Thomas, pp. 421–472.

Maguire, M. (1991), The needs and rights of victims of crime. *Crime and Justice, 14*, 363–433.

Maxwell, C. D., Robinson, A. L., & Post, L. A. (2003). The nature and predictors of sexual victimization and offending among adolescents. *Journal of Youth and Adolescence, 32*(6), 465–477. Retrieved from http://0-search.proquest.com.wncln.wncln.org/docview/204646203?accountid=8337

Moracco, K., Runyan, C., Bowling, J., & Earp, J. A. (2007). Women's experiences with violence: A national study. *Women's Health Issues, 17*, 3–12.

Norris, F. H., Kaniasty, K. Z., & Scheer, D. A. (1990). Dating, drinking, and rape: Effects of victim's and assailant's alcohol consumption on judgments of their behavior and traits. *Psychology of Women Quarterly, 16*, 179–191.

Oppenlander, N. (1982). Coping or copping out. *Criminology, 20*(3–4), 449–465.

Pennebaker, J. W., Kiecolt-Glaser, J. K., & Glaser, R. (1988). Disclosure of traumas and immune function: Health implications for psychotherapy. *Journal of Consulting and Clinical Psychology, 56*, 239–245.

Roberts, A. (1990). *Helping crime victims: research, policy, and practice*. Newbury Park, CA: Sage Publications.

Roberts, A. (1996). *Helping battered women: New perspectives and remedies*. New York: Oxford University Press.

Sherman, L. (1992). *Policing Domestic Violence*. New York: The Free Press.

Sims, B., Yost, B., & Abbott, C. (2005). Use and nonuse of victim services programs: Implications from a statewide survey of crime victims. *Criminology & Public Policy, 4*(2), 361–383. Retrieved from http://0-search.proquest.com.wncln.wncln.org/docview/200116293?accountid=8337

Skogan, W. G. (1977). Dimensions of the dark figure of unreported crime. *Crime and Delinquency, 23*, 41–50.

Skogan, W. G., Davis, R. C., & Lurigio, A. J. (1990). *Victim's needs and victim services: Final report to the National Institute of Justice*. Washington, D.C.: Crime Victims Institute.

Spitzberg, B. H. (1999). An analysis of empirical estimates of rape and sexual coercion. *Violence and Victims, 14*, 241–260.

Stalans, L., & Lurigio, A. (1995). Responding to domestic violence against women. *Crime and Delinquency, 41*(4), 387–398.

Stewart, B. D., Hughes, C., Frank, E., Anderson, B., Kendall, K., & West, D. (1987). The aftermath of rape: Profiles of immediate and delayed treatment seekers. *Journal of Nervous and Mental Disease, 175*, 90–94.

Teske, R. (1995). *Crime and Justice in Texas*. Huntsville, TX: Sam Houston Press.

Ullman, S. E. (1996). Do social reactions to sexual assault victims vary by support provider? *Violence and Victims, 11*, 143–156.

Ullman, S. E. (1999). Social support and recovery from sexual assault: A review. *Aggression and Violent Behavior: A Review Journal, 4*, 343–358.

Ullman, S. E., & Filipas, H. H. (2001). Correlates of formal and informal support seeking in sexual assault victims. *Journal of Interpersonal Violence, 16*, 1028–1047.

Ullman, S. E., & Siegel, J. M. (1993). Victim-offender relationship and sexual assault. *Violence and Victims, 8*, 121–134.

U.S. Department of Justice. (2000). *Denver victim services 2000 needs assessment*. Washington, D.C.: Crime Victims Institute.

Wilt, S., & Olson, S. (1996). Prevalence of domestic violence in the United States. *Journal of the American Medical Women's Association, 51*(3), 77–82.

4
VICTIMS IN CRIMINOLOGICAL THEORY

Tusty ten Bensel and Dana L. Radatz

Keywords

victim–offender overlap, routine activities, lifestyle perspective, symbolic interaction, neighborhood factors, life course theory

Objectives

By the end of this chapter, you should be able to:

- Discuss the victim–offender overlap for victimization.
- Explain and distinguish between routine activities and lifestyle theory.
- Discuss how social interactional perspective applies to victimization.
- Explain the role of peers, parents, and neighborhood context in relation to victimization.
- Discuss and compare the two life course perspectives that has been applied to victimization.

Introduction

For decades, criminologists have explored the overarching question of *why do we have crime*? Under this umbrella, various bodies of research have focused on understanding offenders, their typologies, behavioral patterns, pathways, motivations, and other individualistic characteristics. However, the causes of crime are more complex than simply focusing on offenders. Victimologists have focused on theories that explain why certain individuals are likely to become targets, or "victims." This chapter will explain the victim-offender overlap, situational and social interactionist theories, as well as social and structural processes. In addition, we discuss the role of life course perspective in the understanding of victimization.

Victim–offender Overlap

Previous research has found empirical support that indicates victims and offenders share many similarities.[1] For instance, victimization surveys, official statistics, and various empirical studies have demonstrated that violent offenders and victims of violent offenses tend to be young (ages 16 to 24) and male, which are both characteristics of one's likelihood of being a victim.[2] To some extent, this could be explained by the principle of homogamy. In 1978, Hindelang, Gottfredson, and Garofalo explained that an individual's risk for victimization and his or her level of exposure to potential offenders can depend on personal behaviors. For instance, young males who frequently associate with other young males have an increased likelihood of victimization. Sampson and Lauritsen (1990) identified several similar characteristics between victims and offenders, such as age, being male, low educational attainment, and single marital status. Even further, they determined behavioral patterns, like spending evenings away from home or engaging in drinking, were also shared similarities between victims and offenders. These are just a few examples of shared characteristics and behavioral patterns of offenders and victims that explain the victim–offender overlap.

Aside from these shared similarities, victim and offender identities have also been found to overlap, meaning those who are offenders can also be victims. Broidy and colleagues (2006) conducted a study on homicides between 1996 and 2001 in Bernalillo County, New Mexico. They reported many of the victims and offenders of homicide in their study lived in and commuted through disadvantaged neighborhoods, had prior arrest histories and involvement in nonviolent behaviors, and engaged in risky behavioral patterns, assuming dual roles. In addition, Sampson and Lauritsen (1990) examined lifestyles and victimization and found offenders who engaged in deviant lifestyles, such as using drugs, were more likely to experience personal victimization than those who did not. Further, Lauritsen, Sampson, and Laub (1991) indicated students who engaged in delinquent behavior were more likely to be victims of assault, robbery, larceny, and vandalism than their non-delinquent peers.

The victim–offender overlap could also be attributed to a larger sociological perspective, in which violence is viewed as an acceptable response to disrespect. In 1967, Wolfgang and Ferracuti developed the subculture of violence theory, which posited some subgroups of individuals, such as gangs, often value violence and they use violent behaviors to retaliate against those that have disrespected them. Further, Singer (1981) reasoned within a subculture where violence is normative and acceptable, individuals could interchangeably be both a victim and an offender. For example, members of a street gang may attack members from an opposing street gang for trespassing on proclaimed territory. In retaliation, opposing gang members may retaliate by attacking the enemy gang who originally targeted them. Essentially, individuals who engage in gang activity have higher rates of victimization due to their risky lifestyles and use of violence in their everyday lives.

Victimization can also be seen as a precursor for criminal behavior. For instance, several scholars have examined female victimization through the "pathways perspective," which examines life histories and subsequent criminal behavior.[3] More specifically, some have argued young girls, who have been victimized, often go on to engage in criminal activities (e.g., prostitution, theft, drug use) later in life as a way to survive and cope with their victimizations. DeHart (2008) conducted qualitative interviews with 60 incarcerated women and found victimization was both directly and indirectly related to their criminality, such as prostitution, theft, and drug addiction. Some of the women in this study claimed they had developed a substance abuse problem as a way of coping with their victimizations, which may also have contributed to their risky behaviors. Further, Salisbury and van Voorhis (2009) found empirical support for three gendered pathways between victimization and female offending. The first pathway identified childhood victimization as a catalyst for mental health problems, which later culminated in five indirect pathways to reoffending. The second pathway demonstrated an indirect link between difficulties in relationships (i.e., lack of power; unsupportive significant other; painful) and subsequent criminality. The third pathway revealed women who had lower educational achievements, dysfunctional intimate partner relationships, low self-efficacy, or minimal familial support, experienced employment and financial challenges, which then directly linked to incarceration. These pathways can be viewed as having a cumulative effect. Although the victim–offender overlap perspective provides some insight into victimization, the context in which such incidents occur is also important.

Situational Theories

Situational theories of victimization and crime, sometimes referred to as opportunity or environmental theories, emphasize the intersection between the victim, offender, and environmental or situational characteristics of crime. Proponents of situational theories suggest personal characteristics and lifestyle activities correlate with one's risk of victimization. Routine activities theory and lifestyles theory are two of the most common situational theories for victimization.

In 1979, Cohen and Felson proposed the routine activity approach to understand crime rate trends following World War II. While many criminological theories focus on offender motivations as explanations for criminal acts, Cohen and Felson posited attention should also be placed on the circumstances surrounding the criminal act. From this perspective, routine activity theory was based on two main principles. First, most criminal acts depend on the concurrence of motivated offenders, suitable targets, and the lack of capable guardianship. Second, the likelihood for a criminal act to occur is related to the routine activities of a suitable target.

Cohen and Felson (1979) explained that for a criminal act to occur, a motivated offender must have both a criminal intent and the opportunity to commit a crime. While there is an adequate amount of motivated offenders with intent to commit criminal acts, the opportunity to commit crimes lies in the necessity and availability of a suitable target and lack of guardianship. A suitable target not only refers to an individual, but also to things that hold value (i.e., materialistic or symbolic). A motivated offender determines a target's suitability based on a wide variety of factors, such as value, availability, and accessibility. Further, a motivated offender's decision to select a particular suitable target is influenced by whether or not a capable guardian is present and able to prevent a criminal act. Capable guardianship can be provided by an individual or by other means of prevention. For example, a police officer, a security system, and a dog can all be considered capable guardians. This framework focuses on the merging of space and time of motivated offenders, an attractive target, and a lack of adequate guardianship to determine one's risk of victimization.

Under the routine activities framework, Cohen and Felson also argued that an individual's routine activities—or daily lifestyle decisions—are correlated with his or her risk of victimization. The extent to which an individual's routine activities and daily lifestyle lend him or herself to interact or be near motivated offenders affects the likelihood of becoming a victim. For instance, an individual who works in the service industry may have a higher likelihood of victimization than an individual who works from home. The individual working in the service industry would have more interactions with potentially motivated offenders than the individual who works from home and has fewer interactions with others.

In 1978, Hindelang, Gottfredson, and Garofalo developed the lifestyles theory, which is similar to the routine activity approach in many aspects. In fact, many scholars have frequently combined routine activity and lifestyles theory when explaining victimization. Hindelang and his colleagues (1978) theorized particular lifestyles, personal characteristics, and behaviors can be correlated with one's risk for victimization. They postulated individuals may willingly and/or innocently engage in lifestyle choices that generate more or less opportunities for offenders to commit a crime against them. For example, a man who works the evening shift at a retail store would have a higher risk of victimization compared with a man that works the day shift. An individual's risk of victimization increases as the amount of time he or she spends outside the home increases, especially at night. However, Hindelang and his colleagues stated an individual's lifestyle is not solely dictated by personal decisions, as lifestyle is also impacted and controlled by role expectations and structural constraints, such as age and sex. For instance, an older individual is more likely to fall victim to telemarketing fraud because elderly persons tend to be at home and have a landline compared with younger individuals. The elderly individual may answer a landline phone call and subsequently be taken advantage of by a scam artist claiming to sell a false insurance policy. This is also evident in sexual assault victimizations, as the risk for sexual assault victimization significantly increases if an individual is a female.

In addition, the lifestyles theory is also based on the principle of homogamy. As discussed above, an individual's level of victimization risk increases as his or her frequency of exposure to potential offenders increases in similar demographic groups (Hindelang, Gottfredson, & Garofalo, 1978). Previous studies have shown younger individuals are more likely to be offenders than older individuals; therefore, a young adult who spends time with other young adults increases his or her risk for victimization. Empirical support for the routine activities theory and the lifestyles theory has been found in a numerous studies, across several different types of offenses.[4] Thus, the logical approach to crime prevention and victimization reduction is to lessen the opportunities for offending to occur. To reduce offending opportunities, attention is placed on manipulating lifestyle and/or environmental factors, such as walking in well-lit pathways late at night, or installing a home alarm system.

Social Interactionist Perspective

Within the social interactionist perspective, emphasis is focused on the interaction between a perpetrator and victim to explain violence and victimization. In their book on aggression and violence, Felson and Tedeschi (1993) explained the social interactionist approach encompasses four key principles. First, aggressive behavior is viewed as goal-oriented and instrumental. For instance, an individual may use aggression to dissuade someone's actions to achieve his end goal. Second, aggressive behavior is perceived as a natural response to employ when a conflict arises between individuals. In essence, the individual deems aggression as a viable, acceptable tactic to obtain his desired outcome. Third, situational and interpersonal influences during the interaction are crucial factors in inciting an individual's aggression. For instance, a victim's behavior, such as being disrespectful or offensive, could elicit an aggressive response from the offender. Fourth, focus is placed on the perspective of the aggressor, which can be used to explain the decision-making process, and thus behavior.

The degree to which a victim is culpable for his or her own victimization, also known as victim precipitation, is an important component of the social interactionist perspective. In 1958, Wolfgang coined the term victim precipitation during his review of Philadelphia police homicide records from 1948 to 1952. Wolfgang determined approximately a quarter of the homicides within the five-year span were victim precipitated, meaning the victims of homicides had been the first to display or use a weapon, strike a punch, or engage in physically assaultive behavior. When examining the relationship between stress and victimization, Felson (1992) determined a distressed individual (as a result of experiencing a negative life event such as the death of a close family member or marital troubles) could, through his aggressive behavior, elicit an aggressive response from others, resulting in his or her own victimization. Felson argued the stress one experiences from a negative life event (e.g., financial concerns) could impact behavior, including violating social rules (i.e., social control processes) and becoming aggressive. Consequently, distressed individuals may become a victim, as initial aggressive and irritating behaviors could evoke aggressive responses from others nearby. For example, a man who was recently fired from his job decided to drink alcohol at a local bar until he became intoxicated. When the drunken man tried to leave with his car keys in hand, another bar patron interjected and took the man's keys as a way to stop him from driving while intoxicated. The drunken man saw the bar patron's behavior as offensive, and began to verbally berate him. The bar patron responded by physically assaulting the drunken man, and a physical altercation ensued. Thus, the drunken man's actions evoked the bar patron's assault. In short, the findings of Felson's study demonstrated individuals who experience negative life events are more likely to be victimized than those that do not experience negative life events, in part due to their own irritating and aggressive behaviors that precede their victimization.

Social and Structural Process

Thus far, we have discussed different theories for why some individuals are more susceptible to victimization than others. Particularly, we have focused on theories that link victims and offenders, personal lifestyles and activities, and social interactions; however, processes and relationships that influence lives, such as peers and family members, can also impact the risk of victimization.

Peer Relationships

Studies have shown peer relationships can be very influential on adolescent behaviors. Involvement in peer groups, especially delinquent peer groups, has been found to increase the likelihood of being victimized for a number of reasons.[5] First, youth who are in delinquent peer groups are more likely to be exposed to motivated offenders. This closely aligns with the "principle of homogamy," in the sense that when adolescents spend time with peers who engage in risky behaviors and have criminal records, they are not only within proximity of a motivated offender, but also exposed to situations that make them vulnerable.

Second, when adolescents spend a lot of time with peers, they are likely to create social bonds, protect each other, and become guardians. When youth are in prosocial peer groups, they are likely to spend time with others who are engaged in positive social activities, limiting the amount of exposure to risky behaviors and situations. On the other hand, when adolescents spend time with delinquent peers, who are often selfish, impulsive, and less likely to protect their peers, adolescents are left vulnerable in risky situations. Lastly, youth who are involved in delinquent peer groups, such as gangs, are likely to participate in criminal activities themselves and become attractive targets for retaliation.

While participating in criminal activities, especially against a rival gang, youths place themselves in risky situations, which can often led to victimization; however, the mere association with a delinquent group, can also make youth an attractive target. For example, Papachristos, Braga, Piza, and Grossman (2015) conducted a study to understand the likelihood of getting shot if an individual is associated with a gang member. The study examined 10,531 youth during a one-year timeframe in Newark and found there was a spillover effect of violence from gang members to non-gang members. Social connections with gang members increased exposure to risk places, activities, and people, but peer associations are not the only relationships that can impact risk of victimization. A study by Schreck and Fisher (2004) found similar results. Spending time with delinquent peers increased the likelihood of victimization for several reasons including exposure to retaliation by rivals, motivated offenders, and lack of capable guardianship. Negative influences of delinquent peers, however, can be evaded through strong parental attachment.

Family Attachment and Supervision

During childhood, bonds to family members, especially parents, can play a pivotal part in adolescent experiences, behaviors, and social interactions. A strong social attachment to family can shield youth from having negative experiences, specifically victimizations. Parents who provide a structured lifestyle (i.e., rules, close supervision, model good behavior, and control bad behavior) for their youth are likely to keep their children closer to home and divert them from risky situations.[6] Parents who have strong attachments to their families, especially their children, may be compelled to supervise and regulate their children's peer network, social activities, and are more likely to get acquainted with individuals who spend time with their children.

Previous research has consistently found a link between importance of family attachment and victimization. For example, a study by Borawski, Ievers-Landis, Lovegreen, and Trapl (2003) examined 692 adolescents who were enrolled in the 9th or 10th grade in six urban high schools. They examined two parenting supervision measures: the degree to which parents knew the whereabouts of their children, and the degree to which children were able to negotiate unsupervised time with their friends. They found adolescents who had decreased levels of parental supervision and increased levels of negotiated unsupervised time were more likely to engage in risk behaviors (i.e., alcohol and drug abuse, sexual activity). Such risky behaviors are likely to place adolescents in situations where victimization is prone to occur.

Parents and children with strong social attachment are likely to spend more time together engaging in family activities; thus, decreasing the likelihood of being exposed to a motivated offender. Also, these youth are less likely to place themselves in risky situations or get involved in risky behaviors in fear of disappointing their parents. Although parents who are negative role models may place their children in dangerous situations, it is typically much more dangerous to be outside the home among strangers.[7]

Neighborhood Factors

While positive role models, attachments, and peer networks are important factors, an individual's surroundings areas can also play a crucial role in understanding risk of victimization. Some neighborhoods are high crime areas and/or areas with higher victimization rates. Not surprisingly, individuals who reside in these areas are at higher risk of exposure to victimization than those who live in less crime/victimization prone neighborhoods.

Previous studies have found a positive relationship between disadvantaged neighborhoods and crime.[8] Areas that are economically underprivileged and socially isolated are tainted with high rates of crime and disorder, unemployment, single-parent households, residential mobility, high rates of drug addiction, and incarceration. Thus, individuals residing in these areas often have difficulty developing collective, informal social control within a neighborhood to guard against victimization and protect the residents in the area. The lack of guardianship and mechanisms to maintain safety, order, and stability within disadvantaged communities decreases the chances that offenders will get caught, and increases the likelihood of victimization.

As discussed earlier, criminal behavior and victimization are strongly correlated (Berg & Loeber, 2011; Hindelang et al., 1978; Sampson & Lauritsen, 1990) and several studies have found that social structural neighborhood factors impact risk of victimization (Lauritsen, 2001; Miethe & McDowall, 1993; Sampson, 1985). Studies on victimizations often integrate routine activities theory and the lifestyle perspective with the social and structural elements of neighborhood disadvantage or social disorganization. Pioneered by Shaw and McKay (1942) and later extended by others,[9] social disorganization theory is commonly explained as areas that exhibit high poverty rates, ethnic heterogeneity, and residential mobility (Sampson, 2006; Shaw & McKay, 1942). Such neighborhoods often have high crime rates and violence, which leads to a higher risk of victimization. For example, Sampson and Wooldredge (1987) conducted a study on personal victimization using the British Crime Survey and found risk of victimization was most prevalent among single and young individuals, and those who regularly go out at night or leave their residences empty. Even after accounting for these individualistic factors, they found victimization was directly correlated with neighborhood factors, such as unemployment, family disruption, housing density, and residential mobility. Focusing specifically on individual factors (routine activities and lifestyle) and neighborhood factors (ethnic heterogeneity, disorders, neighborhood density), they found both violent and property victimization was strongly correlated with neighborhoods conditions. In summary, there is plenty of literature that indicates neighborhood disadvantage is a strong predictor of risk of victimizations. Within a broader scheme, risk of victimization is a complex issue and researchers have been attempting to understand it through various theoretical lenses, including the life-course perspective.

Life-course Perspective

The life-course perspective emerged in criminological studies in the 1990s, focusing specifically on understanding the development of criminal behaviors over time. Thus far, there has been growing interest among criminology researchers as to why individuals begin, continue, and desist from offending. Although this body of research primarily focuses on criminal offending, victimologists have also applied and tested the life-course perspective in relation to victimization.

General Theory of Crime

In 1990, Gottfredson and Hirschi proposed the general theory in crime, in which they argued criminal offending can be explained by low self-control. Given the opportunity, individuals with low self control will engage in criminal activities, such as drug use, sexual promiscuity, or aggravated assault. They argued low-self control is not an innate characteristic genetically passed down from parents, but a learned behavior cultivated through parental socialization. Essentially, individuals with low self-control will be impulsive and will be unable to delay gratification. They will engage in risky-thrill seeking behaviors, with little to no consideration of the outcome. These individuals will typically lack long-term goals and tend to engage in physical activities instead of mental activities. They will exhibit low tolerance to frustration, which can result into sudden anger. Lastly, individuals with low self control will tend to lack empathy towards others.

Towards the end of the 1990s, victimologists started to predict connections between various aspects of low-self control and risk of victimization.[10] For example, individuals with low self control tend to be impulsive and likely to engage in self gratifying behaviors, which leaves little room for individuals to consider the consequences of their actions. When these individuals make instant behavioral decisions, they eliminate the opportunity to protect themselves from victimization. One of the first researchers to apply the principles of low self-control to victimization risk was Christopher Schreck in 1999. He conducted a survey of 959 undergraduate students at the University of Arizona and found low self control increased the likelihood of personal and property victimizations, even after controlling for criminal behaviors. Recent studies have also found low self-control can influence re-victimization. For example, Turanovic and Pratt (2014) found low self control not only increased the likelihood of victimization, but also predicted whether victims were likely to makes lifestyle changes post victimization. If the victim made little to no changes in their lifestyles, then they were likely to be repeat victims. The general theory of crime is one of the perspectives of life course theory, while the other theory is known as age-graded informal social control.

Age-graded Informal Social Control

Sampson and Laub (2003) proposed social bonds could protect individuals from engaging in criminal activities. One of their primary principles asserted criminal behavior is closely linked to whether "an individual's bond to society is weak or broken" (p. 305). They proposed that when individuals lack social capital and investment, they turn to a life of crime and deviance. Further, offenders can change their life trajectories through various transitions in their lives. Such transitions include marriage, employment, joining the military, new peers, and/or children. These transitions could lead offenders through a process of desistance from criminal involvement. For example, when offenders stabilize new employment, they are more likely to cut off old delinquent peers and replace them with new work associates. After a period of time, it allows the offenders to realize the commonality between their new work peers and themselves. This also provides offenders with different viewpoints of how others behave and operate. Offenders, as a result, want to "fit in" and are more likely to change their perspective on life.

Although age-graded informal social control perspective has primarily been applied and tested for offending behaviors, Daigle, Beaver, and Hartman (2008) focused on the role of marriage and employment on desistance from delinquent behaviors and victimization. Using the National Longitudinal Study of Adolescent Health (Add Health), they found getting married predicted a desistance from victimization as adolescents emerged into adulthood, while employment reduced the likelihood of desistance from victimization. The authors concluded their findings were consistent with routine activities theory and the life course perspective. The more individuals spend time at home with their spouse and/or, the less likely that individual will be victimized, but employment is another story since jobs require individuals to leave the house. This is another example of how different theoretical perspectives (in this case, life course perspective, routine activity theory, and lifestyle perspective) are integrated to explain the likelihood of victimization.

Conclusion

As indicated in this chapter, there are plenty of explanations for why individuals fall prey to victimization. Although the prevailing theories are routine activities and the lifestyle perspectives, other theories that focus on social and structural factors have played an important role in understanding risk of victimization. Understanding and explaining criminal offending and victimization is complex in nature and as discussed in this chapter, there is rarely ever one clear explanation for a phenomenon. It can take both micro and macro level explanations to provide a robust picture.

Discussion Questions

1. What are the individual and social/structural factors that put an individual in risk of victimization?
2. Explain how and why criminal offending and victimization often overlap.
3. Think about your own activities and neighborhood dynamics. What factors about your life put you at risk of victimization?
4. What are different strategies you can implement that will decrease your risk of victimization?

Notes

1 Several studies have reported that victims and offenders have significant similarities with each other (Broidy, Daday, Crandall, Sklar, & Jost, 2006; Lauritsen & Laub, 2007; Mustaine & Tewksbury, 2000; Wolfgang, 1958).

2 Results from the 2013 National Crime Victimization Survey indicated that individuals aged 12 to 17 had the highest rate of prevalence for violence compared with all other age groups, and males had a higher likelihood of being victims of violence crimes compared with females (Truman & Langton, 2014). 2013 Uniform Crime Report data indicate a higher number of males than females committed murder, and the majority of the homicide offenders were under the age of 30 (U.S. Department of Justice, 2014). Uniform Crime Report arrest trends show that males are arrested for a wider variety of violent offenses (e.g., murder, forcible rape, aggravated assault) than females (U.S. Department of Justice, 2013).

3 For studies related to victimization and the "pathways perspective," see: Belknap (2001); Bloom, Owen, and Covington (2003; Chesney-Lind and Pasko (2004, 2012); Chesney-Lind and Sheldon (1992).

4 For studies that show empirical support for the routine activities theory and/or the lifestyles theory, see: Fisher, Cullen, and Turner (2002); Lauritsen, Sampson, and Laub (1991); Mustaine and Tewksbury (1999); Osgood, Wilson, O'Malley, Bachman, and Johnston (1996); Sampson and Lauritsen (1990).

5 For studies on peer influence on victimization, see Delisi, Barnes, Beaver, and Gibson (2009); Gibson, Miller, Jennings, Swatt, and Gover (2009); Papachristos, Braga, Piza, and Grossman (2015); Schreck and Fisher (2004).

6 For studies on parental attachment and its impact on victimization, see Esbensen, Huizinga, and Menard (1999); Pratt, Turner, and Piquero (2004); Schreck and Fisher (2004).

7 Felson, M. (1998). *Crime and everyday life.* Thousand Oaks, CA: Pine Forge Press.

8 See Pratt and Cullen (2005); Sampson, Morenoff, and Gannon-Rowley (2002).

9 For more information on social disorganization, see Bursik (1988); Rose and Clear (1998); Sampson and Groves (1989); Sampson, Morenoff, and Gannon-Rowley (2002); Shaw and McKay (1942).

10 For studies on low self-control and victimization, see Evans, Cullen, Burton, Dunaway, and Benson (1997); Pratt, Turnaovic, Fox, and Wright (2014); Schreck (1999); Turanovic, Reisig, Pratt (2015).

References

Belknap, J. (2001). *The invisible woman: Gender, crime, and justice.* (2nd ed.). Belmont, CA: Wadsworth.

Berg, M. T., & Loeber, R. (2011). Examining the neighborhood context of the violent offending–victimization relationship: A prospective investigation. *Journal of Quantitative Criminology, 27*(4), 427–451.

Bloom, B., Owen, B., & Covington, S. S. (2003). *Gender-responsive strategies: Research practice and guiding principles for women offenders.* Washington, DC: National Institute of Corrections.

Borawski, E. A., Ievers-Landis, C. E., Lovegreen, L. D., & Trapl, E. S. (2003). Parental monitoring, negotiated unsupervised time, and parental trust: The role of perceived parenting practices in adolescent health risk behaviors. *Journal of Adolescent Health, 33*(2), 60–70.

Broidy, L. M., Daday, J. K., Crandall, C. S., Sklar, D. P., & Jost, P. F. (2006). Exploring demographic, structural, and behavioral overlap among homicide offenders and victims. *Homicide Studies, 10*(3), 155–180.

Bursik, R. J. (1988). Social disorganization and theories of crime and delinquency: Problems and prospects. *Criminology, 26*(4), 519–552.

Chesney-Lind, M. & Pasko, L. J. (2004). *The female offender: Girls, women and crime.* (2nd ed.). Thousand Oaks, CA: Sage.

Chesney-Lind, M. & Pasko, L. J. (2012). *The female offender: Girls, women and crime.* (3rd ed.). Thousand Oaks, CA: Sage.

Chesney-Lind, M., & Sheldon, R. G. (1992). *Girls, delinquency, and juvenile justice.* Pacific Grove, CA: Brooks/Cole.

Cohen, L. E., & Felson, M. (1979). Social change and crime rate trends: A routine activity approach. *American Sociological Review, 44*(1), 588–608.

Daigle, L. E., Beaver, K. M., & Hartman, J. L. (2008). A life-course approach to the study of victimization and offending behaviors. *Victims and Offenders, 3*(4), 365–390.

DeHart, D. D. (2008). Pathways to prison: Impact of victimization in the lives of incarcerated women. *Violence Against Women, 14*(2), 1362–1381.

Delisi, M., Barnes, J. C., Beaver, K. M. & Gibson, C. L. (2009). Delinquent gangs and adolescent victimization revisit: A propensity score matching approach. *Criminal Justice and Behavior, 36*, 808–823.

Esbensen, F. A., Huizinga, D., & Menard, S. (1999). Family context and criminal victimization in adolescence. *Youth & Society, 31*(2), 168–198.

Evans, T. D., Cullen, F. T., Burton, V. S., Dunaway, R. G., & Benson, M. L. (1997). The social consequences of self-control: Testing the general theory of crime. *Criminology, 35*(3), 475–504.

Felson, M. (1998). *Crime and everyday life.* Thousand Oaks, CA: Pine Forge Press.

Felson, R. B. (1992). "Kick 'em when they're down": Explanations of the relationship between stress and interpersonal aggression and violence. *The Sociological Quarterly, 33*(1), 1–16.

Felson, R. B., & Tedeschi, J. T. (1993). Social interactionist perspectives on aggression and violence: An introduction. In R. B. Felson & J. T. Tedeschi (Eds.), *Aggression and violence: Social interactionist perspectives* (pp. 1–10). Washington, DC: American Psychological Association.

Fisher, B. S., Cullen, F. T., & Turner, M. G. (2002). Being pursued: Stalking victimization in a national study of college women. *Criminology & Public Policy, 1*(2), 257–308.

Gibson, C. L., Miller, J. M., Jennings, W. G., Swatt, M., & Gover, A. (2009). Using propensity score matching to understand the relationship between gang membership and violent victimization: A research note. *Justice Quarterly, 26*(4), 625–643.

Gottfredson, M. R., & Hirschi, T. (1990). *A general theory of crime.* Stanford, CA: Stanford University Press.

Hindelang, M. J., Gottfredson, M. R., & Garofalo, J. (1978). *Victims of personal crime: An empirical foundation for a theory of personal victimization.* Cambridge, MA: Ballinger.

Lauritsen, J. L. (2001). The social ecology of violent victimization: Individual and contextual effects in the NCVS. *Journal of Quantitative Criminology, 17*(1), 3–32.

Lauritsen, J. L., & Laub, J. H. (2007). Understanding the link between victimization and offending: New reflections on an old idea. *Crime Prevention Studies, 22*, 55–75.

Lauritsen, J. L., Sampson, R. J., & Laub, J. H. (1991). The link between offending and victimization among adolescents. *Criminology, 29*(2), 265–292.

Miethe, T. D., & McDowall, D. (1993). Contextual effects in models of criminal victimization. *Social Forces, 71*(3), 741–759.
Mustaine, E. E., & Tewksbury, R. (1999). A routine activity theory explanation for women's stalking victimizations. *Violence Against Women, 5*(1), 43–62.
Mustaine, E. E., & Tewksbury, R. (2000). Comparing the lifestyles of victims, offenders, and victim–offenders: A routine activity theory assessment of similarities and differences for criminal incident participants. *Sociological Focus, 33*(3), 339–362.
Papachristos, A. V., Braga, A. A., Piza, E., & Grossman, L. S. (2015). The company you keep? The spillover effects of gang membership on individual gunshot victimization in a co-offending network. *Criminology, 53*(4), 624–649.
Pratt, T. C. & Cullen, F. T. (2005). Assessing marco-level predictors and theories of crime: A meta-analysis. *Crime and Justice, 32*, 373–450.
Pratt, T. C., Turanovic, J. J., Fox, K. A., & Wright, K. A. (2014). Self control and victimization: A meta analysis. *Criminology, 52*(1), 87–116.
Pratt, T. C., Turner, M. G., & Piquero, A. R. (2004). Parental socialization and community context: A longitudinal analysis of the structural sources of low self-control. *Journal of Research in Crime and Delinquency, 41*(3), 219–243.
Osgood, D. W., Wilson, J. K., O'Malley, P. M., Bachman, J. G., & Johnston, L. D. (1996). Routine activities and individual deviant behavior. *American Sociological Review, 61*(4), 635–655.
Rose, D. R., & Clear, T. R. (1998). Incarceration, social capital, and crime: Implications for social disorganization theory. *Criminology, 36*(3), 441–480.
Salisbury, E. J., & Van Voorhis, P. (2009). Gendered pathways a quantitative investigation of women probationers' paths to incarceration. *Criminal Justice and Behavior, 36*(6), 541–566.
Sampson, R. J. (1985). Neighborhood and crime: The structural determinants of personal victimization. *Journal of Research in Crime and Delinquency, 22*(1), 7–40.
Sampson, R. J. (2006). How does community context matter? Social mechanisms and the explanation of crime rates. *The Explanation of Crime: Context, Mechanisms, and Development*, 31–60.
Sampson, R. J., & Groves, W. B. (1989). Community structure and crime: Testing social-disorganization theory. *American Journal of Sociology, 94*(4), 774–802.
Sampson, R. J., & Laub, J. H. (2003). Life-course desisters? Trajectories of crime among delinquent boys followed to age 70. *Criminology, 41*(3), 555–592.
Sampson, R. J., & Lauritsen, J. L. (1990). Deviant lifestyles, proximity to crime, and the offender–victim link in personal violence. *Journal of Research in Crime and Delinquency, 27*(2), 110–139.
Sampson, R. J., Morenoff, J. D., & Gannon-Rowley, T. (2002). Assessing "neighborhood effects": Social processes and new directions in research. *Annual Review of Sociology, 28*, 443–478.
Sampson, R. J., & Wooldredge, J. D. (1987). Linking the micro-and macro-level dimensions of lifestyle-routine activity and opportunity models of predatory victimization. *Journal of Quantitative Criminology, 3*(4), 371–393.
Schreck, C. J. (1999). Criminal victimization and low self-control: An extension and test of a general theory of crime. *Justice Quarterly, 16*(3), 633–654.
Schreck, C. J., & Fisher, B. S. (2004). Specifying the influence of family and peers on violent victimization extending routine activities and lifestyles theories. *Journal of Interpersonal Violence, 19*(9), 1021–1041.
Shaw, C. R., & McKay, H. D. (1942). *Understanding deviance: Connecting classical and contemporary perspective*, edited by Tammy Anderson. New York, NY: Routledge Publishing.
Singer, S. I. (1981). Homogeneous victim–offender populations: A review and some research implications. *Journal of Criminal Law and Criminology, 72*(2), 779–788.
Turanovic, J. J., & Pratt, T. C. (2014). "Can't stop, won't stop": Self-control, risky lifestyles, and repeat victimization. *Journal of Quantitative Criminology, 30*(1), 29–56.
Turanovic, J. J., Reisig, M. D., & Pratt, T. C. (2015). Risky lifestyles, low self-control, and violent victimization across gendered pathways to crime. *Journal of Quantitative Criminology, 31*(2), 183–206.
Truman, J. L., & Langton, L. (2014). *Criminal victimization, 2013.* (NCJ 247648). Washington, DC: Bureau of Justice Statistics.
U.S. Department of Justice (2013). Uniform Crime Report: Crime in the United States, 2012.
U.S. Department of Justice. (2014). Uniform Crime Report: Crime in the United States, 2013.
Wolfgang, M. E. (1958). *Patterns in criminal homicide.* Montclair, NJ: Patterson Smith.
Wolfgang, M. E., & Ferracuti, F. (1967). *The subculture of violence.* London, UK: Travistock Publications.

5

VICTIMS' RIGHTS LEGISLATION

Comparative Assessment and Implementation Issues

Francis D. Boateng

Keywords

victims; rights; legislation; Europe; America; victimology; criminal justice; system

Objectives

After reading this chapter, readers will:

- Understand the historical development of victims' rights from a comparative perspective.
- Identify and discuss specific issues hindering the implementation of victims' rights legislation across cultures.
- Develop a conceptual framework of the role of victims in the criminal justice system.

Introduction

On July 30, 2015, a Florida judge, Jerri Collins, berated a domestic violence victim and sentenced her to jail for failing to testify against a man she had a child with, who allegedly abused her and threatened her with a knife. Judge Collins's behavior was an abuse of authority, with serious implications for domestic violence reporting; it exemplifies the numerous abuses that victims of crime face during criminal proceedings. This and other similar behaviors—as in the Oklahoma City bombing trial—raise thought-provoking questions about the status of crime victims in the criminal justice system.

Historically, the United Nations, as an international organization, has been at the forefront of the fight against the maltreatment of crime victims (Burgess, Regehr, & Roberts, 2013; García-Godos, 2013; Maguire & Shapland, 1997). To address the plight of victims, the United Nations (1985) passed into effect the Declaration of the Basic Principles of Justice for Victims of Crime and Abuse of Power, which required member nations to protect the rights of victims of crime. It obligated states to (a) guarantee victims' access to justice and fair treatment, (b) require offenders to make restitution for their criminal behaviors, (c) endeavor to provide financial compensation to victims, and (d) provide material, medical, psychological, and social assistance to victims. The principles outlined in the Declaration had great significance for the development of victims' rights and the protection of victims. First, they formed the foundation of victims' rights legislation in several countries across the globe.

Second, as noted by García-Godos (2013), they established what were to be understood as victims' rights: access to justice and fair treatment, restitution, compensation, and assistance. Thanks to the work of the United Nations and victims' rights advocacy groups, many countries today have some form of legislation that addresses the concerns of victims of crime (Joutsen, 1987; Krainz, 1991; Spinellis, 1997).

This chapter offers a global discussion on victims' rights legislation in the U.S. and Europe, with the aim of identifying and addressing some of the issues embedded in the implementation of the legislation. For a thoughtful presentation, the paper is broadly organized in this order: following the introduction are assessments of victims' rights in the U.S. and in Europe, while the next two sections discuss implementation issues from a global perspective and ways to address the issues.

Victims' Rights Legislation in the U.S.: A Historical Analysis

Traditionally, the criminal justice system in America has largely recognized the rights of the defendant in all criminal proceedings (Blondel, 2008), with apparent lack of recognition for the rights of crime victims (Kyl, Twist, & Higgins, 2005). Victims' rights advocates argue that the rights of victims of crime must be recognized during criminal proceedings, since these individuals have a unique interest in such proceedings (Cassell, 2009; Pizzi, 1999), and have heavily criticized this behavior of the system. The major concern of the advocates is that victims of violent or nonviolent criminal acts have a stake in the criminal proceedings that is different from that of the public or non-victims. Therefore, their rights must be recognized and respected in court.

Officially, the victims' rights movement started in the mid-1960s (Kyl et al., 2005) with the establishment of victim assistance programs in states like California and Missouri. At the same time, several other movements were taking place, such as the Civil Rights Movement of 1964 and the women's movement. These other movements were part of the development of the victims' rights movement and played significant roles (Young & Stein, 2004). However, the movement gained momentum in the 1970s and 1980s (Tobolowsky, 2001), especially with the establishment of the President's Task Force on Victims of Crime by President Ronald Reagan in 1982. This development, according to victimologists, formed the root of the modern victims' rights movement in America.

The task force was commissioned to investigate the treatment of victims in federal courts and recommend strategies to reform the criminal justice system (Giannini, 2008). After extensive hearings and interviews, it produced a final report (President's Task Force on Victims of Crime, 1982) that concluded that victims of crime were not only persecuted in court but also denied the opportunity to speak and to participate in criminal proceedings. Following this observation, the task force made several recommendations aimed at transforming the American criminal justice system. These recommendations, according to Cassell (2009), included the following: courts should receive victim impact evidence at sentencing, restitution should be ordered in most cases, victims and their families should be allowed to attend trials, and prosecutors must be responsible for notifying victims of all court proceedings. It is worth mentioning that the task force recommendations focused mainly on victims of rape, armed robbery, murder, and similar violent offenses, without any recognition for victims of other types of crimes, such as environmental and nonviolent offenses. The exclusive focus on violent crime victims has been a key criticism of the work of the President's Task Force.

Despite their exclusive nature, several federal legislative frameworks were enacted in response to the task force's recommendations. These enactments sought to redefine and broaden the scope of victims' rights in the criminal justice system (Cassell, 2009; Kyl et al., 2005). The initial legislative efforts included the passage of the Victim and Witness Protection Act (VWPA) in 1982 by the U.S. Congress. The VWPA was intended to (a) enhance and protect the necessary role of crime victims and witnesses in the criminal justice process, (b) ensure that the federal government did everything within limits of available resources to assist victims and witnesses of crime without infringing on the constitutional rights of the defendant, and (c) provide a model for legislation for state and local governments. Although the VWPA was concerned with victims' and witnesses' rights, it also put in place mechanisms to avoid infringing defendants' rights in the process of recognizing and respecting the rights of victims and witnesses. The VWPA offered numerous rights to crime victims, including the right to make an impact statement during the sentencing phase of the criminal proceedings and an expanded right to receive restitution (Cassell, 2009; Heinz, 1983; VWPA, 1982). In cases of restitution, the VWPA required that it should be made directly to the victim or an organization designated by the victim (Heinz, 1983).

Subsequent to the passage of the VWPA, several other laws were passed by Congress to expand the protection accorded to victims. These laws included the Victims of Crime Act of 1984, the Victims' Rights and Restitution Act of 1990, the Violent Crime Control and Law Enforcement Act of 1994, the Antiterrorism and Effective Death Penalty Act of 1996, and the Victims' Rights Clarification Act of 1997. Unfortunately, these 1980s and 1990s victims' rights legislative efforts failed to achieve their intended purpose of ensuring maximum protection for crime victims in the courtroom. Even under this legislation, many victims were still mishandled, and criminal justice professionals constantly trampled upon their rights. A case in point is how victims of the Oklahoma City bombing were treated by judges and prosecutors during the trial of the bombers. The absolute failure of this legislation to guarantee victims' rights throughout the stages of the criminal justice process was due in part to the lack of enforcement mechanisms to provide recourse for victims (Beloof, 2006).

In response to the failures of the earlier laws, Congress passed the Crime Victims' Rights Act (CVRA) in 2004 (Cassell & Joffee, 2011; Jarrell & Ozymy, 2012). The CVRA, which was purported to empower crime victims and expand and define the role of victims in criminal proceedings (Jarrell & Ozymy, 2012), focused mainly on protecting the rights of victims of the most egregious crimes. It was perhaps the most comprehensive legislative effort to address the needs of crime victims, and defined a crime victim strictly as a person directly and proximately harmed because of the commission of a federal offense. This definition excludes persons harmed because of the commission of state offenses from the purview of who is considered a crime victim. The Crime Victims' Rights Act of 2004 (as part of the Justice for All Act) provides eight fundamental rights to victims, as defined in Section 377(a):

1. "to be reasonably protected from the accused"
2. "to reasonable, accurate, and timely notice of any public court proceeding, or any parole proceeding, involving the crime or of any release or escape of the accused"
3. "not to be excluded from any such public court proceeding, unless the court, after receiving clear and convincing evidence, determines that testimony by the victim would be materially altered if the victim heard other testimony at that proceeding"
4. "to be reasonably heard at any public proceeding in the district court involving release, plea, sentencing, or any parole proceeding"
5. the "reasonable right to confer with the attorney for the Government in the case"
6. "to full and timely restitution as provided in law"
7. "to proceedings free from unreasonable delay"
8. "to be treated with fairness and with respect for the victim's dignity and privacy."

As noted by Cassell and Joffee (2011), the CVRA allows crime victims the right to be heard as well as the right to confer with the prosecution. To ensure that victims' rights are safeguarded, CVRA requires district courts to respect and recognize the rights of victims and provides recourse for victims if they feel their rights have been violated. Today, almost all 50 U.S. states and Washington, DC, have enacted legislation in the nature and spirit of the Federal Victims' Bill of Rights that secures victims' rights to participate in criminal proceedings and to be heard. The analysis that follows comparatively assesses victims' rights legislation in all 50 U.S. states plus the District of Columbia.

Victims' Rights Legislation: States Analysis

This section provides a brief analysis of legislative protections and guidelines for crime victims at the state level. State initiatives to guarantee victims' rights mirror the efforts of the federal government (Doerner & Lab, 2015) in four significant ways:

1. The passage of victims' bills of rights in every state to provide a certain number of entitlements to victims of crime.
2. The provision of victim–witness assistance programs to help victims of crime navigate how the criminal justice system works.
3. Establishment of victim compensation funds to oversee the provision of financial compensation to victims for the losses suffered due to the commission of the crime.
4. The lack of enforcement mechanisms to uphold and protect victims' rights.

According to the National Crime Victim Law Institute (2011), most U.S. states (about 33 states) have incorporated victims' bills of rights into their state constitutions, while the rest have specifically enacted victims' rights legislation. Table 5.1 is a chronological representation of state enactments of victims' bills of rights in the United States; the state of Wisconsin was the first to make a legislative attempt to protect victims, in 1980.

Although variations exist in victims' bills of rights across the states, there is some common ground (Tobolowsky, Gaboury, Jackson, & Blackburn, 2010). Table 5.2 presents a statutory analysis of victims' rights across the 50 U.S. states plus the District of Columbia. It indicates that victims of crime in most states are afforded the following set of rights:

1. The right to be present at all stages of the criminal justice processes.
2. The right to be compensated for losses suffered.
3. The right to be heard.
4. The right to be informed about the criminal justice processes and other services.
5. The right to be treated fairly and respectfully, and with dignity and privacy.
6. The right to be protected against humiliation from the offender and any other person.
7. The right to restitution.

Table 5.1 State Enactment of Crime Victims' Bills of Rights

Year of Enactment	*State(s)*
1980	Wisconsin
1982	California
1986	Rhode Island
1988	Florida; Michigan
1989	Texas; Washington
1990	Arizona
1991	New Jersey
1992	Colorado; Illinois; Kansas; Missouri; New Mexico
1994	Alabama; Alaska; Idaho; Maryland; Ohio; Utah
1996	Connecticut; Indiana; Nebraska; Nevada; North Carolina; Oklahoma; South Carolina; Virginia
1998	Louisiana; Mississippi; Montana; Tennessee
1999	Oregon (originally enacted in 1996, repealed in 1998, and reenacted in 1999)

Source: NCRVW Resource Guide, 2014

Table 5.2 Victims' Rights Analysis in All the U.S. States and the District of Columbia

States	*Crime Victims' Right to:*									
	Be present at all stages	*Be compensated*	*Be heard*	*Be informed*	*Treated fairly and respectfully, with dignity and privacy*	*Protection*	*Restitution*	*Return of property*	*Speedy trial*	*Confer with prosecution*
Total	44	43	37	48	32	37	34	22	21	22
Alabama	x	x	x	x				x		x
Alaska	x	x	x	x	x	x	x		x	x
Arizona	x	x	x	x	x		x		x	x
Arkansas	x	x			x	x	x	x		
California		x		x	x	x	x			
Colorado	x	x	x	x						
Connecticut	x	x		x	x	x	x		x	
Delaware	x	x			x	x		x	x	
DC	x			x	x	x	x			x
Florida	x	x	x	x					x	
Georgia	x	x	x	x	x		x			
Hawaii	x	x		x	x	x		x		
Idaho	x	x	x	x	x		x		x	x
Illinois	x	x		x	x	x	x		x	x
Indiana	x	x	x	x	x	x	x			x
Iowa	x	x		x	x		x			
Kansas	x	x	x		x	x	x		x	x
Kentucky		x	x	x	x	x		x	x	
Louisiana	x	x	x	x	x		x	x	x	
Maine		x		x	x	x	x			
Maryland	x	x	x	x	x		x			x
Massachusetts	x	x	x	x		x				x
Michigan	x		x	x	x	x	x		x	x

Minnesota	x	x		x		x	x			
Mississippi	x		x	x					x	x
Missouri	x			x		x	x	x	x	x
Montana	x	x	x	x				x		x
Nebraska	x	x	x	x		x		x	x	
Nevada		x	x	x		x	x			
New Hampshire	x		x	x	x	x	x	x		x
New Jersey	x	x	x	x	x	x		x		x
New Mexico	x	x	x	x	x	x	x	x	x	x
New York		x		x	x	x	x	x		
North Carolina	x	x	x	x			x			x
North Dakota	x	x	x	x		x		x	x	
Ohio	x	x	x	x	x	x		x		
Oklahoma	x		x	x	x	x	x	x		
Oregon	x		x	x		x	x			x
Pennsylvania		x	x	x			x			
Rhode Island		x	x	x		x		x		
South Carolina	x		x	x	x	x	x		x	
South Dakota	x	x		x	x	x	x			x
Tennessee	x	x	x	x		x	x		x	x
Texas	x	x	x	x		x		x		
Utah	x	x	x	x	x	x	x		x	
Vermont	x	x		x	x		x	x	x	
Virginia	x	x	x	x	x	x	x	x		
Washington	x	x	x	x		x		x		
West Virginia	x	x	x	x	x	x	x			
Wisconsin	x	x	x	x	x	x	x		x	x
Wyoming	x	x	x	x		x		x		

Comparatively, about 44 states guarantee victims the right to be present at all stages of the criminal justice proceedings. The significance of this right is that it offers victims the opportunity to see firsthand how the criminal justice system operates. States that provide this right to victims include Alabama, Alaska, Arizona, Arkansas, Colorado, Connecticut, Delaware, Florida, Georgia, Hawaii, Idaho, and Indiana (see Table 5. 2). Similarly, under some state laws, crime victims have the right to financial compensation to cover losses they suffered from the occurrence of the crime. Most of these states have set up special compensation funds, administered by a board that is in charge of disbursing the funds. For instance, under Washington State law, financial compensation is paid to victims through the Washington State Crime Victim Compensation Program (WSCVCP) to cover expenses relating to medical treatment, loss of financial support, and funeral arrangements. Moreover, states like California, Iowa, Kansas, Maryland, Maine, Minnesota, Montana, Nebraska, and Ohio provide compensation to victims. It should be noted that the eligibility criteria for compensation vary from state to state. For example, Alaska law requires victims to report a crime to the police within five days of its occurrence to be eligible for compensation, while Arizona requires reports to be made within 72 hours of discovery of the crime.

The rights to be heard and to be informed are guaranteed by 37 and 48 states respectively. States such as Kansas, Kentucky, Louisiana, Maryland, Massachusetts, Michigan, New Jersey, and North Carolina afford victims the opportunity to be heard during the criminal process. This opportunity usually takes the form of a victim impact statement, which is included in the pre-sentence investigation report presented to the judge. In 47 states, victims of crime have the right to be informed about the criminal justice process, their rights, the release of the offender, and any available services that might help them go through the ordeal successfully. See Table 5. 3 for an assessment of specific rights offered to victims in each U.S. state.

However, according to some critics, states' efforts to expand and redefine victims' rights have created problems for the criminal justice system (Calcutt, 1988; Office for Victims of Crime, 2002; Tobolowsky, 2001). The lack of enforcement strategies, the overloading of criminal justice professionals leading to delays and greater costs, and the lack of recourse for victims if their rights are violated are some of the issues raised by critics against states' efforts to protect and expand victims' rights.

Victims' Rights Legislation in Europe: A Historical Analysis

Like America, Europe has made considerable efforts in the area of protecting victims and expanding their rights, leading to the enactment of much legislation and promotion of best practices (Aa, 2015; Buczma, 2013; Joutsen, 1987, 1994; Kaiser, Kury, & Albrecht, 1991; Maguire & Shapland, 1997). Historically, this began in the mid-1980s, with European countries adopting many legal instruments to further the emancipation of crime victims and define their role in the criminal justice system (Aa, 2015). While some of the legal instruments were binding, others were non-binding initiatives. The Europeans' efforts to set guidelines for the treatment of victims came from different facets. However, for the purpose of the current analysis, attention will be limited to the legislative efforts made by the Council of Europe and the European Union.

On September 28, 1977, the Council of Europe, through its Committee of Ministers, adopted a legal text dealing with the situation of victims of crime: Resolution (77) 27 on the compensation of victims of crime. The Resolution offered several guiding principles to harmonize national provisions in the protection of victims by member states. These principles included:

1. When compensation cannot be ensured by other means the state should contribute to compensate:
    a. anyone who has sustained severe bodily injury as a result of crime,
    b. the dependents of any person who died as a result of crime;

2. As regards the crimes, which caused the bodily injury, at least all intentional crimes of violence should be covered even if the offender could not be prosecuted;
3. The compensation might be effected either within the framework of the social security system, or by the setting up of a special compensation scheme or by recourse to insurance;
4. The compensation should be the fullest and fairest possible, taking into account the nature and the consequences of the injury;
5. The compensation should include, in appropriate cases, at least loss of past and future earnings, increase of expenses, medical expenses, expenses of medical and professional rehabilitation, and funeral expenses;
6. For practical or economic reasons, the compensation scheme might make provision for a minimum or a maximum. It might also be fixed based on prefixed scales or of a percentage assessment of the injury. The payment of compensation might be limited to victims who are in a serious material situation;
7. The compensation might take the form of a lump sum or of periodic payments;
8. The compensation scheme should provide for the possibility of granting in urgent cases interim awards when there would be delay in determining the compensation;
9. With a view to avoiding double compensation, any amount of money received or obtainable from other sources such as the offender, social security or private insurance might be deducted or reclaimed;
10. The scheme might subrogate in the victim's claims, as far as possible without impairing the rehabilitation of the offender;
11. The compensation might be reduced or refused on account of the victim's conduct and his relationship to the offender and his milieu;
12. Except when special conventions apply, compensation shall be paid by the state on whose territory, including its ships and aircraft, the crime was committed;
13. In respect of foreigners, the principle of reciprocity might be wholly or partially applied.

Apart from making the effort to ensure uniformity in national legislation, this legal text laid the foundation for the adoption of the European Convention on Compensation of Victims of Violent Crimes (ECCVVC) in 1983. Buczma (2013) has noted that this convention was the first legally binding victims' rights instrument in Europe.

In the years ahead, the Council of Europe adopted several other legal frameworks focusing on meeting the needs of victims. For instance, in 1985, two years after the adoption of the ECCVVC, the Council of Europe adopted Recommendation No. R (85) 11 on the position of the victim in the framework of criminal law and procedure, which specified that the fundamental function of the criminal justice system is to meet the needs and to safeguard the interests of victims (Muller-Rappard, 1990). In addition to providing guidelines to meet the needs of victims, Recommendation R (85) 11 emphasized the importance of enhancing victims' confidence and encouraging their cooperation in the system. The subsequent effort, Recommendation R (87) 21 on assistance to victims and the prevention of victimization, outlined rules relating to support services. About two decades later, Recommendation R (87) 21 was updated, leading to the adoption of Recommendation R (2006) 8 on assistance to crime victims.

In addition to the numerous initiatives taken by the Council of Europe to safeguard the rights of victims, another important milestone in addressing the problems of victims and protecting their interests was the 2001 EU Framework Decision on the Standing of Victims in Criminal Proceedings. Although this decision made a significant contribution to expanding protection for victims, critics accused it of being preoccupied with law enforcement purposes instead of demonstrating genuine concern for victims (Wieczorek, 2012). Specifically, scholars believed that its emphasis on the right to information and participation without creating obligations regarding rights to protection and support was problematic. Later, in 2012, the Framework Decision was replaced by Directive 2012/29/EU, which established minimum standards on the rights and protections of victims of crime in the European Union. This directive addressed some of the criticisms of the Framework Decision and made significant improvements in the areas of rights to protection, reparation, and support (Wieczorek, 2012). Generally, victims of crime in the European Union enjoy the following rights:

1. Right to have access to justice;
2. Right to be offered support in accessing justice;
3. Right to protection;
4. The right to an effective remedy;
5. Right to fair trial and public hearing;
6. Right to be advised and represented;
7. Right to legal aid.

Victims' Rights Legislation in Select European Countries

Member states of the European Union are obliged to follow and adhere to the EU Directives and Recommendations for establishing protections and guidelines for victims in their respective criminal justice systems. This obligation is to ensure uniformity in victims' rights legislation across all member states. However, despite these efforts, it seems that the goal of uniformity is far from achieved. There are noticeable differences in the rights provided to victims of crime across member states. These differences are mainly due to the different roles victims play in the criminal justice systems in various European countries, as well as the varying ways that a victim is conceptualized by these countries. The definition of *victim*, which varies across national legal systems, determines the role that victims play in the system, which in turn affects the rights and support they will receive during criminal proceedings. The existing variation in victims' rights further leads to differences in the number of rights that each member state affords to victims. Some member states offer more rights to victims than others.

The analysis in Table 5.3 details specific rights that 28 member states of the European Union provide to crime victims. Overall, victims enjoy the following seven rights across the member states analyzed:

1. The right to be heard, provided by 22 member states, including Estonia, Greece, Spain, and Finland.
2. The right to supply evidence, provided by 22 member states, including Austria, Belgium, Czech Republic, and Germany.
3. The right to be questioned and testify, provided by 24 member states, including France, Croatia, Hungary, and Ireland.
4. The right to a separate waiting area at court, provided by 14 member states, including Netherlands, Sweden, and United Kingdom.
5. The right to be accompanied at trial by support persons, provided by 17 member states, including Romania, Malta, and Slovakia.
6. The right to access and copy trial records, provided by 23 member states, including Luxembourg, Latvia, and Poland.
7. The right to ask for compensation during a criminal trial, provided by 22 member states, including Portugal, Slovenia, and Slovakia.

While six (Austria, Belgium, Czech Republic, Germany, Finland, and France) of the 28 member states analyzed afford victims all seven rights during a criminal trial, countries like Bulgaria, Cyprus, Denmark, Ireland, Italy, Lithuania, Romania, and the United Kingdom provide fewer than five rights to victims during criminal proceedings.

Table 5.3 Victims' Rights Analysis of European Countries

Country	*Rights to:*						
	Be heard	*Supply evidence*	*Be questioned and testify*	*Separate waiting area at court*	*Accompanied at trial by support persons*	*Access and copy trial records*	*Ask for compensation during criminal trial*
Total	22	22	24	14	17	23	22
Austria	x	x	x	x	x	x	x
Belgium	x	x	x	x	x	x	x
Bulgaria	x			x		x	
Croatia	x	x	x		x	x	x
Cyprus			x	x	x		
Czech Republic	x	x	x	x	x	x	x
Germany	x	x	x	x	x	x	x
Denmark			x		x		x
Estonia	x	x	x			x	x
Greece	x	x	x			x	
Spain	x	x	x	x		x	x
Finland	x	x	x	x	x	x	x
France	x	x	x	x	x	x	x
Hungary	x	x	x	x		x	x
Ireland			x	x	x		
Italy		x	x			x	x
Latvia	x	x	x		x	x	x
Lithuania	x	x				x	x
Luxembourg	x	x			x	x	x
Malta	x	x	x		x	x	
Netherlands	x	x	x	x		x	x
Poland	x	x	x			x	x
Portugal	x	x	x			x	x
Romania			x		x		x
Slovakia	x	x			x	x	x
Slovenia	x	x	x			x	x
Sweden	x	x	x	x	x	x	x
United Kingdom			x	x	x		

Source: Data used in this analysis was obtained from the European Union Agency for Fundamental Rights (FRA), 2014.

Despite the differences in the type and number of rights accorded to crime victims, most jurisdictions in the European community provide victims the opportunity to question the decision of prosecutors not to continue with the case (Spinellis, 1997). This measure is put in place to ensure that prosecutors are accountable to the victims and to protect victims' right to a fair trial. It must be acknowledged that even though only 22 member states provide victims the right to ask for compensation during a criminal trial, all member states guarantee victims' right to ask for compensation in civil proceedings.

Issues Impeding Effective Implementation of Victims' Rights

A number of countries have made enormous efforts aimed at expanding the role of victims in the criminal justice system. These efforts are evident in the countless laws passed to guarantee protections for victims of crime. Inasmuch as these country-level initiatives are appealing and appreciated, the core problem remains—victims' rights have not been fully and globally recognized, leading to the existence of misconceptions about the status of crime victims in the criminal justice system.

The lack of global recognition is due in part to the lack of workable guidelines for the treatment of victims and their witnesses in some countries. Many countries, notably African countries, have made little or no effort to offer protections for victims of crime, and in such countries, victims have no entitlements and play no role in criminal justice processes. This is problematic because it undermines the global effort to achieve uniform protection for all victims irrespective of jurisdiction.

Apart from the blatant lack of effort on the part of some countries to protect victims, there are multiple issues affecting the effective implementation of victims' rights in countries that have legislative frameworks. Professional knowledge is a major driver of effective and successful implementation of victims' rights laws, and the lack of it causes significant drawbacks. Criminal justice professionals have been criticized for lacking adequate knowledge about victims' rights, which leads to inability to properly advise victims of their rights (Kury, Kaiser, & Teske, 1994). Subsequently, victims get less information, are not adequately notified, and are unable to access the rights they are afforded by law (Wemmers, 1995).

The implementation of victims' rights legislation is further affected by the lack of stringent mechanisms to enforce victims' rights. Most states and countries do not have remedial provisions that allow victims to hold officials responsible for not respecting their rights. Crime victims therefore have no legal standing to enforce their rights in the criminal justice system (U.S. Department of Justice, 1997). This lack of legal recourse means that officials are not legally obliged to protect victims and cannot be held accountable if victims' rights are violated. To ameliorate this issue, provisions have to be made to ensure compliance with the legislation.

Another significant issue hindering the global acceptance of victims' rights is the stringent criteria used to disqualify victims from accessing compensation. The idea that not all victims qualify to receive compensation for their suffering is antagonistic to the fight for victims' status. Across all the U.S. states, for instance, victims must meet certain criteria in order to be eligible for financial compensation. For example, in Arizona and Alaska, victims must cooperate with law enforcement officials and prosecutors to be eligible for compensation. The decision about who has cooperated is a discretionary one made by the board in charge of the compensation program. Moreover, Arizona and other states require victims to report the crime within 72 hours to be eligible to receive financial compensation. This criterion denies victims who fail to report within the set time the opportunity to recover financially from their losses.

Another problem hindering the general recognition of victims' rights has to do with the operational definition of who is a victim (Elster, 2004; García-Godos, 2008a, 2008b). The definition of a victim varies by jurisdiction and by legal framework. The varying definitions not only undermine approaches designed to support victims but also limit our overall understanding of the role of victims in the criminal justice system. Recognizing the damaging nature of this issue, García-Godos (2013) cautioned against allowing the different legal definitions to blind us to the heterogeneity in the universe of victims in any jurisdiction. A related problem is the limited scope of most victims' rights provisions, which exclude victims of certain offenses. For instance, under most state laws, victims of violent crimes are considered for protection, but victims of fraud and other nonviolent crimes are largely excluded from any protection. Moreover, in several states and countries, victims of environmental crimes are also forgotten (Jarrell & Oznmy, 2012) or face challenges in getting recognition (Atkins, 2010; Starr, Flack, & Foley, 2009).

Addressing the Issues: What Has to Be Done?

Criminal justice officials "are the implementers of laws that provide victims access to information and facilitate victims' participation in the criminal justice process" (Kilpatrick, Beatty, & Howley,

1998, p. 2). For this reason, officials need to be properly trained and educated on victims' rights. The training—which should be compulsory for all professionals likely to have contact with victims—will increase the knowledge base of the officials, as well as make them aware of the needs of victims of crime. Ensuring professionals are knowledgeable in this arena of their profession enables them to provide victims with accurate information about their rights and what they need to do during criminal proceedings.

Moreover, it is highly suggested that mechanisms need to be in place to ensure that victims' rights are enforceable. Now, most countries do not have provisions empowering victims to file a liability suit against departments or professionals for violating their rights. This issue has to be remedied in order to achieve full compliance with legislation protecting the interests of victims. Victims should be able to file an injunction with a higher authority to order the professionals violating their rights to comply. Even if victims decide not to use this avenue to demand respect for their rights, the threat of its existence alone will be enough to force officials to comply with the legislation. Alternatively, a designated office could be established to receive complaints of violations from victims and subsequently pursue violations on behalf of the victims. This special office would serve as an external oversight board with the aim of increasing compliance with victims' rights laws among criminal justice professionals.

Some critics argued that the implementation of victims' rights legislation would affect the effective functioning of the criminal justice system. On the contrary, the existence of strong victims' rights laws would strengthen the operation of the system, because it ensures that all parties, including victims, are given the opportunity to play their rightful roles in the system's processes. Crime victims have a unique status in the criminal justice system, and that has to be respected, protected, and recognized at all times.

Summary

This chapter offered a critical assessment of victims' rights legislation in U.S. states and European countries. As discussed, many victimologists agree that efforts have been made to guarantee the status of crime victims in the criminal justice system. Currently, several states and countries have mechanisms for safeguarding the rights of victims and expanding the role victims play in the criminal justice system. In the U.S. for instance, about 33 states have amended their constitutions to include victims' rights provisions, while the remaining states have passed legislation outlining principles for the treatment and handling of crime victims. However, the ultimate goal of providing a voice to and expanding the role played by this population is still a dream, due mainly to the absence of effective implementation mechanisms of victims' rights laws. Issues such as the lack of professional knowledge, the lack of enforcement mechanisms, strict eligibility criteria for compensation, varying definitions of victim across jurisdictions, and the limited scope of most crime victim legislation all undermine the effort to successfully protect victims and achieve a global recognition of the status of victims in the criminal justice system. Until these problems are resolved, victims of crime will forever remain the forgotten parties in the criminal justice system.

Discussion Questions

1. Outline the historical development of victims' rights legislation in US. and Europe.
2. Identify and discuss the major issues hindering the successful implementation of victims' rights legislation in any given jurisdiction.
3. Why have victims not been fully recognized in the criminal justice system?
4. In what ways can we achieve a global acceptance of victims of crime?

References

Aa, S. (2015). Post-trial victims' rights in the EU: Do law enforcement motives still reign supreme?. *European Law Journal, 21*(2), 239–256.

Atkins, A. (2010). A complicated environment: The problem with extending victims' rights to victims of environmental crimes. *Washington and Lee Law Review, 67*(4), 1623–1658.

Beloof, D. E. (2006). Judicial leadership at sentencing under the Crime Victims' Rights Act: Judge Kozinski in Kenna and Judge Cassell in Degenhardt. *Federal Sentencing Reporter, 19*(1), 36–43.

Blondel, E. C. (2008). Victims' rights in an adversary system. *Duke Law Journal, 58*, 237–274.

Buczma, S. R. (2013). An overview of the law concerning protection of victims of crime in the view of the adoption of the Directive 2012/29/EU establishing minimum standards on the rights, support and protection of victims of crime in the European Union. In *ERA Forum* (Vol. 14, No. 2, pp. 235–250). Berlin; Heidelberg: Springer.

Burgess, A., Regehr, C., & Roberts, A. (2013). *Victimology: Theories and applications*. Burlington, MA: Jones & Bartlett Learning.

Cassell, P. G. (2009). In defense of victim impact statements. *Ohio State Journal of Criminal Law, 6*, 611.

Cassell, P. G., & Joffee, S. (2011). The crime victims' expanding role in a system of public prosecution: A response to the critics of the Crime Victims' Rights Act. *Northwestern University Law Review Colloquy, 105*, 164–183.

Calcutt, P. (1988). The Victims' Rights Act of 1988, the Florida constitution and the new struggle for victims' rights. *Florida State University Law Review, 16*, 811.

Doerner, G. W., & Lab, P. S. (2015). *Victimology*. Waltham, MA: Anderson Publishing.

Elster, J. (2004). *Closing the books. Transitional justice in historical perspective*. Cambridge: Cambridge University Press.

FRA (2014). Victims of crime in the EU: the extent and nature of support for victims. Retrieved on April 13, 2016 at http://fra.europa.eu/en/publication/2014/victims-crime-eu-extent-and-nature-support-victims

García-Godos, J. (2013). Victims' rights and distributive justice: In search of actors. *Human Rights Review, 14*(3), 241–255.

García-Godos, J. (2008a). Victim reparations in the Peruvian Truth Commission and the challenge of historical interpretation. *International Journal of Transitional Justice, 2*(1), 63–82.

García-Godos, J. (2008b). Victim reparations in transitional justice: What is at stake and why. *Nordisk tidsskrift for menneskerettigheter, 26*, 111.

Giannini, M. M. (2008). Equal rights for equal rites? Victim allocution, defendant allocution, and the Crime Victims' Rights Act. *Yale Law & Policy Review, 26*(2), 431–484.

Heinz, J. (1983). Victim and Witness Protection Act of 1982. *Practical Lawyer, 29*, 13–18.

Jarrell, L. M., & Ozymy, J. (2012). Real crime, real victims: Environmental crime victims and the Crime Victims' Rights Act (CVRA). *Crime Law Social Change, 58*, 373–389.

Joutsen, M. (1987). Listening to the victim: The victim's role in European criminal justice systems. *Wayne L. Rev., 34*, 95.

Joutsen, M. (1994). Victim participation in proceedings and sentencing in Europe. *International Review of Victimology*, 3, 57.

Kaiser, G., Kury, H., & Albrecht, J. (Eds.). (1991). *Victims and criminal justice*. Freiburg: Max-Planck-Institut.

Kilpatrick, D. G., Beatty, D., & Howley, S. S. (1998). *The rights of crime victims: Does legal protection make a difference?* Washington, DC: National Institute of Justice, U.S. Department of Justice, 1–11.

Krainz, K. W. (1991). The position of injured parties in the Austrian criminal procedure—First results of an empirical investigation. In G. Kaiser, H. Kury, & J. Albrecht (Eds.), *Victims and criminal justice*. Freiburg: Max-Planck-Institut, p. 778.

Kury, H., Kaiser, M., & Teske, R. (1994). The position of the victim in criminal procedure: The results of a German study. *International Review Victimology, 3*, 69.

Kyl, J., Twist, S. J., & Higgins, S. (2005). On the wings of their angels: The Scott Campbell, Stephanie Roper, Wendy Preston, Louarna Gillis, and Nila Lynn Crime Victims' Rights Act. *Lewis & Clark L. Rev., 9*, 581.

Maguire, M., & Shapland, J. (1997). Provision for victims in an international context. In R. Davis, A. Lurigio, & W. Skogan (Eds.), *Victims of crime*. Thousand Oaks: Sage, pp. 211–230.

Muller-Rappard, E. (1990). Perspectives on the Council of Europe's approach to the issue of basic principles of justice for victims of crime. *Human Rights Quarterly, 12*(2), 231–245.

National Crime Victim Law Institute (NCVLI). (2011). *History of NCVLI and victims' rights*. Retrieved April 09, 2016, from http: law.lclark.edu/centers

National Crime Victims' Right Week. (2014). Landmarks in victims' rights and services: An historical overview. Retrieved on April 13, 2016 at http://victimsofcrime.org/docs/default source/ncvrw2014/2014ncvrw_section5_landmarks.pdf?sfvrsn=2

Office for Victims of Crime. (2002). *Ordering restitution to the crime victim*. Legal Series Bulletin #6. Washington, D.C: Office for Victims of Crime.

Pizzi, W. T. (1999). Victims' rights: Rethinking our adversary system. *Utah Law Review*, 349–361.

President's Task Force on Victims of Crime (1982). Final report. Available at http://www.ojp.gov/ovc/publications/presdntstskforcrprt/ 87299.pdf

Spinellis, D. (1997). Victims of crime and the criminal process. *Israel L. Rev.*, *36*, 337.

Starr, J. W., Flack, B. L., & Foley, A. D. (2009). A new intersection: Environmental crimes and victims' rights. *Natural Resources and Environment*, 23, 41–46.

Tobolowsky, P. M. (2001). *Crime victim rights and remedies* (pp. 36–39). Durham, NC: Carolina Academic Press.

Tobolowsky, P. M., Gaboury, M. T., Jackson, A. L., & Blackburn, A. G. (2010). *Crime victim rights and remedies*. Durham, NC: Carolina Academic Press.

United Nations. (1985). *Declaration of basic principles of justice for victims of crime and abuse of power*. G.A. 40/34, annex, 40 U.N. GAOR Supp. (No.530 at 214, U.N. Doc. A/40/53).

U.S. Department of Justice. (1997). *New directions from the field*. Washington, DC: U.S. Department of Justice, Office of Justice Programs.

Victim and Witness Protection Act (1982), Pub. L. No. 97–291, § 5, 96 Stat. 1248, 1253–55.

Wemmers, J. (1995). Victims in the Dutch criminal justice system: The effects of treatment on victims' attitudes and compliance. *International Review Victimology*, *3*, 323.

Wieczorek, I. (2012). A needed balance between security, liberty and justice. Positive signals arrive from the field of victims' rights. *European Criminal Law Review*, *2*(2), 141–157.

Young, M., & Stein, J. (2004). *The history of the crime victims movement in the United States*. Washington, DC: Office of the Victims of Crime.

PART II

Victim Issues Regarding Specific Types of Victimization

In Part II of the handbook, the victim issues regarding specific types of victimization are explored. Chapter 6 examines an under researched population, that of secondary victims or secondary survivors of sexual assault. Secondary survivors include the family, spouses and/or friends of the person who was sexually victimized (i.e., the victim or survivor). The chapter discusses how secondary survivors suffer in their own unique ways as a result of having a loved one sexually assaulted. The chapter also provides an overview of the existing literature of secondary sexual assault victims, providing information on their experiences. Finally, the chapter discusses the implications for assisting secondary survivors of sexual assault victims is also discussed.

Chapter 7 describes how neoliberal political ideologies affect perceptions of individuals who experience partner sexual assault, physical assault, or stalking. The chapter contends that compared with targets of stranger violence, targets of intimate partner violence (IPV) receive less sympathy and more blame. Feelings of sympathy and judgments of blame are shaped, in part, by neoliberal ideologies that affect judgments of individuals who experience IVP.

In Chapter 8, the authors discuss cybercrime victimization and how the evidence suggests that victims of interpersonal cybercrime like cyberbullying, cyberabuse, and cyber identity theft can have their lives virtually decimated by perpetrators. The authors note that the onus is on academics and practitioners to keep pace with technology in order to continue informing best practices on how to reduce one's risk of victimization.

The authors in Chapter 9 discuss hate crimes as an area of justice and social policy. They point out that hate crimes have a relatively recent history, although it's not a new phenomenon. Drawing on evidence primarily from the United Kingdom and United States, this chapter also examines four issues of particular salience to understanding hate crime victimization policy and practice: how hate crime is defined; how hate crime is measured; why victims under-report hate crime and how to encourage victims to report; and the effectiveness of services for hate crime victims.

Chapter 10 discusses the issues involved in counseling family members of murdered victims. The authors note that losing a loved one through homicide is devastating, and survivors go through many painful moments. Homicide has significant impact on survivors and the bereavement period can last between three and five years.

Chapter 11, the final chapter in this section, focuses on members of the lesbian, gay, bisexual, and transgender (LGBT) community as victims of crime. After first defining the LGBT community and examining applicable theoretical explanations of victimization, the chapter reviews statistics and demographics of hate crimes and other violent or serious crimes against members of the LGBT community across the nation as published by the FBI's UCR Hate Crimes Statistics. Additionally, the chapter evaluates the impact of crimes against special populations of the LGBT community, focusing on transgender and gender-nonconforming individuals, its youth, the homeless, those incarcerated, and sex workers.

6

EXPANDING THE CONCEPTUALIZATION OF SURVIVOR IN SEXUAL ASSAULTS

Shelly Clevenger and Jordana N. Navarro

Keywords

secondary victim/secondary survivor; sexual assault; trauma contagion model; threatened beliefs-shattered assumptions; chronic stress; repetition and reenactment; self-blame/guilt; suffering; anger; stress; anxiety; victim service organizations

Objectives

After studying this chapter, the reader should be able to:

- Broadly describe the literature regarding sexual assault victims' family/spouses.
- Understand the experiences of the family and spouses of sexual assault survivors.
- Recognize the struggles that family and spouses encounter when a loved one is sexually assaulted.

Introduction

In the victimization literature, scholars have mainly focused on the primary victims or primary survivor of sexual assault, the individual who the crime was committed directly against. However, a dearth of information exists on the secondary victims, or secondary survivors, of sexual assault. These are the individuals who are the loved ones of the victim. This can include anyone in the support system of the victim, such as family members, friends and also spouses or significant others. They suffer, oftentimes in silence, next to the victim. There is a limited amount of research on the impact of sexual assault on secondary survivors. If loved ones are addressed in research, it is often from the vantage point of how family members assist survivors of sexual assault, and not the impact of the crime on these individuals. This lack of understanding is all the more important to address the experiences of the loved ones of sexual assault survivors. This chapter will present an overview of the literature relating to secondary survivors, including the family members, spouses and friends of sexual assault victims with the intent of making known the experiences these individuals have in dealing with the victimization of someone they love.

Secondary Survivors of Sexual Assault

Sexual assault is a crime that affects many individuals across the nation. According to the FBI's 2014 Uniform Crime Report, there were 116,645 reported forcible rapes in the United States[1]. One cannot completely understand the prevalence and scope of rape from reported crime, however, as sexual assault is often an underreported crime. Data from the 2012 *National Crime Victimization Survey* underscores this point as 346,830 women reported being raped, but not all these survivors necessarily reported that information to the police[2]. In terms of child victimization, 62,939 cases of child sexual abuse were reported in 2012(the most recent year available)[3]. Looking at the number of victimized individuals, we can assume that there is at least one person (often more) who loves and cares for the victim whom also experiences the ramifications of these crimes. When victimization occurs, it sends out a ripple effect, affecting those that care about the victim. In terms of raw numbers of victims then, in a case of sexual assault, there is likely a doubling (or tripling or quadrupling) of the number of victims in each case that is suffering and coping. Given the aforementioned, it is incumbent of researchers to recognize this large number of secondary survivors and begin investigating their experiences in conjunction with the impact on the primary survivor.

Impact on Significant Others

Research on the experiences of the significant other themselves is limited. The bulk of the literature, which does mention significant others, typically only addresses how they help the victims and/or problems they face in assisting the victim through the recovery process.[4, 5, 6, 7, 8, 9, 10, 11, 12, 13, 14, 15, 16, 17, 18, 19] The literature has led to some important findings about how this type of victimization affects the relationship. One important finding, that has immediate implications for service provides, is that there is often an effect on the relationship, in general, beginning right with the disclosure of the sexual assault. A common initial response of anger by the partner is often seen with male partners including expressions of desire of wanting to harm the perpetrator.[20] The initial disclosure also can be followed by a period of crisis and disorientation, in which the significant other must adjust to the news that their partner was victimized.[21] Research indicates that there can be emotional and sexual intimacy issues within couples after a disclosure, whether it was an assault that recently occurred or the disclosure of child sexual abuse, can impact the relationship and can include problems with establishing and maintaining sexual relationships.[22, 23, 24, 25, 26, 27, 28] Additionally, partners of sexual assault victims often report that they have experienced significant stress and anxiety,[29] unhappiness and discontent[30]as well feelings of guilt and shame.[31]

In relationships where one partner has suffered child sexual abuse, there is particular risk for secondary trauma, in which the partner who was not victimized suffers emotional distress and reactions along with the partner. Maltas and Shay contend that the partner of the survivor also suffers trauma and have created what they refer to as the *trauma contagion model*.[32] The idea behind this model is that trauma is transmitted, like a virus, from one intimate sexual partner to the other due to the nature and closeness of that relationship. The intimate partner of the victim of child sexual abuse thereby suffers in a way that is different than other people in the life of the victim. This model has three parts. First is *threatened beliefs–shattered assumptions*. In this part of the model, the partner realizes that what they thought about their partner and their relationship thus far has not been reality, as their whole relationship leading up to the point of disclosure was impacted by the sexual assault and they did not know it. They must completely readjust their views of their partner's past, their relationship history and even the world. The initial reaction may be denial that the abuse happened to their partner or that it will affect the relationship or even for the partner to leave the relationship as to not have to deal with what they are feeling.

The second part of the model is *chronic stress*. The partners of the victims are suffering from a variety of emotions, stress, irritability and often anxiety. Now that they are aware of their partner's victimization, they may be worried about saying the wrong thing or if an item, event or conversation may trigger them. This can also be avoidance of intimacy as now that they know about the sexual abuse of their partner, they may not want to engage in sexual activities. Partners of the victims suffer in a variety of ways as a result of the chronic stress they feel. They may be distracted at work, have difficulty sleeping, and become depressed and even physically ill from pushing their feelings inward. They may seek solace in alcohol, smoking or food and might dread coming home to face their partner.

The final part of the *trauma contagion model* is *repetition and reenactment*. Survivors of child sexual abuse may be unconsciously drawn to repeat behaviors. Levine asserts that primitive and dissociated parts of the personality are continually trying to work out trauma until it is resolved or corrected.[33] Chu,[34] in similar vein to Freud,[35] contends that what is dissociated will be repeated until it is remembered and resolved. The need of the victim to repeat and reenact the abuse they suffered in some capacity can be very upsetting for the partner as sometimes they may unknowingly take on the role of the abuser or aggressor and become that way even if they are not so inclined. This can occur if their partner is casting them in the role of villain and unfairly blaming them and abandoning them. This can be the case for the survivor of child sexual abuse in which there are flashbacks and memories that can be triggered. This can be very stressful for the partner of the victim.

If the couple has children, this victimization of one partner can influence parenting. It can lead to disagreements as well as poor communication patterns[36] and a decrease in the cohesion of the family in general.[37] The degree to which the relationship is influenced is contingent upon many factors, such as the type and extent of sexual victimization that occurred, as well the support that the partner provided to the victim after the incident and/or the disclosure.[38]

While the literature regarding significant others has illuminated part of the picture of what it is like to have someone you are romantically involved with experience sexual victimization, it does not truly capture what struggles they deal with from their own point of view, without the context of the relationship. The research does not adequately address how people cope individually with this news. Another key component that is missing is how the significant other deals with the formal adjudication (or lack thereof) of the offender. The research looks at secondary survivors as an extension of the primary victim, but does not seek to identify their experiences as victimizations in their own right.

Impact on Parents of Victimized Children

In addition to the significant others of sexual assault victims, some research has also considered the impact of this crime on parents of victimized children. However, as is the case with significant other research, there has been a lack of focus on the reaction, adjustment, and coping of the parents themselves. Most studies that involved parents have included them in order to assess the impact of sexual assault on the child and the child's functioning rather than studying the impact to the parents directly.[39, 40, 41, 42] In other words, there have been few studies that directly addressed the impacts of the sexual abuse of a child has on parents.

The initial reactions of parents are similar to that of significant others as the parents often have the desire to harm the person who abused their child. Additionally, parents may displace anger at a family member, blaming that family member for their child's victimization. This has occurred even if that family member was not the offender, because the parent believed they played a role in the child's harm.[43] The parents also may blame themselves, especially if a family member or friend was the offender. Parents also reported feeling helpless, vulnerable, and panic-stricken.[44] The sexual abuse of a child also exacerbates marital problems.[45, 46, 47] These consequences also impact the relationship between the parent and the child as well.[48, 49, 50]

The gender of a parent, or if a parent themselves had been victimized, also influence how they react and cope with their child's victimization. Evidence indicates that female parents, or parents that had been previously victimized, experience increased anxiety and stress.[51, 52] Research has found that mothers suffer more than fathers and this finding has been attributed to the child-rearing roles, as well as the fact that mothers usually provided the main support network to the child while dealing with the recovery post-victimization.[53, 54, 55, 56]

In terms of the types of suffering a mother experiences, research has found that assisting a child through the recovery process also affects the mother's own self-esteem, her feelings about herself as a caregiver and her perception of her ability to protect her children.[57, 58] Mothers have reported that they felt like they have failed in their duty or role of mother because they were not able to protect their child from harm. They often blame themselves for what has happened and sometimes even commit acts of self-punishment to atone for their perceived mistakes.[59] This is not to suggest that fathers do not also suffer. However, unlike mothers, fathers may experience delayed reactions because of suppressing their feelings and/or dealing with the situation at hand.[60] Also, fathers were found to be absent from much of the aftercare in cases where a child had been sexually assaulted.[61]

While the family research has provided insight into the emotions and reactions of parents, the literature falls short on illustrating how the parents dealt with these emotions, and what their overall experience was like helping their child and themselves recover from the trauma. In addition, there is a dearth of information on the impacts of crime on adult siblings of the victim. Adult siblings, and other family members like grandparents, may have a completely different, or similar, experience compared with the victim's parents. Without this critically needed research, it is not possible to know how siblings or grandparents of sexual assault survivors react, adjust, and cope as secondary survivors. Addressing this gap in the literature is vastly important in order to gauge the initial reaction of the family, but also learn how family members cope with, or are coping with, victimization. Learning about crime victims' families, and the impacts of trauma on secondary victims, will add to the limited existing research and assist practitioners in knowing how to help family members in dealing with a loved one's victimization. This is especially prudent in today's society in which there are non-traditional families and/or child victims who may not reside in a traditional nuclear family situation.

Impact on Friends of Victims

In addition to just examining family or spouses, little is known about how victimization affects the friends of a survivor. Yet, this is an important population that needs to be studied as friends play a pivotal role in the lives of adolescents and adults. Research has shown that adolescents who are sexually assaulted often turn to their friends or peers[62, 63, 64, 65] and disclose to them first.[66, 67] One such reason is that adolescents feel that they can trust their friends and feel close to them. Research has shown that peers usually respond with empathy and are nurturing unless the assault involves physical violence that is very severe, then the adolescent may not know how to respond or can withdraw from victims.[68] An issue with disclosing to adolescent friends is that the friend will not keep it a secret and there can be rumor-spreading and gossip, damaging social relationships.[69, 70] The response of the friends (and also family) was found to be paramount in the deciding factor of the victim to report or enter any formal system after the assault.[71]

Adult survivors of sexual assault also primarily seek the support of their friends as well.[72] The limited research that does exist that examined the emotional experiences of friends of survivors, has shown that they felt good about helping their friend through their recovery and that they did not experience extreme distress, but that they did feel anger towards the perpetrator and wanted revenge. They also most often reported that they did not think the friendship would be changed as a result of the assault.[73, 74]

While the research provides insight into how friends of victims behave, it does not paint a clear picture of the thought processes or emotional experiences that friends have after someone close to them is assaulted. Attention to this additional component is relatively absent in the current literature despite the fact that these are the people who assist survivors through the recovery process and may be closer to them than their actual family. Arguably, this could be the case for college-aged individuals, as their friends may be who they rely upon the most. The literature on secondary survivors has not examined this friend component thoroughly enough. Particular attention needs to be paid to how the friends, as members of the support system of the victim, experience dealing with their friend's sexual assault. Friends, just as significant others and family, may suffer in their own ways because of their friend's victimization.

Primary and Secondary Victims' Experiences with Obtaining Help

After victimization occurs, or an individual has been victimized in the past but is currently prepared to heal, survivors are often reeling with deciding the "next steps" of what to do or where to go get assistance. The family, spouses and friends are often the ones who are putting their needs on the sidelines to assist the victim first and then thinking about their needs later. One of the main goals of victim service organizations (VSO) is to help these individuals. Additionally, victim service organizations are, and should be, simply sources of support in the aftermath of crime and network victims to critical resources within the community (e.g., counseling, medical care, etc.) to aid in the healing process. Unfortunately, research has identified several barriers that hinder the effectiveness of VSOs, particularly in cases of sexual assault. These barriers that impact victims have the potential to impact the loved ones who are assisting the victim and ultimately the loved ones' own access to treatment and resource if they chose to seek it out. It is important for victims and their loved ones to be aware of the potential road blocks they could face in seeking help with healing and recovery.

Research has identified several barriers that hinder victims in the accessing of VSO and these challenges largely center on: (1) availability, (2) accessibility, (3) affordability, and (4) acceptability.[75] Unfortunately, perspectives from secondary sexual assault victims in accessing services are largely unknown at this time as research on this topic is nonexistent (to the best of our knowledge). In considering these barriers, research by Logan and colleagues[76] indicates that geography also matters when assessing the overall effectiveness of VSO. In terms of geography, sociocultural differences between rural and urban communities, and how these differences affect crime victims, exist[77, 78] and should be considered. In terms of affordability, Logan and colleagues[79] found that victims often did not access services because of the perceived costs. Moreover, some victims reported concerns surrounding the need for multifaceted care (e.g., prescription medication and victim advocacy), which entailed the involvement of multiple agencies, and how the involvement of these various partners could quickly grow financial obligations.[80] This is aside from the related concern that each new organization that became involved in the victims' care likely entailed a retelling and revisiting of the details of the victimization.[81] Even if financials were not an issue, the perceived availability and accessibility—or lack thereof—of victim services was a barrier encountered by many victims.

Evidence of the aforementioned was readily seen in statements made by victims who reported extensive wait times to access services from medical personnel and VSO.[82] For victims located in rural communities, the inability to call for help or secure reliable transportation was an added complication.[83] However, in ideal situations where these factors (i.e., costs, availability, and accessibility) were not constraints, victims reported encountering other challenges that acted as discouragers to reporting.

Perhaps the most known barrier to reporting a sexual assault is the overall lack of understanding and sensitivity from various sources of informal and formal social support (i.e., acceptability). Indeed, research has found that victims greatly fear how others will react upon disclosure, whether it be family members or agents of the criminal justice system.[84, 85, 86] For instance, in research conducted by Logan and colleagues,[87] some survivors reported experiencing a lack of overall sensitivity among medical personnel and law enforcement in the aftermath of the crime. Victims residing in rural communities also noted the fear of the potential of "politicking" in the courtroom if their case made it to trial.[88] In other words, given the small social and close-knit setting of many rural communities, victims expressed fear that the outcomes of their cases could vary greatly depending on the perpetrators' connections.[89] Given the aforementioned, some victims held the perception that sexual assault was treated as a less serious crime and questioned whether it was even worth reporting.[90] Unfortunately, as previously mentioned, information on how and what services secondary victims access to help their loved ones (or themselves) through the recovery process following this type of crime is unknown. However, upon looking at the limited research on secondary victims involved in other types of crimes, such as homicide, the evidence overwhelmingly indicates that these services are sorely needed as best practices despite what type of incident has taken place.

Secondary Victims in Violent Crime

Although it may not initially appear as if there are any similarities between secondary victims involved in cases of homicide versus sexual assault, one can indeed draw parallels. For example, one seemingly obvious difference between the two is that homicide cases result in the literal removal of the loved one from his/her family and social network. However, in reviewing qualitative data on how sexual assault affects family members and loved ones of the victim, evidence of a similar type of loss is readily apparent. For example, in Clevenger's[91] work on mothers of sexually victimized children, the author poignantly states, "Women did not think about retreating, taking time to *grieve for the loss of the innocence* of their child. . ." (p. 12; emphasis added). This statement, along with the following, demonstrates that although the primary victims were alive, some would likely never be the person they were before the assault took place:

> For 91 days, I would drive an hour one way to see 'Sophia' while she was in that place [mental health facility]. Some days she was sedated and did not wake up. . .others she would not speak. . .but every day I drove and I saw her.[92]

Aside from the perception of an unrecoverable loss, secondary victims involved in these two crimes may also encounter negative reactions from laypersons in the form of blame and shame as they navigate their communities and social service agencies.

As documented in research on sexual assault, homicide studies—particularly focusing on femicide—have noted that victim blaming occurs even in this type of depraved crime. Indeed, in her analysis of nearly 300 newspaper articles, Taylor found that femicide victims often were portrayed as responsible for their own deaths either directly or indirectly.[93] This overall finding was supported in a later study involving a much broader sample although the authors noted the problem was "not as pervasive as found in previous studies" (p. 178).[94] Thus, given these similarities and in reflection of the absence of information on secondary victims of sexual assault, we can look to the limited literature on secondary victims of homicide to inform best practices within formal institutions of social support (e.g., criminal justice agencies, social services).

Although information on the interaction between secondary victims and the criminal justice system is limited, even in homicide research, several studies have produced noteworthy findings that inform best practices when assisting these individuals in dealing with the aftermath of crime overall. In reviewing several past studies, the two prominent themes that emerged were secondary victims feeling largely devalued and, at times, marginalized by the criminal justice system.[95, 96, 97] More specifically, secondary victims reported negative interactions with the early processing of their cases with law enforcement, with later experiences at the trial stage, and with their interactions with victim advocates.[98, 99, 100] Several of these experiences closely mirror the negative experiences primary victims of sexual assault also report experiencing.

In terms of the initial report stage, secondary victims of homicide noted that interactions with law enforcement were largely unsatisfactory, with the questioning style of these agents spanning abrasiveness to accusatory.[101, 102] Again, this mirrors the experiences of primary victims of sexual assault who have noted this finding as a barrier to reporting.[103] In two horrifying cases, secondary victims of homicide reported that law enforcement officers actually victim-blamed the deceased loved one of the secondary victim,[104] which is a factor (i.e., victim blaming) that affects sexual assault survivors and their loved ones as well.[105, 106] Other findings indicated that secondary victims often struggled with law enforcement to obtain updates on the processing of their cases, which one woman (of a murdered child) attributed to the rapid health decline and ultimate death of her husband.[107] These experiences did not improve for secondary victims of homicide once cases proceeded to trial.

As cases progressed to the trial phase, secondary victims of homicide noted their overall frustration with the lack of control over the direction of their loved ones' cases.[108, 109] As documented in research on primary victims of sexual assault,[110] secondary victims of homicide felt their desires and opinions were subordinated to the decisions of criminal justice agents (i.e., prosecutors, judges).[111, 112] Moreover, restrictions placed upon secondary victims of homicide in terms of emotional restraint within the courtroom and what victim impact statements could and could not say further compounded the perception that the trial process deemphasized the emotional damage the accused had perpetrated against the family.[113, 114] This perception was, unfortunately, magnified for some secondary victims of homicide when sentencing was completed and some offenders were given only short-sentences—leading to the belief that their loved ones' lives had been grossly devalued.[115] This finding also echoes research on primary victims of sexual assault and the fear of coming forward given that community dynamics, particularly in rural locations, may result in cases not being taken seriously in court.[116]

Although the noted research centers largely on secondary victims of homicide and these individuals' experiences with seeking help through the criminal justice system, the findings are parallel with the challenges identified among primary survivors of sexual assault. Thus, one can logically conclude that although there is a dearth of research on this topic, secondary victims of sexual assault likely also encounter these same barriers as they navigate the criminal justice process with their loved ones. Given these concerns, this line of research is especially ripe for investigation so that services can be expanded to all survivors of crime. In order to begin addressing this gap in the literature, research conducted by the first-author of this chapter (S. Clevenger) has begun delving into the experiences of secondary victims of sexual assault as they both deal with the ramifications of the crime as victims themselves and serve as an emotional support system for their loved one. The ultimate hope of conducting this research is to give secondary victims of violent crime, and particularly rape, a voice in the processing of these cases. In doing so, the onus is on academics, practitioners, and stakeholders alike to recognize that we need to broaden our conceptualization of "victim" and "survivor" to include all individuals left behind in a perpetrator's wreckage.

Summary

Research often looks at significant others and family in terms of what role they play with regards to the victim instead of victims in their own right as secondary survivors. There are a small number of studies that have researched how secondary survivors have dealt with the sexual assault of a loved one, but this topic remains largely unexplored. Although the aforementioned studies are noteworthy, more in-depth research is needed in order to fully understand the suffering of these individuals, their methods of coping, and how victimization has affected their lives. While the voices of primary victims are critically important to inform the literature, secondary survivors also deserve to be heard and acknowledged.

Discussion Questions

1. Thinking about the research presented on secondary victims/survivors, was the findings different or similar to what you would have thought before reading this chapter? Why or why not?
2. Do you believe that trauma can act as a contagion as described in the trauma contagion model? Please explain your answer.
3. What services do you think would be beneficial for secondary victims/survivors of sexual assault?

Notes

1 Uniform Crime Report (2016). www.fbi.gov/about-us/cjis/ucr/

2 U.S. Department of Justice. *National Crime Victimization Survey.* 2012.

3 "Child Maltreatment 2012," U.S. Department of Health and Human Services, Administration for Children and Families, Administration on Children, Youth and Families, Children's Bureau.

4 Bass, E., & Davis, L. (1988). *The courage to heal: A guide for women survivors of child sexual abuse.* New York: Harper and Row.

5 Brittain, D. E., & Merriam, K. (1988). Groups for significant others of survivors of child sexual abuse. *Journal of Interpersonal Violence, 3,* 90–101.

6 Burge, S. K. (1983). Rape: Individual and family reactions. In C. R. Figley & H. I. McCubbin (Eds.), *Stress and the family: Coping with catastrophe* (Vol. 2, pp. 103–119). New York: Bruner/Mazel.

7 Burgess, A. W., & Holstrom, L. L (1979a). Adaptive strategies and recovery from rape. *American Journal of Psychiatry, 136,* 1278–1982.

8 Burgess, A. W., & Holstrom, L. L (1979b). *Rape: Crisis and recovery.* Bowie, MD: Robert J. Brady.

9 Cohen, L. J. (1988). Providing treatment and support to partners of sexual assault survivors. *Psychotherapy, 25,* 94–98.

10 Crenshaw, T. L. (1978). Counseling the family and friends. In S. Harper (Ed.), *Rape: Helping the victim* (pp. 51–65). Oradell, NJ: Medical Economics Book Division.

11 Downing, N. E. (1988). A conceptual model for victim services: Challenges and opportunities for counseling psychologists. *The Counseling Psychologist, 16,* 531–595.

12 Feinauer, L. (1982). Rape: A family crisis. *American Journal of Family Therapy, 10(4)* 35–39.

13 Figley, C. R. (1985). Traumatic stress: The role of the family and social support system. In C. R. Figley (Ed.) *Trauma and its wake: Vol. 2, the study and treatment of posttraumatic stress disorder* (pp. 39–54). New York: Bruner/Mazel.

14 Herndon, A. D., & Law, Jr. J. G. (1985). Post-traumatic stress and the family: A multimethod approach to counseling. In C. R. Figley (Ed.) *Trauma and its wake: Vol. 2, the study and treatment of posttraumatic stress disorder* (pp. 39–54). New York: Bruner/Mazel.

15 Miller, W. R., Williams, A. M., & Bernstein, M. H. (1982). The effects of rape on marital and sexual adjustment. *The American Journal of Family Therapy, 10,* 51–58.

16 Orzeck, A. M. (1983). Sexual assault: The female victim, her male partner and their relationship. *The Personnel and Guidance Journal, 62,* 143–146.

17 Silverman, D. C. (1978). Sharing the crisis of rape: Counseling the families and victims. *American Journal of Orthopsychiatry, 48,* 166–173.

18 Sutherland, S., & Sherl, D. J. (1970). Patterns of response among victims of rape. *American Journal of Orthopsychiatry, 48,* 166–173.

19 White, P. N, & Rollins, J. C. (1981, January). Rape: A family crisis. *Family Relations, 30,* 103–109.

20 Holstrom, L. L. & Burgess, A. W. (1979). Rape: The husband's and boyfriend's initial reactions. *The Family Coordinator, 28,* 321–330.

21 Remer, R., & Ferguson, R. A. (1995). Becoming a secondary survivor of sexual assault. *Journal of Counseling and Development, 73*(4), 407– 413.

22 Bacon, B., & Lein, L. (1996). Living with a female sexual abuse survivor: Male partner's perspectives. *Journal of Child Sexual Abuse, 5*, 1–16.
23 Finkelhor, D., Hotaling, G., Lewis, I., & Smith, C. (1989). Sexual abuse and its relationship to later sexual satisfaction, marital status, religion and attitudes. *Journal of Interpersonal Violence, 4*, 379–399.
24 Gill, M., & Tutty, L. (1999). Male survivors of childhood sexual abuse: A qualitative study and issues or clinical consideration. *Journal of Child Sexual Abuse*, 7, 19–33.
25 Holstrom, L. L. & Burgess, A. W. (1979). Rape: The husband's and boyfriend's initial reactions. *The Family Coordinator, 28, 321–330.*
26 Jacquet, S. (1999). Sexual abuse experiences and family environment in childhood as predictors of sexual dysfunction and premarital relationships in adulthood. *Dissertation Abstracts International, 60*(9), 4501B.
27 Jacob, C., & Veach, P. (2005). Intrapersonal and familial effects of child sexual abuse on female partners of male survivors. *Journal of Counseling Psychology, 52*, 284–97.
28 Nelson, B., & Wampler, K. (2002). Further understanding the systematic effects of childhood sexual abuse: A comparison of two groups of clinical couples. *Journal of Child Sexual Abuse, 11*, 85–106.
29 Nelson, B., & Wampler, K. (2002). Further understanding the systematic effects of childhood sexual abuse: A comparison of two groups of clinical couples. *Journal of Child Sexual Abuse, 11*, 85–106.
30 Champion De Crespingy, J. (1996). The experiences of couples in intimate relationships when the woman is a survivor of child sexual abuse. A phenomenological study. *Dissertation Abstracts International, 58*(9), *5109B.*
31 Chauncy, S. (1994). Emotional concerns and treatment of male partners of female sexual abuse survivors. *Social Work, 39*, 669–676.
32 Maltas, C. P., & Shay, J. (1995) Trauma contagion in partners of survivors of childhood sexual abuse. *American Journal of Orthopsychiatry, 65*(4), Oct 1995, 529–539.
33 Levine, H. (1993). Clinical analysis in adults who were sexually abused as a child. In H. Levine (Ed.), *Adult analysis and child sexual abuse* (pp. 197–213). Hillside, NJ: Analytic Press.
34 Chu, J. A. (1991). The repetition convulsion revisited: Reliving dissociated trauma. *Psychotherapy, 28*, 327–332.
35 Freud, S. (1978). *The basic works of Sigmund Freud*. Franklin Center, PA: The Franklin Library. Original work published in 1920.
36 Champion De Crespingy, J. (1996). The experiences of couples in intimate relationships when the woman is a survivor of child sexual abuse. A phenomenological study. *Dissertation Abstracts International, 58*(9), *5109B.*
37 Nelson, B., & Wampler, K. (2002). Further understanding the systematic effects of childhood sexual abuse: A comparison of two groups of clinical couples. *Journal of Child Sexual Abuse, 11*, 85–106.
38 Denkers, A. (1999). Factors affecting support after criminal victimization: Needed and received support from partner, the social network and distant support providers. *The Journal of Social Psychology, 139*, 191–201.
39 Finkelhor, D. (1984). *Child sexual abuse: New theory and research*. New York: Free Press.
40 Friedrich, W. (1991). Mothers of sexually abused children: An MMPI study. *Journal of Clinical Psychology, 47*, 778–783.
41 Gomes-Schwartz, B., Horowitz, J., & Cardarelli, A. (1990). *Child sexual abuse: The initial effects*. Newbury Park, CA: Sage.
42 Rivera, M. (1988). Social systems' intervention in families of victims of child sexual abuse. *Canadian Journal of Community Mental Health*, 7, 35–51.
43 Clevenger, S. (2015). Mothers of sexual assault victims: How women "do mother" after their child has been sexually assaulted. *Feminist Criminology, 11*(3), 227–252.
44 Clevenger, S. (2015). Mothers of sexual assault victims: How women "do mother" after their child has been sexually assaulted. *Feminist Criminology, 11*(3), 227–252.
45 Burgess, A., Hartman, C., Kelley, S., Grant, C., & Gray, E. (1990). Parental response to child sexual abuse trials involving day care settings. *Journal of Traumatic Stress, 3*, 395–405.
46 Finkelhor, D., Williams, L., & Burns, N. (1988). *Nursery crimes: Sexual abuse in day care*. Newbury Park, CA: Sage.
47 MacFarlane, K. J. (1986). Helping parents cope with extrafamilial molestation. In K. MacFarlane, J. Waterman, S. Connerly, L. Damon, M. Durfee, & S. Long (Eds.), *Sexual abuse of young children* (pp. 299–311). New York: Guilford Press.
48 Burgess, A., Hartman, C., Kelley, S., Grant, C., & Gray, E. (1990). Parental response to child sexual abuse trials involving day care settings. *Journal of Traumatic Stress, 3*, 395–405.
49 Esquilin, S. (1987). Family responses to the identification of extra-familial child sexual abuse. *Psychotherapy in Private Practice, 5*, 105–113.
50 Regehr, C. (1990). Parental responses to extrafamilial child sexual assault. *Child Abuse & Neglect, 14*, 113–120.

51 Breckenridge, J. (2006). "Speaking of mothers most": How does the literature portray mothers who have a history of child sexual abuse? *Journal of Child Sexual Abuse, 15*, 52–74.
52 Manion, I., McIntyre, J., Firestone, P., Ligenzinska, M., Ensom, R., & Wells, G. (1996). Secondary traumatisation in parents following disclosure of extrafamilial child sexual abuse: Initial effects. *Child Abuse & Neglect, 20*(11), 1095–1109.
53 Burge, S. K. (1983). Rape: Individual and family reactions. In C. R. Figley & H. I. McCubbin (Eds.), *Stress and the family: Coping with catastrophe* (Vol.2, pp.103–119). New York: Bruner/Mazel.
54 Clevenger, S. (2015). Mothers of sexual assault victims: How women "do mother" after their child has been sexually assaulted. *Feminist Criminology, 11*(3), 227–252.
55 Figley, C. R. (1985). Traumatic stress: The role of the family and social support system. In C. R. Figley (Ed.) *Trauma and its wake: Vol. 2, the study and treatment of posttraumatic stress disorder* (pp. 39–54). New York: Bruner/Mazel.
56 Manion, I., McIntyre, J., Firestone, P., Ligenzinska, M., Ensom, R., & Wells, G. (1996). Secondary traumatisation in parents following disclosure of extrafamilial child sexual abuse: Initial effects. *Child Abuse & Neglect, 20*(11), 1095–1109.
57 Clevenger, S. (2015). Mothers of sexual assault victims: How women "do mother" after their child has been sexually assaulted. *Feminist Criminology, 11*(3), 227–252.
58 Manion, I., McIntyre, J., Firestone, P., Ligenzinska, M., Ensom, R., & Wells, G. (1996). Secondary traumatisation in parents following disclosure of extrafamilial child sexual abuse: Initial effects. *Child Abuse & Neglect, 20*(11), 1095–1109.
59 Clevenger, S. (2015). Mothers of sexual assault victims: How women "do mother" after their child has been sexually assaulted. *Feminist Criminology, 11*(3), 227–252.
60 Manion, I., McIntyre, J., Firestone, P., Ligenzinska, M., Ensom, R., & Wells, G. (1996). Secondary traumatisation in parents following disclosure of extrafamilial child sexual abuse: Initial effects. *Child Abuse & Neglect, 20*(11), 1095–1109.
61 Clevenger, S. (2015). Mothers of sexual assault victims: How women "do mother" after their child has been sexually assaulted. *Feminist Criminology, 11*(3), 227–252.
62 Kogan, S. M. (2004). Disclosing unwanted sexual experiences: Results from a national sample of adolescent women. *Child Abuse and Neglect, 28*, 147–165.
63 Rickert, V. I., Wiemann, C. M., & Vaughan, R. D. (2005). Disclosure of date/acquaintance rape: Who reports and when. *Journal of Pediatric Adolescent Gynecology, 18*, 17–24.
64 Stein, R. E., & Nofziger, S. D. (2008). Adolescent sexual victimization: Choice of confidant and the failure of authorities. *Youth Violence and Juvenile Justice, 6*(2), 158–177.
65 Weisz, A., Tolman, R. M., Callahan, M. R., Saunders, D. G., & Black, B. M. (2007). Informal helpers' response when adolescents tell them about dating violence or romantic relationship problems. *Journal of Adolescence, 30*, 853–868.
66 Boldero, J., & Fallon, B. (1995). Adolescent help-seeking: What do they get help for and from whom? *Journal of Adolescence, 18*(2), 193–209.
67 Sullivan, K., Marshall, S. K., & Schonert-Reichl, K. A. (2002). Do expectancies influence choice of help-giver? Adolescents' criteria for selecting an informal helper. *Journal of Adolescent Research, 17*(5), 509–531.
68 Weisz, A., Tolman, R. M., Callahan, M. R., Saunders, D. G., & Black, B. M. (2007). Informal helpers' response when adolescents tell them about dating violence or romantic relationship problems. *Journal of Adolescence, 30*, 853–868.
69 Neal, J. W. (2010). Social aggression and social position in middle childhood and early adolescence: Burning bridges or building them? *Journal of Early Adolescence, 30*(1), 122–137.
70 Staller, K. M., & Nelson-Gardell, D. (2005). "A burden in your heart": Lessons of disclosure from female preadolescent and adolescent survivors of sexual abuse. *Child Abuse and Neglect, 29*, 1415–1432.
71 Fehler-Cabral, G., Campbell, R., & Patterson, G. (2011). Adult sexual assault survivors' experiences with sexual assault nurse examiners (SANEs). *Journal of Interpersonal Violence, 26*, 3618–3639.
72 Ullman, S. E., & Filipas, H. H. (2001). Correlates of formal and informal support seeking in sexual assault victims. *Journal of Interpersonal Violence, 16*, 1028–1047.
73 Ahrens, C. E., & Campbell, R. (2000). Assisting rape victims as they recover from rape: The impact on friends. *Journal of Interpersonal Violence, 15*(9), 959–986.
74 Ullman, S. E., & Filipas, H. H. (2001). Correlates of formal and informal support seeking in sexual assault victims. *Journal of Interpersonal Violence, 16*, 1028–1047.
75 Logan, T., Evans, L., Stevenson, E., & Jordan, C. E. (2005). Barriers to services for rural and urban survivors of rape. *Journal of Interpersonal Violence, 20*(5), 591–616.

76 Ibid.
77 Edwards, K. M. (2014). Intimate partner violence and the rural–urban–suburban divide: Myth or reality? A critical review of the literature. *Trauma, Violence, & Abuse*, *16*(3), 359–373.
78 Logan, T., Evans, L., Stevenson, E., & Jordan, C. E. (2005). Barriers to services for rural and urban survivors of rape. *Journal of Interpersonal Violence*, *20*(5), 591–616.
79 Ibid.
80 Ibid.
81 Ibid.
82 Ibid.
83 Ibid.
84 Ibid.
85 Goodman, L. A. & Smyth, K. F. (2011). A call for a social network oriented approach to services for survivors of intimate partner violence. *Psychology of Violence*, *1*(2), 79–92.
86 Clevenger, S. (2015). Mothers of sexual assault victims: How women "do mother" after their child has been sexually assaulted. *Feminist Criminology*, *11*(3), 227–252.
87 Logan, T., Evans, L., Stevenson, E., & Jordan, C.E. (2005). Barriers to services for rural and urban survivors of rape. *Journal of Interpersonal Violence*, *20*(5), 591–616.
88 Ibid.
89 Ibid.
90 Ibid.
91 Clevenger, S. (2015). Mothers of sexual assault victims: How women "do mother" after their child has been sexually assaulted. *Feminist Criminology*, *11*(3), 227–252.
92 Ibid.
93 Taylor, R. (2009). Slain and slandered: A content analysis of the portrayal of femicide in crime news. *Homicide Studies*, *13*(1), 21–49.
94 Richards, T. N., Gillespie, L. K., & Smith, M. D. (2011). Exploring news coverage of femicide: Does reporting the news add insult to injury? *Feminist Criminology*, *6*(3), 178–202.
95 Englebrecht, C., Mason, D. T., & Adams, M. J. The experience of homicide victims' families with the criminal justice system: An exploratory study. *Violence and Victims*, *29*(3), 407–421.
96 Gekoski, A., Adler, J. R., & Gray, J. M. (2013). Interviewing women bereaved by homicide: Reports of secondary victimization by the criminal justice system. *International Review of Victimology*, *19*(3), 1–23.
97 Morrall, P., Hazelton, M., & Shackelton, W. (2011). Homicide and its effect on secondary victims. *Mental Health Practice*, *15*(3), 14–19.
98 Englebrecht, C., Mason, D. T., & Adams, M. J. The experience of homicide victims' families with the criminal justice system: An exploratory study. *Violence and Victims*, *29*(3), 407–421.
99 Gekoski, A., Adler, J. R., & Gray, J. M. (2013). Interviewing women bereaved by homicide: Reports of secondary victimization by the criminal justice system. *International Review of Victimology*, *19*(3), 1–23.
100 Morrall, P., Hazelton, M., & Shackelton, W. (2011). Homicide and its effect on secondary victims. *Mental Health Practice*, *15*(3), 14–19.
101 Englebrecht, C., Mason, D. T., & Adams, M. J. The experience of homicide victims' families with the criminal justice system: An exploratory study. *Violence and Victims*, *29*(3), 407–421.
102 Gekoski, A., Adler, J. R., & Gray, J. M. (2013). Interviewing women bereaved by homicide: Reports of secondary victimization by the criminal justice system. *International Review of Victimology*, *19*(3), 1–23.
103 Logan, T., Evans, L., Stevenson, E., & Jordan, C. E. (2005). Barriers to services for rural and urban survivors of rape. *Journal of Interpersonal Violence*, *20*(5), 591–616.
104 Gekoski, A., Adler, J. R., & Gray, J. M. (2013). Interviewing women bereaved by homicide: Reports of secondary victimization by the criminal justice system. *International Review of Victimology*, *19*(3), 1–23.
105 Logan, T., Evans, L., Stevenson, E., & Jordan, C. E. (2005). Barriers to services for rural and urban survivors of rape. *Journal of Interpersonal Violence*, *20*(5), 591–616.
106 Clevenger, S. (2015). Mothers of sexual assault victims: How women "do mother" after their child has been sexually assaulted. *Feminist Criminology*, *11*(3), 227–252.
107 Gekoski, A., Adler, J. R., & Gray, J. M. (2013). Interviewing women bereaved by homicide: Reports of secondary victimization by the criminal justice system. *International Review of Victimology*, *19*(3), 1–23.
108 Ibid.
109 Englebrecht, C., Mason, D. T., & Adams, M. J. The experience of homicide victims' families with the criminal justice system: An exploratory study. *Violence and Victims*, *29*(3), 407–421.
110 Logan, T., Evans, L., Stevenson, E., & Jordan, C. E. (2005). Barriers to services for rural and urban survivors of rape. *Journal of Interpersonal Violence*, *20*(5), 591–616.

111 Gekoski, A., Adler, J. R., & Gray, J. M. (2013). Interviewing women bereaved by homicide: Reports of secondary victimization by the criminal justice system. *International Review of Victimology, 19*(3), 1–23.
112 Englebrecht, C., Mason, D. T., & Adams, M. J. The experience of homicide victims' families with the criminal justice system: An exploratory study. *Violence and Victims, 29*(3), 407–421.
113 Gekoski, A., Adler, J. R., & Gray, J. M. (2013). Interviewing women bereaved by homicide: Reports of secondary victimization by the criminal justice system. *International Review of Victimology, 19*(3), 1–23.
114 Englebrecht, C., Mason, D. T., & Adams, M. J. The experience of homicide victims' families with the criminal justice system: An exploratory study. *Violence and Victims, 29*(3), 407–421.
115 Ibid.
116 Logan, T., Evans, L., Stevenson, E., & Jordan, C. E. (2005). Barriers to services for rural and urban survivors of rape. *Journal of Interpersonal Violence, 20*(5), 591–616.

7

INTIMATE PARTNER VIOLENCE, NEOLIBERAL IDEOLOGIES, AND CONTROVERSIES ABOUT VICTIMHOOD

Jennifer Katz and Hillary Rich

Keywords

domestic violence; intimate partner violence; neoliberal beliefs; rape; sexual assault; stalking; victim blame

Objectives

After studying this chapter, the reader should understand:

- How U.S. laws about different forms of intimate partner violence (IPV) shifted over time, along with perceptions of legitimate victimhood.
- The major tenets of neoliberalism as applied to individual lives, morality, and responsibility.
- The three major dimensions of neoliberal victim theory suggested by Rebecca Stringer (2014): victim blame, reverse victimization, and resentment, as reflected in the IPV literature.
- How neoliberal victim theory may affect views of women of color, lesbians, and men who experience sexual or intimate partner sexual assault, physical violence, or stalking.
- The multiple, complex, sometimes paradoxical ways in which actual and perceived agency are related to an individual's status as a victim.
- Stigma associated with a victim identity and negative consequences of both identifying and not identifying as a victim.

Introduction

You are not a victim. No matter what you have been through, you're still here. You may have been challenged, hurt, betrayed, beaten, and discouraged, but nothing has defeated you. You are still here! You have been delayed but not denied. You are not a victim; you are a victor. You have a history of victory.

(Steve Maraboli, Unapologetically You: Reflections on Life and the Human Experience, http://www.stevemaraboli.com/)

If you know and admit that you're in an abusive relationship, then you are no longer a victim. You are a survivor *of domestic abuse.*

(Posted on June 23, 2013 by Kellie Jo Holly, Top 3 Things I Know That an Abuse Victim Does Not)

The primary purpose of this chapter is to explore the application of neoliberal victim theory to the ways in which targets of intimate partner violence (IPV) are recognized and identified as victims. Identifying victims "takes place within a historical, cultural, and organizational context shaped by multiple perspectives on what it means to be a 'true' victim" (Dunn, 2001, p. 287). From a constructionist perspective, social processes of interpretation determine whether a person may be *recognized* as a victim, either by oneself or by observers (e.g., law enforcement officers). Loseke (2003), as cited by Leisenring (2006), suggests that such interpretations recognizing victimhood are based on whether a person is deemed worthy of sympathy. In general, sympathy is reserved for innocent people who have been unjustly injured. That is, the label of victim and the benefits of victim assistance are offered to "morally good people" who "are greatly harmed through no fault of their own" (Leisenring, 2006, p. 79). As we show throughout this chapter, neoliberal ideologies profoundly affect how people understand morality and responsibility; thus, neoliberal ideologies affect judgments of sympathy and shape processes of victim recognition and identification.

Victimization is a broad topic. Our focus here is on acts of assault (sexual or physical) or stalking perpetrated by intimate or sexual partners (or ex-partners). Historically, in the U.S. and similar cultures, such acts have been minimized as typical of private heterosexual relationships in which women fail to meet the needs of their male partners. In contemporary times, perceptions of IPV and victimhood are also affected by evolving societal recognitions of different types of couples and different types of individuals who may be considered victims. Yet, both historically and today, IPV is perceived as less serious and worthy of criminal prosecution than assault, violence, or stalking perpetrated by a stranger. Even after partner sexual assault, physical assault, or stalking were eventually recognized by law as criminal activities, police officers, prosecutors, courts, and juries have not tended to regard such acts as "real crimes."

Legal Acknowledgement of IPV: Historical and Cultural Shifts

Understandings of IPV, including sexual assault, physical assault, and stalking, have evolved over time. For many years in the U.S., rape was legally understood as an act of physically forced vaginal penetration committed by a man against a woman to whom he is not married (e.g., McMahon-Howard, Clay-Warner, & Renzulli, 2009). Originally, rape laws were enacted to protect women as men's "property;" rape penalties were intended to punish men for harming other men's property, and as property owners, husbands could not be charged (Bergen, 1996). Although laws were later revised to allow women to own property, theoretically invalidating the legal impossibility of marital rape, marital rape remained legal for most of the twentieth century (Bennice & Resick, 2003) and was typically dismissed as a "private matter" (Caringella-MacDonald, 1988, p. 175).

Once recognized as a crime by all 50 U.S. states in the late twentieth century, marital rape was often placed in a different penal category from other general rape statutes (Caringella-MacDonald, 1988), with the tacit understanding that marital rape wasn't "real rape" (Bennice & Resick, 2003, p. 231). Even after marital rape was criminalized, police were reluctant to make arrests. In addition, courts were often unwilling to prosecute given that prosecution generally required third-party witnesses or evidence that the rape was life threatening (MacManus & Van Hightower, 1989). Importantly, marriage is not the only type of relationship in which a relationship between the perpetrator and victim diminishes the perceived severity of rape. For example, a former United States Penal Code provision stipulated if a rape victim had "previously permitted him [the perpetrator] sexual liberties," then there would be a lesser potential punishment (Denno, 2009, p. 54). Clearly, these types of stipulations also adversely affected the perceived legitimacy of "real rape" among those who were cohabiting, engaged, dating, or casually involved in a sexual relationship.

Like rape, battering and other forms of physical assault within intimate relationships in the U.S. have long been deemed tolerable or even acceptable. In some cases, physical assault may have been expected; when women are seen as the property of/belonging to a man (such as a husband), violence has been seen as a tool of legitimate control, discipline, or chastisement. Over time, even as U.S. courts in the twentieth century began to reject the notion of husband chastisement, a common law doctrine of family privacy was substituted in order to justify legal non-intervention despite evidence for physical abuse of the wife by the husband (Goldfarb, 2005).

In the U.S., partner (i.e., domestic) violence began to be recognized as a potential crime in the 1970s during the second wave feminist movement. Yet in their classic book, *Intimate Violence*, Gelles and Straus (1988) wryly refer to the marriage license as "a hitting license" (p. 26). Gelles and Straus also cite research suggesting that a) police respond more slowly to domestic than public disturbances, b) calls for police intervention may anger the perpetrator and encourage further violence, and c) law enforcement systems are reluctant to prosecute men for domestic violence because doing so may "break up families" (p. 24). In another classic book, *Next Time, She'll be Dead*, Jones (2000) argues that domestic violence must be viewed as a crime rather than a marital or interpersonal relational problem. She bemoans the dismissive ways cases of marital or other intimate assault are typically treated by law enforcement, even after necessary legal reforms recognizing violence between intimate partners as a crime (see also Goldfarb, 2005).

Compared with sexual and physical assault, recognition of stalking as a crime has a different but similarly troublesome legal history. Stalking was not legally criminalized in the U.S. until the early 1990s. This change was in response to the murder of actress Rebecca Schaeffer by an obsessed fan, Robert John Bardo. Bardo had written the actress multiple letters, and his obsession culminated in a visit to her home where he shot her (Coleman, 1997; Meloy, 1998). Schaeffer's death prompted California to institute the first anti-stalking legislation in 1990; the rest of the nation soon followed suit with relatively similar statutes (Meloy, 1998). Rebecca Schaeffer's specific plight shaped the conceptualization of the stalker as an obsessed and insane stranger, a conceptualization, which has influenced subsequent laws (McCann, 1998). Yet, cases like Schaeffer's are relatively unusual, and the most common stalker is a former intimate partner (Fox, Gover, & Kaukinen, 2009).

Unfortunately, this most prevalent form of stalking, by an ex-partner, is also mistakenly perceived as less serious than stalking by a stranger. Furthermore, the victim of stalking by an ex-partner is also perceived as more blameworthy. In a study of attitudes about stalking behavior, when the stalker was an ex-partner, rather than a stranger, observers regarded the pursuit as less indicative of stalking and less likely to require police intervention; these victims also were seen as more responsible for encouraging the stalker's behavior (Sheridan, Gillett, Davies, Blaauw, & Patel, 2003). Furthermore, in interviews with women who were stalked and seeking support from the courts, victims report being asked by family and friends "what they had done to encourage their former partners' attention" (Dunn, 2001, p. 292) and being accused by lawyers of "leading him on" (p. 293). Finally, it should be noted that most states necessitate that behaviors must be unwanted, repeated, and fear-inducing to legally qualify as stalking (Davis, Ace, & Andra, 2000; Meloy, 1998; Mullen, Pathé, & Purcell, 2000). In fact, stalking is unique in the U.S. as one of the only crimes in which the legality of a behavior is dependent on the victim's reaction: fear (Cass & Rosay, 2012; Mullen, Pathé, Purcell, & Stuart, 1999). Therefore, the fear requirement essentially demands that the target of unwanted, repeated pursuit behaviors acknowledge fear and accept the label of victim before the stalking behaviors are considered criminal (Dunn, 2001).

Overall, in contemporary times, legal reforms have successfully allowed for better recognition of various types of IPV, including sexual assault (e.g., Schulhofer, 2003; Randall, 2010), partner violence and stalking (Goldfarb, 2005). Nonetheless, many individual experiences are not acknowledged or legitimized as "real" victimization. We argue in this chapter that obstacles to improved reform and understandings of victimization often directly or indirectly involve the workings of neoliberal ideologies as applied to individual lives. As described below, neoliberal ideologies shift focus away from the perpetrator and the crime and instead assign blame to the target of partner IPV. According to neoliberal victim theory, a target of violence is a person who has a personal or interpersonal problem warranting privacy rather than a person experiencing a social problem that could be resolved or prevented via collective action, legal reform, and socio-cultural change.

Neoliberal Victim Theory: Choice, Morality, and Personal Responsibility

Rebecca Stringer (2014) defines "anti-victimism" as "the notion that one should 'choose to refuse to be a victim'" (p. 3). This idea of choice shows that anti-victim talk locates the problem of victimization within the individual, and not within the individual's experience of violation, injury, or other harm within a situation or set of circumstances. This idea of choice also is reflected in concerns about the allegedly widespread problem of victim identities. Some social commentators in the U.S. and similar contexts complain about becoming a "victim society" (Sykes, 1992) in which "citizens take up victim identity instead of taking personal responsibility, seeking 'special treatment'" (Stringer, 2014, p. 3). Consequently, individuals who describe a curtailment of their human rights to bodily integrity and safety often are criticized as "doing it to themselves" or "playing the victim." Such criticism presumes that claims of victimhood reflect an individual's unique, potentially distorted thoughts and feelings about their experiences rather than the actual situation or circumstances that led to violation, injury, or other harm.

Regarding the victimization of women specifically, some feminists' desires to ascribe agency to women have turned into anti-victimism when they reject the word victim (Stringer, 2014). This is especially true when the term victim is replaced with the term "survivor" after non-life-threatening experiences (Lamb, 2015). Recognizing and acknowledging that girls and women are empowered, rational people who have personal and behavioral agency to meaningfully affect their lives is a worthy cause. Yet, denying victimization experienced by girls and women fails to support the social changes needed to end various circumstances that cause victimization in the first place. For example, the sociocultural belief or expectation that women owe men sexual access to their bodies or that women should defer to men's interests can increase risk for men's violence against women (e.g., Harding, 2015, Hester, 2014). Furthermore, systems of oppression related to gender, race, and class increase risks for violence against marginalized women of color (e.g., Richie, 2012). Although neoliberalists and feminists might agree that girls and women should have behavioral/psychological agency, in reality, not all girls and women do have agency, at all times. Recognizing this fact does not require a belief that an individual who has been victimized lacks agency in general, across all situations.

Nonetheless, anti-victim talk seems grounded in a neoliberal framing of the definition of victimization as involving an immoral lack of personal agency and responsibility. On a macro level, neoliberal economic and social policies are designed to support the expansion of capital markets while restricting government regulations and social welfare systems. Neoliberal policies are founded on a belief that rational, self-interested systems (including nations, governments, and individuals) should compete on an even playing field to maximize gains and reduce losses (e.g., Harvey, 2005). According to Brown (2003), the neoliberal ideals of competition and a free market are achieved "through economic deregulation, elimination of tariffs, and a range of monetary and social policies favorable to business and indifferent toward poverty" (p. 38). In the U.S. economic neoliberal ideology emerged in the 1970s and was pervasive by the 1990s (Bay-Cheng et al., 2015). Such ideologies have been used to critique domestic social policies and government programs that attempted to reduce social inequality. Ostensibly, such programs are antithetical to outcomes based on merit and individual work ethic.

Scholars have become increasingly focused on the ways in which macro level neoliberal policies affect individuals and perceptions of individuals in their everyday lives. That is, neoliberal ideologies shape how people make sense both of their own lived experiences and the experiences of others. For example, Luxton (2010) writes that neoliberal beliefs promote a focus on individuals as "responsible for themselves" and "the choices they make determine the outcome of their lives" (p. 173). She found that neoliberal beliefs affected how people made sense of their need for informal caregiving by family, friends, or community members after either a medical emergency or unemployment. These individuals blamed themselves for their difficult situations because they had made choices to work in dangerous or difficult fields. These same individuals seemed unaware of how these contexts of danger or difficulty also affected them. Luxton's (2010) findings match with the suggestion by Brown (2003) that "[neoliberalism] figures individuals as rational, calculating creatures whose moral autonomy is measured by their capacity for self-care" (p. 42).

From a neoliberal perspective, individuals are expected to pursue their own rational self-interests, accept potential risk, and exert and maintain control over themselves and their lives. As applied to individuals in the U.S. and other similar cultures, Bay-Cheng (2015) argues that these neoliberal principles are moral obligations for good citizens. That is, a person's failure to exert her own free will de-legitimizes her as a person – regardless of social, economic, or cultural circumstances. Agency is a mandate, even for the powerless. Therefore, a person faced with unexpected or undesirable outcomes is perceived as lacking worth and dignity. Bay-Cheng (2015) also argues that, from a neoliberal perspective, there is no excuse for a failure of personal responsibility. Thus, experiences of sexual helplessness such as rape reflect "a manifestation of one's ineptitude as an agent" and not "violation by another person, systemic injustice, or even bad luck" (Bay-Cheng, 2015, p. 286). By casting victims as making bad choices, morally deficient, and lacking in agency by virtue of their victimization, neoliberal beliefs erode sympathy for targets of assault, violence, and stalking pursuit. In so doing, such beliefs adversely affect the identification of victimization by intimate partners or ex-partners.

Neoliberal Victim Theory and IPV

As suggested by Rebecca Stringer (2014), there are three major dimensions of neoliberal victim theory: victim blame, reverse victimization, and resentment. The social science literatures on sexual assault, physical assault, and stalking by current or former partners show both direct and indirect evidence for these dimensions in controversies regarding which individuals can be legitimately considered victims.

First, victim blame is a primary part of neoliberal victim theory. The central idea, as posed by Stringer (2014), is that victims are seen as having a specific type of "personality" (p. 9) rather than having had a specific type of experience or situation. The victim personality is incompetent in managing risks and avoiding negative outcomes. In this way, the neoliberal paradigm is fundamentally "punitive," because if successes reflect the workings of meritocracy, in which people get what they deserve, failures reflect personal ineptitude (Baker, 2008, p. 59).

These tendencies to blame victims also are supported by multiple general cognitive biases that are well-established in the psychological literature (Lamb, 2015). According to the Just World Hypothesis, because we are motivated to perceive the world as fair, we are motivated to believe that those who have positive experiences are good people, and those who have negative experiences are bad people (Lerner, 1980). Similarly, according to System Justification Theory, we are motivated at both conscious and unconscious levels to view a given situation as legitimate, fair, natural, desirable, and inevitable (Jost, Banaji, & Nosek, 2004). Similarly, the Fundamental Attribution Error describes the tendency for observers to ascribe the causes of events to the characteristics of those people who experience them (Reber, Allen, & Reber, 2009).

Randall (2010, p. 409) describes victim-blaming in the context of sexual assault against women as explicitly related to neoliberal attitudes:

> Women are, and should be, responsible for navigating their own safety, for managing men's sexual attention and aggression, and also for accurately assessing and avoiding risk. Such forms of victim-blaming have most recently been associated with the neo-liberal strategy of "responsibilization," which is itself a project of privatization that deviates away from recognizing public responsibility for social problems such as violence against women and, instead, endorses a radically decontextualized, de-gendered focus on "problematic" individuals.

In other words, within the context of an intimate or sexual relationship, an assault can be seen as a logical result of having selected a problematic partner. More informally, choosing a partner means choosing the consequences of that partner's behavior. This idea converges with research by Jones (2000), who reported that law enforcement officers regard battered women as at least partly responsible for the attacks they suffer, which adversely affects police response to domestic violence calls. Importantly, apparent individual mistakes in partner selection are not easily undone because IPV by both current and former partners is minimized. Experimental research on perceptions of IPV suggests that a target of sexual assault (e.g., Ben-David & Schneider, 2005) or of stalking (e.g., Sheridan et al., 2003) is held more responsible if the act was perpetrated by an ex-partner than a stranger.

A second tenet of neoliberal victim theory is "reverse victimology." According to Stringer (2014), this refers to the tendency of perpetrators and others to invert the positions of perpetrator and victim. More generally, Stringer suggests that observers sometimes consider "those claiming victim status for themselves or for others. . . as non-credible victimizers" (p. 10). Often, the victims are described as the "true perpetrators." This type of reverse victimology is seen when rape victims make police reports and are then referred to as "accusers" of potentially innocent men (Harding, 2015). Similarly, the last dimension of the "Deny, Attack, and Reverse Victim and Offender" (DARVO) model has been proposed by trauma researcher Jennifer Freyd (2015). The offender may a) Deny the behavior, b) Attack the individual doing the confronting, and c) Reverse the roles of Victim and Offender. In this last part, the offender identifies as the actual victim and names the actual victim as the "true offender." For example, Freyd (2015) cites the case of a guilty sexual offender who claims to be falsely accused and attacks the credibility of the person whom the perpetrator violated.

Reverse victimology also affects perceptions of physical assault. For example, evidence for reverse victimology was shown by men interviewed for a qualitative study about how heterosexual couples made sense of the man's violence against his female partner. Men commonly described that their female partner had emasculated and wounded them, for example, by being critical. This victimized, wounded state led to the men's violent behavior (Boonzaier, 2008). Similarly, Goldfarb (2005) found that a third of women who are convicted of homicide have killed a partner who had been physically violent toward them. Goldfarb argues that many women treated as perpetrators experience repeated, severe physical violence and become desperate to defend themselves; their actions, however, lead to prosecution and the label of perpetrator, with the physically violent partner identified as the victim of their crime. Given that many couples show patterns of reciprocal or mutual violence; reciprocal violence may be viewed as acts of agentic self-defense or as acts of perpetration; the latter view would be most in accord with reverse victimology.

A third tenet of neoliberal victim theory, according to Stringer (2014), is "resentment." Resentment involves the idea that a victim has pathological thoughts and feelings, and these internal experiences constitute the victim identity. This part of neoliberal victim theory reduces victimization to a state of mind involving irrational anger and perhaps entitlement for justice or change. In this way, anger, a common emotional consequence of being a target of harm, can be used to individualize and discredit the veracity of the claim that victimization occurred. The general tendency for those who are victimized to be diagnosed as pathological has been critiqued by feminist scholars such as Jane Ussher (2011). Diagnosing individuals, including women, who are coping with victimization implies that the understandable distress that occurs following being violated, injured, or both is a product of the individual's mind rather than a product of the individual's life experience. Similarly, Goldfarb (2005) describes "battered women's syndrome" as a limited legal defense to the degree that it focuses attention on the battered woman's mental state and behavior rather than the perpetrator's role in affecting her mental state and behavior.

To avoid resentment, individuals can re-interpret for themselves and others the experience of victimization in a way that minimizes or neutralizes the experience. For example, when a person uses physical force against an intimate partner, the partner may reinterpret the force as due to "joking" (Arriaga, 2002). Such a reinterpretation neutralizes the perceived deviance of the act and minimizes blame assigned to the forceful partner. These types of reinterpretations mitigating resentment starkly contradict the interpretations that Dunn (2001, 2010) found central to the process of identifying oneself as a victim of stalking. That is, in order to consider oneself a "victim," one who is stalked must interpret the stalker's actions as deviant, cease to neutralize those behaviors, and blame the stalker for enacting unwanted, repeated pursuit behaviors. Because ex-partner stalkers are the type of stalker most likely to escalate to violence (Dietz & Martin, 2007), minimizing or neutralizing pursuit experiences to avoid appearing resentful may preclude individuals from seeking potential legal action and even place them in greater danger.

Identifying Victims across Diverse Identity Categories

Neoliberal ideologies also appear to interfere with the identification of victims across diverse identity categories related to gender, race, sexual orientation, and other factors. Men in both same- and mixed-sex relationships, lesbians, and women of color have all been targets of intimate partner violence, yet such experiences have not always been perceived as reflecting victimization. According to Bay-Cheng et al. (2015), neoliberal policies and beliefs "presume institutionalized discrimination to be largely eradicated" and reflect a view of society as "meritocratic, post-racial, [and] post-feminist" (p. 73). These neoliberal assumptions contrast with clear empirical evidence that some groups of people are seen as more credible and are more valued within society than others, including certain victims of IPV. For example, compared with white women who are sexually assaulted, black women who are sexually assaulted are judged more negatively (e.g., Donovan, 2007; Randall, 2010) and are often not considered to be legitimate victims (Richie, 2012). Similarly, battered women who are black, lesbian, or both have been dismissed or devalued judged negatively for not displaying the culturally expected, traditionally feminine victim profile of passivity and male deference (Goldfarb, 2005).

Neoliberal beliefs also affect perceptions of men who are targets of IPV. To the degree that institutionalized discrimination has been largely eradicated in contemporary times, as suggested by a neoliberal perspective, IPV scholars and advocates should focus on spousal or partner violence, with no special attention needed for violence against girls and women specifically (e.g., Straus, 2008). Some argue that both women and men perpetrate violence against partners, and thus partner violence is a symmetrical problem across gender. Others argue that IPV reflects both structural and interpersonal power differences, and because men tend to be more powerful and dominant than their female partners, violence is asymmetrical across gender. Debates about gender symmetry and asymmetry and the context of perpetration represent longstanding controversies in the field of IPV (e.g., Johnson, 2005, 2006, 2008). At the same time, behavioral or psychological agency is viewed as a traditionally masculine quality (e.g., Katz & Tirone, 2015). Therefore, if victims are understood to be people lacking in agency, men may be unfairly dismissed as incapable of being victimized by intimate partners. Alternatively, men may be seen as emasculated, or "not real men," if they are targets of IPV and claim victim status.

Victims or Agents? A False Binary

Neoliberalism frames and defines victimhood as involving an absence of agency. This framing is inherently problematic and relies on a false binary: the victim/agent dichotomy. According to this binary position, one cannot be a victim and demonstrate agency (Stringer, 2014). Yet, there are cases in which agentic behavior is required in order for victimhood to be established. In addition, there are cases in which agentic behavior is viewed as an inappropriate reaction to one's experiences of being violated or injured, possibly increasing an individual's risk for continued victimization. Clearly, the binary is paradoxical. Furthermore, maintaining a focus on the victim/agent binary requires a focus on the individual and how s/he responds to situations rather than a focus on both the individual as well as the situation in which s/he is targeted and harmed.

One clear example of the false victim/agent binary involves historical definitions of sexual assault requiring active resistance (Stringer, 2014). Active resistance on the part of the sexual assault victim has long been considered necessary in order for an assault to be considered legitimate. As Randall (2010, p. 415) writes:

> underpinning the stereotype of an "ideal" and "real" victim of sexual assault, then, is the assumption that, when being sexually assaulted, violated, or raped, a woman who is truly unwilling will vigorously verbally and/or physically resist the attack or the coercive or unwanted sex. Not only should "ideal" victims resist, but this resistance should also be evident or capable of proof somehow in order to provide validation of non-complicity. This has not only been a social expectation, but it has also been embedded historically in legal requirements.

Another example of the false victim/agent binary is the framing of domestic couple violence. When violence is one-sided, individuals who respond passively, such as by minimizing conflict or attempting to appease the partner may be blamed for "putting up with" partner violence. Yet, individuals who show agentic responses such as fighting back or using self-defense responses may be perceived as perpetrators, and not victims, consistent with the ideas underpinning "reverse victimology." This paradox for women in domestically abusive relationships was summed up by Langan, Hannem, and Stewart (2014, p. 14): "socially dominant, victim-blaming discourse holds women responsible if they do not try to protect themselves (i.e. if they are perceived to be victims), and if they do try to protect themselves (i.e. if they are perceived to be perpetrators)."

Furthermore, in some cases, a neoliberal view holding individual targets of IPV as responsible for managing risk within their environments may prove dangerous. Pacifying a violent partner to avoid violence may reduce immediate risk but also reinforce broader patterns of instrumentally aggressive behavior over time (Gelles & Straus, 1988). Yet, assertive expressions of dissatisfaction with a partner's behavior can lead to conflict escalation. For instance, targets of stalking often continuously confront their stalkers, resort to threats, or attempt reconciliation (Bjorklund,

Hakkanen-Nyholm, Sheridan, & Roberts, 2010; Meloy, 1997). In fact, as many as 90 percent of stalking victims continue to interact with their stalker in some way (Dunn, 2001). However, these approaches actually provide powerful intermittent reinforcement to a stalker by demonstrating that enough persistence elicits a response from the victim (Meloy, 1997). Instead, experts advise victims to straightforwardly inform the stalker that they do not want any further contact and not to engage with the stalker again (Mullen et al., 2000). This ostensibly passive approach is incompatible with neoliberalism and is in direct contrast to the ideal victim who shows forceful resistance (Randall, 2010).

Finally, rather than being lauded for agentic actions in which targets of violence try to correct social wrongs, victims instead may be punished as showing "inappropriate" reactions to victimization. Expressions of anger and active attempts to seek retribution or justice may be seen as particularly abnormal among women who have been victimized because such women are violating the prescribed feminine role. As noted by Goldfarb (2005, p. 222):

> the battered woman stereotype has worked to the particular disadvantage of black women, lesbians, women perceived to have assertive personalities, women with substance abuse histories, and others who for a variety of cultural reasons may not be readily perceived to embody the passive virtues that fit constrained understandings of the battered woman profile.

Paradoxically, beliefs about "appropriate" reactions to victimization often punish individuals both for their expressions of agency as well as for expressions of passivity. For example, in Jane Doe v. Metropolitan Toronto (Municipality) Commissioners of Police, the complainant (a rape victim) successfully sued the police for negligence. This suit occurred after a serial rapist sexually attacked five women at knifepoint. The first two women who were attacked reported their assaults to law enforcement; unfortunately, their reports had been discounted. Jane Doe, one of the rape victims who was attacked after the police failed to investigate, "was pathologized by a psychiatrist called by the defence, who claimed that Jane Doe was 'malingering' and that the civil action could be seen as part of a protracted psychological disturbance" (Randall, 2010, p. 421). Jane Doe's agentic response was cast as reflecting resentment rather than as an action to ensure accountability by law enforcement and safety for other women. Yet, Randall (2010) also suggests that law enforcement and others may have difficulties with the credibility of "women who appear to be stoic, calm, and controlled" (p. 427) following an assault, as evidenced by their failure to investigate a report made by one such victim in this specific case.

Stigma, Self-blame, and the Victim Identity

Given the pervasiveness of neoliberal values, the "victim identity" is stigmatized yet often necessary for individuals to adopt in order receive medical, legal, and other needed assistance. For example, an acknowledgement of partner violence is needed to seek refuge in a shelter for battered women, and an acknowledgement of stalking is needed to seek court orders of protection. Yet, being a victim is stigmatized, and stigmatized persons are seen as different, are discriminated against, and feel inferior or damaged (Goffman, 1963). Not surprisingly, many targets of IPV prefer not to acknowledge membership in a stigmatized group and to avoid the adoption of a stigmatized identity. Indeed, research finds that acknowledged rape victims are more likely to feel embarrassed, shamed, "dirtied," "different than other women," and to fear that others may find out about what happened (Gibson & Leitenberg, 2001, p. 1348; Littleton, Breitkopf, & Berenson, 2008). Similarly, based on interviews with women living in shelters, Leisenring (2006) observed that "battered women found it difficult to depict themselves as injured or wronged while acknowledging they were not passive or helpless" (p. 308). In other words, targets of IPV may recognize that what happened to them was traumatic or even a crime, yet downplay the experience as "no big deal" or a "mistake" in order to avoid the distress and stigma associated with a victim identity (Boyle & McKinzie, 2015; Dunn, 2001, 2010; Dunn & Powell-Williams, 2007).

Unfortunately, avoiding claim to a victim identity by blaming oneself does not, in fact, promote better mental or physical health outcomes. In one study of college women who had been raped, self-blame was associated with higher rates of depressive symptoms, lower self-esteem, and lower perceived control (Branscombe, Wohl, Owen, Allison, & N'gbala, 2003). Another study of undergraduate women found that the degree of self-blame endorsed by victims of sexual assault prospectively predicted revictimization at 4-month follow-up (Miller, Markman, & Handley, 2007). Evidently, accepting personal responsibility for victimization may perpetuate risk for future revictimization. Similarly, battered women who report greater self-blame also report more symptoms of depression, obsessive compulsivity, and somatization and are more likely to still be involved in the abusive relationship (O'Neill & Kerig, 2000). Furthermore, female victims of stalking who blamed themselves more reported higher symptoms of anxiety, depression, and PTSD, even when controlling for the severity of stalking (Kraaji, Arensman, Garnefski, & Kremers, 2007). The alleged psychological benefits of taking personal responsibility and learning from one's own mistakes touted by neoliberal victim theory are directly contradicted by research that consistently demonstrates the damaging effects of self-blame.

Summary and Conclusion

This chapter explored some of the ways in which neoliberal victim theory can be used to understand controversies about different types of victimization enacted by sexual or intimate partners and ex-partners. Neoliberal victim theory encourages an overly individualistic, decontextualized, and responsible focus on targets of violence who, by virtue of being targeted, failed to effectively exert rational control over their lives. Such a view, we argue, is myopic and ethically problematic. A person does not become a target of IPV because of a lack of personal responsibility or failure to adequately manage risks. Rather, IPV involves a lack of mutual respect, fairness, and dignity within an intimate relationship.

Lamb (2015) has argued that personal responsibility per se isn't problematic as a moral or ethical position; rather, the problem with neoliberalism, is "uber-responsibility" (p. 292). That is, those who are targets of IPV are held responsible while those who are perpetrators are not, typically within an environment that "gives privilege to certain girls and women over others, and judges women's sexuality in terms of how pleasing it is to men" (p. 295). Furthermore, although individuals may freely make choices that are related to their subsequent victimization (e.g., dating someone who turns out to have problems with impulse control, anger management, or feelings of sexual entitlement to one's body), these choices aren't a direct cause of victimization.

Finally, as Lamb (2015) suggests, a consequence of a neoliberal viewpoint is to over-value strength and under-value both vulnerability and mutuality. Yet, healthy partnerships require some degree of emotional intimacy, vulnerability, trust, and faith – being strong as a couple, not merely as an individual. By holding mutual respect as an ethical value in relationships over individual responsibility, strength, or risk management, we can move beyond the individual victim to consider the relational and social context within which an individual's right to live free from harm has been violated.

Discussion Questions

1. Compare and contrast the neoliberal reaction to a victim raped by a stranger, acquaintance, or an intimate partner.
2. From a neoliberal perspective, is the victim of intimate partner violence more blameworthy than a victim of a property crime such as a theft? Why or why not?

3. What are the implications, positive and negative, of using the term "survivor" for victims of intimate partner violence?
4. How does neoliberal victim theory both converge with and deviate from the empowerment goals of modern feminism?
5. Because targets of IPV must identify a threat or danger to seek legal action, how does a neoliberal perspective affect different types of victims who hope for support from the criminal justice system?
6. In what ways does neoliberalism potentially deny or ignore a perpetrator's agency?

References

Arriaga, X. B. (2002). Joking violence among highly committed individuals. *Journal of Interpersonal Violence, 17*, 591–610.

Baker, J. (2008). The ideology of choice: Overstating progress and hiding injustice in the lives of young women: Findings from a study in North Queensland, Australia. *Women's Studies International Forum, 31*, 53–64.

Bay-Cheng, L. Y. (2015). The agency line: A neoliberal metric for appraising young women's sexuality. *Sex Roles*, 73, 279–291.

Bay-Cheng, L. Y., Fitz, C. C., Alizaga, N. M., & Zucker, A. N. (2015). Tracking homo oeconomicus: Development of the neoliberal beliefs inventory. *Journal of Social and Political Psychology, 3*, 71–88.

Ben-David, S., & Schneider, O. (2005). Rape perceptions, gender role attitudes, and victim–perpetrator acquaintance. *Sex Roles, 53*, 385–399.

Bennice, J. A., & Resick, P. A. (2003). Marital rape: History, research, and practice. *Trauma, Violence, and Abuse, 4*, 228–246.

Bergen, R. K. (1996). *Wife rape: Understanding the response of survivors and service providers*. Thousand Oaks, CA: Sage Publications.

Bjorklund, K., Hakkanen-Nyholm, H., Sheridan, L., & Roberts, K. (2010). Coping with stalking among university students. *Violence and Victims, 25*, 395–408.

Boonzaier, F. (2008). If the man says you must sit then you must sit: The relational construction of woman abuse: Gender, subjectivity, and violence. *Feminism and Psychology, 18*, 183–206.

Boyle, K. M., & McKinzie, A. E. (2015). Resolving negative affect and restoring meaning responses to deflection produced by unwanted sexual experiences. *Social Psychology Quarterly, 78*, 151–172.

Branscombe, N. R., Wohl, M. J. A., Owen, S., Allison, J. A., & N'gbala, A. (2003). Counterfactual thinking, blame assignment, and well-being in rape victims. *Basic and Applied Social Psychology, 25*, 265–273.

Brown, W. (2003). Neoliberalism and the end of liberal democracy. *Theory and Event*, 7, 37–44.

Caringella-MacDonald, S. (1988). Parallels and pitfalls: The aftermath of legal reform for sexual assault, marital rape and domestic violence victims. *Journal of Interpersonal Violence, 3* 174–189.

Cass, A. I., & Rosay, A. B. (2012). College student perceptions of criminal justice system responses to stalking. *Sex Roles, 66*, 392–404.

Coleman, F. L. (1997). Stalking behavior and the cycle of domestic violence. *Journal of Interpersonal Violence, 12*, 420–428.

Davis, K. E., Ace, A., & Andra, M. (2000). Stalking perpetrators and psychological maltreatment of partners: Anger-jealousy, attachment insecurity, need for control, and break-up context. *Violence and Victims, 15*, 407–425.

Denno, D. W. (2009). Selected model penal code provisions. *Fordham University School of Law, 42*, 1–59.

Dietz, N. A., & Martin, P. A. (2007). Women who are stalked: Questioning the fear standard. *Violence Against Women, 13*, 750–776.

Donovan, R. A. (2007). To blame or not to blame: Influences of target race and observer sex on rape blame attribution. *Journal of Interpersonal Violence, 22*, 722–736.

Dunn, J. L. (2001). Innocence lost: Accomplishing victimization in intimate stalking cases. *Symbolic Interaction, 24*, 285–313.

Dunn, J. L. (2010). Vocabularies of victimization: Toward explaining the deviant victim. *Deviant Behavior, 31*, 159–183.

Dunn, J. L. & Powell-Williams, M. (2007). "Everybody makes choices": Victim advocates and the social construction of battered women's victimization and agency. *Violence Against Women, 13*, 977–1001.

Freyd, J. J. (2015). *What is DARVO?* Retrieved from http://pages.uoregon.edu/dynamic/jjf/defineDARVO.html.

Fox, K. A., Gover, A. R., & Kaukinen, C. (2009). The effect of low self-control and childhood maltreatment on stalking victimization among men and women. *American Journal of Criminal Justice, 34*, 181–197.

Gelles, R. J., & Straus, M. J. (1988). *Intimate violence: The definitive study of the causes and consequences of abuse in the American family*. New York: Simon & Schuster.

Gibson, L. E., & Leitenberg, H. (2001). The impact of child sexual abuse and stigma on methods of coping with sexual assault among undergraduate women. *Child Abuse & Neglect, 25*, 1343–1361.

Goffman, E. (1963). *Stigma: Notes on the management of spoiled identity*. New York: Prentice-Hall.

Goldfarb, P. (2005). Intimacy and injury: How law has changed for battered women. In A. Barnes (Ed.), *The handbook of women, psychology, and the law* (pp. 212–264). San Francisco: Jossey-Bass.

Harding, K. (2015). *Asking for it: The alarming rise of rape culture—and what we can do about it*. Philadelphia, PA: Da Capo Press.

Harvey, D. (2005). *A brief history of neoliberalism*. New York, NY: Oxford University Press.

Hester, M. (2014). Theorizing male power and violence against women. Revisiting Millet's *Sexual Politics*. In N. Aghtaie and G. Ganoli (Eds.), *Understanding gender based violence: National and international contexts*. (pp, 17– 30). London and New York: Routledge.

Johnson, M. P. (2005). Domestic violence: It's not about gender—Or is it? *Journal of Marriage and Family, 67*, 1126–1130.

Johnson, M. P. (2006). Conflict and control: Gender symmetry and asymmetry in domestic violence. *Violence against Women, 12*, 1003–1018.

Johnson, M. (2008). *A typology of domestic violence*. Boston: Northeastern University Press.

Jones, A. (2000). *Next time, she'll be dead: Battering and how to stop it*. Boston, MA: Beacon Press.

Jost, J. T., Banaji, M. R., & Nosek, B. A. (2004). A decade of system justification theory: Accumulated evidence of conscious and unconscious bolstering of the status quo. *Political Psychology, 25*, 881–919.

Katz, J., & Tirone, V. (2015). From the agency line to the picket line: Neoliberal ideals, sexual realities, and arguments about abortion in the U.S. *Sex Roles, 73*, 311–318.

Kraaji, V., Arensman, E., Garnefski, N., & Kremers, I. (2007). The role of cognitive coping in female victims of stalking. *Journal of Interpersonal Violence, 22*, 1603–1612.

Lamb, S. (2015). Revisiting choice and victimization: A commentary on Bay-Cheng's agency matrix. *Sex Roles, 73*, 292–297.

Langan, D., Hannem, S., & Stewart, C. (2014). Deconstructing accounts of intimate partner violence: Doing interviews, identities, and neoliberalism. *Applied Linguistics*, 1–21. doi:10.1093/applin/amu019 Advance online publication retrieved from http://applij.oxfordjournals.org/.

Leisenring, A. (2006). Confronting "victim" discourses: The identity work of battered women. *Symbolic Interaction, 29*, 307–330.

Lerner, M. (1980). *The belief in a just world: A fundamental delusion*. New York: Plenum Publishing.

Littleton, H. L., Breitkopf, C. R., & Berenson, A. (2008). Beyond the campus: Unacknowledged rape among low-income women. *Violence against Women, 14*, 269–286.

Loseke, D. R (2003). *Thinking about social problems: An introduction to constructionist perspectives*. New York: Aldine de Gruyter.

Luxton, M. (2010). Doing neoliberalism: Perverse individualism in personal life. In S. Braedley and M. Luxton (Eds.), *Neoliberalism and everyday life* (pp. 163–183). Montreal: CA: Mc-Gill Queen's University Press.

MacManus, S. A., & Van Hightower, N. R. (1989). Limits of state constitutional guarantees: Lessons from efforts to implement domestic violence programs. *Public Administration Review, 49*, 269–277.

McCann, J. T. (1998). Subtypes of stalking (obsessional following) in adolescents. *Journal of Adolescence*, 21, 667–675.

McMahon-Howard, J., Clay-Warner, J., & Renzulli, L. (2009). Criminalizing spousal rape: The diffusion of legal reforms. *Sociological Perspectives* 52, 505–531.

Meloy, J. R. (1997). The clinical risk management of stalking: "Someone is watching over me. . .". *American Journal of Psychotherapy, 51*, 174–184.

Meloy, J. R. (1998). *The psychology of stalking: Clinical and legal perspectives*. San Diego, CA: Elsevier.

Miller, A. K., Markman, K. D., & Handley, I. M. (2007). Self-blame among sexual assault victims prospectively predicts revictimization: A perceived sociolegal context model of risk. *Basic and Applied Social Psychology, 29*, 129–136.

Mullen, P. E., Pathé, M., Purcell, R., & Stuart, G. W. (1999). Study of stalkers. *The American Journal of Psychiatry, 156*, 1244–1249.

Mullen, P. E., Pathé, M., & Purcell, R. (2000). Stalking. *The Psychologist, 13*, 545–549.

O'Neill, M. L., & Kerig, P. K. (2000). Attributions of self-blame and perceived control as moderators of adjustment in battered women. *Journal of Interpersonal Violence, 15*, 1036–1049.

Randall, M. (2010). Sexual assault law, credibility, and "ideal victims:" Consent, resistance, and victim blaming. *Canadian Journal of Women and the Law, 22*, 397–434.

Reber, A., Allen, R., & Reber, E. (2009). Fundamental attribution error. *The Penguin dictionary of psychology*. London, United Kingdom: Penguin.

Richie, B. E. (2012). *Arrested justice. Black women, violence, and America's prison nation*. New York: NYU Press.

Schulhofer, S. J. (2003). Rape-law reform circa June 2002: Has the pendulum swung too far? *Annals of the New York Academy of Sciences, 989*, 276–287.

Sheridan, L., Gillett, R., Davies, G. M., Blaauw, E., & Patel, D. (2003) There's no smoke without fire: Are male ex-partners perceived as more "entitled" to stalk than acquaintance or stranger stalkers? *British Journal of Psychology, 94*, 87–98.

Straus, M. (2008). Dominance and symmetry in partner violence by male and female university students in 32 nations. *Child and Youth Services Review, 30*, 252–275.

Stringer, R. (2014). *Knowing victims: Feminism, agency, and victim politics in neoliberal times*. Hove: Routledge.

Sykes, C. J. (1992). *A nation of victims: The decay of the American character*. New York: St. Martin's Press.

Ussher, J. M. (2011). *The madness of women: Myth and experience*. London: Routledge.

8

WHY ME

Understanding Cybercrime Victimization

Jordana N. Navarro and Shelly Clevenger

Keywords

cybervictimization; cyberbullying; cyberabuse; cyber identity theft; cybercrime

Objectives

After studying this chapter, the reader should be able to:

- Broadly describe three major areas of interpersonal cybercrime research.
- Discuss what actions constitute each type of cybercrime noted.
- Describe the prevalence and risk factors associated with each type of cybercrime.

Introduction

As technology has continued to advance, these tools have seemingly permeated every aspect of social life. Technology enables individuals to communicate, collaborate, and form relationships despite geographic boundary or distance. However, one consequence of these advancements is that interpersonal crime has "gone viral." In other words, perpetrators are exploiting the largely unregulated environment of the Internet to engage in various forms of cybercrime such as cyberbullying, cyber intimate partner abuse, and cyber identity theft. Although cybercrime includes a broad array of crimes ranging across of spectrum of "property cybercrime" to "interpersonal cybercrime," the focus of this chapter will center on examining three large areas within the interpersonal cybercrime research area, as well as how these crimes occur in the digital realm.

Cyberbullying

Definition and Prevalence

Awareness of cyberbullying has steadily grown throughout the years and rapidly accelerated after the tragic suicides of several victimized teenagers (e.g., Megan Meier,[1] Alexis Pilkington,[2] Amanda Todd,[3] etc.). Although research continues to indicate that cyberbullied youth react in a myriad of ways to victimization,[4] with some reporting being unfazed by the events, the aforementioned suicides demand continued efforts to understand and combat this cybercrime. One challenge that the field continues to face is defining what "cyberbullying" includes, which is vastly important to resolve in order to compare prevalence findings.

Within the cyberbullying field, there is an ongoing conversation about the need for a standardized definition to utilize across studies.[5, 6, 7] Patchin and Hinduja[8] made one of the earliest attempts to define cyberbullying by describing it as "willful and repeated harm inflicted through the medium of electronic text" (p. 152). During that same year, Smith and colleagues[9] proposed a similar definition and noted cyberbullying was an "aggressive, intentional act carried out by a group or individual, using electronic forms of contact, repeatedly and over time against a victim who cannot easily defend him or herself" (p. 1). Despite these early attempts to propose a consistent description of cyberbullying, scholars have continued to utilize several definitions across studies, which have led to various challenges.[10] To address this inconsistency and move the field forward, Tokunaga[11] has proposed a broader conceptualization of cyberbullying that encapsulates previous research: "Cyberbullying is any behavior performed through electronic or digital media by individuals or groups that repeatedly communicates hostile or aggressive messages intended to inflict harm or discomfort on others" (p. 278). The importance of establishing a standard definition of cyberbullying cannot be understated, because the lack of a consistent measure across studies has contributed to a wide range of prevalence findings regarding how many youth experience and/or perpetrate cyberbullying.

Although the cyberbullying field is still grappling with some methodological challenges, these issues should not overshadow the point that many youth experience cyberbullying in their daily lives. Indeed, findings indicate that anywhere from less than 10 percent to over 50 percent of youth experience cyberbullying.[12, 13, 14, 15, 16, 17, 18] Compounding this social problem, evidence indicates that a high degree of overlap exists between cyberbullying and "offline" bullying,[19] which again underscores the point that bullying overall is a reality for many youth. Moreover, this problem spans geographic boundaries as studies in various countries have noted a substantial amount of youth respondents experienced cyberbullying.[20] Although some cyberbullying victims report being unfazed by occurrences, studies also indicate these events can have a lasting impact on youth.[21, 22]

Although evidence indicates that some youth are resilient when cyberbullying occurs, studies have also consistently found that some cyberbullied youth can suffer a host of negative consequences.[23] In a recent meta-analysis, Kowalski and colleagues found evidence across the literature of a relationship between experiencing cybervictimization and various behavioral and psychological problems: anxiety, depression, somatic symptoms, and suicidal ideation.[24] Additionally, evidence from across studies indicates a relationship exists between experiencing cybervictimization and engagement in substance use, reduced life satisfaction, and decreases in prosocial behavior.[25] Aside from behavioral and psychological outcomes, evidence indicates that experiencing cyberbullying can also lead to various other negative outcomes.

Recent research has discovered that the negative consequences of experiencing cyberbullying may extend beyond victims' behavioral and psychological well-being. For example, scholars[26] investigated the impact of experiencing cyberbullying on disordered eating among females. While the data failed to indicate a statistically significant relationship between experiencing cyberbullying and disordered eating,[27] the line of research in of itself demonstrates that scholars are increasingly investigating all the various ramifications of experiencing cyberbullying. Given the serious impacts that experiencing cyberbullying can have on victims, scholars have placed a great emphasis on identifying risk factors for experiencing and perpetrating cyberbullying in order to ultimately create effective prevention and intervention programs aimed at stopping the behavior.

Victim Risk Factors

Scholars in the cyberbullying field have placed a great emphasis on identifying victim risk factors that affect the odds of experiencing abuse. In terms of demographic factors, scholars have found a statistically significant relationship between age and experiencing cyberbullying and, specifically, that younger youth are at higher risk compared to older children.[28, 29] Likewise, similar research has focused on whether the frequency of cyberbullying increases at particular grade levels with some evidence indicating that cybervictimization is most prevalent in the eighth grade and then decreases in later grade levels.[30, 31] However, the relationship between age and experiencing cyberbullying is not consistently found across studies and requires further investigation.[32, 33] Unfortunately, the role of gender in assessing the risk of experiencing cyberbullying is also not consistent across studies.

Popular movies depicting cyberbullying, such as *Cyberbully*,[34] often depict females as both perpetrators and victims of abuse; however, research findings remain inconsistent across studies on the importance of gender as a risk factor for experiencing cyberabuse.[35] While some scholars have found no statistically significant relationship between gender and experiencing cyberbullying,[36] others have found that girls are at an increased risk of victimization.[37, 38, 39, 40] Similarly, findings regarding the role of race/ethnicity as a risk factor for experiencing cyberbullying are also inconsistent across studies. Indeed, some scholars have found that there is not a statistically significant relationship between race/ethnicity and experiencing cyberbullying[41, 42, 43] while others have found that youth who do *not* identify as a minority may be at more risk for experiencing cyber victimization.[44] In addition to the aforementioned, cutting-edge research has also highlighted the importance of including sexual orientation as a risk factor for experiencing cyberbullying with results largely indicating that non-heterosexual youth are more at risk of experiencing cyber abuse compared to heterosexual individuals.[45, 46] Aside from these factors, scholars have also focused on determining the risk associated with engaging in different online activities and experiencing cyberbullying.

As technology has evolved, scholars have increasingly investigated the role of various online activities as potential risk factors for experiencing cyberbullying.[47, 48, 49, 50, 51, 52] In general, evidence indicates a positive relationship between online presence and experiencing cyberbullying.[53, 54, 55] In other words, greater Internet usage corresponds with an increased risk of experiencing cyberbullying.[56, 57, 58] In terms of online activities, evidence indicates that using the Internet for social activities increases the risk of experiencing cyberbullying.[59, 60, 61, 62] Specifically, using instant messaging programs and social networking sites has been found to increase the risk of cyberbullying in several studies.[63, 64, 65, 66] Recent research has tried to address what behaviors within social networking sites are particularly risky for youth, and found that posting status updates and using private messages increased the risk of cybervictimization.[67] Scholars have also found that youth who engage in cyberbullying increase their own chances of becoming a victim of bullying as well.[68, 69] Aside from these factors, evidence indicates that other activities—like lying about one's age—may also increase the risk of experiencing cyberbullying.[70] Unfortunately, one consequence of the rapid advancement of technology is that new tools are constantly becoming available, which then may be used for malicious purposes. Indeed, one such consequence of the "technological era" is that perpetrators of intimate partner abuse have utilized these advancements to further their coercive control over partners.

Cyberabuse and Cyberstalking by Intimate Partners

Definition and Prevalence

Intimate partner abuse (IPA) has evolved with technology. In the past, IPA was an offense that took place in person, but it has now gone "virtual" (i.e., cyberIPA). Because cyberIPA is a largely unexplored field of cybercrime research, a standardized definition has not been developed as of yet (to the best of our knowledge). However, cyberIPA can be thought of as any utilization of technology (e.g., the Internet, software, products, etc.) by abusers that furthers the coercive control over survivors. CyberIPA can assume many forms: cyberharassment, cyberstalking, cybersexual exploitation, identity theft, revenge porn, etc. The ability to engage in these exploits is likely the result of the widespread use of various forms of technology (e.g., "smart" cameras, computers, phones), software programs (e.g., "apps," email, instant messaging), and malicious software (e.g., key loggers, spyware) that have provided abusers with new ways to threaten, control, and terrorize their victims.[71, 72] Smartphones, or phones that provide access to the Internet, have become particularly powerful tools for abusers who seek to harass, threaten, and cyberstalk their partners.[73, 74, 75, 76, 77]

Ending and escaping an abusive relationship can be the most dangerous thing a survivor does as she is putting herself at risk of harm from the abuser,[78, 79] and, unfortunately, technological tools compound this risk as they can be utilized to find partners who have fled. For example, malware referred to as "spyware" is used to monitor one's online activities (e.g., sites visited, texts, and instant message conversations) as well as providing GPS coordinates of the target.[80, 81] Given these technological advancements, the ability of victims to ever really feel "safe" is seemingly gone as abusers can cyberstalk, or track their movements or online activity, from anywhere.[82]

While stalking is not a new occurrence, the understanding of this form of cybercrime is still developing as technology and online social life continues to advance.[83] This behavior occurs when a person, that may or may not know the perpetrator, is repetitively followed or monitored using digital or online technology.[84] Cyberstalking can occur in conjunction with offline stalking, but the overlap is not always present.[85] There is also uncertainty surrounding whether cyberstalking and offline stalking are similar in terms of etiology and offender characteristics or somehow different.

There is a debate within the literature and discipline as to whether offline stalking and cyberstalking are similar or different behaviors in terms of characteristics of offenses and offenders.[86, 87] On one hand, both behaviors can involve former partners,[88, 89, 90, 91] as well as involving recurring actions that make an individual feel exposed with less privacy and safety.[92] On the other hand, the two crimes may differ in that cyberstalking does not require a prior relationship between the victim and offender, is not limited by physical constraints or geography, and may have different motivations compared to offline stalking.[93, 94]

Research has shown that cyberstalking affects a significant amount of individuals.[95, 96, 97, 98, 99] Data from the Centers for Disease Control and Prevention (CDC) underscores this point as nearly half (49.7 percent) of female stalking victims reported being watched, followed, or monitored by some form of technology (e.g., a GPS device, spyware, camera, or listening device).[100] The U.S. Department of Justice reported that the average number of stalking and harassment incidents each year totals 5.2 million of cases. Of those cases, 44.1 percent involved the use of spyware, 40.3 percent involved the use of digital cameras or video, 35.8 percent involved the use of listening devices, and 9.7 percent involved the use of GPS monitoring to track victims.[101]

The 2006 *National Crime and Victimization Survey*, which included a supplemental survey on stalking, mirrors the CDC's findings as the data revealed that 1.5 percent of adults were stalked in the year prior to the survey and that 26 percent of those adults experienced cyberstalking.[102] College students, in particular, are a population that has experienced cyberstalking at high rate, although the exact prevalence varies across studies.[103] Indeed, findings from one study estimated 31 percent of college students were cyberstalked[104] and, in another study, 40 percent of the college students sample had experienced some form of cyberstalking throughout their lifetime.[105]

Aside from the ability to monitor survivors who have fled, perpetrators have utilized technology to record and photograph survivors, without their consent, in order to blackmail and stalk them online.[106, 107] The ability of perpetrators to violate survivors in the aforementioned manner puts victims especially at risk for cyberharassment, which involves the sending of menacing messages, or threatening/actually distributing photos to manipulate an individual, or posting personal information publicly in an online space.[108] Many ex-partners also use social network sites, such as Facebook, to victimize their former partners. For example, perpetrators have created fake accounts, masquerading as the survivor, to post embarrassing photos or posts in order to assassinate reputations.[109] Abusers have also engaged in threatening and harassing behavior towards the victim and their family members online through Facebook.[110]

Victim Risk Factors

Most IPA perpetrators are male and the victims are typically female.[111] However, the limited research on cyberIPA does indicate some gender variation among victims and offenders. For example, while some findings show that females are more susceptible to cyberabuse victimization,[112, 113] other studies have found no difference between genders in terms of risk for electronic abuse[114] or aggression.[115] In terms of differences between genders, one study found that women reported checking their partner's emails and phone call history at a significantly higher rate than males.[116] Similarly, in another study, results indicated that women committed non-sexual cyberIPA at a higher rate.[117] On the other hand, findings indicate that males are more likely to use GPS monitoring and concealed cameras to monitor their partners.[118]

Aside from the role of gender, evidence indicates risk may vary among different race/ethnicities and sexual orientations. For example, one study found that non-whites and non-heterosexuals had higher rates of victimization.[119] Moreover, victims were more likely to be cyberstalked by someone that they knew and it was most commonly ex-partners.[120] In terms of risk associated with certain activities, research has revealed that cyberstalking typically involves email (82 percent) in a majority of cases followed by instant messages (35 percent) and then blogs or online message boards (12 percent).[121] As mentioned, cyber identity theft may also be a form of cyberabuse, depending on the motivations of the perpetrator. Regardless of the motivations driving the perpetrator, however, cyber identity theft is a particularly devastating and invasive form of interpersonal violence. As one victim noted: "You are what the Web says you are, and if it misrepresents you, the feeling of having been violated is crushing" (p. 4).[122]

Cyber Identity Theft

Definition and Prevalence

Cyber identity theft is pervasive and costly for all involved. Indeed, evidence indicates that the total losses stemming from identity theft amount to *billions* of dollars lost in the United States.[123] The Identity Theft and Assumption Deterrence Act[124] defines identity theft as:

> Knowingly transferring or using, without lawful authority, a means of identification of another person with the intent to commit, or aid or abet, any unlawful activity that constitutes a violation of Federal law, or that constitutes a felony under any applicable State or local law.

Although this definition provides a broad understanding of identity theft, this crime can assume various forms that involve completely online activities, completely offline activities, or a mixture of both (i.e., hybrid).

In terms of specific forms, identity theft involving financial accounts usually entails the illegal use, or attempted illegal use, of banking and/or credit accounts.[125, 126] This form of identity theft could also include the illegal use, or attempted illegal use, of identifiable information to secure loans (e.g., car, mortgage).[127] Although this is the most frequently reported type of identity theft, identity theft involving the illegal use of identifiable information to obtain social services under the guise of the actual victim (e.g., medical benefits, social services) or to secure employment is also prevalent.[128, 129] Finally, and perhaps most disturbingly, identity theft could also entail the perpetrator creating and masquerading as the victim online in order to simply destroy one's relationships and reputation[130]—as in the horrifying case of James Lasdun.[131] Unfortunately, even though identity theft is a serious social problem, there are several challenges that continue to hamper the ability of scholars to determine prevalence rates.[132]

Determining prevalence rates of identity theft is extremely challenging for several reasons. As White and Fisher note (p. 4), the challenges associated with determining prevalence rates largely stems from four factors: (1) "the limitations of current definitions," (2) "how it [identity theft] is committed, discovered, and reported," (3) "the inconsistent, fragmented response by law enforcement and private industry," and (4) "problems with existing data sources and implications"—each of which will be expanded on in the following section.[133]

In terms of point one, White and Fisher note that while there are several federal laws that address identity theft (e.g., Fair Credit Reporting Act,[134] Gramm-Leach-Bliley Act,[135] etc.), there is great variation in how each state defines this crime.[136] As discussed within the cyberbullying section, various definitions often result in wide prevalence ranges as well. In regards to the second point, unlike other types of crimes, there is often a delay in the detection and reporting of identity theft, which subsequently hinders the ability of scholars to determine prevalence rates. Findings from the 2014 Identity Theft Supplement (conducted as part of the National Crime Victimization Survey) underscore this point as data indicates a majority of identity theft victims only learned of their victimization through contact by a financial institution.[137] Moreover, even after learning that a crime had been committed, only a small fraction of victims (8 percent) notified law enforcement.[138] Unfortunately, even if a victim reports to law enforcement, there are issues that may hinder subsequent investigations—in reference to the third challenge noted by White and Fisher.[139] One such issue is that the crime may involve various jurisdictions and result in confusion about which agency is actually charged with the investigation.[140] Additionally, given the complexity of these crimes, identity theft may only be one "piece" of the overall victimization that involves various offenses.[141] Given the entirety of the aforementioned, it is not surprising that White and Fisher note that the fourth challenge to accurately assessing prevalence rates largely stems from these three identified barriers. Despite these limitations, several studies have provided estimations on the prevalence of identity theft.

As part of the National Crime Victimization Survey in both 2012 and 2014, the Bureau of Justice Statistics gathered data on identity theft through an Identity Theft Supplement survey.[142, 143] Results from the most recent supplement indicate that over 17 million U.S. residents (greater than 15 years of age)experienced a form of identity theft in 2014.[144] In terms of form, identity theft involving financial accounts was the most commonly reported type (e.g., illegal use of existing bank account = 38 percent and/or credit card = 42 percent).[145] Although many respondents reported experiencing other forms of identity theft, the total number of these victimizations was substantially fewer (N = 713,000).[146] Data from countries around the world indicate identity theft is a global problem. For instance, data from various organizations in the United Kingdom indicate that over 200,000 cases of fraud occurred during 2014.[147] In reviewing those reports, identity theft comprised a substantial percentage of cases.[148] Although the scope and severity of the theft varies from case to case, research has found that victims suffer considerable distress in the aftermath of victimization.[149]

Identity theft victims suffer a wide range of consequences. The victims of identity theft involving financial accounts often experience monetary losses or damaged credit. For example, data gathered through the Bureau of Justice Statistics' 2014 Identity Theft Supplement shows that slightly more than 10 percent of victims reported some level of financial loss.[150] Financial loss is just one consequence though as victims also reported losing considerable time simply spent trying to rectify their records with lenders.[151] Indeed, while some victims were able to rectify their records in a relatively short timeframe, other severe cases took considerably longer to reach a resolution.[152] Given these potential financial and personal losses, it is not surprising that a considerable percentage of victims (36 percent) reported experiencing some level of emotional distress.[153] Fortunately, cybercrime scholars have identified several online behaviors that affect the risk of identity theft, which can inform users on how to protect themselves.

Victim Risk Factors

Given the abundance of information online and the relative lack of security in the virtual realm, it is nearly impossible to prevent identity theft entirely. However, scholars generally agree that greater information publication and sharing increases the risk of identity theft.[154, 155, 156] In terms of *who* is more at risk of identity theft, research has found that men, older individuals, and individuals in higher income groups may be particularly vulnerable to this form of victimization.[157, 158] Research also indicates that individuals are at greater risk of identity theft if their personal information was compromised through a hacking or phishing fraud.[159] While the aforementioned factors are important considerations in the safeguarding of personal information, the online activities one engages in are also vastly important.

Although there remains an overall dearth of information about which online activities are the most dangerous for users, cutting-edge research has identified several potentially risky behaviors. Considering that a majority of reported identity theft cases involve financial accounts, it should not be surprising that research has found that utilizing online banking programs heightens the risk of experiencing identity theft.[160, 161, 162, 163] Moreover, engaging in similar behaviors online (i.e., purchasing items) also increases the risk of experiencing identity theft.[164, 165] Although email and instant messaging are ubiquitous communication tools, these programs are not without risk as evidence indicates their utilization increases the chances of experiencing identity theft.[166] Finally, users who downloaded items (e.g., music, movies) from the Internet were more at risk of experiencing identity theft[167]—perhaps not surprising given that malicious software designed to steal personally identifiable information could be hidden within that material.[168] Although malware is one method perpetrators utilize to obtain personally identifiable information, research has also found users can be at risk by simply disclosing too much personal information online that can then be easily aggregated and exploited.[169, 170] For example, using public information from social networking sites, scholars were able to successfully predict partial security numbers of various individuals.[171] Given the ability of perpetrators to target victims remotely through technology, it is vastly important that users remain vigilant at safeguarding their personal information.

Summary

One significant consequence of the rapid advancement of technology is that stakeholders must attempt to keep pace with perpetrators seeking to exploit these tools for malicious purposes. Although this chapter only discussed cyberbullying, cyber IPA, and cyber identity theft, these interpersonal cybercrimes represent some of the largest lines of research within the field. Yet, with each new day, the world of cybercrime could change and these crimes could morph again. For example, one emerging area of cyberbullying research is concerned with how seemingly harmless forms of social media, like Instagram, are utilized in cyberbullying.[172] In another example, scholars that study cyber IPA are beginning to research "revenge porn" and cases where former intimate partners have released photos/videos, which had been recorded privately, to the public in order to enact "revenge" on their ex-partner.[173] Finally, scholars continue to investigate cyber identity theft and the various "high-tech," but also very "low-tech," methods perpetrators utilize to destroy victims. Thus, this chapter should serve as a broad overview of three important areas of interpersonal cybercrime research and the risk factors associated with these crimes. Only by learning and researching the "dark side" of technology, can we hope to reduce the risks of cyber victimization.

Discussion Questions

1. Should cyberbullying be criminalized, particularly if a survivor commits suicide because of the bullying? Why, or why not?
2. Imagine that you are involved in a violent relationship with a partner that uses technology to monitor your movements. How would you escape with the car, cell phone, clothes, money, etc. without accessing technology? Prepare a detailed plan that lists the steps you would take.
3. What responsibility, if any, should system administrators have to safeguard their products from malicious uses by perpetrators? For example, should Facebook be held responsible if a perpetrator establishes a fake Facebook profile to then assassinate the reputation of his former friend?

Notes

1 Maag, C. (2007, November 28). A hoax turned fatal draws anger but no charges. *The New York Times*. Retrieved from: http://www.nytimes.com/2007/11/28/us/28hoax.html?rref=collection%2Ftimestopic%2FMeier%2C%20Megan&action=click&contentCollection=timestopics&region=stream&module=stream_unit&version=latest&contentPlacement=8&pgtype=collection

2 Martinez, E. (2010, March 26). Alexis Pilkington brutally cyber bullied, even after her suicide. *CBS News*. Retrieved from: http://www.cbsnews.com/news/alexis-pilkington-brutally-cyber-bullied-even-after-her-suicide/

3 Dean, M. (2012). The story of Amanda Todd. *The New Yorker.* Retrieved from: http://www.newyorker.com/culture/culture-desk/the-story-of-amanda-todd

4 Kowalski, R. M., Giumetti, G. W., Schroeder, A. N., & Lattanner, M. R. (2014). Bullying in the digital age: A critical review and meta-analysis of cyberbullying research among youth. *Psychological Bulletin, 140*(4), 1073–1137.

5 Smith, P. K., del Barrio, C., Tokunaga, R. S. (2013). Definitions of bullying and cyberbullying: How useful are the terms? In: Bauman, S., Cross, D., Walker J. (Eds.) Principles of cyberbullying research: Definitions, measures and methodology. New York, NY: Routledge, pp. 26–40.

6 Aboujaoude, E., Savage, M.W., Starcevic, V. & Salame, W.O. (2015). Cyberbullying: Review of an old problem gone viral. *Journal of Adolescent Health, 57*(1), 10–18.

7 Tokunaga, R. S. (2010). Following you home from school: A critical review and synthesis of research on cyberbullying victimization. *Computers in Human Behavior, 26*, 277–287.

8 Patchin, J. W., & Hinduja, S. (2006). Bullies move beyond the schoolyard a preliminary look at cyberbullying. *Youth Violence and Juvenile Justice, 4*(2), 148–169.

9 Smith, P. K., Mahdavi, J., Carvalho, M., & Tippett, N. (2006, July). *An investigation into cyberbullying, its forms, awareness and impact, and the relationship between age and gender in cyberbullying.* (Research Brief No. RBX03-06). Retrieved from: http://webarchive.nationalarchives.gov.uk/20130401151715/http://www.education.gov.uk/publications/eOrderingDownload/RBX03-06.pdf

10 Tokunaga, R. S. (2010). Following you home from school: A critical review and synthesis of research on cyberbullying victimization. *Computers in Human Behavior, 26*, 277–287.

11 Ibid.

12 Ackers, M. J. (2012). Cyberbullying: Through the eyes of children and young people. *Educational Psychology in Practice, 28*, 141–157.

13 Gomez-Garibello, C., Shariff, S., McConnell, M., & Talwar, V. (2012). Adolescents' evaluation of cyberbullying events. *Alberta Journal of Educational Research*, 58, 474–477.

14 Navarro, J. N. & Jasinski, J. L. (2012). Going cyber: Using routine activities theory to predict cyberbullying experiences. *Sociological Spectrum, 32*, 81–94.

15 Navarro, J. N. & Jasinski, J. L. (2013). Why girls? Using routine activities theory to predict cyberbullying experiences between girls and boys. *Women & Criminal Justice, 23*, 286–303.

16 Navarro, J. N., Clevenger, S., Beasley, M. E., & Jackson, L. (2015). One step forward, two steps back: Cyberbullying within social networking sites. *Security Journal*, online first. DOI: 10.1057/sj.2015.19
17 Seiler, S. J. & Navarro, J. N. (2014). Bullying on the pixel playground: Investigating risk factors of cyberbullying at the intersection of children's online-offline social lives. *Cyberpsychology: Journal of Psychosocial Research on Cyberspace*, *8*(4).
18 Tomşa, R., Jenaro, C., Campbell, M. & Neacşu, D. (2013). Student's experiences with traditional bullying and cyberbullying: Findings from a Romanian sample. *Procedia - Social and Behavioral Sciences*, *78*, 586–590.
19 Olweus, D. (2012). Cyberbullying: An overrated phenomenon? *European Journal of Developmental Psychology*, *9*, 520–538.
20 Kowalski, R. M., Giumetti, G. W., Schroeder, A. N., & Lattanner, M. R. (2014). Bullying in the digital age: A critical review and meta-analysis of cyberbullying research among youth. *Psychological Bulletin*, *140*(4), 1073–1137.
21 Mishna, F., Cook, C., Gadalla, T., Daciuk, J., & Solomon, S. (2010). Cyber bullying behaviors among middle and high school students. *American Journal of Orthopsychiatry*, *80*(3), 362–374.
22 Dredge, R., Gleeson, J., & de la Piedad Garcia, X. (2014). Cyberbullying in social networking sites: An adolescent victim's perspective. *Computers in Human Behavior*, *36*, 13–20.
23 Kowalski, R. M., Giumetti, G. W., Schroeder, A. N., & Lattanner, M. R. (2014). Bullying in the digital age: A critical review and meta-analysis of cyberbullying research among youth. *Psychological Bulletin*, *140*(4), 1073–1137.
24 Ibid.
25 Ibid.
26 King, R., Moorfoot, R., & Kotronakis, M. (2015). Impact of bullying and cyberbullying on body image and disordered eating in young adult females. *Journal of Eating Disorders*, *3*(Suppl 1), 18.
27 Ibid.
28 Navarro, J. N. & Jasinski, J. L. (2012). Going cyber: Using routine activities theory to predict cyberbullying experiences. *Sociological Spectrum*, *32*, 81–94.
29 Seiler, S. J. & Navarro, J. N. (2014). Bullying on the pixel playground: Investigating risk factors of cyberbullying at the intersection of children's online–offline social lives. *Cyberpsychology: Journal of Psychosocial Research on Cyberspace*, *8*(4).
30 Williams, K. R., & Guerra, N. G. (2007). Prevalence and predictors of internet bullying. *Journal of Adolescent Health*, *41*(6), S14–S21.
31 Schneider, S. K., O'Donnell, L., Stueve, A., & Coulter, R. W. (2012). Cyberbullying, school bullying, and psychological distress: A regional census of high school students. *American Journal of Public Health*, *102*(1), 171–177.
32 Smith, P. K., Mahdavi, J., Carvalho, M., Fisher, S., Russell, S., & Tippett, N. (2008). Cyberbullying: Its nature and impact in secondary school pupils. *Journal of Child Psychology and Psychiatry*, *49*(4), 376–385.
33 Tokunaga, R. S. (2010). Following you home from school: A critical review and synthesis of research on cyberbullying victimization. *Computers in Human Behavior*, 26: 277–287.
34 Prupas, J. (Producer) & Binamé, C. (Director). (2011). *Cyberbully* [Motion picture]. Canada: Muse Entertainment Enterprises.
35 Kowalski, R. M., Giumetti, G. W., Schroeder, A. N., & Lattanner, M. R. (2014). Bullying in the digital age: A critical review and meta-analysis of cyberbullying research among youth. *Psychological Bulletin*, *140*(4), 1073–1137.
36 Hinduja, S., & Patchin, J. W. (2008). Cyberbullying: An exploratory analysis of factors related to offending and victimization. *Deviant Behavior*, *29*(2), 129–156.
37 Smith, P. K., Mahdavi, J., Carvalho, M., Fisher, S., Russell, S., & Tippett, N. (2008). Cyberbullying: Its nature and impact in secondary school pupils. *Journal of Child Psychology and Psychiatry*, *49*(4), 376–385.
38 Navarro, J. N. & Jasinski, J. L. (2012). Going cyber: Using routine activities theory to predict cyberbullying experiences. *Sociological Spectrum*, 32, 81–94.
39 Navarro, J. N. & Jasinski, J. L. (2013). Why girls? Using routine activities theory to predict cyberbullying experiences between girls and boys. *Women & Criminal Justice*, *23*, 286–303.
40 Seiler, S. J. & Navarro, J. N. (2014). Bullying on the pixel playground: Investigating risk factors of cyberbullying at the intersection of children's online–offline social lives. *Cyberpsychology: Journal of Psychosocial Research on Cyberspace*, *8*(4).
41 Hinduja, S., & Patchin, J. W. (2008). Cyberbullying: An exploratory analysis of factors related to offending and victimization. *Deviant Behavior*, *29*(2), 129–156.
42 Schneider, S. K., O'Donnell, L., Stueve, A., & Coulter, R. W. (2012). Cyberbullying, school bullying, and psychological distress: A regional census of high school students. *American Journal of Public Health*, *102*(1), 171–177.

43 Navarro, J. N. & Jasinski, J. L. (2013). Why girls? Using routine activities theory to predict cyberbullying experiences between girls and boys. *Women & Criminal Justice, 23*, 286–303.
44 Seiler, S. J. & Navarro, J. N. (2014). Bullying on the pixel playground: Investigating risk factors of cyberbullying at the intersection of children's online–offline social lives. *Cyberpsychology: Journal of Psychosocial Research on Cyberspace, 8*(4).
45 Schneider, S. K., O'Donnell, L., Stueve, A., & Coulter, R. W. (2012). Cyberbullying, school bullying, and psychological distress: A regional census of high school students. *American Journal of Public Health, 102*(1), 171–177.
46 Hinduja, S., & Patchin, J. W. (2011). Cyberbullying research summary: Bullying, cyberbullying, and sexual orientation. *Cyberbullying Research Center*. Retrieved from: http://cyberbullying.org/cyberbullying_sexual_orientation_fact_sheet.pdf
47 Navarro, J. N. & Jasinski, J. L. (2012). Going cyber: Using routine activities theory to predict cyberbullying experiences. *Sociological Spectrum, 32*, 81–94.
48 Navarro, J. N. & Jasinski, J. L. (2013). Why girls? Using routine activities theory to predict cyberbullying experiences between girls and boys. *Women & Criminal Justice, 23*, 286–303.
49 Seiler, S. J. & Navarro, J. N. (2014). Bullying on the pixel playground: Investigating risk factors of cyberbullying at the intersection of children's online–offline social lives. *Cyberpsychology: Journal of Psychosocial Research on Cyberspace, 8*(4).
50 Navarro, J. N., Clevenger, S., Beasley, M. E., & Jackson, L. (2015). One step forward, two steps back: Cyberbullying within social networking sites. *Security Journal*, online first. DOI: 10.1057/sj.2015.19.
51 Smith, P. K., Mahdavi, J., Carvalho, M., Fisher, S., Russell, S., & Tippett, N. (2008). Cyberbullying: Its nature and impact in secondary school pupils. *Journal of child psychology and psychiatry, 49*(4), 376–385.
52 Park, S., Na, E.Y., & Kim, E. M. (2014). The relationship between online activities, netiquette and cyberbullying. *Children and Youth Services Review, 42*, 74–81.
53 Navarro, J. N. & Jasinski, J. L. (2012). Going cyber: Using routine activities theory to predict cyberbullying experiences. *Sociological Spectrum*, 32, 81–94.
54 Park, S., Na, E.Y., & Kim, E. M. (2014). The relationship between online activities, netiquette and cyberbullying. *Children and Youth Services Review, 42*, 74–81.
55 Navarro, J. N., Clevenger, S., Beasley, M. E., & Jackson, L. (2015). One step forward, two steps back: Cyberbullying within social networking sites. *Security Journal*, online first.
56 Ibid.
57 Navarro, J. N. & Jasinski, J. L. (2012). Going cyber: Using routine activities theory to predict cyberbullying experiences. *Sociological Spectrum, 32*, 81–94.
58 Park, S., Na, E.Y., & Kim, E. M. (2014). The relationship between online activities, netiquette and cyberbullying. *Children and Youth Services Review, 42*, 74–81.
59 Navarro, J. N. & Jasinski, J. L. (2012). Going cyber: Using routine activities theory to predict cyberbullying experiences. *Sociological Spectrum, 32*, 81–94.
60 Navarro, J. N. & Jasinski, J. L. (2013). Why girls? Using routine activities theory to predict cyberbullying experiences between girls and boys. *Women & Criminal Justice, 23*, 286–303.
61 Navarro, J. N., Clevenger, S., Beasley, M. E., & Jackson, L. (2015). One step forward, two steps back: Cyberbullying within social networking sites. *Security Journal*, online first. DOI: 10.1057/sj.2015.19.
62 Park, S., Na, E.Y., & Kim, E. M. (2014). The relationship between online activities, netiquette and cyberbullying. *Children and Youth Services Review, 42*, 74–81.
63 Navarro, J. N. & Jasinski, J. L. (2012). Going cyber: Using routine activities theory to predict cyberbullying experiences. *Sociological Spectrum, 32*, 81–94.
64 Navarro, J. N. & Jasinski, J. L. (2013). Why girls? Using routine activities theory to predict cyberbullying experiences between girls and boys. *Women & Criminal Justice, 23*, 286–303.
65 Navarro, J. N., Clevenger, S., Beasley, M. E., & Jackson, L. (2015). One step forward, two steps back: Cyberbullying within social networking sites. *Security Journal*, online first. DOI: 10.1057/sj.2015.19.
66 Park, S., Na, E.Y., & Kim, E. M. (2014). The relationship between online activities, netiquette and cyberbullying. *Children and Youth Services Review, 42*, 74–81.
67 Navarro, J. N., Clevenger, S., Beasley, M. E., & Jackson, L. (2015). One step forward, two steps back: Cyberbullying within social networking sites. *Security Journal*, online first. DOI: 10.1057/sj.2015.19.
68 Navarro, J. N. & Jasinski, J. L. (2013). Why girls? Using routine activities theory to predict cyberbullying experiences between girls and boys. *Women & Criminal Justice, 23*, 286–303.
69 Seiler, S. J. & Navarro, J. N. (2014). Bullying on the pixel playground: Investigating risk factors of cyberbullying at the intersection of children's online–offline social lives. *Cyberpsychology: Journal of Psychosocial Research on Cyberspace, 8*(4).
70 Ibid.

71 Logan, T. K. (2010). Research on partner stalking: Putting the pieces together. Lexington, KY: University of Kentucky, Department of Behavioral Science and Center on Drug and Alcohol Research. Retrieved from: http://beta.nij.gov/topics/crime/intimate-partner-violence/stalking/documents/research-on-partner-stalking.pdf
72 Southworth, C., Finn, J., Dawson, S., Fraser, C., & Tucker, S. (2007). Intimate partner violence, technology, and stalking. *Violence against Women, 13*(8), 842–856.
73 Belknap, J., Chu, A. T., & DePrince, A. P. (2011). Roles of phones and computers in threatening and abusing women victims of male intimate partner abuse. *Duke Journal of Gender Law & Policy, 19*, 373–406.
74 Burke, S. C., Wallen, M., Vail-Smith, K., & Knox, D. (2011). Using technology to control intimate partners: An exploratory study of college undergraduates. *Computers in Human Behavior, 27*(3), 1162–1167.
75 Dimond, J. P., Fiesler, C., & Bruckman, A. S. (2011). Domestic violence and information communication technologies. *Interacting with Computers, 23*(5), 413–421.
76 Hand, T., Chung, D., & Peters, M. (2009). *The use of information and communication technologies to coerce and control in domestic violence and following separation.* Australian Domestic and Family Violence Clearinghouse, UNSW. http://www.austdvclearinghouse.unsw.edu.au/PDF%20files/Stakeholder%20Paper_6.pdf
77 Hinduja, S., & Patchin, J. (2011). Electronic dating violence: A brief guide for educators and parents. *Cyberbullying Research Center.* Retrieved from: http://cyberbullying.org/electronic_dating_violence_fact_sheet.pdf
78 Fleury, R. E., Sullivan, C. M., & Bybee, D. I. (2000). When ending the relationship does not end the violence women's experiences of violence by former partners. *Violence against Women, 6(12)*, 1363–1383.
79 Johnson, H., & Hotton, T. (2003). Losing control homicide risk in estranged and intact intimate relationships. *Homicide Studies*, 7(1), 58–84.
80 Southworth, C., & Tucker, S. (2006). Technology, stalking and domestic violence victims. *Mississippi Law Journal, 76*, 667–676.
81 Southworth, C., Finn, J., Dawson, S., Fraser, C., & Tucker, S. (2007). Intimate partner violence, technology, and stalking. *Violence against Women, 13*(8), 842–856.
82 Hand, T., Chung, D., & Peters, M. (2009). *The use of information and communication technologies to coerce and control in domestic violence and following separation.* Australian Domestic and Family Violence Clearinghouse, UNSW. http://www.austdvclearinghouse.unsw.edu.au/PDF%20files/Stakeholder%20Paper_6.pdf
83 Reyns, B. W., Henson, B., & Fisher, B. S. (2016). Guardians of the cyber galaxy: An empirical and theoretical analysis of the guardianship concept from routine activity theory as it applies to online forms of victimization. *Journal of Contemporary Criminal Justice, 32*(2), 148–168.
84 Reyns, B. W., Henson, B., & Fisher, B. S. (2012). Stalking in the twilight zone: Extent of cyberstalking victimization and offending among college students. *Deviant Behavior, 33*, 1–25.
85 Sheridan, L. P., & Grant, T. (2007). Is cyberstalking different? *Psychology, Crime & Law, 13*(6), 627–640.
86 McFarlane, L., & Bocij, P. (2003). An exploration of predatory behaviour in cyberspace: Towards a typology of cyberstalkers. *First Monday, 8*(9).
87 Sheridan, L. P., & Grant, T. (2007). Is cyberstalking different? *Psychology, Crime & Law, 13*(6), 627–640.
88 Alexy, E. M., Burgess, A. W., Baker, T., & Smoyak, S. A. (2005). Perceptions of cyberstalking among college students. *Brief Treatment and Crisis Intervention, 5*, 279–289.
89 Cavezza, C., & McEwan, T. E. (2014). Cyberstalking versus off-line stalking in a forensic sample. *Psychology, Crime & Law*, (ahead-of-print), 1–16.
90 Dreßing, H., Bailer, J., Anders, A., Wagner, H., & Gallas, C. (2014). Cyberstalking in a large sample of social network users: Prevalence, characteristics, and impact upon victims. *Cyberpsychology, Behavior, and Social Networking, 17*(2), 61–67.
91 Vasiu, I., & Vasiu, L. (2013). Cyberstalking nature and response recommendations. *Academic Journal of Interdisciplinary Studies, 2*(9), 229.
92 Spitzberg, B. H., & Hoobler, G. (2002). Cyberstalking and the technologies of interpersonal terrorism. *New Media & Society, 4*(1), 71–92.
93 Bocij, P., & McFarlane, L. (2003). Cyberstalking: The technology of hate. *The Police Journal, 76*(3), 204–221.
94 McFarlane, L., & Bocij, P. (2003). An exploration of predatory behaviour in cyberspace: Towards a typology of cyberstalkers. *First Monday, 8*(9).
95 Alexy, E. M., Burgess, A. W., Baker, T., & Smoyak, S. A. (2005). Perceptions of cyberstalking among college students. *Brief Treatment and Crisis Intervention, 5*, 279–289.
96 Baum, K., Catalano, S., Rand, M., & Rose, K. (2009). Stalking victimization in the United States. United States Department of Justice. Retrieved from: https://victimsofcrime.org/docs/src/baum-k-catalano-s-rand-m-rose-k-2009.pdf?sfvrsn=0
97 Finn, J., & Banach, M. (2000). Victimization online: The downside of seeking human services for women on the Internet. *CyberPsychology & Behavior, 3*(5), 785–796.

98 Fisher, B. S., Cullen, F. T., & Turner, M. G. (2002). Being pursued: Stalking victimization in a national study of college women. *Criminology and Public Policy, 1*, 257–308.
99 Spitzberg, B. H., & Hoobler, G. (2002). Cyberstalking and the technologies of interpersonal terrorism. *New Media & Society, 4*, 71–92.
100 Black, M. C., Basile, K. C., Breiding, M. J., Smith, S. G., Walters, M. L., Merrick, M. T., & Stevens, M. R. (2011). The national intimate partner and sexual violence survey (NISVS): 2010 summary report. Atlanta, GA: National Center for Injury Prevention and Control, Centers for Disease Control and Prevention. Retrieved from http://www.cdc.gov/violenceprevention/nisvs/summary_reports.html
101 Baum, K., Catalano, S., Rand, M., & Rose, K. (2009). Stalking victimization in the United States. United States Department of Justice. Retrieved from: http://www.victimsofcrime.org/docs/src/baum-k-catalano-s-rand-m-rose-k-2009.pdf?sfvrsn=0
102 Catalano, S. (2012). *Stalking victims in the United States–Revised* (NCJ 224527). Washington, DC: Bureau of Justice Statistics. Retrieved from: http://www.bjs.gov/content/pub/pdf/svus_rev.pdf
103 Alexy, E. M., Burgess, A. W., Baker, T., & Smoyak, S. A. (2005). Perceptions of cyberstalking among college students. *Brief Treatment and Crisis Intervention, 5*, 279–289.
104 Spitzberg, B. H., & Hoobler, G. (2002). Cyberstalking and the technologies of interpersonal terrorism. *New Media & Society, 4*, 71–92.
105 Reyns, B. W., Henson, B., & Fisher, B. S. (2012). Stalking in the twilight zone: Extent of cyberstalking victimization and offending among college students. *Deviant Behavior, 33*, 1–25.
106 Finn, J., & Banach, M. (2000). Victimization online: The downside of seeking human services for women on the Internet. *CyberPsychology & Behavior, 3*(5), 785–796.
107 Silverstein, L. (2004). Double edged sword: An examination of the global positioning system, enhanced 911, and the internet and their relationships to the lives of domestic violence victims and their abusers, *The Buffalo Women's Law Journal, 13*, 97.
108 Dimond, J. P., Fiesler, C., & Bruckman, A. S. (2011). Domestic violence and information communication technologies. *Interacting with Computers, 23*(5), 413–421.
109 Lyndon, A., Bonds-Raacke, J., & Cratty, A. D. (2011). College students' Facebook stalking of ex-partners. *Cyberpsychology, Behavior, and Social Networking, 14*(12), 711–716.
110 Dimond, J. P., Fiesler, C., & Bruckman, A. S. (2011). Domestic violence and information communication technologies. *Interacting with Computers, 23*(5), 413–421.
111 Hand, T., Chung, D., & Peters, M. (2009). The use of information and communication technologies to coerce and control in domestic violence and following separation: Australian Domestic and Family Violence Clearinghouse, UNSW. http://www.austdvclearinghouse.unsw.edu.au/PDF%20files/Stakeholder%20Paper_6.pdf
112 Burke, S. C., Wallen, M., Vail-Smith, K., & Knox, D. (2011). Using technology to control intimate partners: An exploratory study of college undergraduates. *Computers in Human Behavior, 27*(3), 1162–1167.
113 Zweig, J. M., Dank, M., Lachman, P., & Yahner, J. (2013). Technology, teen dating violence and abuse, and bullying: the urban institute. Retrieved from: https://www.ncjrs.gov/pdffiles1/nij/grants/243296.pdf
114 Hinduja, S., & Patchin, J. (2011). Electronic dating violence: A brief guide for educators and parents. Cyberbullying Research Center. Retrieved from: http://cyberbullying.org/electronic_dating_violence_fact_sheet.pdf
115 Schnurr, M. P., Mahatmya, D., & Basche III, R. A. (2013). The role of dominance, cyber aggression perpetration, and gender on emerging adults' perpetration of intimate partner violence. *Psychology of Violence, 3*(1), 70.
116 Burke, S. C., Wallen, M., Vail-Smith, K., & Knox, D. (2011). Using technology to control intimate partners: An exploratory study of college undergraduates. *Computers in Human Behavior, 27*(3), 1162–1167.
117 Zweig, J. M., Dank, M., Lachman, P., & Yahner, J. (2013). Technology, teen dating violence and abuse, and bullying: The Urban Institute. Retrieved from: https://www.ncjrs.gov/pdffiles1/nij/grants/243296.pdf
118 Burke, S. C., Wallen, M., Vail-Smith, K., & Knox, D. (2011). Using technology to control intimate partners: An exploratory study of college undergraduates. *Computers in Human Behavior, 27*(3), 1162–1167.
119 Reyns, B. W., Henson, B., & Fisher, B. S. (2012). Stalking in the twilight zone: Extent of cyberstalking victimization and offending among college students. *Deviant Behavior, 33*, 1–25.
120 Dreßing, H., Bailer, J., Anders, A., Wagner, H., & Gallas, C. (2014). Cyberstalking in a large sample of social network users: Prevalence, characteristics, and impact upon victims. *Cyberpsychology, Behavior, and Social Networking, 17*(2), 61–67.
121 Baum, K., Catalano, S., Rand, M., & Rose, K. (2009). Stalking victimization in the United States. United States Department of Justice. Retrieved from: http://www.victimsofcrime.org/docs/src/baum-k-catalano-s-rand-m-rose-k-2009.pdf?sfvrsn=0

122 Lasdun, J. (2013). I will ruin him. *The Chronicle of Higher Education*. Retrieved from: http://chronicle.com/article/I-Will-Ruin-Him/136693/
123 Langton, L. (2013). *Identity Theft Reported by Households, 2005–2010*. US Department of Justice, Office of Justice Programs, Bureau of Justice Statistics. Retrieved from: http://www.bjs.gov/content/pub/pdf/vit12.pdf
124 Federal Trade Commission. (1998). Identity Theft and Assumption Deterrence Act. Retrieved from: http://www.ftc.gov/os/statutes/itada/itadact.htm
125 Harrell, E. (2015). *Victims of Identity Theft, 2014*. Department of Justice, Office of Justice Programs, Bureau of Justice Statistics. Retrieved from: http://www.bjs.gov/content/pub/pdf/vit14.pdf
126 Perl, M. W. (2003). It's not always about the money: Why the state identity theft laws fail to adequately address criminal record identity theft. *The Journal of Criminal Law and Criminology (1973–)*, *94*(1), 169–208.
127 Harrell, E. (2015). *Victims of Identity Theft, 2014*. Department of Justice, Office of Justice Programs, Bureau of Justice Statistics. Retrieved from: http://www.bjs.gov/content/pub/pdf/vit14.pdf
128 Ibid.
129 Perl, M. W. (2003). It's not always about the money: Why the state identity theft laws fail to adequately address criminal record identity theft. *The Journal of Criminal Law and Criminology (1973–)*, *94*(1), 169–208.
130 Timm, C., & Perez, R. (2010). *Seven deadliest social network attacks*. Burlington, MA: Syngress.
131 Lasdun, J. (2013). I will ruin him. *The chronicle of higher education*. Retrieved from: http://chronicle.com/article/I-Will-Ruin-Him/136693/
132 White, M. D., & Fisher, C. (2008). Assessing our knowledge of identity theft: The challenges to effective prevention and control efforts. *Criminal Justice Policy Review*, *19*(1), 3–24.
133 Ibid.
134 Fair and Accurate Credit Transactions Act, Public Law 108–159, 111 Stat. 1952 (2003). Retrieved from: https://www.gpo.gov/fdsys/pkg/PLAW-108publ159/pdf/PLAW-108publ159.pdf
135 Gramm-Leach-Bliley Act, Public Law 106-102 (1999). Retrieved from: https://www.gpo.gov/fdsys/pkg/PLAW-106publ102/pdf/PLAW-106publ102.pdf
136 White, M. D., & Fisher, C. (2008). Assessing our knowledge of identity theft: The challenges to effective prevention and control efforts. *Criminal Justice Policy Review*, *19*(1), 3–24.
137 Harrell, E. (2015). *Victims of Identity Theft, 2014*. Department of Justice, Office of Justice Programs, Bureau of Justice Statistics. Retrieved from: http://www.bjs.gov/content/pub/pdf/vit14.pdf
138 Ibid.
139 White, M. D., & Fisher, C. (2008). Assessing our knowledge of identity theft: The challenges to effective prevention and control efforts. *Criminal Justice Policy Review*, *19*(1), 3–24.
140 Ibid.
141 Ibid.
142 Harrell, E. (2013). *Victims of Identity Theft, 2013*. Department of Justice, Office of Justice Programs, Bureau of Justice Statistics. Retrieved from: http://www.bjs.gov/content/pub/pdf/vit12.pdf
143 Harrell, E. (2015). *Victims of Identity Theft, 2014*. Department of Justice, Office of Justice Programs, Bureau of Justice Statistics. Retrieved from: http://www.bjs.gov/content/pub/pdf/vit14.pdf
144 Ibid.
145 Ibid.
146 Ibid.
147 N.A. (2015). *Fraud in 2014: What you need to know. Cifas*. Retrieved from: https://www.cifas.org.uk/secure/contentPORT/uploads/documents/External-A5%20Fraudscape%20insert%20LOW%20RES.pdf
148 Ibid.
149 Harrell, E. (2015). *Victims of Identity Theft, 2014*. Department of Justice, Office of Justice Programs, Bureau of Justice Statistics. Retrieved from: http://www.bjs.gov/content/pub/pdf/vit14.pdf
150 Ibid.
151 Ibid.
152 Ibid.
153 Ibid.
154 Al Hasib, A. (2009). Threats of online social networks. *IJCSNS International Journal of Computer Science and Network Security*, *9*(11), 288–93.
155 Aïmeur, E., & Schonfeld, D. (2011, July). The ultimate invasion of privacy: Identity theft. In *Privacy, Security and Trust (PST), 2011 Ninth Annual International Conference on* (pp. 24–31). IEEE.
156 Lehrman, Y. (2010). The weakest link: The risks associated with social networking websites. *Journal of Strategic Security*, *3*(2), 7.

157 Reyns, B. W. (2013). Online routines and identity theft victimization further expanding routine activity theory beyond direct-contact offenses. *Journal of Research in Crime and Delinquency*, *50*(2), 216–238.

158 Reyns, B. W., & Henson, B. (2015). The thief with a thousand faces and the victim with none: Identifying determinants for online identity theft victimization with Routine Activity Theory. *International Journal of Offender Therapy and Comparative Criminology*, online first.

159 Ibid.

160 Harrell, E. (2015). *Victims of Identity Theft, 2014*. Department of Justice, Office of Justice Programs, Bureau of Justice Statistics. Retrieved from: http://www.bjs.gov/content/pub/pdf/vit14.pdf

161 N.A. (2015). *Fraud in 2014: What you need to know. Cifas*. Retrieved from: https://www.cifas.org.uk/secure/contentPORT/uploads/documents/External-A5%20Fraudscape%20insert%20LOW%20RES.pdf

162 Reyns, B. W. (2013). Online routines and identity theft victimization further expanding routine activity theory beyond direct-contact offenses. *Journal of Research in Crime and Delinquency*, *50*(2), 216–238.

163 Reyns, B. W., & Henson, B. (2015). The thief with a thousand faces and the victim with none: Identifying determinants for online identity theft victimization with Routine Activity Theory. *International Journal of Offender Therapy and Comparative Criminology*, online first. DOI: 10.1177/0306624X1557286

164 Reyns, B. W. (2013). Online routines and identity theft victimization further expanding routine activity theory beyond direct-contact offenses. *Journal of Research in Crime and Delinquency*, *50*(2), 216–238.

165 Reyns, B. W., & Henson, B. (2015). The thief with a thousand faces and the victim with none: Identifying determinants for online identity theft victimization with Routine Activity Theory. *International Journal of Offender Therapy and Comparative Criminology*, online first. DOI: 10.1177/0306624X1557286

166 Reyns, B. W. (2013). Online routines and identity theft victimization further expanding routine activity theory beyond direct-contact offenses. *Journal of Research in Crime and Delinquency*, *50*(2), 216–238.

167 Ibid.

168 Timm, C., & Perez, R. (2010). *Seven deadliest social network attacks*. Burlington, MA: Syngress.

169 Reyns, B. W., & Henson, B. (2015). The thief with a thousand faces and the victim with none: Identifying determinants for online identity theft victimization with Routine Activity Theory. *International Journal of Offender Therapy and Comparative Criminology*, online first.

170 Aïmeur, E., & Schonfeld, D. (2011, July). The ultimate invasion of privacy: Identity theft. In *Privacy, Security and Trust (PST), 2011 Ninth Annual International Conference on* (pp. 24–31). IEEE.

171 Acquisti, A., & Gross, R. (2009, June). Social insecurity: The unintended consequences of identity fraud prevention policies. In Workshop on the Economics of Information Security (pp. 24–25).

172 Li, H. H. S., Yang, Z., Lv, Q., Han, R. I. R. R., & Mishra, S. (2014, December). A comparison of common users across instagram and ask.fm to better understand cyberbullying. In *Big Data and Cloud Computing (BdCloud), 2014 IEEE Fourth International Conference on* (pp. 355–362). IEEE.

173 Burris, A. (2014). Hell hath no fury like a woman porned: Revenge porn and the need for a federal nonconsensual pornography statute. *Florida Law Review*, *66*, 2325.

9
HATE CRIME VICTIMIZATION

Kevin Wong and Kris Christmann

Keywords

hate crime; defining hate crime; under-reporting by victims; victim support services; victim decision making; bias crimes

Objectives

After studying this chapter, the reader should understand:

- Defining hate crime: Be able to define what a hate crime is whilst also appreciating the many definitional difficulties encountered and the deeply contested nature of the concept.
- The prevalence of hate crime: Gain an understanding of how widespread hate crime is and the variable rates of victimization across different protected groups.
- Hate crime reporting: Understand the reasons for the under-reporting of hate crime, as well as the factors influencing reporting, including those measures authorities have in place to try and increase reporting amongst victims and witnesses.
- Supporting hate crime victims: Gain an understanding of the types of support services for victims of hate crime and how these can be sequenced and structured to better meet victims' needs.

Introduction

Hate crimes occur against individuals or certain stigmatized groups because the perpetrator harbors a prejudice, dislike, distrust or hatred towards that group. It has a relatively recent history as an area of justice and social policy. In the United States (US), attention to hate crime by criminal justice policy makers and practitioners originated in the early 1980s when the civil rights, women's rights and victims' rights movement provided the impetus for an anti-hate crime movement.[1] In the United Kingdom (UK), around the same time, ad hoc responses to hate crime were developed against the backdrop of anti-discrimination legislation enacted in the 1970s.[2]

Acts that are currently referred to as hate crime are not a new phenomenon. Similar patterns of motivation, sentiment and victimization have recurred over time. Immigrants to the US in the 1890s were subject to institutional and public forms of discrimination and violence. Former black slaves were subject to intimidation and violence by the Ku Klux Klan when trying to exercise their rights in the antebellum period.[3]

However, it has been argued by Perry (2003) that there is a dramatic difference between the examples drawn from eras preceding the 1970s and 1980s, mainly that these historical acts would not have been perceived of as hate crimes. Instead, they might have been viewed as a normative behavior, representing non-punishable, perhaps even celebrated acts in their time. In contrast, similar acts, occurring in more recent years would be "defined and publicly perceived in a qualitatively different light."[4] Social and cultural contexts are therefore important as determinants of how hate crime is conceptualized, perceived and responded to.

This chapter will examine four issues of particular salience to hate crime victimization, policy and practice:

- Definition—how is hate crime defined?
- Prevalence—how is hate crime measured, what are the trends?
- Under-reporting—why victims under-report hate crime and the efficacy of measures to encourage victims to report; and
- Efficacy of support services—how effective are services for hate crime victims.

Examples and research will be drawn primarily from the US and the UK where the development of hate crime policy and practice are most developed, supplementing this with evidence from other jurisdictions.

Defining Hate Crime

Hate crime is a deeply contested and politically controversial concept. There is no agreed criminological consensus on the definition of the term or even the validity of hate crime as a concept.[5] Neither is it clear what hate as an emotion encapsulates, indeed it has long been recognized that an offender may not be motivated by hate at all but the weaker emotions of bias or prejudice. This is supported by research evidence that suggests that hate itself is apparent in only a small proportion of hate crimes.[6] A finding that has led some academics and practitioners in the US to prefer the term "bias crime." The recognition that much of what passes for hate crime is more accurately prompted by prejudice and hostility held by the offender towards a social group that is seen as having "outsider status"[7] would seem to relegate hate crime to more of a misnomer. Hate crime then would appear to be more about prejudice or bias than about hate.

As others have argued, the notion of hate crime oversimplifies the concept, tending to reduce it to discrete acts of individual pathology which drives violence, rather than reflecting deeper relational structures embedded in some offending communities.[8] Rather than conceiving of hate crimes as discrete isolated incidents, they are more likely to form part of an ongoing process of victimization, one repeated over protracted periods of time.[9] These difficulties of definition become even more complex when one considers international differences. Even if we restrict ourselves to rather narrow legalistic definitions, the element of bias or prejudice in the motivation can be defined in different ways and require different thresholds (i.e., the classification can be partly or wholly motivated by bias). Different aspects of the offense can be emphasized in different countries, for example in Germany legislation tends to focus on the organized nature of violence associated with far right groups, whereas the US emphasizes individual acts.[10] Different countries use a variety of approaches in classifying bias motivations, so for instance bias categories related to racism or xenophobia can include a range of identity characteristics such as race/color, ethnicity/nationality, citizenship or language.[11]

Working Definitions

Unlike social science definitions of hate crime, legal definitions tend to be more narrow in their scope. So, for law enforcement purposes hate crimes are generally deemed to have two essential components.

The first is that an act violates the criminal law in that jurisdiction. The second is that the offender intends to target a protected characteristic shared by a group. Whilst these characteristics can vary widely across different countries, they can include aspects such as a person's race, language, religion, sexuality, ethnicity, nationality or any other similar common factor. For example, if a person is assaulted because of his or her real or perceived religious faith (i.e., being Muslim), this would constitute a hate crime. Hate crimes always require a base offense to have occurred, without which there is no hate crime, as well as a victim who is symbolic of a wider population. By contrast a street robbery on an elderly person who is frail would likely not constitute a hate crime if the target selection was on the basis of perceived vulnerability alone, not because the offender chose the victim because of their group membership. What is distinctive about hate crime is that the victim is targeted *because* of their membership of a social group. Thus, it is the group identity that is being attacked, not the individual, so in theory the victim could be replaced by someone else.[12] The target can be one or more people, or it may be property associated with a group that shares a protected characteristic.

The widespread adoption of the term hate crime internationally in many government, campaigning and academic circles is likely due to its flexibility, being an umbrella term broad enough to cover offenses perpetrated against minority racial groupings, as well as faith based groups and other vulnerable communities.

Once an offense has been reported to the authorities, difficulties can arise in categorizing the type of hate crime, for instance, if an attack takes place on a mosque and is accompanied by theft, the motive may be economic, religious bias or both.[13] Such difficulties can lead to the systematic under-recording of hate crimes by authorities.

There are also marked differences in what class of victims enjoys protected status. Mason[14] has argued that the claim to victim status is the outcome of engendering a form of emotional thinking, one that encourages others to see them as an undeserving victim of prejudice. It is also frequently a product of that group's ability to campaign and lobby for protected characteristics status, or the outcome of a cause célèbre, which can drive public support for change.

In some countries, such as the UK and US, hate crime policy and legislation is well developed and has found a strong foothold. By contrast, in many parts of continental Europe it has struggled to gain a comparable position.

United Kingdom Definition

In the UK, unlike in the US where there are specific statutes, the term "hate crime" has no legal status, but rather denotes a wide range of criminal offenses, from relatively low level harassment motivated by hostility based on personal characteristics at one end of the scale, to organized, premeditated activity designed to incite hatred against a group at the other. So, the term "hate crime" means different things in different contexts. Hate crime is institutionally defined within the criminal justice system in England and Wales: as "any criminal offence which is perceived, by the victim or any other person, to be motivated by a hostility or prejudice [. . .]."[15]

The above definition is also the broad operational definition primarily used for recording practices and was agreed to in 2007 by ACPO (Association of Chief Police Officers) the Crown Prosecution Service (CPS), Prison Service (now the National Offender Management Service NOMS) and other agencies that make up the criminal justice system in the UK. Whilst this definition is widely quoted in the UK literature (particularly government documents), it reflects institutional practice rather than the legal statutes. So, when criminal justice agencies refer to "hate crime," rather misleadingly they are generally not referring specifically to the statutory regimes. Their definition is wider than the terms used in the two groups of statutory offenses (discussed below). Aggravated offenses also provide for sentence enhancements and also re-labeling where the offenses are motivated by *racial or religious* hatred (i.e. the Crime and Disorder Act 1998, which created a new category of racially aggravated criminal offenses (ss. 28–32). The Religious Hatred Act (2006) inserted similar offenses for religious hatred.

It is, therefore, important to note that although hate crimes are recorded for all five of the "protected characteristics" of race, religion, disability, sexual orientation and gender identity, the criminal offenses that specifically deal with hate crime only cover some of the characteristics.[16]

Hate crime comes in two forms, direct and derivative.

Direct Hate Crime (Stirring up Offenses)

One form of hate crime is stirring up hatred. If a person engages in certain forms of threatening, abusive or insulting conduct where the intention is to stir up racial hatred or, having regard to all the circumstances, racial hatred was likely to be stirred up. At present, the stirring up offenses do not cover hatred on grounds of transgender identity or disability, but do cover race (and in a more limited way) religion and sexual orientation.[17] Criminal liability ensues where a person engages in (Law Commission, 2013:4):

- using threatening, abusive or insulting words or behavior or displaying written material that is threatening, abusive or insulting;
- publishing or distributing written material that is threatening, abusive or insulting;
- presenting or directing the public performance of a play involving the use of threatening, abusive or insulting words or behavior;
- distributing, showing or playing a recording of visual images or sounds that are threatening, abusive or insulting;
- providing a program service, or producing or directing a program, where the program involves threatening, abusive or insulting visual images or sounds, or using the offending words or behavior therein;
- possessing written material, or a recording of visual images or sounds, which is threatening, abusive or insulting, with a view to it being displayed, published, distributed, shown, played or included in a cable program service.

Incitement to racial hatred, or religious hatred (extended in 2007) or on grounds of sexual orientation (extended in 2010) are offenses in themselves (Public Order Act 1986, Pts III and IIIA, ss. 17–29A–M) but, for religious hatred and sexual orientation the offenses are narrower in scope:

1. The words or conduct must be threatening (not merely abusive or insulting);
2. There must have been an intention to stir up hatred (a likelihood that it might be stirred up is not enough), and;
3. There are express provisions protecting freedom of expression covering, for example, criticism of religious beliefs or sexual conduct.

(Law Commission, 2013:4)

Consequently, there are fewer prosecutions for stirring up racial hatred on grounds of race, religion or sexual orientation than those for aggravated offenses.

Derivative Hate Crime (Aggravated Offenses)

Derivative hate crimes take the form of aggravated versions of common offenses. These basic offenses that can be aggravated include: common assault; assault occasioning actual bodily harm; maliciously wounding or inflicting grievous bodily harm; destroying or damaging property;

threatening, abusive or insulting conduct towards someone with intent to cause fear of violence or provocation of violence; threatening, abusive or insulting conduct intended to cause harassment, alarm or distress; threatening, abusive or insulting conduct likely to cause harassment, alarm or distress; harassment and stalking; and putting people in fear of violence and stalking involving fear of violence, serious alarm or distress.

In determining guilt the court must be satisfied that both a criminal offense has been committed *and* that it is racially or religiously aggravated (within Section 28 of the 1998 Crime and Disorder Act). Thus, to commit the aggravated offense the offender needs either to demonstrate hostility to the racial or religious group, even if it is a presumed membership (i.e. they can be mistaken but still be guilty). In addition, guilt can also be assigned even if hostility is only partly (rather than wholly) the motivation (s 28, Crime and Disorder Act, 1998). As with instances of direct hate crime, aggravated offenses motivated by *racial or religious* hatred attract a sentence enhancement (ss. 28–32) (Racist or Religious Crime—CPS Guidance).

According to the UK Law Commission (2013) at present, the aggravated offenses do not cover hostility based on sexual orientation, transgender identity or disability, which is curious as hatred on grounds of sexual orientation was added by the Criminal Justice and Immigration Act (2008). The Law Commission's consultation document (2013) proposes extending the aggravated offenses in the Crime and Disorder Act 1998 to include where hostility is demonstrated towards people on the grounds of disability, sexual orientation or gender [i.e. "transgender"] identity; and proposes the case for extending the stirring up of hatred offenses under the Public Order Act 1986 to include stirring up of hatred on the grounds of disability or gender identity.

The definition of racial aggravation is very wide and, according to Burney,[18] it is "not essential to prove a racial motive in order for an offense to be racially aggravated; rather the two-pronged definition (above) was deemed necessary because of the difficulty of proving motive." This last point demonstrates the extraordinary scope of the legislation, and one of the reasons for why it is so politically controversial.

Hate Incidents and Hate crimes

A crucial distinction needs to be made between a "hate crime" and a "hate incident." In the UK a hate incident is: "*Any incident, which may or may not constitute a criminal offence, which is perceived by the victim or any other person, as being motivated by prejudice or hate.*"[19]

Such a definition inevitably draws in a wider range of behaviors than the legal classifications as contained in Home Office list offenses[20] (this needs to be borne in mind when making comparisons between different data sets both within and between jurisdictions) as it can be highly subjective, permissively so. This strategy in the UK derives from the landmark Stephen Lawrence Inquiry Report recommendations and explicitly removes police officer discretion at the point of recording (all hate incidents have to be recorded as such). The aim is to try and prevent inappropriate "no-criming" practices, which can substantially contribute to under-recording of hate crime more generally. Therefore, each police force has an obligation to initially treat all hate incidents as hate crimes and investigate them accordingly.

The Crime Survey England and Wales (CSEW) (which is a national victimization survey) also employs a wider definition of a racially and religiously motivated incident, one broadly in line with that recommended by The Lawrence Inquiry (again, subsequently adopted by the British police). A victim of racially or religiously motivated crime is then defined as anyone who judged that motivation was present in any household or personal crime which they experienced in the relevant year, including threats. By contrast, whether such incidents would be recorded as offenses by the police depends upon whether the offenses meet the Home Office criteria of a racially or religiously motivated offense. Whilst CSEW data is generally considered the more reliable measure of crime nationally than police crime data figures, this subjective element provides a cautionary note when considering prevalence of hate crimes.

Emerging Issues

Online hate crimes/incidents are a developing phenomenon, and there is growing concern about social media platforms acting as a method of victimisation. Online communication can be offensive and in bad taste, but as set out in the UK Crown Prosecution Service guidelines on prosecuting cases involving social media, content has to be more than simply giving offense to be contrary to the criminal law. Only communication that is grossly offensive, indecent, obscene or false is prohibited by legislation.

In principle, there may be other forms of hostility arising from age, gender or appearance, for example, which can also be considered hate crimes, although, for example, in the UK, they are not part of the five centrally monitored strands.[21] A number of other groups could also have claim to being victimized because of a shared identity or characteristic (i.e., certain youth subcultures, the homeless, prostitutes, sectarian groups, asylum seekers etc.) but *may* fall outside of the nationally monitored strands. For instance, in a study of a rural county in the UK.[22] because of the rural nature of significant parts of the county, hate crime victimization towards Travelers and Gypsies was examined (unlike Roma Gypsies, Travelers, especially new travelers, are not subsumed under an ethnic group, and hence racial monitored strand).

This widening about what constitutes a group that is vulnerable to hate crime is further illustrated by the growing variability across the 43 police forces in England and Wales regarding what vulnerable groups are being monitored. Greater Manchester police (GMP) was the first force to record as a hate crime direct and derivative offenses against some subcultural groups (here Goths and Emos[23]), a practice now adopted by several other police forces. The flexible nature of what constitutes hate crime, police force independence, and the influence of local Police and Crime Commissioners is likely to see this variation in monitoring continue. Issues of group classification are important as hate crime policy defines who will be provided with support and as such which local groups will be provided with funding.

Prevalence

It is extremely difficult to establish the precise levels of hate crime across different jurisdictions without a shared transnational definition of what hate crime is, as well as differences in methods to record hate crimes. Even when a definition is imposed, such as in the case of the Organisation for Security and Co-operation in Europe (OSCE) the number of hate crimes that comes to the attention of the respective authorities varies widely. For instance, the OSCE reports that no official data on racist or xenophobic hate crimes were reported to ODIHR for member states such as Italy, Spain and Russia (in respect of the 2012 OSCE Annual Report), whereas in two other member states with smaller populations, 39,906 racist crimes were recorded in the UK and an estimated 3,979 in Sweden. Such stark comparisons only act to highlight the major deficiencies in reporting and recording of hate crime and the definitional problems encountered when trying to make meaningful comparisons between different countries.

Victimization Surveys in the European Union

In response to the glaring inadequacies and absences of publicly available data on hate crime in European Union Member States (EUMS) the Fundamental Rights Agency (FRA) launched its own survey to explore selected immigrant and minority groups victimization. The 2008 European Union

Minorities and Discrimination Survey (EU-MIDIS) interviews some 23,500 respondents with an ethnic minority or immigrant background across 27 Member States and we cite findings from the survey in some detail.

The survey uses a representative sampling approach of minority groups, which chooses interviewees at random, and hence the results do not reflect experiences of a chosen few. The survey highlights that Sub-Saharan Africans and Roma peoples suffer the highest rates of racially motivated crime. Some 18 percent of Roma respondents and 18 percent of Sub-Sahara African respondents said they had experienced at least one racially motivated incident in the last 12 months. Other general groups surveyed showed a lower level of racially motivated crime in the last 12 months, with North Africans (9 percent); Turkish (8 percent); Central and Eastern Europeans (7 percent); Russians (5 percent) and former Yugoslavians (3 percent).[24]

In some EUMS these racially motivated in-person victimization rises to more than 1 in 4 respondents; notably, Roma in the Czech Republic (32 percent), Somalis in Finland (32 percent), Somalis in Denmark (31 percent), Africans in Malta (29 percent) and 26 percent of Roma in Greece, Poland and Sub-Saharan Africa in Ireland. By contrast, hardly any (1 percent) former Yugoslavians in Austria and Luxemburg, Russians in Latvia, or Turkish in Bulgaria said they had been victim to any ethnic or racist motivated crime in the past 12 months.

There was a higher volume of serious harassment compared with assaults or threats of assault across almost every surveyed group (with only a few exceptions). Roma respondents in Greece showed the highest rate of harassment over 12 months (174 incidents per 100 respondents). The survey found other high levels amongst Roma in the Czech Republic (118), Somalis in Denmark (112) and Somalis in Finland (106).

As with racist violence and threats, Roma and Sub-Saharan respondents were especially affected by harassment incidents. As the FRA authors conclude, the survey findings demonstrate the extent to which racially motivated crime is overwhelmingly experienced by the more visible minorities in the EU.

UK and USA

In the UK and the USA there is a relatively well developed legislative program and reporting procedures for hate crime.

In the US, the Hate Crime Statistics Act of 1990 (HCSA) later modified by the Matthew Shepard and James Byrd Jr. Hate Crimes Prevention Act (2009) required the Attorney General to collect data on crimes committed because of the victim's race, religion, disability, sexual orientation, or ethnicity.

In the UK the Crime Survey for England and Wales (CSEW), which is a national victimization survey, provides the most accurate estimates of hate crime prevalence. Estimates for the years 2012/13 to 2014/15 indicate that there were 222,000 hate crimes per year for the five monitored strands,[25] with 0.4 percent of adults (in England and Wales) being victims of any hate crime in the 12 month period prior to the survey.[26] This total figure represents a statistically significant fall of 28 percent from 2007/8 and 2008/09 CSEW, which reflects a similar rate of fall to overall crime.[27]

Some 48 percent of hate crimes came to the attention of the police, more than the 40 percent for volume crime, likely reflecting the greater number of violent crime incidents (49 percent of hate crimes as opposed to 19 percent of overall CSEW crime) which tend to see higher levels of reporting.[28] Of the 52,528 hate crimes in England and Wales that came to the attention of the police, the overwhelming majority (some 82 percent) were race hate crimes, followed by 11 percent being sexual orientation hate crimes, 6 percent religion hate crimes, 5 percent disability hate crimes and 1 percent transgender hate crimes.[29]

Whilst the media in the UK, US and other countries may tend to concentrate on the most extreme expressions of hate motivated violence, as with volume crime more generally, this does not reflect the daily reality. For example, in the UK much hate crime takes the form of "low level" public order offenses (59 percent) such as harassment, verbal abuse, and intimidation.[30] Some 30 percent of incidents are classified as violence against the person offenses (30 percent of which caused injury but the majority, some 70 percent, is violence without injury).[31] The remaining 7 percent constitutes criminal damage/arson offenses, and 3 percent "other notifiable" offenses.

As with volume crime more generally, hate crime victimization is disproportionately concentrated for young males 16 to 24 years old (with 0.5 percent experiencing personal hate crime, being a factor of ten higher than for the over 75s). Socio-demographic characteristics are also important, as social renters (0.4 percent) experience more hate crime than owner occupiers (0.1 percent).[32]

Ethnic minorities such as Black (0.7 percent), Asian (0.5 percent) or Mixed Ethnic (1.4 percent) backgrounds experience more hate crime than White adults (0.1 percent), as do single (0.4 percent) compared to married adults (0.1 percent).[33] This is likely due to their different use of public space and heightened situational risks in their routine activities. Indeed, there is a worrying trend showing a marked increase (37 percent) in race hate crime offenses occurring on public transport over the past five years.[34] Train carriages and buses provide confined spaces and direct contact with visibly different others, where grievances and prejudices can rapidly escalate into violent altercations.[35]

Hate crime victims also suffer higher rates of repeat victimization[36] than do victims of volume crime, particularly for household crime (35 percent) more than personal crime (27 percent).[37]

Under-reporting of Hate Crime

Reasons for Under-reporting

The under-reporting of hate crime needs to be seen within the wider context of low levels of reporting of crime more generally. Using two sweeps of the British Crime Survey (BCS) 2009/10 and 2010/11, Table 9.1 summarizes victims' reasons for not reporting hate crime to the police, compared

Table 9.1 Reasons for Not Reporting Crime Incident to the Police (Amended from Smith and Colleagues)[1]

Reason for not reporting	*All hate crime*	*All BCS crime*	*16 Western nations*
Trivial/no loss/police would not/could not do anything	55	73	84*
Private/dealt with ourselves	19	15	9
Common occurrence	9	3	–
Dislike or fear of the police/previous bad experience with the police or courts	7	2	2
Inconvenient to report	6	6	–
Fear of reprisal	5	2	4
Reported to other authorities	4	5	3
Other	21	6	19**

*Included 'Inappropriate for Police,' which was a category unique to the 16 nation International study.
**This category differs to that of the BCS 'Other' category in its make up (although the expectation would be that similar reasons were cited (no insurance; don't know etc.).
NB: Figures may add to more than 100 as multiple responses were allowed and also due to rounding errors.

1. Smith, K., Lader, D., Hoare, J., Lau, I. (2012). Hate Crime, cyber security and the experience of crime among children: Findings from the 2010/11, British Crime Survey: Supplementary Volume 3 to Crime in England and Wales 2010/11. Home Office Statistical Bulletin. London: Home Office.

with reasons for victims not reporting all BCS crime.[38] The table also provides comparable analysis of reasons given by victims for not reporting all crime to the police across 16 industrialized Western nations (including the UK and US) in a study by Goudriaan and colleagues.[39]

The most frequently mentioned reason for not reporting hate crime (as with other crime) is that the victim perceived the incident as too trivial, no loss was involved, believing that the police would not be bothered or could not do much about the offense, or that the attempt at an offense was unsuccessful,[40] all of which equated to over half (55 percent) of all reasons for non-reporting hate crime.[41] However, despite this representing the most oft given reason for non-reporting, victims of hate crime were less likely than victims of overall BCS crime to say that the incident was too trivial to report to the police (55 percent compared with 73 percent) as they were in comparison with the international data.

The second most frequent reason across all three data sets (19 percent for hate crime) was the victim feeling that the incident was a private matter to be dealt with by them, not the authorities. The third most common reason cited by victims, (9 percent for hate crime) perceived that the incident was a "common occurrence" and so did not report it because of this. The fourth most commonly cited reason cited by hate crime victims (7 percent) was holding some objection to the reporting agency, such as dislike or fear of the police, or having had a previous bad experience with the police or courts as the reason for not reporting the incident. The inconvenience of reporting was cited by some 6 percent, whereas having a fear of reprisal prevented reporting by a further 5 percent. Only 4 percent of responses said they reported to other authorities rather than the police.

The remaining "Other" reasons category for not reporting hate crime represents more than a fifth of all victim responses (some 21 percent). This is not disaggregated in the analysis, collapsing a number of different reasons for non-reporting, such as: something that happens as part of my job; partly my/friend's/relative's fault; offender not responsible for actions; thinking that someone else had reported the incident/similar incidents; in addition to failures on behalf of the reporting agency (i.e. "tried to report but was not able to contact the police"; and, "police not interested") as well as "other" miscellaneous reasons.

Increasing Hate Crime Reporting

Particular efforts have been made by policymakers and practitioners in the UK and US to encourage victims to report hate crimes. This is in part recognition of the vulnerability of particular communities and groups to hate crime and part of a deliberate attempt to address wider issues of discrimination against these groups. These policy and practice responses are considered below.

Building Confidence in the Police

Victims of hate crime are generally likely to be less satisfied than victims of other crime in their interactions with the police. BCS survey results showed that 53 percent of hate crime victims were "very" or "fairly satisfied" compared with the more substantial 69 percent for BCS overall crime.[42] Hate crime victims were also more likely to be "very dissatisfied" (23 percent) with how the police handled the matter compared with overall BCS crime (14 percent). Furthermore, in only 45 percent of hate crime incidents did victims think that the police took the matter as seriously as they should, compared with 65 percent of incidents of BCS crime overall. Similarly, there were lower levels of agreement that the police had treated victims of hate crime fairly (63 percent) when compared with overall BCS crime (79 percent), or treated victims with respect (76 percent compared with 89 percent) of incidents of overall BCS crime.

These findings take on greater weight when considering the impact on citizens of encounters with the police. Skogan's (2006) work in the US (replicated in several other countries, including the UK) suggests that having a bad experience with the police is four to 14 times as great or impactful as that of having a positive experience.[43] Indeed, there appears to be an "asymmetry" between how people perceive they are treated and their general confidence in the police. In addition to this, the way in which victims are updated on the progress of their cases can affect the likelihood that they will report future crimes to the police.[44]

To achieve this requires police forces to build positive relationships with organizations that represent those groups that are vulnerable to hate crime; train all their officers and support staff (such as call handlers) to deal with hate crime incidents appropriately; deploy specialist officers (who have received additional training) to case manage hate crime cases; and more generally improve the way that they maintain contact and communicate the progress of a case with victims.

Third Party Hate Crime Reporting Centers

In the UK, the landmark Lawrence Inquiry report encouraged the reporting of racist incidents to agencies other than the police.[45] The rationale for this was if members of black and minority ethnic communities were reluctant to report racist incidents to the police, fearing police racism and/or indifference, then they should be given the opportunity to report to agencies that they trusted and/or in which they had greater confidence. This established in the UK the principle of "third party" reporting hate crime reporting centers which has been applied to other groups and communities vulnerable to hate crime.

In 2014 the UK Government's Hate Crime Action Plan for England and Wales acknowledged that victims of hate crime were still reluctant to report hate crimes and underreporting remained a problem.[46] The role of the third party reporting centers in contributing to increasing reporting has received limited attention. Research in the UK that has been conducted into the efficacy of these centers, suggests that despite laudable efforts from local authorities in encouraging the establishment of third party reporting centers and NGOs in agreeing to act as third party reporting centers, the performance of these centers has been variable and reporting rates have been low.[47] Based on this

Table 9.2 Dimensions of an Effective Hate Crime Reporting Center

Operating dimension	*List A*	*List B*
Organisational purpose	Hate crime as core business	Hate crime as non-core business
Resourcing	Dedicated funding for hate crime work	Hate crime work resourced from funding that does not specifically cover hate crime work
Capacity/capability	Reporting, support and signposting for other help Reporting, enforcement, support and signposting for other help	Reporting only Reporting and signposting for further help
Types of hate crime dealt with	All	Specific hate crime types
Strength of links to groups vulnerable to hate crime	Well embedded	Limited
Strength of operational and strategic links to police and other key strategic agencies	Good operational links Good strategic links	Limited operational links Limited strategic links

research it is possible to devise a typology of hate crime reporting centers which goes some way to predicting how effective they're likely to be. This is summarized in Table 9.2. Organizations that tick all or most of the boxes from list A are likely to be more effective than those which fall into list B.

Social Context

Goudriaan, Lynch and Nieuwbeerta considered the influence of wider social context on the reporting of crime by examining incident level data from the International Crime Victims Survey (ICVS) for 16 western industrialized countries including the UK and United States.[48] They devised a framework, reproduced below, which makes the distinction between three geographically defined social contexts and two types of considerations. The social contexts cover the micro level, mesmo and macro level, with the corresponding decision gates that an individual engages in. In doing so the authors emphasize the wider social context in which the crime took place. Understanding of these contexts has the potential to provide policy makers with policy and practice responses, which could foster increased reporting of hate crime. To date, there has been limited research into the efficacy of responses that have aimed to influence social context around the reporting of hate crime or for that matter any crime.

Table 9.3 Factors Influencing the Reporting of Crime to the Police: The Effects of Social Context

Level *Geographic entity*	*Cost/benefit consideration*	*Normative consideration*
Micro level Situation	Knowledge about offender Perceived risk of retribution by offender Amount of injury Amount of loss Means of contacting police Distance from event in time or space Perceived likelihood of police response Perceived chance to receive some sort of compensation (e.g., recovery, repair, punishment of offender, payment by insurance company) Guilt Shame	Victim offender relationship Victim precipitation Guilt Shame
Meso-level Family and friends, block, neighbourhood, community, organization, jurisdiction	Availability of (community organizations) for self help Knowledge about area Reputation Knowledge of alternatives Private security	Attachments to family and friends, area or organization Reputation Norms regarding self help Policies for handling crime incidents
Macro level State, nation	Availability of (community organizations) for self help Police competence (responsiveness, efficiency) Social stratification Gender roles Roles of adults and juveniles	Legitimacy of police or government Norms regarding self help (individualism v collectivism) Compliance norm Institutionalization of insurance Gender roles Roles of adults and juveniles

Community Level Factors that Influence Reporting and Responses

Wilson and Ruback[49] examined hate crime incidents reported to the Pennsylvania Human Relations Commission from 1984 to 1998. The Commission is a state agency that enforces laws prohibiting discrimination and records reported bias crime incidents by victims or authorities relating to race, religion and sexual orientation. They found that *rates* of both personal and property hate crimes are significantly higher in rural than urban counties across the state. They attribute this (based on social disorganization theory) to a *"threshold effect"* on the reporting of hate crime. As interactions between races are more frequent in urban areas, hate crimes may be more frequent in urban counties. Therefore, residents may not report these incidents because they consider interracial tension and hate activity so commonplace that agencies will not intervene unless the matter is serious. In rural counties, there may relatively little contact between races, resulting in fewer hate crime incidents, however residents may be more likely to take these events seriously and are more likely than their urban counterparts to report them.

Wilson and Ruback[50] also found that police were more likely to become involved in incidents in counties with large Jewish populations, but less likely in counties with substantial black populations. They suggest that this is also consistent with *social disorganization theory*, i.e. the extent to which these two ethnic groups are organized among themselves and with political forces that control the allocation of resources to and the priorities of local law enforcement agencies. They propose that Jewish communities are better organized than black communities and so are more likely to seek help after a hate crime has occurred.

McVeigh, Welch and Bjarnason[51] conducted an analysis of hate crime recording in the United States in relation to the activity of civil rights organizations and voting. They found that:

- The presence of civil rights organizations and the resources of civil rights organizations can contribute to higher numbers of reported hate crimes in counties with relatively high levels of voting for the Democratic Party.
- The effectiveness of civil rights organizations was affected by the *credibility of hate crime framing* to provide confirmation that hate crime was an important issue. This credibility was influenced by the degree of ethnic heterogeneity in the county, the levels of interracial homicide and the number of racist hate groups.

McVeigh et al.[52] also found that hate crime reporting tended to be higher in politically competitive counties. Overall, these findings demonstrate the importance of having an organizational infrastructure to promote positive reporting messages, channel grievances and advocate on behalf of minority groups.

Support Services for Hate Crime Victims

There is a diverse body of research about the needs of hate crime victims[53] which points to a dual role for hate crime victim support services: supporting individuals, building their confidence to report hate crimes to the police and/other official body; and providing the emotional and practical support to cope with the aftermath of the incident(s). The service model in Table 9.4 devised by Wong, Christmann and colleagues (2013)[54] draws on this literature and maps this across to a victim's journey before, during and after the end of their engagement with the criminal justice system, offering whole system model of support for hate crime victims.

Table 9.4 A Whole System Approach to Supporting Hate Crime Victims

Service stages	*Key service objective*	*Key service elements across all the stages*
Pre-incident	• Providing targeted information to individuals who may be vulnerable to hate crime • Information initiatives targeted at potential perpetrators to deter or prevent hate crimes occurring	Case co-ordination by a 'lead professional' (from a public or VCS agency) who is responsible for managing the individual's case at each or any of these stages
Pre-reporting to the police	• Recording information about hate crimes from individuals who do not feel comfortable/confident to report this to the police • Working with individuals and communities so that they feel able to report incidents to the police	A risk of victimization and needs assessment process that is applied to each case A scaled response to each case based on a red, amber, green (RAG) system of risk of victimization and need
Reporting to the police	• Supporting individuals report hate crime to the police • Managing the expectations of individuals about the types of action that the police can take	(similar to that adopted for the management of prolific offenders) which ensures that community specific support (where required) is provided
Criminal justice system	• Supporting individuals through the criminal justice system, managing their expectations through this process • Protecting individuals from reprisals	A regular case conference and review process (as adopted for the management of prolific offenders) involving all the key
Post criminal justice system	• Providing 'aftercare' support and protection to individuals whether or not perpetrators are convicted	criminal justice and voluntary sector agencies

Summary

Hate crime is a contested and politically controversial concept. In criminology there is no consensus on how it is defined or even its validity. For law enforcement purposes hate crimes are generally deemed to have two essential components. The first is that an act that violates the criminal law in that jurisdiction. The second is that the offender intends to target a protected characteristic shared by a group. Protected characteristics used across jurisdictions include: race, religion, disability, sexual orientation and gender identity and are being widened to include other identified groups that are vulnerable to crime (homeless, a prostitute and belonging to a youth sub-culture group).

Comparing the prevalence of hate crime across jurisdictions is difficult because of a lack of a trans-national definition and differences in methods to record hate crime. A European survey of European Union Member States exploring immigrant and minority group victimization demonstrates that racially motivated crime is overwhelmingly experienced by the more visible minorities in the EU. In the UK, hate crime is measured in two ways, through regular victim surveys, which provide the most accurate estimates of certain hate crimes, and through the police who record as hate incidents (where an incident is perceived by the victim or anyone else to be a hate crime) and hate crimes where an incident is investigated and where deemed to a recordable offense is "crimed"—recorded as a criminal offense.

Hate crimes as with other crimes are underreported. The most frequently given reasons for underreporting by hate crime victims are: the incident was too trivial; the incident was a private matter and the incident was a common occurrence. To encourage victims to report to the police requires: the police to build greater confidence in the police organization among groups vulnerable to hate crime; improving the efficacy of third party reporting centers; official bodies understanding the social context which could support reporting and community factors.

Support services for hate crime victims have a dual role: supporting individuals, building their confidence to report hate crimes to the police and/other official body; and providing the emotional and practical support to cope with the aftermath of the incident(s).

Discussion Questions

1. Can there ever be an internationally agreed definition of hate crime? Would this be desirable? Think about the advantages and disadvantages to this policy goal, including an international legal framework.
2. How prevalent is hate crime? What difficulties do you encounter in trying to provide a robust answer to this question?
3. How can authorities increase the reporting of hate crime?
4. How should hate crime victims be supported? In answering this question think about the diffusion of innovation across other social policy and criminal justice arenas and consider questions of effectiveness.

Notes

1 Jenness, V. (1995). Social movement growth, domain expansion, and framing processes: The gay/lesbian movement and violence against gays and lesbians as a social problem. *Social Problems*, *42*(1), 145–170. Jenness, V. and Broad, K. (1998). *Hate crimes: New social movements and the politics of violence.* New York NY: Aldine de Gruyter.

2 These included: The Equal Pay Act 1970; The Sex Discrimination Act 1975; and The Race Relations Act 1976.

3 Perry, B. (2003). Where do we go from here? Researching hate crime. *Internet Journal of Criminology*, *3*, 45–47.

4 Perry 2003 Supra note 3, p. 6.

5 Hall, N. (2013). *Hate crime.* Abingdon, Routledge; Perry, B. (2003). Where do we go from here? Researching hate crime. *Internet Journal of Criminology*, *3*, 45–47.

6 McDevitt, J., Levin, J., Nolan, J. and Bennett, S. 2010. Hate crime offenders. In Chakraborti, N. ed. *Hate crime: concepts, policy, future directions.* Cullompton: Willan, pp. 124–145.

7 Walters, M. A. (2014). *Hate crime and restorative justice: Exploring causes, repairing harms.* Oxford, Oxford University Press.

8 Ray, L. and D. Smith (2001) Racist offenders and the politics of "hate crime," *Law and Critique*, *12*(3), 203–21.

9 Williams, M. L. and Tregidga, J. (2013). Time for justice: All Wales hate crime research project. Cardiff: Race Equality First; Walters, M. A. (2014). *Hate crime and restorative justice: Exploring causes, repairing harms.* Oxford, Oxford University Press; Walters, M. A. & Paterson, J. L. (2015) *Transphobic hate crime and perceptions of the criminal justice system.* Transgender Equality Inquiry, Women and Equalities Committee, UK Parliament. Walters, M., Brown, R., Wiedlitzka, S. (2016). Hate crime: Causes and perpetrator motivations. Equality and Human Rights Commission Research Report Series. Equality and Human Rights Commission.

10 Perry, B. (2003:7). Where do we go from here? Researching hate crime, *Internet Journal of Criminology.*

11 OSCE (2013). Hate crimes in the OSCE region: Incidents and responses annual report for 2012 (November).

12 Perry, B. (2001). *In the name of hate: Understanding hate crimes.* New York: Routledge.

13 OSCE (2013) Hate crimes in the OSCE region: Incidents and responses annual report for 2012 (November).

14 Mason, G. (2007). Hate crime as a moral category: Lessons from the Snowtown case. *Australian and New Zealand Journal of Criminology*, *40*(3), 249–271.

15 College of Policing. (2014:3–4). *Hate Crime Operational Guidance* 2014. Coventry, UK: College of Policing Limited.

16 Law Commission. (2013). Hate crime: The case for extending the existing offences: A consultation paper.

17 Ibid.

18 Wells C. & Quick, O. (2010) Reconstructing criminal law: Texts and materials. Fourth edition. Cambridge: Cambridge University Press, p. 193.

19 ACPO (2005). *Hate crime: Delivering a quality service.* London: ACPO; Home Office, p. 9.

20 The Home Office lists offenses comprise all those criminal offenses that police forces around the country centrally report. It is important to note that this is not an exhaustive as some more minor offenses are not reported centrally but dealt with at the police force level.
21 There is a fairly substantial body of literature that grapples with the question of what should be classed as hate crime, and there is a potentially very large number of incumbent groups (Travellers, Gypsies, asylum seekers, overseas students, prostitutes, homeless people, to name a few). It is also instructive to examine how the BCS records incidents on whether the victim thought the offender was motivated by the victim's age or gender (categorized as age or gender motivated hate crime) of which there were around 143,000 (0.3 percent) and 120,000 (0.2 percent) perceived incidents for the youngest and oldest age groups (Smith et al. 2012:25). However, these victims may be targeted as much for their vulnerability as the fact that they are old, young, or female, making the ascribed hate element as the defining feature problematic. A number of other groups could also have claim to being victimized because of a shared identity or characteristic (i.e. certain youth subcultures, the homeless, prostitutes, sectarian groups etc.) but may fall outside of the nationally monitored strands. See Smith, K., Lader, D., Hoare, J., Lau, I. (2012). *Hate Crime, cyber security and the experience of crime among children: Findings from the 2010/11*, British Crime Survey: Supplementary Volume 3 to Crime in England and Wales 2010/11. Home Office Statistical Bulletin. London: Home Office.
22 Wong, K. and Christmann, K., Meadows, L., Albertson, K., Senior, P. (2013), *Hate crime in Suffolk: Understanding prevalence and support needs*. Sheffield: Sheffield Hallam University.
23 A subculture group of individuals who generally favor a form of punk music that incorporates more complex arrangements and emotionally wrought lyrics
24 FRA (2009:15–16) *Hate crime in the European Union*. FRA – European Union Agency for Fundamental Rights.
25 The five monitored strands are: race, religion, disability, sexual orientation and gender-identity.
26 Corcoran, H., Lader, D. and Smith, K. (2015). *Hate crime, England and Wales, 2014/15*. London: HMSO.
27 Ibid.
28 Ibid.
29 Ibid.
30 Walters, M., Brown, R., Wiedlitzka, S. (2016) *Hate crime: Causes and perpetrator motivations. Equality and Human Rights Commission Research Report Series*. Equality and Human Rights Commission. Manchester, UK: Equality and Human Rights Commission; Walters, M. A. (2014). *Hate crime and restorative justice: Exploring causes, repairing harms*, Oxford: Oxford University Press; Williams, M. L. and Tregidga, J. (2013), *Time for justice: All Wales hate crime research project*. Cardiff: Race Equality First.
31 Corcoran, H., Lader, D. and Smith, K. (2015). *Hate crime, England and Wales, 2014/15*. London: HMSO.
32 Ibid.
33 Corcoran, H., Lader, D. and Smith, K. (2015). *Hate crime, England and Wales, 2014/15*. London: HMSO.
34 Yeung and Duncan (2016, January 27). Race hate crimes reported on UK railways rise 37% in five years, Guardian Newspaper. (Available at https://www.theguardian.com/uk-news/2016/jan/27/race-hate-crimes-uk-railways-rise-37-per-cent-five-years) (Accessed 27.1.16).
35 Chakraborti, N. and Hardy, S.-J. (2015). *LGB&T hate crime reporting: identifying barriers and solutions*. Leicester, UK: University of Leicester; Walters, M., Brown, R., Wiedlitzka, S. (2016) Hate crime: Causes and perpetrator motivations. Equality and Human Rights Commission Research Report Series. Manchester, UK: Equality and Human Rights Commission.
36 The CSEW defines repeat victimization as being a victim of the same type of any hate crime more than once in the last year.
37 Corcoran, H., Lader, D. and Smith, K. (2015). *Hate crime, England and Wales, 2014/15*. London: HMSO.
38 Table 4.1 displays data combined from two survey years (2009/10 and 2010/11) in order to give more robust estimates by increasing the number of incidents available for analysis. Displayed figures are 12-month averages of the estimates from the two survey years and therefore comparable with 12-month BCS findings more generally.
39 Goudriaan H., Lynch, J. P., Nieuwbeerta P. (2004). Reporting to the police in western nations: A theoretical analysis of the effects of social context, *Justice Quarterly*, *21*(4), 933–969, December 2004.
40 The authors merged a number of similar answer categories: ("Too trivial/not worth reporting," "No loss/damage," "Police would not have been bothered/interested," "Police could not do anything" and "Attempt at offence was unsuccessful") due to the similarity in their definition and end meaning for respondents. This is unfortunate as several of these reasons point to service failures and would more profitably have been disaggregated for finer analysis.
41 Unfortunately, the BCS merges these different reasons due to the perceived similarity for respondents, so we are unable to know whether it is the victim's subjective feelings concerning the crime or alternatively their

assessments of the police response that results in non-reporting—this is especially unhelpful when trying to understand victim decision making.

42 Smith, K., Lader, D., Hoare, J., Lau, I. (2012). *Hate crime, cyber security and the experience of crime among children: Findings from the 2010/11*, British Crime Survey: Supplementary Volume 3 to Crime in England and Wales 2010/11. Home Office Statistical Bulletin. London: Home Office.

43 Skogan, W. G. (2006). Asymmetry in the impact of encounters with police. *Policing & Society 16*(2), 99–126.

44 Victim Support (2011). Left in the dark: Why victims of crime need to be kept informed, Victim Support. Victim Support (2005) The Impact of hate crime: Needs, practical and emotional support for victims, a literature review. London: Victim Support.

45 Recommendation 15 of the Lawrence Inquiry Report stated: "That all possible steps should be taken by Police Services at local level in consultation with local Government and other agencies and local communities to encourage the reporting of racist incidents and crimes. This should include: – the ability to report at locations other than police stations; and – the ability to report 24 hours a day."

46 HM Government (2014) *Challenge it, report it, stop it: Delivering the Government's Hate Crime Action Plan*, London: HM Government.

47 Swift Research (2005). Police hate crime reporting centres. Unpublished Report. West Yorkshire Swift Research; Wong, K. & Christmann, K. (2007). Wakefield Hate Crime Victim Support Needs Project. Unpublished Final Report to Wakefield Council. Wong, K. & Christmann, K. (2008). The role of decision making in reporting hate crimes, *Community Safety Journal*, 7(2) 19–34; Monchuck, L. & Santana-Acosta, J. (2006). An audit of the hate crime reporting centers in [study area] Unpublished report for [study area] Safer Communities Partnership.

48 Goudriaan et al. 2004. Supra note 11.

49 Wilson, M. S. & Ruback, R. B. (2003). Hate crimes in Pennsylvania 1984–99 Case characteristics and police responses, *Justice Quarterly*, *20*(2), June 2003, 373–398.

50 Ibid.

51 McVeigh, R., Welch, M. R. & Bjarnason, T. (2003). Hate crime reporting as a successful social movement, *American Sociological Review*, *68* (December), 843–867.

52 Ibid.

53 Sin, H. C., Hedges, A., Cook, C., Mguni, N. & Comber, N. (2009). Disabled people's experiences of targeted violence and hostility, Office for Public Management, Equality and Human Rights Commission. Research Report 21; Sobsey, D. (1994). Violence and abuse in the lives of people with disabilities: The end of silent acceptance? Baltimore, MD: Paul H. Brookes Publishing. Victim Support 2011 and Victim Support 2005 Supra note 13, Vine, L., The Robert Gordon University (2004). Community Safety for ethnic minority groups in Aberdeenshire, Grampian Racial Equality Council; Willitts, M., Farmer, M., & Gunning, C. (2011). Life Opportunities Survey Wave one results, 2009/11. London, Office for Disability Issues: HM Government; Walters, M., Hoyle, C. (2010). Healing harms and engendering tolerance: the promise of restorative justice for hate crime, In *Hate crime: Concepts, policy and future directions*. N. Chakraborti (ed.), Cullompton: Willan Press, pp. 228–245.

54 Wong, K., Christmann, K., Meadows, L., Albertson, K., & Senior, P. (2013) *Hate crime in Suffolk: Understanding prevalence and support needs*, Sheffield: Hallam Centre for Community Justice, Sheffield Hallam University.

10

COUNSELING FAMILIES OF MURDERED VICTIMS

A Therapeutic Perspective

Nana A. Serwaa Adjekum-Boateng and Francis D. Boateng

Keywords

homicide; survivors; counseling; therapy; victimology; cognitive-behavioral

Objectives

After reading this chapter, readers will:

- Be able to identify and discuss the psychological impacts of homicide on survivors.
- Develop an in-depth understanding of the therapeutic methods used to assist homicide survivors to cope with the tragic event.
- Develop a holistic understanding of the experiences that survivors of homicide go through.

Introduction

In spite of the significant adverse consequences of homicide on families and the community (Green, 2000; McDevitt-Murphy, Neimeyer, Burke, Williams, & Lawson, 2012; Spungen, 1998), little victimological attention has been paid to the experiences of homicide survivors. Instead, most of the extant research has focused on addressing the needs of victims of domestic violence and sexual assault (Campbell, 2001; Warshaw, Sullivan & Rivera, 2013). This exclusion is problematic because of the violent nature of the crime, but also because of the impact of the crime on the group, that Redmond (1989) termed "homicide survivors." This group includes the immediate family, such as children, spouses, and parents; the extended family members, such as grandparents, uncles, nephews, nieces, and aunts; and other loved ones of the deceased, such as friends, co-workers, schoolmates, and neighbors. These individuals go through the ordeal of having a loved one murdered.

Victimologists have argued that homicide causes drastic and permanent changes in the family structure, and these changes are often difficult for survivors to endure. For instance, according to Aldrich and Kallivayalil (2013), homicide shoves survivors into "a terrain that is completely foreign and characterized by an anguish that steadily increases and consumes as the initial shock gradually recedes" (p. 362). This conclusion is the epitome of what survivors of homicide go through: guilt, shock, rage, helplessness, isolation, grief, and posttraumatic stress.

Although homicide has devastating effects on survivors, the extent of the impact and reaction to the crime vary significantly from one person to another. Factors such as family background and personality have been found to determine the level of reaction among survivors. Similarly, demographic factors—gender, age, and race—affect how homicide survivors will react to the loss of their loved ones. For example, in one study, males and females responded differently to the murder of a family member (Kenny, 2003): while women could easily cope with the loss, men, because of their stereotypical gender role and feelings of guilt and self-blame, had trouble coping.

In this chapter, we review and discuss the experiences of survivors of homicide and the various counseling strategies that can be adopted to help these individuals successfully cope with the loss of their loved ones. The chapter is divided into sections on three main topics: the characteristics of homicide victims, the impact of homicide on families, and counseling strategies for survivors. After the discussion of these topics, conclusions are drawn.

Homicide Victims: Who Are They?

While there are no known estimates about the number of family members or survivors that lose their loved ones through homicide, available statistics provide us with estimates and information about people who are murdered in a given year. This information can indirectly give us an idea about the number and type of families that mourn the demise of their members. Statistically, in 2013, the FBI UCR Supplementary Homicide Report estimated the total number of murder victims to be 12,253. Non-familial individuals such as friends, neighbors, romantic partners, and acquaintances killed about 56 percent of these victims, while almost 25 percent of the victims were killed by family members. Moreover, a significant number of these victims (40 percent) were killed in the course of an intense argument, while less than one-third were killed during the committing of a violent crime, such as rape and robbery. The FBI report also suggests significant demographic differences in the numbers of people that were murdered in 2013. The majority of the victims were male (78 percent) and black (52 percent). The increasing murder rate for blacks is troubling; this is evident in Cooper and Smith's (2012) comment that African Americans are killed each year at a rate over six times greater than that of whites. Only about 22 percent of the murder victims were female, and their husbands or boyfriends murdered a majority of these victims.

Impact of Homicide on Families

Homicide has diverse and significant effects on the families of the murdered victims, who, according to Redmond (1989) are called survivors. The level of impact is based on several factors, including the age of the victim, the victim's gender, relationship to the victim, the violent way the victim died, and the intensity of suffering (Redmond, 1989). At times, the presence of a support network, whether the perpetrator is punished, and the availability of family financial resources also determine the degree to which survivors will be affected by the incident.

The pain of losing a loved one through murder, according to Redmond (1989) is more intense and long-lasting than other types of grief, and in some cases, the bereavement can last 3–5 years. Erickson (1976) termed it a chronic and never-ending disaster that can never be forgotten. The survivors' loss disrupts their shared plans and dreams with the victim of homicide. For example, parents may re-experience the feeling of losing a child several times in their lives, especially when they see others' children moving forward in life—graduating from college, getting married, or starting a job. Moreover, siblings and other relatives may feel guilty to be alive and express continued grief, rage, and despair when dealing with their loss. The expression of loss differs and often depends on the closeness to the victim. Rando (1993) affirmed that survivors feel guilty to be alive because they failed to protect the victim. Some survivors reminisce about past events involving the victim and think of ways they could have prevented their death. The loss of a family member may also cause a change in roles played by the other members: survivors might have to take on different responsibilities within the family. In the case of the death of a mother, the father may have to assume additional child-rearing and household duties, and older siblings may assume the responsibility of caring for the younger ones.

The loss of a family member to homicide may also have tremendous financial effects on the family. Apart from the physical absence of their loved one, the survivors may suffer financially, especially when the victim was the sole provider for the family. They may have difficulty affording basic amenities (food, shelter, clothes). In cases where victims survive for a few days or months, medical expenses can cause further financial drain if the victim has no health insurance. The death of the breadwinner in the family may result in children dropping out of school because of the lack of finances to cover educational expenses. Families may also lose their homes or cars because they cannot keep up with the payments.

In addition to the physical loss and financial difficulties, homicide can cause significant psychological problems for those who live to mourn the murdered one. Psychological disorders such as posttraumatic stress disorder (PTSD), depression, anxiety, feelings of hopelessness, and substance abuse are common among survivors. The DSM-IV diagnosis of PTSD is found in survivors of traumatic events (APA, 1994). In addition, Gerber (1995) noted that survivors of murdered relatives experience substantial levels of distress. Rynearson and McCreery (1993) and Thompson et al. (1998) also pointed out that survivors often live in stressful conditions. PTSD is characterized by sleeplessness, nightmares, fatigue, startled reactions, and fears involving situations associated with the murder. Murphy et al. (1999) included denial and numbing as additional effects of PTSD that enable survivors to avoid the pain of the murder.

Homicide can instill a great amount of anger and guilt in survivors. Some survivors feel rage toward the murderer of their loved one that can last for years, even if the culprit is apprehended and receives the due punishment. They sometimes direct their rage toward society or other family members for failing to protect their loved ones. They feel guilt for not alerting or protecting the victim, and blame themselves for not foreseeing the tragedy and not intervening (Bard & Sangrey, 1979). Self-blaming enables survivors to believe that they had control over the situation. Sometimes, they may blame themselves more directly for the death of the victim, such as if the survivor encouraged the victim in inappropriate behavior or failed to direct the victim toward a better path in life.

Related to the above psychological issues are the intrapsychic implications of homicide on survivors. Survivors tend to lose their self-esteem, self-reliance, and feelings of empathy for others. In addition, their sense of security and safety in their surroundings is shattered, resulting in confrontation of their own vulnerabilities and mortality (Amick-McMullan et al., 1989; Armour, 2003; Boss, 2002; Neimeyer et al., 2002; Miller & Schlesinger, 2000). Blum (2003) also shines light on the insecurity felt by survivors after such a tragic loss.

Moreover, the loss of a loved one through such a horrific and tragic event can affect the physical well-being of survivors. Survivors sometimes experience symptoms like gastrointestinal problems and cardiovascular disorders, and are prone to infectious diseases. According to experts, most survivors die within the first few years of any kind of violent criminal homicide (McFarlane et al., 1994; Prigerson et al., 1997; Schlosser, 1997; Sprang & McNeil, 1995). Kenny (2003) identified that male survivors were likely to suffer from heart-related illnesses and early death, whereas female survivors experienced anxiety and depression. He attributed these results to the fact that men are known to repress their emotions or pain, while women are encouraged to be emotional.

Lastly, survivors' traumatic experiences are further exacerbated by specific community reactions (Neimeyer, 2006). Survivors of homicide victims who were considered a menace to society—drug dealers, prostitutes, and gang members—according to Doka (2002), may experience disenfranchised bereavement. They may be stigmatized in the community, and subsequently receive little or no support from the society they live in (Neimeyer & Jordan, 2002). This reception from the community, according to victimology experts, may lead to secondary victimization (Hatton, 2003; Rando, 1993; Rynearson, 1988, 1994). Survivors may feel despair at being prevented from making meaning of the death of their loved one (Armour, 2003). They may try to turn the negative image of their loved one around and argue that the victim's death is tragic and his or her life is worthy.

Counseling Strategies: Therapeutic Approaches

Grief is an intensely personal emotion characterized by disbelief, yearning, isolation, and bitterness related to the death of the loved one. Bereavement can affect one's physical and mental health. Survivors following a tragic encounter may engage in several coping strategies to withstand the aftermath of the death of their loved ones (Sheehan, 1991; Violanti, 2000). Some choose to distance themselves mentally from the traumatic event by channeling their attention to work and family responsibilities. Others may seek social support and sympathy from their friends and family members. Yet others may isolate themselves from their loved ones and social activities. The effect of homicide, according to research, goes on for years, and the request for intervention may be initiated many months or years after the experience. Additionally, Weiner (1992) emphasized the fact that the effects of traumas may be cumulative; therefore, therapy for survivors has to incorporate the resolution of past traumatic events that will trigger the recent trauma of the murder.

There is the need for intervention by a professional after a horrific event like the homicide of a loved one to help alleviate the long-term psychological effects on the survivor. Counseling is very imperative for homicide survivors; it enables them to process their painful emotions after a tragic loss. Therapists or counselors employ various strategies and methods, including cognitive-behavioral therapy (CBT), to help survivors deal with their losses. The choice of strategy can be influenced by the age of the survivor, gender, his or her closeness to the victim, his or her ability to manage stressful events, and the availability of a support network system.

Cognitive-Behavioral Therapy Approach

CBT is a form of psychotherapy used in cases of anxiety disorders, skill training, stress management, and health care problems (Granvold, 1994; Reineke, Dattilio, & Freeman, 1995). CBT entails the application of both cognitive techniques, such as changing of one's thought processes, and behavioral components, such as education and skill development. CBT focuses on correcting irrational, illogical, and faulty thinking (Beck, 1993; Beck, 1995; Day, 2008; Ellis, 1994; Glasser, 2000). This strategy could be adopted to help survivors of a homicide reduce their negative emotional responses by prolonging or repeating the traumatic event (Foa et al., 1999; Resick et al., 2002).

As part of this strategy, the therapist can ask survivors to remember and visualize their fears, and this can consequently help their anxiety. Therapists can also use this approach to help survivors change their thought processes, behavior, and emotional responses. The treatment process is often short-term. The therapeutic session can be a one-on-one session between the therapist and the survivor, or it can be organized as a group session for several family members who have been affected by the tragedy.

Therapists when applying this strategy refer to the therapeutic techniques and procedures developed by the pioneers of this form of psychotherapy. For example, Albert Ellis in 1955 developed rational-emotive behavior therapy (REBT), which indicated that experiences shape the belief system and thinking process of the individual. He outlined the cognitive, emotive, and behavioral techniques and methods that are usually adopted by therapists when dealing with survivors of homicide.

Cognitive Methods

Disputing irrational beliefs. This is an effective method employed by most therapists in assisting survivors. The therapist actively disputes the negative and irrational beliefs of the survivors and encourages them to do the same. The therapist may ask why the survivors have the belief that they are responsible for the loved one's death and why it is a taboo for life not to turn out as planned. The therapist continues asking various questions to help the survivors make their thinking more rational. The therapist urges the survivors to refute every irrational belief in their daily lives.

Cognitive homework. This cognitive method is also widely used by therapists when helping their clients. The survivors are asked by the therapist to list their problems. They dispute their own irrational beliefs at home and document their thought disputation. In addition, the therapist may help the survivors fill their daily activities with things they love and enjoy doing. The survivors are also encouraged to put themselves in risk-taking situations, i.e., using the road or visiting the place where their loved one was murdered; this step can help them challenge their irrational thoughts. The therapist can give the survivors reading assignments and audio tapes to work on their thoughts, feelings, and behavior. The use of cognitive homework enables the survivors to learn new skills and apply them in real-life situations, in addition to learning how to deal with their emotional traumas by carrying out the various assignments proposed by the therapist, either during the therapeutic session or at home when they are faced with their own thoughts.

Changing one's language. Albert Ellis affirmed that language is the basis of irrational or distorted thinking. Language is also seen as a medium of shaping one's own thought processes. A therapist can help survivors modify the way they express themselves. For example, a survivor may use expressions like "I am better off dying," "I cannot live without my loved one," "I let my loved one down," etc. The therapist can help survivors understand that they are not the cause of their loved one's death, and that their presence is important for the family and they are alive for a reason. By doing this, the therapist assists the survivors to shape their narratives, and consequently their ways of thinking.

Use of humor. According to Warren and McLellarn (1987), humor is one of the most used techniques. The therapist can use humor to overturn sadness and anxiety. For example, the therapist could suggest that a survivor sing a humorous song anytime he or she feels depressed, sad, or anxious (Ellis & Yeager, 1989). This approach can help survivors see humor in life despite their traumatic experiences.

Emotive Techniques

These strategies involve the unconditional acceptance of the client. In addition, they help clients to assess the negative effect of undermining themselves. Specific emotive techniques employed are discussed below.

Rational-emotive imagery. The therapist asks survivors to imagine feeling, thinking, or behaving the way they do in their normal daily routine (Maultsy, 1984). The therapist guides them to think about an unpleasant thing that could happen, and to feel upset. Afterward, the therapist directs the survivors to change their feelings to appropriate ones (Ellis & Yeager, 1989). When survivors are able to have appropriate feelings during the situation faced, they can redirect their behavior. The use of rational-emotive imagery several times a week for a few weeks can have a tremendous effect on survivors' ability to manage unpleasant situations (Ellis, 1988).

Role-playing. During the therapeutic session, the therapist can interrupt the survivor and point out what he or she is not doing right and how to achieve an appropriate feeling about himself or herself. The survivor can work to achieve acceptable behavior in a given situation. The aim of this exercise is to help survivors change irrational thoughts, feelings, and behaviors to appropriate ones. Role-playing enables survivors to go through a series of situations in which the therapist directs them to overcome obstacles. This transfers into real life, and it gives survivors the ability and strength to stand tall in unpleasant circumstances.

Use of force and vigor. With this technique, the survivor conveys his or her irrational thoughts and beliefs and strongly denounces them. The therapist can choose to imitate the survivor in these irrational pronouncements, and the survivor then tries to encourage the therapist to let go of these negative thought processes. The use of force and vigor helps survivors to take control and feel that they have the ability to deal with traumatic situations.

Behavioral Techniques

Behavioral techniques encompass a host of related techniques including relaxation techniques, self-management, assertiveness training, desensitization, skill training, modeling, and operant conditioning. In addition, behavioral assignments, which involve real-life circumstances, are also given to clients. These behavioral techniques can help survivors take command of their situation, change negative thought processes, and face traumatic situations squarely. The therapist reinforces progress made by the survivors and helps them to relax, cope with the trauma, and eliminate anxiety.

Meichenbaum's Cognitive Therapy

Aside from REBT techniques and procedures, therapists using CBT also refer to Meichenbaum's cognitive therapy, which focuses on self-verbalization. Self-statements have the same negative effect as statements made by another person (Meichenbaum, 1977). Meichenbaum (1986) proposed that clients need to interrupt the scripted nature of their behavior in order to evaluate their behaviors in situations for the purpose of change. In homicide cases, therapists try to help homicide survivors change their thought processes and behaviors. There are three phases of behavioral change that the therapist can adopt (Meichenbaum, 1986): self-observation, starting a new internal dialogue, and learning new skills.

The self-observation phase enables survivors to observe their own behavior, which before therapy is characterized by negative thoughts and statements. In addition, it helps them be sensitive to their own feelings, actions, and thoughts. In this process, survivors come to see themselves not only as victims but as people who can change their thoughts. Then, in the new internal dialogue phase, they learn new adaptive behaviors. With the help of the therapist, the survivors learn to change their internal dialogue, which promotes desirable behavior. In the learning new skills phase, the therapist teaches the survivors new coping skills to deal with traumatic situations. The survivors practice the new behavior, and this consequently helps them combat the traumatic situation.

Meichenbaum's (1985) stress inoculation program is a coping skill program used to help survivors overcome the trauma surrounding their loss. This procedure involves modifying beliefs and self-statements in stressful situations through information giving, cognitive restructuring, problem solving, relaxation training, self-reinforcement, and self-monitoring. The stress inoculation program has three stages (Meichenbaum, 1985). During the first stage, termed the conceptual phase, both the therapist and the survivors go through the nature of the problem. The survivors become sensitive to the role of cognition and emotion in the creation and maintenance of stress, and become aware of their own contributions to the creation of the stress.

The second stage, the skills-acquisition and rehearsal phase, helps survivors address stressful situations using both behavioral and cognitive coping techniques. The therapist assists the survivors to gather information about their fears and situations that enforce stress, and to find appropriate methods of relaxation such as meditation, yoga, walking, jogging, breath control, and other physical activities. The therapist also helps the survivors change negative self-statements by introducing new self-statements to rehearse. This helps eliminate maladaptive behaviors and thoughts, which are linked to inner dialogue.

The final stage, which is the application and follow-through phase, involves the transition into the real world. The survivors are faced with the task of applying their new skills to real-life situations. The therapist gives them behavioral homework and goes through it in subsequent meetings. The therapist also follows up with the survivors to make sure that they are putting the coping skills into practice.

Summary

Homicide survivors—a group that includes family members, friends, co-workers, schoolmates, and neighbors of homicide victims—go through many traumatic experiences following the murder. Homicide has a dreadful impact on survivors, and there is an urgent need for intervention to enable family members and others to cope successfully. The physical loss of a loved one, financial difficulties, and psychological disorders such as PTSD, depression, anxiety, hopelessness, guilt, and anger can weigh heavily on survivors and might eventually lead to total isolation in the family or the community. Psychological counseling is one way to provide support for survivors. Therapists employ various strategies and methods, including CBT approaches, to help survivors deal with their losses.

Discussion Questions

1. Discuss the psychological, social, and economic impacts of homicide on survivors, such as family members and other relatives.
2. From a therapeutic approach, how can experts assist homicide survivors to cope with the tragic event?
3. Who is a homicide survivor?

References

Aldrich, H., & Kallivayalil, D. (2013). The impact of homicide on survivors and clinicians. *Journal of Loss and Trauma, 18*(4), 362–377.

American Psychiatric Association. (1994). *Diagnostic and statistical manual of mental disorders* (4th ed.). Washington DC: Author.

Amick-McMullan, A., Kilpatrick, D., Veronon, L., & Smith, S. (1989). Family survivors of homicide victims: Theoretical perspectives and an exploratory study. *Journal of Traumatic Stress, 2*, 21–35.

Armour, M. (2003). Meaning making in the aftermath of homicide. *Death Studies, 27*, 519–540

Bard, M., & Sangrey, D. (1979). *The crime victims book*. New York: Basic Books.

Beck, A. T. (1993). Cognitive therapy: Past, present, and future. *Journal of Consulting and Clinical Psychology, 61*, 194–198.

Beck, J. S. (1995). *Cognitive therapy: Basics and beyond*. New York: Guillard.

Blum, H. (2003). Psychic trauma and traumatic object loss. *Journal of the American Psychoanalytic Association, 51*, 415–431.

Boss, P. G. (2002). Ambiguous loss: Working with families of the missing. *Family Process, 41*, 14–17.

Campbell, R. (2001). Mental health services for rape survivors: Current issues in therapeutic practice. *Violence against women online resources*. Available from: http://www. mincava. umn. edu/documents/commissioned/campbell/campbell. html. [24.6.2011].

Cooper, A., & Smith, E. L. (2012). *Homicide trends in the United States, 1980–2008*. Washington, DC: BiblioGov.

Day, S. X. (2008). *Theory and design in counseling and psychotherapy* (2nd ed.). Boston: Houghton Mifflin.

Doka, K. (2002). *Disenfranchised grief*. Champaign, IL: Research Press.

Ellis, A. (1955). What is REBT? Available from: http://rebtnetwork.org/[10.4.2016]

Ellis, A. (1988). *How to stubbornly refuse to make yourself miserable about anything—Yes, anything!* Secaucus, NJ: Lyle Stuart.

Ellis, A. (1994). *Reason and emotion in psychotherapy: A comprehensive method of treating human disturbances.* New York: Kensington.

Ellis, A., & Yeager, R. J. (1989). *Why some therapies don't work.* Buffalo, NY: Prometheus Books.

Erickson, K. (1976). *Everything in its path, destruction of community in the Buffalo Creek flood.* New York: Simon and Schuster.

Foa, E. B., Davidson, Frances, J. R. T., Culpepper, L., Ross, R., & Ross, D. (Eds.). (1999).The expert of consensus guideline series: Treatment of posttraumatic stress disorder. *Journal of Clinical Psychiatry, 60,* 4–76.

Gerber, F. S. (1995). The relationship of posttraumatic stress disorder and grief in family survivors of homicide victims. *Dissertation Abstract International, 56,* 28–64.

Glasser, W. (2000). *Reality therapy in action.* New York: Harper Collins.

Granvold, D. K. (Ed.). (1994). *Cognitive and behavioral treatment: Method and applications.* Pacific Grove, CA: Brooks/Cole.

Green, B. L. (2000). Traumatic loss: Conceptual and empirical links between trauma and bereavement. *Journal of Personal & Interpersonal Loss, 5*(1), 1–17.

Hatton, R. (2003). Homicide bereavement counseling: A survey of provider. *Death Studies, 27,* 427–448.

Kenny, J.S. (2003). Gender roles and grief cycles: Observations on models of grief and coping in homicide cases. *International Review of Victimology, 10,* 19–47.

Maultsy, M. C., Jr. (1984). *Rational behavior therapy.* Englewood Cliffs, NJ: Prentice-Hall.

McFarlane, A. C., Atchison, M., Rafalowicz, E., & Papay, P. (1994). Physical symptoms in posttraumatic stress disorder. *Journal of Psychosomatic Research, 38,* 715–726.

McDevitt-Murphy, M. E., Neimeyer, R. A., Burke, L. A., Williams, J. L., & Lawson, K. (2012). The toll of traumatic loss in African Americans bereaved by homicide. *Psychological Trauma: Theory, Research, Practice, and Policy, 4*(3), 303.

Meichenbaum, D. (1977). *Cognitive and behavior modification: An integrative approach.* New York: Plenum.

Meichenbaum, D. (1985). *Stress inoculation training.* New York: Pergamon Press.

Meichenbaum, D. (1986). Cognitive and behavior modification. In F.H. Kanfer & A.P. Goldstein (Eds.), *Helping people change: A textbook of methods* (pp. 346–380). New York: Pergamon Press.

Miller, L., & Schlesinger, L. B. (2000). Survivors, families, and co-victims of serial offenders. In L. B. Schlesinger (Ed.), *Serial offenders: Current thought, recent findings, unusual syndromes* (pp. 309–334). Boca Raton, FL: CRC Press.

Murphy, S. A., Braun, T., Tillery, L., Cain, K. C., Johnson, L. C., & Beaton, R. D. (1999). PTSD among bereaved parents following the violent deaths of their 12–18 year old children: A longitudinal prospective analysis. *Journal of Traumatic Stress, 12,* 273–29.

Neimeyer, R. A. (2006). Complicated grief and the reconstruction of meaning: Grief therapy and the process of reconstruction. *Death Studies, 24,* 541–550.

Neimeyer, R. A., & Jordan, J. R. (2002). Disenfranchisement as empathic failure. In K. Doka (Ed.), *Disenfranchised grief: New directions, challenges, and strategies for practice* (pp. 95–117). San Francisco: Jossey-Bass.

Neimeyer, R. A., Prigerson, H. G., & Davies, B. (2002). Mourning and meaning. *American Behavioral Scientist, 46,* 235–251.

Prigerson, H. G., Bierhals, A. J., Stanislav, V. K., Raynolds, C. F., Shear, M. K., Day, N., Beery, L. C., Newsom, J. T., & Jacobs, S. (1997). Traumatic grief as a risk factor for mental and physical morbidity. *American Journal of Psychiatry, 154,* 616–623.

Rando, T. A. (1993), *Treatment of complicated mourning.* Champaign, IL: Research Press.

Redmond, L. (1989). *Surviving: When someone you love was murdered.* Clearwater, FL: Psychological Consultation and Educational Services.

Reineke, M., Dattilio, F. M., & Freeman, A. (Eds). (1995). *Casebook of cognitive behavior therapy with children and adolescents.* New York: Guilford Press.

Resick, P. A., Nishith, P., Weaver, T. L., Astin, M. C., & Feuer, C. A. (2002). A comparison of cognitive-processing therapy with prolonged exposure and a waiting condition for the treatment of chronic post-traumatic stress disorder in female rape victims. *Journal of Consulting & Clinical Psychology, 70,* 867–879.

Rynearson, E. K. (1988). The homicide of a child. In F. M. Ochberg (Ed.), *Post-traumatic therapy and victims of violence* (pp. 213–224). New York: Brunner/Mazel.

Rynearson, E. K. (1994). Psychotherapy of bereavement after homicide. *Journal of Psychotherapy Practice and Research, 3,* 341–347.

Rynearson, E. K. & McCreery J. M. (1993). Bereavement after homicide: A synergism of trauma and loss. *American Journal of Psychiatry, 150,* 258–261.

Schlosser, E. (1997). A grief like no other. *Atlantic Monthly*, September, pp. 37–76.
Sheehan, P. L. (1991). Critical incident trauma and intimacy. In J. T. Reese, J. M. Horn, & C. Dunning (Eds.), *Critical incidents in policing* (pp. 331–334). Washington, DC: Federal Bureau of Investigation.
Sprang, G., & McNeil, J. (1995). *The many faces of bereavement: The nature and treatment of natural, traumatic, and stigmatized grief.* New York: Brunner/Mazel.
Spungen, D, (1998). *Homicide: The hidden victims: A guide for professionals*. Thousand Oaks, CA: Sage Publications, Inc.
Thompson, M., Norris, F., Ruback, B. (1998). Comparative distress levels of inner-city family members of homicide victims. *ISTSS*, *11*(2), 223–242.
Violanti, J. M. (2000). Scripting trauma: The impact of pathogenic intervention. In J. Violanti, D. Paton & C. Dunning (Eds.), *Posttraumatic stress intervention: Challenges, issues, and perspectives* (pp. 153–165). Boca Raton, FL: Charles C. Thomas.
Warren, R., & McLellarn, R. W. (1987). What do RET therapists think they are doing? An international survey. *Journal of Rational-Emotive Therapy*, *5*(2), 92–107.
Warshaw, C., Sullivan, C. M., & Rivera, E. A. (2013). *A systematic review of trauma-focused interventions for domestic violence survivors*. National Center on Domestic Violence, Trauma & Mental Health.
Weiner, H. (1992). *Perturbing the organism: The biology of stressful experience*. Chicago: University of Chicago Press.

11

MEMBERS OF THE LGBT COMMUNITY AS VICTIMS OF CRIME

David P. Weiss

Keywords

LGBT; hate crime(s); youth; transgender; sexual orientation; gender identity

Objectives

After studying this chapter, the reader should understand:

- The prevalence of victimization that members of the LGBT community face.
- The impact such crimes have on the members of the LGBT community.
- The systemic barriers and challenges faced by members of the LGBT community as victims of crime, including the three criminal justice subsystems of cops, courts, and corrections.
- The legal rights, protections, and recourses available to LGBT crime victims.
- Resources and services offered to LGBT crime victims.

Introduction

Members of the lesbian, gay, bisexual, and transgender (LGBT) community are exposed to criminal victimization just like all members of the broader community, yet have the added risk of being victims of hate crimes, too. Criminal victimization issues for the LGBT community can become even more complex, depending upon whether one's identity is linked to the victimization, and, if so, if it's based on one's sexual orientation (i.e., lesbian, gay, bisexual) or gender identity (i.e., transgender or gender nonconforming). In many cases, the crime committed has no connection to the victim's LGBT identity, such as a residential burglary while the victim is at work, while in too many other victimizations the crime committed is based solely on the victim's LGBT identity, thereby ostensibly making it a potential hate crime (depending upon how a particular state delineates the elements of a hate crime). Further, other crimes, such as same-sex interpersonal violence determined by police to be domestic violence based upon the relationship between the perpetrator and victim, may directly involve members of the LGBT community, yet the victim's sexual orientation or gender identity is secondary or simply not germane to the crime itself. In other words, police should, in theory, treat the crime of domestic violence the same whether the couple is straight or gay, cisgender or transgender.

Given these various complexities (recognizing only a few of the obvious ones), identifying, measuring, and responding to criminal victimizations for members of the LGBT community becomes fraught with challenges. Further, while society has continued to make great strides in the acceptance of, and rights for, members of the LGBT community, individual attitudinal hurdles and bureaucratic-institutional hurdles of bias remain within the criminal justice system.

Yet, all of this begets several questions: How does one begin to comprehend the impact of criminal victimization on the LGBT community? Should we concern ourselves *only* with hate crimes? Should we attempt to respond to LGBT victims of *all* different types of crime, even if one's sexual orientation or gender identity is secondary to the victimization? And what of those LGBT victims who are unwilling to self-identify as LGBT for fear of being outed, "read," or victimized again due to further bias or discrimination? While all of these challenges cannot be adequately addressed in one reference book chapter, creating awareness of these challenges, while exploring the fundamentals of LGBT victimization (hate crime or otherwise), is both right and proper in advancing justice and providing services for LGBT victims of crime.

Historical Context

According to Quinn and Brightman (2015, 10), the study of the crime victim came about in the 1920s because of the burgeoning awareness of the lack of attention paid to such victims, with the term "victimology" coined by Benjamin Mendelsohn, a lawyer, in 1947. Further, in 1980, Quinn and Brightman note that "Wisconsin was the first state to enact a crime victims' bill of rights" (2015, 186), and, in 1981, was also the first state to pass hate crime legislation in the U.S. (2015, 162), while California established the first monetary compensation program for victims of crime in 1965 (2015, 197). At the federal level, White House recognition of crime victims gained momentum in the early 1980s, with passage of the Victims of Crime Act (VOCA) in 1984, and eventual establishment of the federal Office for Victims of Crime (OVC) under the umbrella of the U.S. Department of Justice.

Official collection and recording of hate crime data across the United States came about in the 1990s. According to the FBI's website,

> On April 23, 1990, Congress passed the Hate Crime Statistics Act. . .which required the Attorney General to collect data "about crimes that manifest evidence of prejudice based on race, religion, sexual orientation, or ethnicity." The Attorney General delegated the responsibilities of developing the procedures for implementing, collecting, and managing hate crime data to the Director of the FBI, who, in turn, assigned the tasks to the Uniform Crime Reporting (UCR) Program. Under the direction of the Attorney General and with the cooperation and assistance of many local and state law enforcement agencies, the UCR Program created a hate crime data collection to comply with the congressional mandate.
>
> *(www.fbi.gov/about-us/cjis/ucr/hate-crime/2014/resource-pages/about-hate-crime)*

The Hate Crime Statistics Act was amended at various times since its passage in 1990 to include bias against persons with disabilities, as well as amended to include the collection of data for crimes motivated by bias against a particular gender or gender identity; collection of the gender and gender identity bias data did not begin by the FBI until 2013 (www.fbi.gov/about-us/cjis/ucr/hate-crime/2014/resource-pages/about-hate-crime).

Review of the Literature

An abbreviated review with regard to criminal victimization of members of the LGBT community found the literature divided into five main categories: 1) literature focused on specific crimes, particularly same-sex domestic violence or intimate partner violence; 2) special populations, such as transgender and gender nonconforming individuals, our youth, including homeless and incarcerated youth, and sex workers; 3) writings on the various institutions of the criminal justice system, especially with regard to the two subsystems of policing and institutional corrections (with very little on the criminal courts or the court process); 4) hate crime laws and other applicable legal matters; and, 5) theoretical explanations of LGBT victimization, or, conversely, perpetrator-defense theories.

First, over the past few decades, much has been written on the issue of domestic violence, now more broadly referred to as intimate partner violence. While terms such as spousal abuse and domestic violence were originally intended for heterosexual couples in traditional marriages, with the male as perpetrator and the female as victim, today's terminology of intimate partner violence, or IPV for short, more broadly encompasses straight, gay, lesbian and bisexual couples, trans men, trans women and gender nonconforming persons, those both married and unmarried, and couples either living together or living separately and in an intimate relationship. Further, IPV is also more inclusive in terms of victimizing behaviors other than physical abuse or assault, including such victimizations as sexual assault, emotional and verbal abuse. Additionally, according to the Council on Crime and Justice's website, while the literature throughout the 1980s and into the 1990s was focused primarily on straight couples, the past dozen years or so have seen an increase in the inclusion of nontraditional couples in the IPV literature (www.crimeandjustice.org/councilinfo.cfm?pID=60). Messinger also conducts a comprehensive review of the same-sex IPV literature over the past 35 years, but notes that greater scholarship is needed in this area for sexual minorities outside of the LGB communities, as well as expanding the scholarship to other international countries (Messinger 2014, 78–9).

Second, there are what could be considered "special populations" when exploring crime victimization within the LGBT community. Such populations are special in the sense that their challenges as crime victims are unique even among the LGBT community itself.

Most recently, social and news media have focused on the plight of members of the transgender community as they struggle for equality in everything from the use of public restrooms to housing, employment, and serving in the military. Gender nonconforming individuals, too, are caught up in reports of perceived "gay bashing," when, in fact, such identity formation themes center on issues of gender and not that of sexual orientation. In looking at these challenges for the transgender and gender nonconforming community, Perry and Dyck (2014) focus their research on trans women's experiences of violence, while Buist and Stone (2014) write about the failures of the criminal justice system for transgender victims and offenders alike. Further, Witten and Eyler (1999) take on the early research of hate crimes and violence against transgender males and females, while Forbes (2014) surveys recent legal outcomes for transgender individuals in the U.S. Yet, with the bellicose political hyperbole continuing at the state and local levels of government over the proper use of public restrooms for transgender women and men, one can anticipate that the struggle for victims' rights for these much-maligned individuals will be continued far into the future.

Other special populations of crime victims within the LGBT community include incarcerated youth (Belknap *et al.* 2014), homeless young people (Frederick 2014, 477–81), and sex workers, both home (Saunders and Kirby 2010) and abroad (Nichols 2014). Additionally, there is a substantive body of literature concentrated generally on LGBT youth as victims of crime (Dwyer 2014b), while also focused on specific victimization matters such as homophobic bullying (Hobson 2012; Warbelow and Cobb 2014), criminal victimizations involving transgender young people (Dwyer 2011), adolescent experiences of violence in LGB romantic attraction (Russell *et al.* 2001), and youth dating violence and mental health (Gillum and DiFulvio 2014).

Third, the literature on the various institutions and subsystems of the criminal justice system with regard to LGBT victims of crime is rather disparate, with especially voluminous scholarship on police and policing institutions (Lyons *et al.* 2005; Miles-Johnson 2013; Johnson 2014; Dwyer 2014a; Colvin 2014), and a literature on prisons and larger jail systems (Dolovich 2012), yet little scholarship on the courts or the daunting legal process faced by LGBT victims of crime. Additionally, more narrowly defined topics were also addressed in the literature, such as police working with victims of same-sex domestic violence (Tesch *et al.* 2010), or transgender correctional policy (Sumner and Jenness 2014). Another division of this literature took a broader systems approach in studying the intersection of the LGBT community with the criminal justice system (Mogul, Ritchie and Whitlock 2011; Noga-Styron, Reasons and Peacock 2012). Yet, as noted above, a lacuna in the literature exists when it comes to LGBT victims of crime intersecting with the adult criminal courts and the convoluted court system. Navigating this subsystem is difficult enough for most folks, but members of the LGBT community may find the criminal legal process so intimidating and complex as to be an institutional and bureaucratic barrier to seeing justice served.

Fourth, the literature on hate crime victimizations and hate crime laws runs the gamut from an early look at these topics (Herek and Berrill 1992; Jenness 1995) to a more recent twenty-first-century review (Rose and Mechanic 2002; Rayburn and Davison 2002; Dunbar 2006; Chakraborti 2010; Stotzer 2014). Additionally, many national advocacy groups, such as the National LGBTQ Task Force, as well as Human Rights Campaign (to name just two of the larger national organizations), publish numerous online pieces on a regular basis addressing issues of LGBT victimization from bias crimes, as well as publish online articles addressing the current state of legal affairs throughout all 50 states and also at the federal level. Of particular interest are two journal articles published in 2007 and 2014. Woods, writing in 2007, argued for expansion of federal hate crime legislation to include gender identity and sexual orientation. In fact, President Obama did just that on October 28, 2009 (www.cnn.com/2009/POLITICS/10/28/hate.crimes/). Yet, Meyer, writing in 2014, argued that such expansion of hate crime laws have only added to police and prosecutorial powers, thereby aiding in the burgeoning of incarcerated individuals and further reinforcing race and social class inequalities.

Fifth, and last, many of the theoretical explanations of criminal victimization against members of the LGBT community focus primarily on the perpetrator. Tejeda (2004) explores the notions of sex-role egalitarianism and self-esteem as correlated to anti-gay/lesbian hatred, while Tilleman (2009) takes on the provocation defense theory. Further, Reasons and Hughson (2000) take on the homosexual panic defense theory, while Mison (1992) and Smyth (2006) explicate the theory of the homosexual advance defense. Additionally, Cramer *et al.* (2013) look at perpetrator blame attribution theory, while it should also be noted that early feminist theory, emanating out of critical criminology, studied victimization against lesbians and trans women (Woods 2014, 28–9). Yet a broader, more explanatory, look elucidating antigay violence was taken on by Waldner and Berg (2008) using Finkelhor and Asdigian's (1996) revised routine activities theory.

To help better understand youth victimization, Finkelhor and Asdigian (1996) moved beyond lifestyle theory and routine activities theory—two theories that can be construed to embody a level of victim culpability or victim blaming in them—to a revised routine activities theory and target congruence process (in addition to consideration of environmental factors). The authors' revised routine activities theory with target congruence incorporated three specific types of victim characteristics which they believed to be congruent to the deleterious desires of the offender, thereby increasing one's risk of victimization. The three characteristics that make up Finkelhor and Asdigian's offender–victim target congruence process include: 1) target vulnerability, or characteristics that compromise the potential victim's ability to resist or deter victimization; 2) target gratifiability, or characteristics the potential victim possesses that the offender wants to violate; and, 3) target antagonism, or characteristics that the potential victim has that stirs up negative impulses in the offender toward the intended victim (Finkelhor and Asdigian 1996, 6–7).

In their 2008 study, Waldner and Berg apply this revised routine activities theory using target congruence to explain antigay violence and victimization. Succinctly summarizing the theory, the authors state, "Quite simply, offenders need a vulnerable victim that somehow gratifies them and provides an excuse for the [antigay] attack" (Waldner and Berg 2008, 269). In applying the revised routine activities theory, the authors explored various predictors of antigay violence to their three dependent variables of physical assault, sexual assault, and property damage. Such predictors stemmed from the theory's target congruence process and included, among others, potential target vulnerability predictors of public drinking, gay stereotypes, gay identification, and gender; potential target antagonism predictors of being more open or out of the closet; and, potential target gratification predictors of perceived wealth or financial privilege of the victim, as well as establishment of heterosexual credentials among peers by the perpetrator.

Of the acceptable 297 mail-survey respondents, wherein 167 males identified as gay or bisexual and 130 females identified as lesbian or bisexual, the authors found that 49.8 percent of the total sample, or 148 individuals, experienced at least one of the three bias incidents, while 50.1 percent, or 149 individuals, reported having experienced none of the three targeted behaviors. Further, of the half who did experience at least one antigay incident, threat of physical assault or physical assault itself was the most common experience, followed by property damage and then sexual assault. Moreover, of the 148 individuals that experienced antigay victimization, 74 of them reported one type of victimization only, while 54 folks reported experiencing two of the target behaviors, and 20 people reported experiencing all three types of victimizations (Waldner and Berg 2008, 277).

Of the three models used to predict antigay victimization based on Finkelhor and Asdigian's revised routine activities theory, Waldner and Berg found some support for the use of the theory with regard to physical victimization and property damage, while their sexual assault model was not significant. More specifically, individuals who were open about their sexual orientation, those who had greater contact with known gay organizations, and those who drank more frequently to levels of intoxication were at "higher risk of experiencing antigay motivated physical assault" (Waldner and Berg 2008, 278). Similarly, out-of-the-closet individuals and folks who had greater contact with gay or lesbian organizations were also at increased risk of experiencing property damage (Waldner and Berg 2008, 279–80). Yet, even with their study's limited support of revised routine activities theory with regard to physical assault and property damage, Waldner and Berg believe there are tangible, real-world applications for the gay and lesbian community—which is to now say the LGBT community—which may address issues of target vulnerability and, to a lesser degree, target antagonism. For example, beefing up visible police patrols in residential neighborhoods and business districts frequented by members of the LGBT community would help to provide for greater capable guardianship. Reducing alcohol consumption and travelling in groups are two additional suggestions also made by the authors (Waldner and Berg 2008, 283).

In all, Finkelhor and Asdigian's revised routine activities theory, as studied by Waldner and Berg, helps to better understand criminal victimization of members of the LGBT community while keeping the onus of the criminal act squarely on the shoulders of the perpetrators themselves, thereby better thwarting any ill-perceived stance of victim-blaming or victim culpability in such serious acts.

Statistics and Demographics

An online survey of LGBT Americans conducted in 2013 by Pew Research Center found that 30 percent of those surveyed claimed to have been physically attacked or threatened, while nearly 60 percent of those surveyed indicated they were the target of slurs or jokes (www.pewsocialtrends.org/2013/06/13/a-survey-of-lgbt-americans/). Official statistics from the FBI's Hate Crimes Statistics report and the Bureau of Justice Statistics' National Crime Victimization Survey bolster the Pew Research Center's findings.

Hate Crime Statistics

In April 1990, Congress passed the Hate Crime Statistics Act, which required the U.S. Department of Justice to collect information on crimes that "manifest evidence of prejudice based on race, religion, sexual orientation, or ethnicity" (www.fbi.gov/about-us/cjis/ucr/hate-crime/2014/resource-pages/about-hate-crime). The first report was subsequently released on 11 states that collected such data in 1990. The Act has been expanded since its initial passage to now include data on persons with disabilities (1994), and, as amended in 2009, to include hate crimes committed by or perpetrated against juveniles, as well as "the collection of data for crimes motivated by bias against a particular gender and gender identity" (www.fbi.gov/about-us/cjis/ucr/hate-crime/2014/resource-pages/about-hate-crime).

In 2013—the first year for official statistics on crimes based on the victim's gender identity and gender nonconformity—the FBI reported that transgender and gender nonconforming individuals were the targets of 0.5 percent of all reported hate crimes motivated by a single bias. Of the 5,928 hate crime incidents reported by law enforcement agencies nationwide to the FBI, nearly 21 percent were motivated by a victim's sexual orientation. Further, of the 1,402 hate crime offenses based on sexual orientation, nearly 61 percent of those were targeted against gay males. Yet, according to Human Rights Campaign (HRC), a national civil rights organization serving the LGBT community, thousands of law enforcement agencies across the nation did not submit crime data on hate crime incidents targeting transgender and gender nonconforming individuals, with eight of those police agencies serving populations of 100,000 or more residents (www.advocate.com/crime/2014/12/09/us-1-5-reported-hate-crimes-target-gay-or-bi-victims). As such, the national advocacy organization believes that the reported number of hate crime incidents perpetrated against transgender and gender nonconforming folks was low for the reported year.

In 2014, according to the FBI, 15,494 law enforcement agencies from across the nation—out of an estimated 18,000 total law enforcement agencies in the U.S.—participated in the Hate Crime Statistics Program. Of the agencies reporting to the FBI in 2014, "1,666 [law enforcement agencies] reported 5,479 hate crime incidents involving 6,418 offenses" (www.fbi.gov/about-us/cjis/ucr/hate-crime/2014/topic-pages/incidentsandoffenses_final). Law enforcement agencies also reported 1,178 hate crime offenses based on sexual-orientation bias, with gay males being the victim in 58 percent of them. Further, in 2014, there were 40 offenses of gender bias reported, wherein 28 of the victims were female, and the remaining 12 victims were male. As for incidents of gender identity bias, there were 109 offenses committed, with 69 offenses against transgender folks, and 40 offenses perpetrated against victims perceived by the offender as gender nonconforming (www.fbi.gov/about-us/cjis/ucr/hate-crime/2014/topic-pages/victims_final).

While the FBI's Hate Crime Statistics report begins to paint a picture of hate crime victimization across America, the challenge with this data collection system is that reporting by law enforcement agencies is voluntary, as pointed out by HRC. Generally speaking, only approximately 40 percent of all crimes are reported to police, leaving roughly 60 percent of crimes unreported—what is often referred to as the "dark figure of crime." What is believed by many to be a more accurate portrayal of crime victimization across the nation is that of the U.S. Department of Justice Bureau of Justice Statistics' National Crime Victimization Survey, an annual survey of homes across the nation measuring both violent and property victimizations.

National Crime Victimization Survey

Begun in 1973, the Bureau of Justice Statistics' National Crime Victimization Survey (NCVS), under the umbrella of the U.S. Department of Justice, is another official governmental source of criminal victimization measurement of nonfatal crimes across the country, both reported and unreported to law enforcement agencies. Annual data collection is conducted by the U.S. Census Bureau for the Bureau of Justice Statistics from a nationally representative sample of households across the nation on individuals aged 12 or older. Criminal victimization data is collected on all nonfatal personal crimes and property crimes which may or may not have been reported to police. Because this is survey data that gets to the "dark figure" of unreported crime to the police, NCVS tends to show higher volumes of criminal victimization across the U.S. than does the FBI's annual Uniform Crime Reporting Program.

In November of 2005, the Bureau of Justice Statistics (BJS) published a special report titled "Hate Crime Reported by Victims and Police" wherein BJS used self-reported NCVS survey data from July of 2000 through December of 2003, and also from police reports provided by law enforcement agencies to the FBI's Uniform Crime Reporting Program in 2002, to describe the characteristics of hate crimes. With regard to members of the LGB community, the special report found that approximately 18 percent of all hate crime victimizations during the reported period of time were motivated by perpetrator's perception of the victim's sexual orientation (www.bjs.gov/content/pub/pdf/hcrvp.pdf).

Another special report published in March of 2013 by BJS on hate crime victimizations spanned the years of 2003 through 2011. This report found that U.S. residents experienced just shy of 260,000 hate crimes annually between 2007 and 2011, and further reported for that, for the same time-period, 65 percent of all hate crime victimizations went unreported to law enforcement agencies. Reasons for non-reporting included rationales such as: police could not or would not help (24 percent); the victimization was dealt with another way or was believed to be a private or personal matter (23 percent); other unspecified reasons given (20 percent); it was believed to be not important enough to report or there was no insurance gain from reporting (18 percent); and, finally, the victim was afraid of reprisal, did not want to get the offender in trouble, or was advised not to report the hate crime to police (15 percent). The typology of victims of violent hate crimes from 2007 through 2011 was that of male (61 percent), white (65 percent), between the ages of 12 and 17 (23 percent), with a household income of less than $25,000 (31 percent) (www.bjs.gov/content/pub/pdf/hcv0311.pdf).

The most recent BJS report on hate crime victimizations was released in February of 2014, covering the years 2004 through 2012. This most recent report estimated that nearly 294,000 hate crime victimizations involving both violent and property crimes occurred in 2012 against individuals aged 12 and older throughout the country. Further, the percentage of hate crimes motived by gender bias doubled from 12 percent in 2004 to 26 percent in 2012, while the percentage of violent hate crimes increased from 78 percent in 2004 to 90 percent in 2012. Additionally for 2012, approximately 60 percent of hate crimes were not reported to law enforcement agencies. In all, hate crime victimizations accounted for 1.2 percent of all victimizations in 2012, 4.2 percent of violent victimizations, and less than 1 percent of property victimizations (www.bjs.gov/content/pub/pdf/hcv0412st.pdf).

Of particular interest are the trends of victimization based on sexual orientation and gender (or, rather, victims' perceptions of offender bias with regard to these two hate crime characteristics) when comparing 2012 with 2004. Criminal victimization based on sexual orientation decreased to 13 percent in 2012 from 22 percent in 2004, while criminal victimization based on gender increased to 26 percent in 2012 from 12 percent in 2004 (www.bjs.gov/content/pub/pdf/hcv0412st.pdf). While it is unwise to draw broad conclusions based on these victim characteristics for only one period of time, it does appears at first glance that members of the LGB community may have become safer, or at less victimized, while women, transgender, and gender nonconforming individuals were at higher risk of hate crime victimization over more recent years.

Although comparisons between hate crime victimization data reported by police agencies to the FBI and survey data produced by BJS is difficult, both forms of official governmental reporting clearly demonstrate the breadth and depth of criminal victimization against members of the LGBT community. Moreover, who these LGBT crime victims are, how they navigate the criminal justice system, what legal protections they are afforded, and what resources might be available to them as victims of crime are all topics to be addressed in the remainder of this chapter.

Special Populations of Victims within the LGBT Community

To refer to the LGBT community in the singular is a bit of a misnomer. Rather, it is made up of several communities—plural—including, but not limited to, the broader LGBTQ community ("Q" for those who identify as queer), the LGB community (based on sexual orientation), the transgender and gender nonconforming community (based on gender and gender identity), the elderly, those incarcerated, sex workers, those who are homeless, and our youth. However individuals might identify, all of these communities are especially vulnerable to being criminally victimized, preyed upon, or having a violent hate crime committed upon them.

While it is beyond the scope of this chapter to address all of the aforementioned LGBT communities, a significant public and scholastic focus has been placed on LGBT youth who also find themselves traversing several of these worlds, including being homeless, being incarcerated, or forced into sex work for the sole sake of survival.

LGBT Youth

Even though society as a whole is becoming far more accepting of LBGT individuals, several members of that community still suffer from homophobia, bigotry, bullying, hate crimes, other criminal victimizations, challenges in employment and housing, and the loss of love and support from family members. LGBT youth especially are at risk for a myriad of difficulties, including being kicked out of their house and the resulting homelessness, bullying in school, use of drugs and alcohol as a response to peer pressure or as a coping mechanism, mental health issues, suicidal ideations, attempts, or suicide itself, and being subjected to acts of physical or sexual victimization and other criminal violence.

In a longitudinal Dutch cohort study involving 1,738 respondents focusing on the differences in symptoms of depression between heterosexual youth and LGB youth, Roi *et al.* (2016) acknowledge that LGB youth have greater levels of depressive symptoms when compared with their heterosexual youth counterparts (Marshal *et al.* 2011; Wang *et al.* 2014), and examine how these differences develop in both straight and LGB youth from late childhood to early adulthood (Roi *et al.* 2016). The authors found that lesbian and bisexual youth were especially at risk for greater symptoms of depression, based, in part, on peer victimization and parental rejection (Roi *et al.* 2016, 453). Additionally, Anita Hobson of the Centre for Crime and Justice Studies out of London looked at the issue of homophobic bullying in schools and noted that even the straightforward, non-bullying use of the word "gay" by students and peers as a pejorative—meaning to refer to something as bad, dumb, stupid or awkward—promoted undesirable feelings of isolation and fear for LBG youth (Hobson 2012, 6). Further, a 2001 study by Russell *et al.* found that, when compared with their heterosexual youth counterparts, LGB youth are at higher risk for being jumped or attacked and/or for being in physically dangerous fights (Russell *et al.* 2001, 905). Finally, with regard to greater risks faced by LGBT youth, Newcomb *et al.* (2012) noted in their longitudinal study of LGBT youth that said youth are at an increased risk for improper use of alcohol, with further results showing that drinking increased significantly over time for such youth, with said increase growing more rapidly among male LGBT youth when compared to their youthful female counterparts. Psychological distress and sexual orientation-based victimization were associated with increased use of alcohol for youthful lesbians, while perceived family support was associated with increased alcohol use of all LGBT youth (Newcomb *et al.* 2012).

When it comes to LGBT youth and victimization (criminal or otherwise), Button (2016), in her study of 484 lesbian, gay, bisexual and queer youth, observed that criminal victimization for these youth reliably predicted negative outcomes such as poor academic performance, substance use, and suicidality (Button 2016). D'Augelli *et al.* (2006) explored the intersection of gender identity/conformity and sexual orientation with verbal, physical, and sexual victimization in 528 LGB youth. Of these young people, 80 percent experienced verbal victimization, 11 percent physical victimization, and 9 percent sexual victimization, with youthful males reporting significantly more victimization overall. Youth who were perceived as gender nonconforming reported greater levels of victimization and struggled with mental health issues. Moreover, post-traumatic stress disorder, or PTSD, was found in 9 percent of the LGB youth, which was associated with past physical victimization (D'Augelli *et al.* 2006, 1462).

Although there are many communities or special populations that live under the broader umbrella of the LGBT community, our LGBT youth may especially be susceptible to criminal victimization due to their age, vulnerability, lack of brain development, isolation, and a shortage or absence of financial, social, familial, or emotional support. Furthermore, because of these various vulnerabilities, assistance, help or intervention from the criminal justice system in addressing the criminal victimizations of our LGBT youth may be slow in coming—or, sadly, nonexistent altogether.

Barriers and Challenges Facing LGBT Victims of Crime

As for all victims of crime, navigating the criminal justice system is more manageably understood when the larger, often-overwhelming system is deconstructed into its three subsystems of cops, courts, and corrections. However, unlike many other victims of crime, members of the LGBT community who are thrust into the bureaucracy and complexity of the criminal justice system can face additional daunting challenges unique to them.

Cops

As noted at the start of this chapter, less than half of all crime is reported to police—ominously referred to as the "dark figure of crime." Further, according to the U.S. Justice Department's Bureau of Justice Statistics, 65 percent of all hate crimes from 2007 through 2011 went unreported to law enforcement agencies across the U.S. For a myriad of reasons, it appears that crime victims across the board are hesitant to report their criminal victimizations to police authorities.

Yet, in an effort to assist LGBT victims of crime move toward a minimal level of comfort in reporting their criminal victimizations, starting with the point of entry into the criminal justice system—which is to say our cops—is key. However, as Dwyer points out, "the history of police interactions with LGBT communities is one fraught with contradiction and tension" (Dwyer 2014a, 150), and that recent progress in community relations between police and the LGBT community "cannot be categorized as linear historical progress towards a more liberated, productive end point" (Dwyer 2014a, 158). In short, more work is to be done.

In a survey of 134 lesbian and gay police officers, Colvin (2014) noted that "cultural competence for officers and good police skills—regardless of sexual orientation—are the most important factors for being an effective officer" (Colvin 2014, 183). Although Colvin's study was focused on the philosophy and techniques of community policing, the broad findings of "cultural competence" and "good police skills" for effective policing may be applicable to the LGBT community, too, and, as such, its victims of crime.

Yet, in implementing community policing across the U.S., Weiss (2010) found that more than just training and resources are needed for its successful implementation. Over and above the elements of training and resources, effective leadership, officer accountability, and meeting community expectations were paramount in the successful implementation of community policing.

Taken together, these ingredients—cultural competence, good policing skills, effective police leadership, officer accountability, and the meeting of community expectations—may pave the way for greater victimization reporting and involvement in the criminal justice system by members of the LGBT community.

Courts

Little has been written on the adult criminal court experiences of LGBT victims of crime. However, for most victims of crime who have formally engaged the criminal justice system, the adult criminal court process is a confusing labyrinth of courthouse security procedures, door after door of courtrooms and offices, stodgy uniformed personnel, robed judges, well-heeled attorneys, other criminal justice system professionals, indecipherable legal jargon bandied about, and, oftentimes, the setting of future court dates for unknown reasons or for unfamiliar hearings—all of it immensely intimidating for a crime victim.

Yet, a well-trained and well-prepared victim advocate from a nonprofit agency or from a victim-witness assistance program based out of the prosecutor's office can go a long way in helping the crime victim navigate the criminal court process. Such advocates can help victims of crime locate much-needed resources, such as medical assistance, lodging, clothing, or even short-tern financial help; they can help the survivor write a victim impact statement; they can explain what took place at a court hearing and interpret the legalese used in the courtroom; and, they can inform the victim of future court dates and the necessity of being present at important future court hearings.

More specific to LGBT victims of crime, including hate crimes perpetrated against such individuals, having a victim advocate who is either a member of the LGBT community or who is very familiar with resources in that community could go a long way in putting such victims of crime at ease throughout the criminal court process.

Corrections

While there is a body of literature on LGBT offenders and their interactions with the institutional and community corrections subsystems (Dolovich 2012; Stohr 2015; Sumner and Jenness 2014), little has been written on LGBT victims of crime and their interactions with those same two corrections subsystems.

When it comes to correctional institutions, whether at the level of city and county jails or state and federal prisons, crime victims have a right to know where their perpetrator is geographically located, when he or she is moved, and the new location of the offender's institution. Additionally, if the offender has an opportunity to be released on pre-trial supervision (pre-plea or before a finding of guilt), probation (after serving time in jail as a condition of probation), or parole (upon serving one's prison sentence), the victim has a right to that information, too, as well as to the offender's conditions of release and any stay-away orders. Because the victim's safety is paramount, such basic offender information—location of incarceration, anticipated release date, and conditions of release—is absolutely necessary in helping to ensure the victim's safety, the victim's sense of well-being, and any hope of being made whole.

Further, while the release of an offender back into the community may provide him or her with greater opportunities for rehabilitation, employment, and a pro-social change in behavior, such release of one's offender back into the community can heighten concerns of personal safety and bring about a greater sense of anxiety for the victim. Establishing and maintaining ongoing communications with the community supervision officer is essential. Moreover, if the offender has completed the carceral portion of his or her sentence, the crime victim can reasonably expect payment by the offender toward restitution in the criminal case, if ordered by the court. Victim-offender remediation programs, too, can be accessed in the community, assuming, of course, both parties enter into such a restorative program under their own volition.

As noted in the sections above, having an open or out member of the LGBT community assist an LGBT victim of crime can put such a crime victim at ease, not only at the individual level of interacting with the criminal justice system and its three subsystems, but also at the greater institutional level, thereby helping to restore LGBT crime victims' sense of trust and legitimacy in the broader institutions of a seemingly unwieldy criminal justice system.

Legal Protections, Rights, Recourses, and Resources

Although entire volumes have been, and can continue to be, published on the quickly changing legal landscape impacting the LGBT community, this section provides a cursory overview of the legal protections, rights, recourses, and resources for LGBT victims of crime, both at the federal level and throughout the various states. Although the focus of LGBT victims of crime tends to be on hate crimes committed throughout the country, as well as on crimes of interpersonal violence and sexual assault, such legal protections can be applied to all crimes committed against members of the LGBT community.

Five stellar national sources that provide legal, policy, advocacy, and other educational information in layman's terms to members of the LGBT community include: The Williams Institute, a think tank housed within U.C. Berkeley's School of Law; Human Rights Campaign (HRC), an LGBTQ civil rights organization based in Washington, D.C.; National LGBTQ Task Force, an advocacy group also located in Washington, D.C.; Lambda Legal Defense and Education Fund, a civil rights organization headquartered in New York City; and, the Matthew Shepard Foundation, a national outreach and advocacy foundation based on the life and death of 21-year-old hate crime victim Matthew Shepard, located in Denver, CO.

Legal Protections, Rights, and Recourses

With the Matthew Shepard and James Byrd, Jr., Hate Crimes Prevention Act of 2009 signed into federal law by President Obama on October 28, 2009, the FBI was given authorization to investigate federal hate crimes against the LGBT community based on perceived sexual orientation and gender identity or expression. According to the Matthew Shepard Foundation website, from the Act's passage in 2009 through year-end 2013, the U.S. Department of Justice reported that "44 people in 16 states had been convicted under the Shepard-Byrd Act" (www.matthewshepard.org/blog/sixth-anniversary-shepard-byrd-act/).

At the state level, according to the Anti-Defamation League's website, as of August 2015, five states were still without any hate crime legislation whatsoever, including Arkansas, Georgia, Indiana, South Carolina, and Wyoming.

Yet, within the adult criminal court system itself, all victims of crime are entitled to restitution, if ordered by the judge in the case, and also access to the state's victim assistance program. Additionally, restorative justice programs can strive to make the victim and the community whole again, with the potential for civil legal action should the criminal court not properly or fully address victim loss in a criminal case.

Resources and Services for LGBT Victims of Crime

At the federal level, assistance and services to victims of federal crimes can be accessed and addressed through the U.S. Attorney's Office which has jurisdiction over prosecuting the federal crime. As such, victims of federal crimes have the full weight of the federal Victims' Rights and Restitution Act behind them, as well as access to the Federal Crime Victim Assistance Fund and the federal Crime Victims' Rights Ombudsman.

Further, each state has established some form of a crime victim assistance or victim compensation program, providing financial assistance and other tangible support both directly to victims of crimes and to governmental and nonprofit agencies who serve crime victims.

In addition to victim services at the federal and state levels of government, many private organizations and nonprofit agencies also serve victims of crime. Specific to the LGBT community, larger cities have LGBT community centers that can be a wealth of information and assistance to members of the LGBT community who have suffered criminal victimization.

Summary

Like all residents of our broader society, members of the lesbian, gay, bisexual, and transgender community are exposed to criminal victimization, too, yet such victimizations have the potential to carry a greater level of complexity based on the victim's sexual orientation, gender identity, or gender expression. Now, however, through passage of seminal federal hate crime legislation in both 1990 and 2009, victimologists and criminal justice system professionals have a clearer understanding of the breadth and depth of criminal victimization perpetrated against the LGBT community. Further, more recent theories of victimization, such as Finkelhor and Asdigian's revised routine activities theory, help us to better comprehend and respond to hate crimes committed against the LGBT community.

Yet, even with recent developments in the expansion of rights for LGBT individuals, such as marriage equality, and even with society's overall greater acceptance and support of the LGBT community, LGBT individuals still continue to be targeted for criminal victimization, as was tragically demonstrated at the Pulse nightclub in Orlando, Florida, on June 12, 2016, with the slaughter of 49 innocent individuals. Providing for a proper response for these and other criminal victimizations against members of the LGBT community, both within the criminal justice system and also in our broader community, is imperative. Tearing down the last vestiges of the criminal justice system's institutional and attitudinal barriers, while providing for the legal, educational, and, when appropriate, financial support of these crime victims through governmental agencies and community-based organizations, must become and remain a priority for all professionals working in the criminal justice system, as well as for today's victimologists.

Discussion Questions

1. Why might it be important to differentiate between violent and serious crimes in general, hates crimes, and, more specifically, hate crimes which target members of the LGBT community?
2. How does Finkelhor and Asdigian's revised routine activities theory help us better understand criminal victimization in the LBGT community?
3. What is the "dark figure of crime?" How is it applicable to LGBT victims of crime, and why should criminal justice professionals be concerned about it?
4. Why are LGBT youth especially at risk for criminal victimization?
5. What barriers or challenges do members of the LGBT community face as crime victims when working with police, the criminal court system, and institutional or community correctional agencies?

6. Describe the Hate Crime Statistics Act of 1990 and the Matthew Shepard and James Byrd, Jr., Hate Crimes Prevention Act of 2009 and discuss the impacts these Acts have had on identifying LGBT victims of crime. What is transpiring at the state level with regard to hate crime legislation?
7. What are some national and local organizations, either governmental or nonprofit, that assist LGBT victims of crime? What types of resources are available to LGBT crime victims through these agencies or organizations?

References

Belknap, J., K. Holsinger, and J. S. Little. 2014. "Lesbian, Gay, and Bisexual Youth Incarcerated in Delinquent Facilities." In *Handbook of LGBT Communities, Crime, and Justice*, edited by D. Peterson and V.R. Panfil, 207–228. New York: Springer.

Buist, C. L., and C. Stone. 2014. "Transgender Victims and Offenders: Failures of the United States Criminal Justice System and the Necessity of Queer Criminology." *Critical Criminology*, Vol. 22, No. 1, 35–47.

Button, D. M. 2016. "Understanding the Effects of Victimization: Applying General Strain Theory to the Experiences of LGBQ Youth." *Deviant Behavior*, Vol. 37, No. 5, 537–56.

Chakraborti, N. 2010. "Crimes against the 'Other': Conceptual, Operational, and Empirical Challenges for Hate Studies." *Journal of Hate Studies*, Vol. 8, No. 1, 9–28.

Colvin, R. 2014. "Policing the Gay and Lesbian Community: The Perceptions of Lesbian and Gay Police Officers." In *Handbook of LGBT Communities, Crime, and Justice*, edited by D. Peterson and V.R. Panfil, 183–205. New York: Springer.

Cramer, R. J., E. L. Gorter, M. D. C. Rodriguez, J. W. Clark, A. K. Rice, and M. R. Nobles. 2013. "Blame Attribution in Court: Conceptualization and Measurement of Perpetrator Blame." *Victims and Offenders*, Vol. 8, No. 1, 42–55.

D'Augelli, A. R., A. H. Grossman, and M. T. Starks. 2006. "Childhood Gender Atypicality, Victimization, and PTSD among Lesbian, Gay, and Bisexual Youth." *Journal of Interpersonal Violence*, Vol. 21, No. 11, 1462–82.

Dolovich, S. 2012. "Two Models of the Prison: Accidental Humanity and Hypermasculinity in the L.A. County Jail." *The Journal of Criminal Law and Criminology*, Vol. 102, No. 4, 965–1117.

Dunbar, E. 2006. "Race, Gender, and Sexual Orientation in Hate Crime Victimization: Identity Politics or Identity Risk?" *Violence and Victims*, Vol. 21, No. 3, 323–37.

Dwyer, A. 2011. "Policing Lesbian, Gay, Bisexual and Transgender Young People: A Gap in the Research Literature." *Current Issues in Criminal Justice*, Vol. 22, No. 3, 415–33.

Dwyer, A. 2014a. "Pleasures, Perversities, and Partnerships: The Historical Emergence of LGBT-Police Relations." In *Handbook of LGBT Communities, Crime, and Justice*, edited by D. Peterson and V.R. Panfil, 149–164. New York: Springer.

Dwyer, A. 2014b. "'We're Not Like These Weird Feather Boa-Covered AIDS-Spreading Monsters': How LGBT Young People and Service Providers Think Riskiness Informs LGBT Youth-Police Interactions." *Critical Criminology*, Vol. 22, No. 1, 65–79.

Finkelhor, D., and N. L. Asdigian. 1996. "Risk Factors for Youth Victimization: Beyond a Lifestyles/Routine Activities Theory Approach." *Violence and Victims*, Vol. 11, No. 1, 3–19.

Forbes, A. 2014. "Define 'Sex': Legal Outcomes for Transgender Individuals in the United States." In *Handbook of LGBT Communities, Crime, and Justice*, edited by D. Peterson and V.R. Panfil, 387–403. New York: Springer.

Frederick, T. 2014. "Diversity at the Margins: The Interconnections Between Homelessness, Sex Work, Mental Health, and Substance Use in the Lives of Sexual Minority Homeless Young People." In *Handbook of LGBT Communities, Crime, and Justice*, edited by D. Peterson and V.R. Panfil, 473–501. New York: Springer.

Gillum, T. L., and G. T. DiFulvio. 2014. "Examining Dating Violence and Its Mental Health Consequences Among Sexual Minority Youth." In *Handbook of LGBT Communities, Crime, and Justice*, edited by D. Peterson and V.R. Panfil, 431–448. New York: Springer.

Herek, G. M., and K. T. Berrill. 1992. *Hate Crimes: Confronting Violence Against Lesbians and Gay Men*. Newbury Park, CA: Sage.

Hobson, A. 2012. "The Political (Mis)Management of (Homo)Sexuality and (In)Securities." *Criminal Justice Matters*, Vol. 88, No. 1, 4–6.

Jenness, V. 1995. "Social Movement Growth, Domain Expansion, and Framing Processes: The Gay/Lesbian Movement and Violence Against Gays and Lesbians as a Social Problem." *Social Problems*, Vol. 42, No. 1, 145–70.

Johnson, D. E. 2014. "When They Tell You Who You Are: Lesbian Resistance to the Policing of Multiple Identities." In *Handbook of LGBT Communities, Crime, and Justice*, edited by D. Peterson and V. R. Panfil, 103–119. New York: Springer.

Lyons, P. M., C. M. Anthony, K. M. Davis, K. Fernandez, A. N. Torres, and D. K. Marcus. 2005. "Police Judgements of Culpability and Homophobia." *Applied Psychology in Criminal Justice*, Vol. 1, No. 1, 1–14.

Marshal, M. P., L. Dietz, M. Friedman, R. Stall, H. Smith, J. McGinley, B. C. Thoma, P. J. Murray, A. R. D'Augelli, and D. A. Brent. 2011. "Suicidality and Depression Disparities Between Sexual Minority and Heterosexual Youth: A Meta-analytic Review." *Journal of Adolescent Health*, Vol. 49, No. 2, 115–23.

Messinger, A. M. 2014. "Marking 35 Years of Research on Same-sex Intimate Partner Violence: Lessons and New Directions." In *Handbook of LGBT Communities, Crime, and Justice*, edited by D. Peterson and V.R. Panfil, 65–85. New York: Springer.

Meyer, D. 2014. "Resisting Hate Crime Discourse: Queer and Intersectional Challenges to Neoliberal Hate Crime Laws." *Critical Criminology*, Vol. 22, No. 1, 113–25.

Miles-Johnson, T. 2013. "Confidence and Trust in Police: How Sexual Identity Difference Shapes Perceptions of Police." *Current Issues in Criminal Justice*, Vol. 25, No. 2, 685–702.

Mison, R. B. 1992. "Homophobia in Manslaughter: The Homosexual Advance as Insufficient Provocation." *California Law Review*, Vol. 80, No. 1, 133–78.

Mogul, J. L., A.J. Ritchie, and K. Whitlock. 2011. *Queer (In)Justice: The Criminalization of LGBT People in the United States*. Boston, MA: Beacon Press.

Newcomb, M. E., A. J. Heinz, and B. Mustanski. 2012. "Examining Risk and Protective Factors for Alcohol Use in Lesbian, Gay, Bisexual, and Transgender Youth: A Longitudinal Multilevel Analysis." *Journal of Studies on Alcohol and Drugs*, Vol. 73, No. 5, 783–93.

Nichols, A. J. 2014. "Intersections of Gender and Sexuality in Police Abuses Against Transgender Sex Workers in Sri Lanka." In *Handbook of LGBT Communities, Crime, and Justice*, edited by D. Peterson and V. R. Panfil, 165–182. New York: Springer.

Noga-Styron, K. E., C. E. Reasons, and D. Peacock. 2012. "The Last Acceptable Prejudice: An Overview of LGBT Social and Criminal Injustice Issues Within the USA." *Contemporary Justice Review*, Vol. 15, No. 4, 369–98.

Perry, B., and D. R. Dyck. 2014. "'I Don't Know Where it is Safe': Trans Women's Experiences of Violence." *Critical Criminology*, Vol. 22, No. 1, 49–63.

Quinn, E., and S. Brightman. 2015. *Crime Victimization: A Comprehensive Overview*. Durham, NC: Carolina Academic Press.

Rayburn, N. R., and G. C. Davison. 2002. "Articulated Thoughts about Antigay Hate Crimes." *Cognitive Therapy and Research*, Vol. 26, No. 4, 431–47.

Reasons, C. E., and Q. Hughson. 2000. "Violence against Gays and Lesbians." In *Race, Ethnicity, Sexual Orientation, Violent Crime: The Realities and the Myths*, edited by N. J. Pallone, 137–59. Hawthorne, NJ: The Hawthorne Press.

Roi, C. L., T. Kretschmer, J. K. Dijkstra, and R. Veenstra. 2016. "Disparities in Depressive Symptoms between Heterosexual and Lesbian, Gay, and Bisexual Youth in a Dutch Cohort: The TRAILS Study." *Journal of Youth and Adolescence*, Vol. 45, No. 3, 440–56.

Rose, S. M., and M. B. Mechanic. 2002. "Psychological Distress, Crime Features, and Help-Seeking Behaviors Related to Homophobic Bias Incidents." *The American Behavioral Scientist*, Vol. 46, No. 1, 14–26.

Russell, S. T., B. T. Franz, and A. K. Driscoll. 2001. "Same-Sex Romantic Attraction and Experiences of Violence in Adolescence." *American Journal of Public Health*, Vol. 91, No. 6, 903–6.

Saunders, P., and J. Kirby. 2010. "Move Along: Community-based Research into the Policing of Sex Work in Washington, D.C." *Social Justice*, Vol. 37, No. 1, 107–27.

Smyth, M. A. 2006. "Queers and Provocateurs: Hegemony, Ideology, and the 'Homosexual Advance' Defense." *Law and Society Review*, Vol. 40, No. 4, 903–30.

Stohr, M. K. 2015. "The Hundred Years' War: The Etiology and Status of Assaults on Transgender Women in Men's Prisons." *Women and Criminal Justice*, Vol. 25, No. 1–2, 120–29.

Stotzer, R. L. 2014. "Bias Crimes Based on Sexual Orientation and Gender Identity: Global Prevalence, Impacts, and Causes." In *Handbook of LGBT Communities, Crime, and Justice*, edited by D. Peterson and V.R. Panfil, 45–64. New York: Springer.

Sumner, J., and V. Jenness. 2014. "Gender Integration in Sex-segregated U.S. Prisons: The Paradox of Transgender Correctional Policy." In *Handbook of LGBT Communities, Crime, and Justice*, edited by D. Peterson and V. R. Panfil, 229–259. New York: Springer.

Tejeda, M. J. 2004. "Egalitarianism and Self-Esteem as Correlates of Hate Ideation against Gay Men and Lesbians." *The Journal of Multicultural Nursing and Health*, Vol. 10, No. 1, 42–50.

Tesch, B., D. Bekerian, P. English, and E. Harrington. 2010. "Same-sex Domestic Violence: Why Victims Are More at Risk." *International Journal of Police Science and Management*, Vol. 12, No. 4, 526–35.

Tilleman, M. 2009. "(Tans)Forming the Provocation Defense." *The Journal of Criminal Law and Criminology*, Vol. 100, No. 4, 1659–88.

Waldner, L. K., and J. Berg. 2008. "Explaining Antigay Violence Using Target Congruence: An Application of Revised Routine Activities Theory." *Violence and Victims*, Vol. 23, No. 3, 267–87.

Wang, J., M. Dey, L. Soldati, M. Weiss, G. Gmel, and M. Mohler-Kuo. 2014. "Psychiatric Disorders, Suicidality, and Personality Among Young Men by Sexual Orientation." *European Psychiatry*, Vol. 29, No. 8, 514–22.

Warbelow, S., and T. Cobb. 2014. "Bullying of LGBT Youth in America: Prevalence, Effects, and Government Responses." In *Handbook of LGBT Communities, Crime, and Justice*, edited by D. Peterson and V.R. Panfil, 405–427. New York: Springer.

Weiss, D. 2010. *The Evolution of Community Policing from Theory to Implementation: A Process Evaluation*. Lewiston, NY: Edwin Mellen Press.

Witten, T. M., and A. E. Eyler. 1999. "Hate Crimes and Violence against the Transgendered." *Peace Review*, Vol. 11, No. 3, 461–8.

Woods, J. B. 2007. "Reconceptualizing Anti-LGBT Hate Crimes as Burdening Expression and Association: A Case for Expanding Federal Hate Crime Legislation to Include Gender Identity and Sexual Orientation." *Journal of Hate Studies*, Vol. 6, No. 1, 81–115.

Woods, J. B. 2014. "'Queering Criminology': Overview of the State of the Field." In *Handbook of LGBT Communities, Crime, and Justice*, edited by D. Peterson and V. R. Panfil, 15–41. New York: Springer.

PART III

Victim Services

Chapter 12 provides the readers with a firm understanding of the heterogeneous nature of victimization so that they eschew a "one size fits all" approach and instead are able to differentially work to meet the individualized need of the victims/survivors of homicide, intimate personal violence/domestic violence (IPV/DV) and trafficking. The chapter also discusses the ability to apply a trauma-informed approach to service delivery with victims and their families.

In Chapter 13, the author concludes that the numbers of elders will increase dramatically, which will result in more elderly victimization. Yet, victim services for the elderly are not keeping up with the pace of the growth trend. Elder abuse is a complicated matter in which such risk factors as age-related factors, especially one's health conditions; the relationship with family members; and culture are intricately intertwined. Elderly victims tend not to report an incident due to protecting family members, stigma and shame, denial of the incident, or being cognitively unable to report the case. Furthermore, many elder abuse cases are overlooked by the mainstream culture, for example, by failing to recognize elderly sexual abuse cases. The shortage of available services for elderly victims is another concern discussed in Chapter 13.

Chapter 14 is the report of a study that investigated the challenges that battered undocumented Latinas face when seeking help from advocacy organizations, as well as the problems that advocates encounter as they try to perform outreach to and serve this population. Drawing on 18 in-depth interviews and one focus group, the authors examine how intersectional factors such race, gender, class and legal status intersect and constrain the context and experiences of battered undocumented Latinas as they try to secure their safety. Findings indicate that the barriers to help seeking that are specific to battered undocumented Latina immigrants, as identified by the women themselves and by the advocates, include legal status and lack of English language proficiency.

Chapter 15 discusses the development of victim's impact statement and its history in the court system. The chapter also discusses how the statements may be improved.

Chapter 16 discusses the needs of crime victims and how restorative justice may help victims. In addition, the chapter discusses the legal basis and empirical research regarding victim restitution and restorative justice conferences.

In Chapter 17, the authors discuss how sexual assault affects different populations and what services are available to help victims deal with these consequences. The roles of the local, state, and federal government in assisting sexual assault victims are outlined, as well as the process that victims must go through in order to receive resources. The chapter also provides information regarding victim assistance on college and university campuses. Finally, we explain that men are affected differently by sexual assault than their female counterparts, and discuss how resources for sexual assault victims can take these differences into account.

Chapter 18 is the last chapter in Part III. In the chapter, the author discusses victim witnesses' role in the investigative and court processes. The chapter discusses the differences between the United States and the United Kingdom in these processes and the growing appetite for procedural change in criminal justice systems where the evidence base supports such amendment be made and this chapter outlines some of those developments which have taken place in the UK jurisdiction, where the applications of new insights have been applied, and where potential modifications are being considered. The chapter also discusses the current position of victim witnesses (as vulnerable witnesses) in the U.K. in, a) investigative interviews, and b) in procedures and examination in the courtroom.

12
ENHANCING SERVICE PROVIDER SYSTEMS

Jed Metzger

Keywords

victimization; homicide; trafficking; intimate partner violence

Objectives

- Readers will have a firm understanding of the heterogeneous nature of victimization so that they eschew a "one size fits all" approach and instead are able to differentially work to meet the individualized need of the victims/survivors of homicide, intimate personal violence/domestic violence (IPV/DV) and trafficking.
- Readers will understand and be able to apply a trauma-informed approach to service delivery with victims and their families.
- Readers will understand, appreciate and be able to effectively work with cultural differences that are brought forward in working with victims and survivors.

Introduction

Recent years have seen an increased commitment, both by the public (governmental) and the private (not for profit) service sector to provide an evidence-informed if not evidenced-based service delivery system to victims of various types of violence. A part of this commitment has been efforts to reach the underserved, often communities of color, sexual minorities and those with immigrant status. At the most basic level, being victimized by crime, especially violent crime, has negative effects on human beings and represents a public health issue for the society at large (Satcher, 1995). Effectively addressing the physical, emotional, fiscal and other needs of victims through accessible and effective services is the best way to mitigate the effects of victimization (Wallace & Roberson, 1998). This chapter aims to address the specific victim service needs through a trauma-informed lens, examining some the specific needs of victims related to the type of victimization, while maintaining a proactive cultural diversity mindset.

Overview of Trauma-informed Approaches

The very nature of victimization results in a multitude of unmet needs (Brickman et al., 2002). Federal response to the needs of victims of crime is handled through the Office for Victims of Crime (OVC).

The OVC has identified that victims of crime have far reaching needs and that the needs vary by a numbers of factors related to type of crime, gender, age, ethnicity (Newmark et al. 2003). Newmark's (2006) large study codified service needs into the three main categories of emotion/psychological recovery, information/advocacy and concrete/tangible. This knowledge is useful in helping to direct service providers to address these larger categorical challenges. The other critical finding of the Newmark study was that despite some success and a degree of satisfaction by victims, there was still considerable unmet need (2006). In relation to the needs of the victims the Newmark study highlighted systemic issues with access to services and gaps in community integration of services as the two most prominent (2006). These access gaps differ by class and ethnicity. Collectively, the individual and systemic issues combine to create inequality in the health status of victims.

Inequality in health status of victims is largely related to the compounding of factors such as poverty, racism, and sexism. These factors interact with the victimization experience to create a public health issue (Israel et al., 1998). A public health perspective is invaluable when looking at victimization (DeGue et al., 2012). This perspective encourages a more constructionist understanding (Israel et al., 1998). In doing so, practitioners and systemic thinkers alike are afforded a view of the nuances involved in victimization. This viewpoint protects against reductionist approaches and prescriptive interventions. Instead, practitioners are directed to consider critical concepts such as identity, assets in face of significant challenge and the ecology in the environment around the victim (Israel et al., 1998). A socially constructed public health perspective when applied to work with victims on an individual and family level helps to direct practitioners and service providers to be sensitive to the effects of class, race, gender and minority status on how the victim is processing the on-going experience of victimization. As each person's story is given value, empowerment opportunities are a created, so necessary in the healing and justice processes (Madsen, 2007). By using trauma-informed practices intervention and services can meet the compounding of needs of victims effectively (Pynoos et al., 2008).

Trauma-informed approaches have been gaining traction in service systems where victimized individuals are frequently serviced. Given the huge numbers of children in the child welfare system (CWS) whose backgrounds are full of trauma and complex trauma, the CWS largely has moved to a trauma-informed model across the U.S. (Klein & White, 2013). Trauma-informed practices include a number of approaches but share the common ground of not trying to focus on maintaining presenting behavior but going after the root causes, which are often related to the prior victimization (Bloom, 2013). In addition, several of the practices have risen to the level of an approved evidenced-based practice such as trauma-focused cognitive-behavioral therapy (TFCBT) (Cohen, Mannarino & Deblinger, 2006) and child–parent psychotherapy (Herschell et al., 2003). These approaches share a belief in the importance of psychoeducation, proper assessment (Klein & White, 2013) and holistic/whole system approaches (Bloom, 2013). Playing a central role to promote this empowerment based approach to victimization of children and youth has been the National Child Traumatic Stress Network (Pynoos et al., 2008). The way the CWS has approached the need of their service recipients for a trauma-informed service is a model that can be and is being used by services for those victimized by homicide, IPV/DV and trafficking.

Current Thinking on the Service Needs Involving Homicide

With the U.S. homicide rate averaging roughly 45 homicides a day (U.S. Department of Justice, 2012), homicide has become a major public health issue (Satcher, 1995). As a public health issue the response of service providers to the specific, complex needs of the surviving victims of each homicide requires a holistic mindset (Mastrocinque et al., 2014). Special attention is required to address the nuances of ethnicity, age, gender, income level, spiritual practice and type of homicide (Metzger et al., 2014). As such, in order to meet the real needs of the family and friends of homicide victims

(FFHV), service providers in the criminal justice system, the medical system, and the behavioral health system need the knowledge followed by the applied policy and practice skills that reflect this type of integrated approach (Hertz, Prothrow-Smith & Chery, 2005).

The devastating consequences associated with the sudden and traumatic loss that defines homicide has been well documented (McDevitt-Murphy et al., 2012). Research has documented the physical and psychological effects of homicide on FFHV (Hertz, Prothrow-Smith & Chery, 2005). For instance, post-traumatic stress disorder (PTSD) as well as complicated grief has been found in rigorous testing showing the compounding of mental health challenges with FFHV (McDevitt-Murphy et al., 2012). In addition, common issues that survivors of homicide often face include fiscal challenges, stigmatization, guilt, media interactions (which is different from most other crimes), and grief (Stern, 2010; Hertz, Prothrow-Smith & Chery, 2005). Understanding these far reaching consequences is essential to successfully meeting the needs.

Having a bio-psycho-social, spiritual framework is a way to use a research information knowledge base to deliver excellence in service delivery to FFHV (Metzger et al., 2014). Ethnicity has been shown to be an important consideration both with regard to victimization and to service delivery (Sharpe & Boyas, 2011; McDevitt-Murphy et al., 2012). Specifically, African Americans are over represented as homicide victims yet not well studied, which has created response gaps (Sharpe & Boyas, 2011). Ethnicity has been shown to effect coping with homicide by FFHV in terms of how events are processed (Sharpe & Boyas, 2011). Homicide presents numerous challenges; one particularity important challenge relates to coping with what is usually an unexpected traumatic event. A person's sense of control is often threatened. In response, Caucasian FFHV tend to favor individualistic coping strategies whereas African American FFHV favor more collaborative approaches (Sharpe & Boyas, 2011). As such, provider networks need to be able to assess for coping approaches considering ethnically informed stylistic approaches without judgment. Doing so promotes a more robust sense of empowerment in a highly disempowered time. An example of this is the historically different relationship with the deceased by race. In this author's experience in working with FFHV, African American survivor victim groups tend to use more public display of grief with tee shirts of the deceased, more public display of emotion at funerals, videotaping of funeral, and public vigils at the spot of the homicide than other ethnic groups. Understanding ethnic difference helps providers avoid homogenized service delivery approaches.

In a related way, the age of the victim has an important role in how the homicide is responded to be FFHV (Rheingold et al., 2012) and thereby should inform the service provider system. For instance, age has been shown to be a factor with adolescent survivors showing greater PTSD (Rheingold et al., 2012). Given the developmental wider networks that youth tend to have, a more community based youth intervention approach using peer mentors, midnight basketball, music and food is suggested, especially in youth communities of color. Children, too, have specific needs based on their developmental position in understanding and responding to homicide (Hertz, Prothrow-Smith & Chery, 2005). The evidence is clear in pointing to the need of service providers with the FFHV population to be trained in developmental theory and how to apply that theory into policy and practice.

While homicide happens in all communities there is evidence to show that homicide, especially when intimate partner and drunken driving homicide are statistically removed from the analysis, does tend to cluster in lower income communities (Jones-Webb & Wall, 2008). The higher frequency of homicide in some lower income communities produces greater numbers of indirect victims, which has been shown to produce a type of collective PTSD (Sharpe & Boyas, 2011). In a related way, McDevitt-Murphy et al. (2012) found more complicated grief in FFHV of lower income (2012). Knowing this, the more service providers can consider macro (community) interventions as well as individualized approaches, the better the overall service provision will be able to meet the larger needs. An example of this in the author's community are the community response teams that are based in the law enforcement department but include members of the clergy, victim advocates and community mental health workers who are called in once a homicide has been identified to bring a holistic, community based response directly to the scene and the survivors.

Spirituality has been identified as an important coping element for FFHV (Metzger et al., 2014; Sharpe & Boyas, 2011). This is particularly true in communities of color (Sharpe & Boyas, 2011). There is some evidence that supports the idea that communities of color may be less likely to seek professional helpers for grief and more likely to use spiritual providers (Laurie & Neimeyer, 2008). This thereby requires all clergy but especially African American clergy to have skill sets to effectively respond to the needs of FFHV. Training on both the individual pastor level as well higher (bishop level) macro intervention strategies will assist in promoting effective service delivery response. At the same time, it is important to be mindful that there is no one "black church" so that training is not over simplified. Additionally, law enforcement, medical and behavioral health providers need to be knowledgeable, comfortable and skilled with regard to the use of spirituality in relation to FFHV (Sharpe & Boyas, 2011). This has direct implications for law enforcement, social work, medical and counseling programs to include spirituality into curriculum. For instance, guilt is an emotional byproduct of homicide (Mastrocinque et al., 2014); as such, providers need to have the skill set to empathically work with guilt to lessen guilt contributing to PTSD (Stern, 2010).

A final factor type consideration is type of homicide. A general recommendation throughout this section of the chapter is that all homicides should not be seen or treated in a similar manner. The nature of the homicide is especially relevant. While there are multiple factors that can be considered with this regard, it is important to distinguish drunken driving homicides and intimate partner homicides separately from other homicides. For too long, drunken driving homicides were not included in the general homicide literature. This has changed recently and has allowed lessons to be learned from the grassroots interventions gained by activist advocacy groups such as Mothers Against Drunk Driving (Stern, 2010). Targeted efforts such as these have been shown to be useful in getting affected individuals to reach out for and receive important post homicide support (Stern, 2010). Homicide due to intimate partner (IPV/DV) also has been shown to have some specific response considerations.

The first glaring issue in IPV/DV homicide is that overwhelmingly the victim in an IPV/DV murder is female, while in non-IPV/DV homicide the victim is male (Juodis et al., 2014). IPV/DV homicide cuts across every demographic group and is very much a heterogeneous issue, other than the victim is usually female. The heterogeneous nature of IPV homicide has resulted in some service gaps as it is hard to target a population that is this diverse. Collaboration by service providers who interact with IPV victims will directly improve gaps in service and folks slipping between those gaps. Clearly, there is room for prevention of IPV homicide. Perpetrators of IPV homicide have often had prior law enforcement involvement, thereby opening up an avenue for prevention (Juodis et al., 2014). There are screening instruments that when administered by law enforcement officers can direct lifesaving intervention. When health care providers screen for violence in family history, they are in a better position to help people link to need sources (Hertz, Prothrow-Smith & Chery, 2005).

While systemic response needs to consider the aforementioned factors, some issues tend to cut across all homicide response. The first relates to the challenge of having to deal with service providers related to the justice system at a stressful time. Many FFHV have had limited dealing with the legal system and yet now need assistance from what is often seen as a daunting system (Stern, 2010; Metzger et al., 2014). Court watch programs where FFHV are matched with a court watch advocate that goes through the court process with the FFHV have been found to be very helpful as long as the court watch advocate is experienced and preferably a victim themselves (Mastrocinque et al., 2014; Metzger et al., 2014). As more PTSD is clinically found in the first six months post homicide, there is a direct need for early behavioral health intervention

(McDevitt-Murphy et al., 2012). Providers need to be able to both get close to the wish to avoid or deny the loss and be able to sit with raw pain in an empathic way, careful not to pry, but open to the nuances of an FFHV's experience (Mastrocinque et al., 2014; Metzger et al., 2014). First responders play a critical role in sensitively handling FFHV on the scene of a homicide and in the sensitive informing of FFHV before events are learned on social media (Mastrocinque et al., 2014; Metzger et al., 2014). In fact, helping FFHV think about how to handle social media is an emerging issue for many FFHV. FFHV have consistently noted that the return of property that has been cleaned of body fluids in a timely manner is important in the grief process (Mastrocinque et al., 2014; Metzger et al., 2014). Finally, community-wide resource guides for both FFHV and the service providers have proven to be an invaluable community asset (Stern, 2010).

Needs of Victims/Survivors of Intimate Partner Violence

One well documented challenge related to IPV/DV victimization is the hidden nature of the epidemic. Stigma of victimization continues to block individuals from accessing the services they need (Trevillion et al., 2012). There are a variety of reasons for this. As the majority of the violence is perpetrated against women, power and sexism needs to be considered as a major factor (Kulkarni, Bell, & McDaniel Rhodes, 2012). A perfect example was the high profile double murder followed by suicide at Geneseo College in January of 2016. The perpetrator came from a well-known family in the Geneseo community and this was translated by the media as a "crime of passion." The inability to face domestic violence as a power and control issue as opposed to some type of Romeo and Juliet gone bad tragedy, traps victims and obscures the truth. This is not to say that heterosexual men (violence in the LGBT community will be considered separately so as not to confound the critical variables) are not victims of partner violence but the power dynamics of violence against women is essential to understand (Caldwell, Swan & Woodbrown, 2012). Ensuring victim safety has both policy and practice implications.

Given the repetitive and escalating nature of IPV/DV victimization (Rennison, 2003), more stringent policy needs to be enacted to assist law enforcement with clarity to help victims gain safety (Lippman, 2012). One such idea which has been put into practice are so-called "no-drop" policies that mandate prosecution even if the victim does not wish to press charges and keeps the case open with the district attorney to guard against future victimization (Lippman, 2012). IPV/DV courts, specialized youth IPV/DV courts and training for judges on IPV/DV in the LGBT community are also important policy and practice considerations. Another source of good information is currently being found in the Domestic Violence Fatality Review Teams (DVFRT).

The DVFRT literature provides insight not just into situations that involve homicide but into the factors involved in all IPV/DV situations. Namely, that IPV/DV is not a homogenized issue, it occurs across all communities and as such community-based coordinated efforts are needed to address the issue (Chanmugam, 2014). At the same time, the literature points to greater risk of IPV fatality for poor women of color (Bent-Goodley, 2013; Richie, 2012). This leads to systemic, policy and practice considerations (Bugeja et al., 2013). It is important for service providers to not victimize the victims, to not blame poor women of color. Historical racism and sexism fuel violence (Krueg et al., 2002). A word of caution is necessary to not treat all women of color as one group, as there are differences in help seeking behavior within the women of color sub group (Cho & Kim, 2012). Clearly historically poor relationships between communities of color and law enforcement, social service and mental health need to be improved so that more women victimized by IPV/DV can chose to access needed services (Bent-Goodley, 2013).

Increasingly, the research has shown an increase in IPV/DV in the lesbian, gay, bisexual and transgender (LGBT) communities (Goldberg & Meyer, 2012). As with other victimized populations, violence in the LGBT community is associated with poorer health outcomes and negative coping behaviors (Butler et al., 2014). Applying lessons being learned in communities of color in other areas of victimization, leads to the recommendation for more empowerment and holistic approaches in the LGBT community. This includes training in working with LGBT populations for law enforcement, medical and behavioral health practitioners. Specifically, these trainings should address the intersection of the diversity needs and the IPV/DV experiences.

As providers adopt more holistic models, the compounding of positive intervention approaches lessens the tendency to blame victims and opens up possibility for empowerment (Madsen, 2007). This includes a collaborative mindset and a commitment by providers to continuously work to develop their own cultural competency skills sets (Bent-Goodley, 2013; Websdale, Town & Johnson, 1999). In addition to cultural competency, strong developmental knowledge is also essential as children and youth exposed to IPV/DV have some specific developmental needs (Carlson, 2000). Fortunately, the evidenced-based trauma-informed interventions all have strong content for working with children and youth victimized by IPV/DV (Pynoos et al., 2008).

These empowerment based approaches are needed especially when child protection services interact with IPV/DV victims. Again, the effect of sexism is clearly seen (Macy, Ermentrout & Rizo, 2012). Women are too frequently held responsible for the children when trying to survive IPV/DV (Alaggia et al., 2012). This has service implications. The more IPV/DV programs can be welcoming and empowering, the more likely victims will engage in the service (Macy, Ermentrout & Rizo, 2012). When social services and family courts mandate abused women to parenting classes it reinforces the message that the women (mothers) are to blame (Simmons, Lehmann & Dia, 2010). The current literature strongly supports moving away from directing IPV/DV victim women into prescriptive parenting programs and into more empowerment based approaches.

Empowerment is a multistep process. Social service agencies, understanding the need to engage women of color more proactively and being mindful of the stigma of IPV/DV should follow a practice of screening everyone for IPV/DV (McDevitt-Murphy et al., 2012). Next, service providers can work to be more welcoming and mix positive psychoeducation into the content of interactions (Macy, Ermentrout & Rizo, 2012). To the extent possible service providers are encouraged to adopt differential response approaches to lessen the blaming of victimized women and ensure that the target of the threat towards children is correctly leveled on perpetrators (Alaggia et al., 2012; Humphreys & Absler, 2011). Differential response is predicated on good screening and follows an understanding of providing what is specifically needed as opposed to a more "cookie cutter" approach.

When intervention is indicated, the evidence strongly supports a comprehensive, integrated and early onset of abuse approach to achieve best results (Saltzman et al., 2000; Wisner et al., 1999). It is important to screen for PTSD especially with people who live (or lived) with the victim or were very close to the victim (Hertz, Prothrow-Smith & Chery, 2005). Victims/survivors of IPV/DV have mental health service needs; historically there has not been good coordination between mental health and IPV/DV services, so referral mechanisms need to be more straightforward (Trevillion et al., 2012). This includes having highly trained therapists on staff at IPV/DV centers, which increases access to quality mental health treatment. Across all victim service provider interactions, the literature supports the continued need for professional services that are respectful, empowering and resist blaming victims (Kulkarni, Bell & McDaniel Rhodes, 2012).

One final emerging issue has to do with the challenge of family pets in situations of IPV/DV (Ascione, et al., 2007). The issue has several layers. First, is the evidence that links male IPV/DV perpetrators with animal abuse, creating a safety issue for the family pets (Febres, et al., 2014). The other huge issue is what to do with the pets. In a time when safety is at a premium, having a way to ensure the safety of the pets is essential so that the victim can make the difficult but necessary decisions for the themselves and the children (McGraw & Jeffers, 2015). Increasingly, this is being addressed by IPV/DV shelters accepting pets.

Needs of Those Victimized by Trafficking, Sexual and Labor Related Crime

The rise in globalization of the world economy combined with instability due to natural disaster, famine, economic disparity, governmental instability and war has come together to support an increase in human trafficking from developing world to developed world (Hoff, 2009). At the same time, the developed world, fearful of the rise in global terrorism, has a safety first mindset that causes the needs of trafficked individuals to be missed or ignored due to the focus on national security (Farrell & Fahy, 2009). Trafficking has become a leading international and national criminal enterprise (Okech, Morreau & Benson, 2011). As the trafficking experience is often filled with traumatic experiences, it is a "perfect storm" for victimization. Effective intervention requires an understanding of social policy environment as well as understanding the specific nature of victimization.

The centerpiece of the United States policy in this area is the Trafficking Victims Protection Act (TVPA). While the Act has its strengths, it is not effective enough as a protective policy (Okech, Morreau & Benson, 2011). One key concern is that the Act does not delineate sex from labor trafficking (Roby, Turley & Cloward, 2008). Trafficking is not just about sex trafficking, as people from the developing world are trafficked as workers to the developed world to do the jobs that people in the developed world no longer want to do (Okech, Morreau & Benson, 2011). The Act also does not mandate a comprehensive data collection system, so necessary with a crime in which so many fall through the cracks and do not get the services they need (Macy & Graham, 2012; Green, 2008). Trafficking advocates consistently note the need to move from a law that focuses on the crime and towards laws that also include provision for support for victims (Hardy, Compton & McPhatter, 2013).

A major suggestion in this section of the chapter is to advocate that the focus of attention moves to where the issue truly lies with the needs of the trafficked individuals. There is a question of if human trafficking needs to be viewed as a human rights issue not just a criminal one (Okech, Morreau & Benson, 2011). Moving to human rights focus would direct attention away from prosecution of traffickers to strategies for victim protection and reintegration. This clearly is a complex political argument. For instance in the United States, the southern border with Mexico remains a political hot potato. The basic thrust of the TVPA is on enforcement and protecting national security, again important issues, however what gets lost is victim issues (Okech, Morreau & Benson, 2011). Moving past the public policy issues directs attention at the victims of trafficking and how best to serve them.

The first issue in improving services for trafficked individuals is for service providers to become more adept at identification of trafficked individuals (Okech, Morreau & Benson, 2011). As human service providers often are some of the first service providers to have contact with trafficked individuals, they need to understand and screen for trafficking (Macy & Graham, 2012). Service providers need to understand trafficking as an economic issue that involves both labor trafficking and sex trafficking, and that trafficking occurs both as an international and a domestic issue (Hardy, Compton & McPhatter, 2013). Within this discussion is the need to delineate and work with labor and sex trafficked individuals differently (Macy & Graham, 2012). The needs of individuals who are picking tomatoes in the panhandle of Florida in virtual slavery are different from that of runaway youth lured into the sex trade business in New York City. By the same token, it is important for service providers to be able to recognize that sex trafficking is a domestic as well as an international issue (Okech, Morreau & Benson, 2011). As trafficked individuals are known to present to social service workers, child welfare workers and homeless service sectors workers, these services are strongly advised to screen minors for sex trafficking. Workers in child welfare or youth homeless services are encouraged to adopt a screening practice for trafficking (Macy & Graham, 2012).

This includes the request to screen minors for sex trafficking in child welfare or youth homeless services (Hardy, Compton & McPhatter, 2013). Victim identification works hand in hand with the need for rapid and sensitive intervention.

The comprehensive literature review published by Macy and Graham (2012) points to several critical themes in working with trafficked individuals once they have been identified. First and foremost is the need for workers to consciously focus on developing a safe and trusting relationship with the trafficked individual. Fear of retaliation or deportation for internationally trafficked individuals weighs heavily, so workers must be sensitive to these very real pressures (Macy and Graham, 2012). This includes connecting without labeling people (Hardy, Compton & McPhatter, 2013). At its core trafficking is an economic issue and the perpetrators of such do not want to lose their "investment", causing legitimate fear in the trafficked population. Human service workers need to understand to needs of trafficked individuals including direct skills, trauma processing, medical, and gainful and legal employment skills (Hardy, Compton & McPhatter, 2013). Trafficked individuals have needs related to the demands of the trafficked experience; these include the need to deal with or work through: isolation, IPV/DV, rape, and loosening the bond that has been forced on them with their perpetrators (Hardy, Compton & McPhatter, 2013). This collection of therapeutic tasks directly relates to the importance of a trauma-informed service.

Macy and Graham (2012) have used their extensive literature review to call for the best practice of a trauma-informed, victim-centered approach to working with trafficked individuals. For many trafficked individuals, the trafficking experience has been an on-going and complex process that has resulted in what is now known as "complex trauma" (Van Der Kolk, 2014). As such, interventions should be empowerment based and focused on the development of systems of support; in short to be victim centered (Hardy, Compton & McPhatter, 2013). This may even include the development of a specific shelter system as is currently seen in the intimate partner violence service system (although placement of trafficked individuals in IPV/DV shelters is discouraged as the issues are different) (Okech, Morreau & Benson, 2011). This also directly includes services to individuals older than 18 as much of the current focus does seem to be with trafficked youth (Okech, Morreau & Benson, 2011). The Polaris project is an example of holistic care approach for training human service workers so that it becomes more of a trauma informed service (Ahn et al., 2013).

The final major pressing need with regard to individual who have survived trafficking is to improve their access to social service benefits. Personal economic instability makes people vulnerable to being trafficked and exploited. Trafficked people need health care as well as access to social service benefits (ASPE, 2012). The U.S. social service system is so state determined there are wide differences in benefit access by state. These differences make it difficult to comment on specifics, but in general access to SNAP, HEAP and other benefits becomes a safeguard against further trafficking. Having access to fiscal stability helps to prevent exposure to future exploitation. Additionally, there are access barriers for trafficked people due to multitude of factors related to migration such as language and cultural issues, literacy, fear of deportation and lack of access to birth records and such (ASPE, 2012). The more service systems can recognize these factors as legitimate and build intervention practices that support empowerment and independence, the less likely the individual will be re-trafficked. Finally, system workers may not understand the needs of trafficked people well and may have limited access to interpreters. The host of issues brought forth by sex and labor trafficking requires a well-trained and trauma-informed service delivery system, especially at the touchpoints where the population is most likely to first come in contact with providers (Macy and Graham, 2012). These training needs include understanding the various types of trafficking, cultural considerations as well as understanding the nature of trauma and how the effects of trauma are expressed behaviorally (Palmer, 2010).

Summary

Homicide, intimate partner violence/ domestic violence and trafficking experiences frequently result in victimization and trauma. As such, collectively they represent a public health challenge to service providers. The advantage of a public health response to this challenge is that it implicitly rejects reductionistic thinking in favor of nuanced approaches targeted at the individualized true needs of victims. When providers and service systems can be trained in culturally and trauma-informed interventions and then implement services that reflect these holistic understandings, then these needs have a fair chance at being addressed.

Discussion Questions

1. Given that exposure to violence and victimization often leads to an imbalance between social/ emotional and concrete/tangible needs, how should practitioners and social services orient themselves so that they can be best able to assist people in addressing the complexity of needs?
2. Increasingly the trauma-informed literature has been brought forward as having a strong evidence base behind it. What are the real training needs in law enforcement, medical and behavioral health that all practitioners need and in what ways must their related systems change in order to embrace these evidenced-based models?
3. Given that race, ethnicity, age, sexual orientation and other factors including differences related to type of victimization lead to different understandings of that victimization and different strategies to address the victimization, how do practitioners and service providers train themselves to be able to successfully understand and meet the variety of needs through culturally-informed approaches?

References

Ahn, R., Alpert, E., Purcell, G., Konstantopoulos, W., McGahan, A., Cafferty, E., & Burke, T. (2013). Human trafficking: Review of educational resources for health professionals. *American Journal of Preventive Medicine, 44*, 3, 283–289.

Alaggia, R., Gadalla, T., Shlonsky, A., Jenny, A., & Daciuk, J. (2012). Does differential response make a difference: Examining domestic violence cases in child protection services. *Child and Family Social Work.* Doi: 10.1111/cfs.12058.

Ascione, F., Weber, C., Thompson, T., Heath, J., Maruyama, M., & Hayashi, K. (2007). Batteredpets and domestic violence animal abuse reported by women experiencing intimate violence and by nonabused women. *Violence Against Women, 13*, 4, 354–373.

ASPE Issue Brief. (2012). Barriers to immigrants' access to health and human service programs. *U.S. Department of Health and Human Services.* 1–19.

Bent-Goodley, T. (2013). Domestic violence fatality reviews and the African American community. *Homicide Studies. 17*, 4, 375–390.

Bloom, S. L. (2013). *Creating Sanctuary: Toward the Evolution of Sane Societies.* NY: Routledge.

Brickman, E., Davis, R., Rabinovich, B., Cantor, D., and Shapiro, G. (2002). *Victims Needs and Victim Assistance.* Report to the National Institute of Justice. NY: Safe Horizon.

Bugeja, L., Dawson, M., McIntryre, S-J. & Walsh, C. (2013). *Trauma, Violence & Abuse.* 20, 10, 1–9.

Butler, A., Devries, K., Howard, L. & Bacchus, L. (2014). Associations between intimate partner violence and health among men who have sex with men: A systematic review and meta-analysis. *PLOS Medicine.* Doi: 10.1371/journal.pmed.1001609.

Caldwell, J., Swan, S. & Woodbrown, D. (2012). Gender differences in intimate partner violence outcomes. *Psychology of Violence. 2*, 1, 42–57.

Carlson, B. (2000). Children exposed to intimate partner violence: Research findings and implications for interventions. *Trauma, Violence and Victims. 1*, 4, 321–342.

Chanmugam, A. (2014). Social work expertise and domestic violence fatality review teams. *Social Work.* Doi:10.1093/sw/swt048.

Cho, H. & Kim, W.J. (2012). Racial differences in satisfaction with mental health services among victims of intimate partner violence. *Community Mental Health Journal*. 48, 84–90.

Cohen, J., Mannarino, A. & Deblinger, E. (2006). *Treating Trauma and Traumatic Grief in Children and Adolescents*. NY: Guilford.

DeGue, S., Simon, T., Basile, K., Yee, S., Lang, K. & Spivak, H. (2012). Moving forward by looking back: Reflecting on a decade of CDC's work in sexual violence prevention, 2000–2010. *Journal of Women's Health*. *21*, 12, 1211–1218.

Farrell, A. & Fahy, S. (2009). The problem of human trafficking in the U.S.: Public frames and policy responses. *Journal of Criminal Justice*. *37*, 620–622.

Febres, J., Brasfield, H., Shorey, R., Elmquist, J., Ninnemann, A., Schonbrun, Y. & Stuart, G. (2014). Adulthood animal abuse among men arrested for domestic violence. *Violence Against Women*. *20*, 9, 1059–1077.

Goldberg, N. & Meyer, I. (2012). Sexual orientation disparities in history of intimate partner violence: Results from the California health interview survey. *Journal of Interpersonal Violence*. Doi: 10.1177/0886260512459384.

Green, S. (2008). Protection for victims of child sex trafficking in the United States: Forging the gap between U.S. immigration laws and human trafficking laws. *UC Davis Journal of Juvenile Law & Policy*. *12*, 2, 302–380.

Hardy, V., Compton, K. & McPhatter, V. (2013). Domestic minor sex trafficking: Practice implications for mental health professionals. *Journal of Women and Social Work*. *00*, 0, 1–11.

Herschell, A. D., Calzada, E. J., Eyberg, S. M., & McNeil, C. B. (2003). Parent–child interaction therapy: New directions in research. *Cognitive and Behavioral Practice*, *9*, 1, 9–16.

Hertz, M., Prothrow-Smith, D. & Chery, C. (2005). Homicide survivors: Research and practice implications. *American Journal of Preventive Medicine*. *29*, 582, 288–295.

Hoff, L. A. (2009). *Violence and Abuse Issues: Cross-cultural Perspectives for Health and Social Services*. NY: Routledge.

Humphreys, C. & Absler, D. (2011). History repeating itself: Child protection responses to domestic violence. *Child and Family Social Work*. *16*, 4, 464–473.

Israel, B., Schulz, A., Parker, E. & Becker, A. (1998). Review of community-based research: Assessing partnership approaches to improve public health. *Annual Review of Public Health*. *19*, 173–202.

Jones-Webb, R. & Wall, M. (2008). Neighborhood racial/ethnic concentration, social disadvantage, and homicide risk: An ecological analysis of ten U.S. cities. *Journal of Urban Health*. *85*, 5, 662–676. Doi:10.1007/s11524-008-9302-y.

Juodis, M., Starzomski, A., Porter, S. & Woodworth, M. (2014). A comparison of domestic and non-domestic homicides: Further evidence for distinct dynamics and heterogeneity of domestic homicide perpetrators. *Journal of Family Violence*. *29*, 299–313.

Klein, E. & White, A. (2013). Implementing trauma-informed practices in child welfare. *ABA Center on Children and the Law*. 1–15.

Krueg, E., Mercey, J., Dahlberg, L. & Zwi, A. (2002). The world report on violence and health. *The Lancet*. *360*, 1083–1088.

Kulkarni, S., Bell, H. & McDaniel Rhodes, D. (2012). Back to basics: Essential qualities of services for survivors of intimate partner violence. *Violence Against Women*. *18*, 1, 85–101.

Laurie, A. & Neimeyer, R. (2008). African Americans in bereavement: Grief as a function of ethnicity. *Omega: Journal of Death and Dying*. *57*, 173–193. Doi:10.2190/OM.57.2.d.

Lippman, J. (2012). Ensuring victim safety and abuser accountability: Reforms and revisions in New York courts' response to domestic violence. *Albany Law Review*. *76*, 1417–1443.

Macy, R., Ermentrout, D. & Rizo, C. (2012). An innovative program for justice-involved partner violence victims: "No man is worth me getting locked up". *Journal of Family Violence*. *27*, 453–464.

Macy, R. & Graham, L. (2012). Identifying domestic and international sex-trafficking victims during human service provision. *Trauma, Violence & Abuse*. *13*, 2, 59–76.

Madsen, W. (2007). *Collaborative Therapy with Multi-stressed Families*. NY: Guilford.

Mastrocinque, J., Metzger, J., Maderia, J., Lang, K., Pruss, H., Navratil, P., Sandys, M. & Cerulli, C. (2014). I'm still here with the pain: Exploring the health consequences of homicide *On families and friends*. Homicide Studies. *Published online June 10, 2014*. Doi: 10.1177/1088767914537494.

McDevitt-Murphy, M., Neimeyer, R., Burke, L., Williams, J. & Lawson, K. (2012). The toll of traumatic loss in African Americans bereaved by homicide. *Psychological Trauma: Theory, Research, Practice and Policy*. *4*, 3, 303.

McGraw, C., & Jeffers, S. (2015). The importance of considering the treatment and care of family pets in domestic violence risk assessments. *Journal of Health Visiting*, *3*, 9, 483–488.

Metzger, J., Mastrocinque, J., Navraitil, P. & Cerulli, C. (2014). *Improving systematic response in the face of homicide: Family and friends of homicide victims service needs.* Violence and *Victims. 29*, 522–532

Newmark, L. (2006). Crime victim needs and VOCA-funded services: Findings and recommendations from two national studies. *Report to the National Institute of Justice.* Alexandria, VA: Institute for Law and Justice.

Newmark, L., Bonderman, J., Smith, B. & Liner, B. (2003). *The National Evaluation of State Victims of Crime Act Assistance and Compensation Programs: Trends and Strategies for the Future.* Report to the National Institute of Justice. Washington, DC: The Urban Institute.

Okech, D., Morreau, W. & Benson, K. (2011). Human trafficking: Improving victim identification and service provision. *International Social Work. 55*, 4, 488–503.

Palmer, N. (2010). The essential role of social work in addressing victims and survivors of trafficking. *Journal of International & Comparative Law. 17*, 43–56.

Pynoos, R., Fairbank, J., Steinberg, A., Amaya-Jackson, L., Gerrity, E., Mount, M., & Maze, J. (2008). The National Child Traumatic Stress Network: Collaborating to improve the standard of care. *Professional Psychology: Research and Practice, 39*, 4, 389–395.

Rennison, C. (2003). *Intimate Partner Violence, 1993–2001 (NCJ 197838).* Washington, DC: Bureau of Justice Statistics.

Rheingold, A., Zinzow, H., Hawkins, A., Saunders, B. & Kilpatrick, D. (2012). Prevalence and mental health outcomes of homicide survivors in a representative U.S. sample of adolescents: Data from the 2005 national survey of adolescents. *Journal of Child Psychological Psychiatry. 53*, 6, 687–694.

Richie, B. (2012). *Arrested Justice: Black Women, Justice and America's Prison Nation.* NY: New York University Press.

Roby, J., Turley, J. & Cloward, J. (2008). U.S. response to human trafficking: Is it enough? *Journal of Immigrant and Refugee Studies. 6*, 4, 508–525.

Saltzman, L., Green, Y., Marks, J. & Thacker, S. (2000). Violence against women as a public Health issue: Comments from the CDC. *American Journal of Preventive Medicine. 19*, 4, 325–329.

Satcher, D. (1995). Violence as a public health issue. *Bulletin of the New York Academy of Medicine. 72*, 1, 46–56.

Sharpe, T. & Boyas, J. (2011). We fall down: The African American experience of coping with the homicide of a loved one. *Journal of Black Studies. 20*, 10, 1–19.

Simmons, C., Lehmann, P. & Dia, D. (2010). Parenting and women arrested for intimate partner violence. *Journal of Interpersonal Violence. 25*, 1429–1448.

Stern, S. (2010). Immediate aftercare program for survivors and families of homicide victims: The case of Cobb County government. *Dissertations, Thesis, Capstone Projects* Paper 227, Kennesaw State University.

Trevillion, K., Howard, L., Morgan, C., Feder, G., Woodall, A., & Rose, D. (2012). The response of mental health services to domestic violence: A qualitative study of service users' and professionals' experiences. *Journal of the American Psychiatric Nurses Association.* 18, 6, 326–336.

U.S. Department of Justice, Bureau of Justice Statistics (2012). *Homicide Trends in the United States 1980–2008.* U.S. Department of Justice Office of Justice Programs Bureau of Justice Statistics November 2011, NCJ 236018 BJS PATTERNS & TRENDS Homicide Trends in the United States, 1980–2008 Annual Rates for 2009 and 2010 Alexia Cooper and Erica L. Smith, BJS Statisticians.

Van Der Kolk, B. (2014). *The Body Keeps Score: Brain, Mind, and Body in the Healing of Trauma.* New York, NY: Viking.

Wallace, H., & Roberson, C. (1998). *Victimology: Legal, Psychological, and Social Perspectives* Boston, MA: Allyn and Bacon.

Websdale, N., Town, M, & Johnson, B. (1999). Domestic violence fatality reviews: From a culture of blame to a culture of safety. *Juvenile & Family Court Journal. 50*, 2, 61–74.

Wisner, C., Gilmer, T., Saltzman, L. & Zink, T. (1999). Intimate partner violence against Women: Do victims cost health plans more? *Journal of Family Practice. 48*, 439–443.

13
SPECIAL NEEDS OF ELDERLY VICTIMS

Yoshiko Takahashi

Keywords

aging; elderly; elder abuse; physical abuse; sexual abuse; financial or material exploitation; emotional or psychological abuse; neglect; self-neglect; abandonment

Objectives

After studying this chapter, the reader should be able to:

- Define and explain elder abuse.
- List the various types of elder abuse.
- Explain the leading issues and special needs of elderly victims.
- Identify the effective response for elderly victims.

Introduction

The population in the world is aging. According to the World Health Organization (WHO), it is estimated that those age 60 and older in the world population will double from about 12 percent to 22 percent between 2000 and 2050 (WHO, n.d.). Among the elderly population, the "oldest old," or people older than age 80, is the most rapidly increasing age group (Patterson & Malley-Morrison, 2006). In the United States, individuals age 55 and older reached 67.1 million in 2005, and the growth rate of the older population is much faster than that of those under age 55 (Krienert, Walsh, & Turner, 2009). The baby-boomer generation, or the 76 million children who were born from 1946 to 1964, is reaching retirement age, and it is estimated that more than 20 percent of the U.S. population will be age 60 and older by 2030. Furthermore, a rapid increase is expected among those Americans age 85 or older (Himes, 2002).

Aging brings individuals insecurity and vulnerability, which could generate an overall increased risk of victimization. To prepare for the inevitable challenge in this population, it is important to determine what can be done to prevent such victimization. This chapter highlights the definitions and prevalence of elder abuse and then discusses the research regarding age-related risk factors, as well as the characteristics and relationships that increase the probability of abuse, to better understand the dynamics and special needs of elderly victims.

Definitions and Prevalence of Elder Abuse

Definitions

Defining the elderly can be a challenge as grouping such a diverse population into one group could do "more disservice than good" (Doerner & Lab, 2005, p. 278). In fact, the definition of *elderly* differs by country and culture, but in the United States, federal law defines age 60 or older as older individuals (Heisler, 2013) and the U.S. Census defines elderly as 65 or older (U.S. Census Bureau, 2011). Although elderly victimization can be discussed from two perspectives—victimization of conventional crimes and abuse and mistreatment (James, 1992)—the main focus of this chapter is abuse and mistreatment. In general, elder abuse includes all types of mistreatment or abusive behaviors toward elders, yet the scope of the definition varies depending on the discipline and research purpose (Krienert et al., 2009). In the United States, the National Center on Elder Abuse and the National Elder Abuse Incidence Study have standardized the definition as physical abuse, sexual abuse, financial or material exploitation, emotional or psychological abuse, neglect and self-neglect, and abandonment (Gorbien & Eisenstein, 2005).

According to the National Center on Elder Abuse, *physical abuse* includes inflicting, or threatening to inflict, physical pain or injury on a vulnerable elder, or depriving an elder of a basic need. *Sexual abuse* includes nonconsensual sexual contact of any kind or coercing an elder to witness sexual behaviors. *Financial or material exploitation* includes illegal taking, misuse, or concealment of funds, property, or assets of a vulnerable elder. *Emotional or psychological abuse* includes inflicting mental pain, anguish, or distress on an elder person through verbal or nonverbal acts. *Neglect* includes refusal or failure by those responsible to provide food, shelter, healthcare, or protection for a vulnerable elder. *Abandonment* includes the desertion of a vulnerable elder by anyone who has assumed the responsibility for care or custody of that person.

Some scholars have more broadly defined the concept of elder abuse including other forms of abuse such as the violation of basic human rights, abductions, and abandonment (Nerenberg, 2008). Self-neglect is sometimes excluded from the definition, and other studies distinguish self-neglect from self-abuse (Choi & Mayer, 2000). Other researchers prefer to use *mistreatment* rather than *abuse* as the term *mistreatment* could include "a broader perspective on behavior perceived as inappropriate" (Bowes, Avan, & Macintosh, 2012, p. 252).

Extent of Elder Abuse

Elder abuse is not a new crime, but empirical research and financial support for studies were relatively limited until recently. Elder abuse is considered as the newest form of intrafamilial violence following the formal introduction of child abuse and spousal abuse, which resulted from the feminist and women's liberation movements in the late 1960s and early 1970s (Krienert et al., 2009). With a growing elder population on the rise, elder abuse, although typically underreported, has gradually become more prevalent within the past two decades. It is estimated that 1 million–2 million Americans age 65 or older have been injured, exploited, or mistreated by someone on whom they depended for care or protection (Bonnie & Wallace, 2003). A summary of prior studies indicated that estimates of the frequency of elder abuse ranged from 2 percent to 10 percent depending on the sampling and survey methods and the case definitions (Lachs & Pillemer, 2004). According to a National Institute of Justice telephone survey conducted in January 2008, 11 percent of persons age 60 and older reported some form of abuse in the previous year (Norman, 2010). Another national elder abuse study in the United States, conducted by Acierno et al. (2010), showed a similar result. Based on 5,777 samples collected via a computer-assisted telephone interviewing methodology, the authors found that the one-year prevalence of emotional abuse was 4.6 percent, 1.6 percent for physical abuse, 0.6 percent for sexual abuse, 5.1 percent for potential neglect, and 5.2 percent for financial abuse by a family member. In sum, 10 percent of the overall respondents indicated that they experienced some form of abuse in the past year. The typical age that made elders more likely to become targets of abuse was 70–81 years old, or "the oldest old" (Schiamberg et al., 2012).

Elder abuse is not selective and could happen to anyone regardless of gender or socioeconomic status (Oh, 2003). Nevertheless, elderly victims are classified as a group with similar vulnerabilities as other groups such as children and mentally ill victims (Marchiori, 2009). For older adults, vulnerability comes from age-related variables. In this sense, exploring the age-related risk factors of elder victimization becomes a valuable reference to explain the dynamics of victimization among elders.

Risk Factors Influencing Victimization

Individual Risk Factors

Individual risk factors associated with aging could be attributed to the prevalence of victimization. Previous research indicated that intra-individual factors (e.g., health conditions, socioeconomic status), social-relational factors (e.g., family relationship, isolation), and geographical factors (e.g., urban versus rural) are associated with the risk of victimization among the elderly. Among those, one of the most age-specific risk factors is health conditions. The aging process brings various physical and cognitive challenges. Roberts and Willits (2012) note that in 2000, 42 percent of individuals age 65 and older had interference with daily activities due to physical or mental disability. Such health issues increase the risk of mistreatment. Much research has found that dementia-related behavior increases the risk of abuse (Hansberry, Chen, & Gorbien, 2005; Wiglesworth et al., 2010). Particularly, older adults with Alzheimer's disease have a high correlation with physical abuse (Pillemer & Suitor, 1992).

In discussing social-relational factors, social exchange theory could help in understanding elderly mistreatment caused by the power imbalance among family members (Doerner & Lab, 2005). This theory is based on the idea that social interaction involves the exchange of rewards and punishments between at least two individuals. The parties interact appropriately when both parties hold equitable power or resources. However, when people get older, they are more likely to depend on others and have increasingly less to offer in an exchange relationship. Under an imbalance exchange relationship, the older parents might feel guilt or distress as they recognize that they no longer have the power to control the relationship. Furthermore, children who become a caregiver of older parents might recognize that the imbalance in the relationship is unfair. Under such circumstances, mistreatment is more likely to happen.

Communication problems increase the frustration in both parties. Many people do not have sufficient knowledge about physiological health issues, and ignorance and unrealistic expectations can increase the likelihood of anger and abuse. Elders who have trouble with daily chores must depend on family members or caregivers. In doing so, the elder parents authorize family members, often their children, to take care of the money to pay the bills. Under such circumstances, financial abuse or systematic theft is more likely to occur (Ottley, 2009). Ironically, many perpetrators of elder abuse are persons who depended on the abused elderly for housing and financial support (Payne, 2005).

The availability of social networks for the elderly is critical as isolation from society is one of the risk factors for victims. Oh (2003) discusses that the various stages of the life cycle affect social networks. During early and middle adulthood, people are exposed to many opportunities to create social networks such as entering the labor force, getting married, and having children. However, those opportunities and interactions decline as people get older. Older people are more likely to withdraw from work, to lose close family members, and to have a limited sphere of activity. They also tend to live alone. According to the 2000 U.S. Census, 30 percent of Americans age 65 and older lived alone (Roberts & Willits, 2012). Consequently, older people have fewer friends than younger people, and those friends tend to be found in their neighborhood (Oh, 2003). Weak social networks of older people can cause social isolation, which could lead to elder abuse. Vandecar-Burdin and Payne (2010) cited a study on the impact of social networks and isolation conducted by Phillips in which abused elders had fewer friends to call on the phone, to correspond with, and to seek support from compared to non-abused elders.

It has been found that geographical factors affect the type of victimization. Comparing the difference of experiences of substantiated elder abuse, neglect, and exploitation in rural and urban areas, Dimah and Dimah (2004) found that even though both rural and urban elder victims had a similar demographic profile, there was a significant difference in emotional abuse, passive neglect, and deprivation between rural and urban samples. More specifically, more rural older adults were subject to emotional abuse and deprivation than their urban counterparts; in contrast, more urban older adults had experience with passive neglect than rural ones. For that reason, such various factors as the homogeneity of rural dwellers as opposed to the diverse population in urban areas, accessibility to social services, and traditional family ties and values could affect outcomes (Dimah & Dimah, 2004).

Characteristics of Perpetrators

The characteristics of perpetrators, along with the relationship with their victims, cannot be ignored for the effective interventions. Although the perpetrators of elderly victimization could be anyone including spouses, family members, doctors, caregivers, or employees in the care faculties, a vast majority of perpetrators are family members, especially adult children (National Center on Elder Abuse, 1998). The risk of victimization is higher if those family members are unemployed, unmarried, and dependent on their victims (Pillemer & Finkelhor, 1988). Not surprisingly, 60 percent of APS-substantiated financial abuse cases are committed by adult children (National Center on Elder Abuse, 1998). Perpetrators are more likely to have mental health, substance abuse, and behavioral problems (Anetzberger, 2005). Although both females and males are almost equally preyed upon as victims (52.5 percent male perpetuators), males are more likely than females to commit certain types of abuse, for example, 83 percent of abandonment, 63 percent of physical abuse, and 60 percent of emotional abuse are committed by males (National Center on Elder Abuse, 1998).

When looking at victimization within care facilities, abusers are direct care providers, support staff, and temporary employees, as well as other residents and visitors (Nerenberg, 2008). Abusive employees tend to be younger and more likely to have negative attitudes toward residents (Pillemer & Moore, 1989) with inadequate training and often experiencing burnout (Payne & Cikovic, 1995). Neglect and verbal abuse are the most common forms of abuse in nursing homes (Goergen, 2001). Common types of physical abuse in nursing homes are excessive restraints, shoving, pinching or grabbing, hitting or slapping, and throwing something at a patient (Pillemer & Moore, 1989).

Cultural and Social Norms

Along with micro or individual risk factors, much larger-scale macro perspectives, or how one's culture and social norms influence lifestyle and daily activities, could increase the risk of particular crime victimization. For example, interdependency is highly valued and observed in many ethnic communities. In some Native American families, for example, sharing a pension and the social security of elders among family members is an accepted way to share resources (Brown, 1989). Black, Hispanic, and Asian and Pacific Islander elderly are more likely than White elderly to live with their children and grandchildren. Although such a multigenerational family support system could provide stability to family members, such mutually dependent relationships could also increase the risk of abuse (Brown, 1989). For example, in South Korea, older parents commonly live with married children, and the burden of caring for older parents rests with the oldest son and his wife. After surveying

15,230 persons at their homes, Oh, Kim, Martins, and Kim (2006) found that the most common abuser was a son followed by a daughter-in-law and emotional abuse is the most common type; more than 3 percent of the sample experienced such abuse.

Cultural and social factors in respective ethnic groups also affect attitudes about abuse and help-seeking behavior. For example, it is acceptable for many Korean elders when the husband controls the family financial resources and limits those available to his wife. Korean American elders are more tolerant of financial exploitation than White elders (Nerenberg, 2008). Asian and Hispanic elders prefer to seek assistance and help from family or friends, whereas African American and White elders prefer to use third-party intervention (Lee & Lightfoot, 2014).

As seen, individual risk factors, the characteristics of perpetuators and their relationship with victims, and cultural norms and customs could significantly affect the detection of abuse and intervention in those situations. This is particularly true for ethnic minority groups where formal intervention and mainstream services do not meet the needs of the respective culture.

Elderly Victims of Specific Crimes

Physical Crime Victimization

Identifying physical abuse cases is a challenge as medical conditions and age-related factors sometimes make it difficult to identify abuse (Dyer, Connolly, & McFeeley, 2003). Although there is limited research on bruising or other injuries associated with elder abuse cases, there are some indications for susceptive cases. For example, a study of bruising in older adults indicated that abused adults are more likely to have bruises 5 cm or greater and abuse is suspected if those appear on the head, neck, lateral right arm, or posterior torso (Wiglesworth et al., 2009). Hair loss could be natural, but it is also possible that the abuser has grabbed the victim by the hair. Also, any observed indications of disengagement, poor health, isolation, depression, and/or alcohol abuse require further attention (Flynn, 2000).

Physical elderly abuse has been further studied relative to domestic violence, elder homicide, and homicide–suicide. Reports of spouse abuse between older couples increased dramatically in the 1980s, likely due to the increased awareness of domestic violence (Buzawa & Buzawa, 2003). In examining the 1985 Family Violence Survey, Harris (1996) found that a majority of older victims of spouse abuse had been physically abused over a period of several years. An analysis of the National Violence Against Women Survey indicated that African Americans and Hispanics are more likely to be victims of elder spouse abuse than their White counterparts (Jasinski & Dietz, 2004).

Elder homicide is sometimes called "gray death" as it might appear to be natural death (Collins & Presnell, 2006). Strangulation and suffocation account for a high percentage of elder homicides, both of which can leave no apparent injuries to find during an autopsy (McClane, Strack, & Hawley, 2001). The prevalence of homicide–suicide is much higher in the population age 55 and older than among younger adults (Malphurs & Cohen, 2001). Among those homicide–suicides, approximately 30 percent of the cases had histories of domestic violence; 50 percent were dependent/protective long-term relationships, where the man was dominant and one or both parties had been ill; and 20 percent were symbiotic relationships characterized by extreme interdependence (Cohen, 2000). The same author noted that men are typically the perpetrator and in a vast majority of the cases guns are used. A high percentage of untreated and undetected psychiatric problems, especially depression, was observed.

A particular concern for elderly domestic violence victims is interdependence with the perpetrator. An Australian study found that the most important concern for elderly victims was to be believed by their spouse or significant other (Schaffer, 1999). In many cases, the victim finds it difficult to escape the abuse because of financial ties to the perpetrator. The victim might be isolated from social, community, and institutional support (Buzawa & Buzawa, 2003). Furthermore, the services and interventions for elderly domestic violence victims are particularly challenging. At domestic violence shelters, there has been an increase in the number of older women victims in recent years. This development presents a challenge to domestic violence shelters as the needs of older female victims are significantly different than those of younger victims.

Protective orders can protect a victim from future harassment or abuse. Such orders can be particularly effective for victims of elder abuse. However, such victims cannot always obtain a protective order. Also, protective orders do have some limitations. The level of protection could be insufficient to the needs of the victim. The order might also be specific to a spouse, when there are also other victims. Depending on the state, the order itself could be temporary. A protective order in and of itself does not address the often complicated financial issues that must be unraveled in resolving an abusive relationship (Buzawa & Buzawa, 2003).

It is important to ensure a victim's safety, reduce trauma, and secure assets when agencies advocate in working with vulnerable and abused victims with crises and emergencies. Despite the problems that exist with protective orders, they remain a key tool in protecting elderly abuse victims. As a first step, such orders can remove the abuser's power over the victim.

Sexual Abuse Victimization

Elder sexual abuse includes various nonconsensual sexual acts, including but not limited to rape, sodomy, molestation, and coerced nudity (National Center on Elder Abuse, n.d.), which could be the most hidden and underreported type of abuse. The National Center on Elder Abuse estimates that sexual abuse cases account for 0.3 percent of elder abuse cases (Payne, 2010). Caution is needed for these statistics as the numbers only capture reported cases and there is the possibility that a sexually assaulted elderly victim chose not to report an incident due to stigma and shame, denial of the incident, or being cognitively unable to report the case (Payne, 2010). Society also has failed to address such issues. In explaining why elderly sexual assault victims have been overlooked and underserved, Vierthaler (2008) noted that popular culture does not acknowledge elderly victims and, as a result, far fewer services are available to address their needs than those available for younger victims.

To understand the dynamics of elder sexual abuse, Payne (2010) compared a sample of 127 elder sexual abuse cases and 314 elder physical abuse cases. The findings indicate that a much higher percentage of the perpetuators in sexual abuse cases are male (78 percent of the elder sexual abuse offenders are male, whereas 26 percent of the physical abuse offenders are male) and the victims are female (67 percent of the elder sexual abuse victims are female, whereas 50.9 percent of physical abuse victims are female). The same study also indicates that victims with cognitive impairment are much higher among the sexual assault victims (44.9 percent for sexual abuse victims, whereas 29.9 percent for physical abuse victims). The vulnerability of the elderly with mental impairment was also found in research conducted by Burgess and Phillips (2006). They found that 60 percent of 284 victims of sexual abuse had suffered from some form of dementia.

Ramsey-Klawsnik and Brandl (2010) discussed sexual abuse issues relative to an intimate partner, incestuous abuse, and sexual assault in care facilities. In the case of intimate partner sexual abuse, the relationship could be short or long, but a long-term domestic violence situation is more common with some women reporting having been sexually abused for 40 or more years. Incestuous elder abuse involves adult children, grandchildren, or other relatives. The perpetuators attempt to control the victims using various abusive tactics including emotional, physical, and financial means in addition to sexual coercion. These victims tend to be too inhibited to protect themselves or to seek help for their often complex traumas (Chihowski & Hughes, 2008). In studies of sexual assault cases in care facilities, Ramsey-Klawsnik, Teaster, Mendiondo, Marcum, and Abner (2008) found that the largest alleged perpetuators were facility staff followed by facility residents. Many of the victims experienced disabilities including dementia and major psychiatric illness, and some had communication problems. Only 27 percent of the cases were substantiated, which is remarkably lower than for all types of elder abuse cases.

As more elder abuse incidents are reported and professionals encounter suspicious elder sexual abuse cases, trainings for professionals in understanding elderly sexual abuse and utilizing assessment tools such as the SPAN scale to assess the impact of sexual assault on elderly women (Burgess & Clements, 2006) would be beneficial for effective crisis intervention.

Financial Abuse and Exploitation

Financial abuse and exploitation is one of the most common and fastest growing forms of elder abuse (Mihaljcic & Lowndes, 2013). The extent of this form of abuse is greater than previously believed, and it is expected to increase with the rising number of older people in the population. Financial abuse accounts for 26–38 percent of all reported cases of elder abuse (Mihaljcic & Lowndes, 2013). The perpetuators of financial abuse could be family members, contractors, salespersons, attorneys, caregivers, insurance agencies, clergy, accountants, bookkeepers, or friends (Kemp & Mosqueda, 2005).

The risk of financial abuse is closely linked to age-related factors. For example, a study conducted by James, Boyle, and Bennett (2014) looked at how people are susceptible to financial abuse in a longitudinal study called the Memory and Aging Project, which started in 1997. From an analysis of individuals in retirement and subsidized housing facilities in the Chicago area, James et al. (2014) found that older persons with low levels of cognitive ability and psychological well-being, poor health, and low financial literacy were prone to being victims of financial fraud. Similarly, research of the financial abuse done by family members in Australia revealed that the elderly with dementia are especially vulnerable to being victims of financial abuse (Adams, Bagshaw, Wendt, & Zannettino, 2014). Financial abuse is a difficult crime to detect and prosecute (Gibson & Greene, 2013). Adult children might not consider borrowing money from their parents as financially abusive behavior, and parents tend to agree that they lend money to their children without expecting any interest or return of payment. In fact, sometimes financial abuse is alleged in situations where the exchange of funds was thought to be a gift or loan from the victim. To ensure such transactions are not financial abuse, there must be an expectation that the person making said gift or loan is capable of making that decision logically and coherently (Nerenberg, 2008). Moreover, some fraudulent schemes might seem legitimate on the surface. Jointly held titles, deeds, or bank accounts, for example, could appear legitimate but might have been created under the threat of coercion. Perpetrators are subtly and effectively manipulative in gaining control over victims and their financial assets (Gibson & Green, 2013).

Another area of growing concern is the elderly as a target of identity theft and fraud. Often extending beyond family members, a variety of scams and frauds threaten the elderly. Scams or frauds related to foreign lotteries, tax or Social Security benefits, Medicare, precious metals, sweepstakes, charities, and home repairs are increasingly common (Myers, 2015).

In response to the financial exploitation of the elderly, measures to effectively address this epidemic need to be implemented. Such measures include the following (Rabiner, Brown, & O'Keeffe, 2004).

- Enhance the understanding of how to prosecute financial abuse crimes effectively.
- Improve the process for the selection and monitoring of financial guardians.
- Establish and follow through on restitution programs.
- Provide training on the signs of and dealing with financial exploitation.

At the national level, the U.S. Government Accountability Office has made a number of recommendations to address financial abuse. These include assisting states with handling mass marketing fraud, providing information about the qualifications of financial services providers, and funding background checks of in-home caregivers (California Elder Justice Coalition, 2016). Furthermore, it was recommended that a national repository be created of contacts for the fraud departments of major financial institutions; incentives be implemented to ensure that financial institutions take financial abuse seriously; and support services be provided for victims (California Elder Justice Coalition, 2016).

Special services for victims of financial abuse could include 1) counseling and advocacy to deal with debt collectors, restructure debt, and handle related issues; 2) protecting assets, recovering losses, securing protective orders, and stopping evictions; 3) advising on money management to prevent future abuse; 4) instructing victims of cybercrime scams on safe computer use; and 5) assisting family members in offering support and protection (California Elder Justice Coalition, 2016).

Psychological and Emotional Abuse

Psychological and emotional abuse can take different forms. Verbal assaults, insults, threats, intimidation, humiliation, and harassment are included in this category. Also, treating an older person like an infant and isolating an elderly person from family members, friends, and society are considered psychological abuse (Nerenberg, 2008). Acierno et al. (2010) found that the prevalence of emotional mistreatment, including verbal abuse, humiliation, harassment/coercing, or being ignored, was 4.6 percent in a study of 5,777 elderly in the United States. Another study, conducted by Laumann, Leitsch, and Waite (2008), sampled 3,005 seniors ages 57 to 85 and found a prevalence rate of 9 percent for verbal abuse, which was defined differently from the Acierno et al. (2010) study.

Along with a lack of clarity, the subjective nature of abuse makes it difficult to address the issue (Nerenberg, 2008). Psychological and emotional abuse were not considered as criminal conduct in the past (Heisler, 2013), and incidents have been somehow overlooked or discounted in the past (Fulmer, Rodgers, & Pelger, 2014). However, that does not necessarily mean that psychological and emotional abuse is less serious than other types of abuse. For example, a study comparing the impact of verbal and physical abuse alone found that verbal abuse leads to greater declines in mental health than physical abuse (Fulmer et al., 2014). Another study recognized the impact of such abuse on elderly depression, nervous disorders, fearfulness, physical illness, and even suicide (Moskowitz, 2003). Furthermore, psychological abuse can often occur simultaneously with other forms of abuse. A study found that in a vast majority of elder abuse cases (89.7 percent), psychological abuse occurred along with neglect and financial abuse (Anetzberger, 1998). In citing the Humane Society of the United States, Nerenberg (2008) notes that stalking and pet abuse have been increasingly reported, and there are some indications of a correlation between those offenses and subsequent acts of domestic violence. Without proper intervention, psychological and emotional abuse could accelerate to physical abuse, which can have a lethal outcome. Mental health professionals and healthcare providers have a critical role in identifying and intervening to curb or eliminate such abuse.

Neglect, Self-neglect, and Abandonment

A National Elder Abuse Incidence Study found that neglect is in general the most common type of abuse reported to Adult Protective Services (APS), accounting for nearly half of substantiated reported incidents (48.7 percent). The largest age group of victims of neglect was elders age 80 and older (51.8 percent; National Center on Elder Abuse, 1998). Although neglect tends to be considered less serious than other forms of abuse, it can be extremely damaging, life threatening, or even have lethal consequences (Nerenberg, 2008).

Neglect is generally defined as the refusal or failure to fulfill any part of a person's obligations or duties to an elder. Those obligations and duties include providing such life necessities as medical care, mental healthcare, assistance with bathing and toileting, personal hygiene, food and water, and protection against safely hazards (Nerenberg, 2008). However, the legal definition of a *caregiver* varies by state; in some states, adult children have a legal duty to care for aging parents, whereas other states do not have such a requirement (Heisler, 2013). In Massachusetts and North Carolina, for example, a person age 18 or older with sufficient means himself who neglects to support a disabled or destitute parent could be fined or imprisoned. In California, conversely, a court ruled that only if an adult child accepts responsibility for care of a parent is she then criminally liable for that parent's care (Nerenberg, 2008).

The diagnosis of neglect is also controversial. Detecting the signs of neglect is not always easy as the aging process could mask the marks. According to practical guidelines (Strasser & Fulmer, 2007), such signs of neglect might include dehydration, poor personal hygiene, oversensitivity, lack of essential accessories such as eyeglasses and hearing aids, unclean bed sheets, and the absence of a minimal standard of living. Moreover, a person who is left home alone could experience psychological neglect. Such neglect might occur in the elderly person's home or in a care facility (Winterstein, 2012).

Self-neglect is a condition in which an elder fails to satisfy his own needs and places his own health or safety at risk (Nerenberg, 2008). Some scholars disagree as to whether this should be an elder abuse category. In fact, there are no perpetuators of self-neglect, and no one will be prosecuted. However, self-neglect is included in mandatory reporting statutes and other policies and research on elder abuse. Research on self-neglect has found certain characteristics of individuals who are susceptible to self-neglect. Payne and Gainey (2005) explained that self-neglect occurs among older persons who are more likely to live alone, refuse services offered by social services, and have psychiatric and alcohol problems. Ernst and Smith (2011) found that older adults who have a poor diet, arthritis, vision problems, and need significant assistance with the key activities of daily living (ADL), including housekeeping, meal preparation, and money management, are susceptible to self-neglect. A clinical study of the elderly who are living in senior public and private housing indicated that the prevalence of clinically significant depressive symptoms and cognitive impairment are good indicators of self-neglect (Abrams, Lachs, McAvay, Keohane, & Bruce, 2002).

A National Elder Abuse Incidence Study (National Center on Elder Abuse, 1998) found that reports of self-neglect derived primarily from hospitals (19.8 percent), friends/neighbors (19.1 percent), police/sheriff's departments (11.7 percent), and family members (6.5 percent). Other reporters included parties with which the elderly come into frequent contact such as churches, apartment managers, and landlords.

Some research indicates that elder self-neglect is associated with increased risk for subsequent elder abuse, specifically financial exploitation and caregiver neglect (Dong, Simon, & Evans, 2013). Payne and Gainey (2005) found that 10 percent of their self-neglect sample was at risk for exploitation of any kind. Therefore, intervening in elder self-neglect can potentially decrease incidents of future elder abuse.

Elderly persons in general are at increased risk of abuse and neglect, but those concerns are exacerbated when those persons are depressed, have symptoms of mental illness, and/or have difficulty caring for themselves. To better recognize this problem and respond with adequate support, community organizations and healthcare workers could be better informed of the warning signs and better prepared with where to refer victims for support services (National Center on Elder Abuse, 1998).

Abandonment is similar in definition and symptoms to neglect. In fact, in determining abandonment, the same standard is used as for neglect, that is, what a reasonable person under like circumstances would do. A major difference would be willfulness; unlike neglect, which might or might not be willful, abandonment typically refers to willful conduct (Nerenberg, 2008).

Special Needs for Elderly Victims

Collaborative Responses

As we have seen, elder abuse has a complex nature with a web of actions or failures to act that have worsened harm to the elderly. As many professionals are involved in identifying and intervening with incidents, coordinating and achieving collaborative responses is crucial. Similar to the partnership of law enforcement and community advocacy groups in intervening with domestic violence issues, elderly victimization requires the involvement of multiple disciplines.

Collaborations could take many different forms, but under a multidisciplinary team, each discipline provides information relevant to the case, whereas an ultimate decision is made by one person. In contrast, under an interdisciplinary team, professionals from a wide variety of disciplines such as physicians, nurses, social workers, pharmacists, chaplains, and others share information and decisions are made collectively (Nerenberg, 2008).

Collaborations would benefit the team members as they could increase their own knowledge of available options and be able to respond to issues more quickly and in appropriate ways. The team members are also more aware of their roles and limitations and seek support from other disciplines for better solutions (Nerenberg, 2008). Collaborations would provide cost savings by reducing the duplication of services. Collaboration also would help in collecting evidence. For example, physicians could make more accurate diagnoses and social service agencies could obtain documentation and identify available witnesses to help make prosecutions easier. Finally, society as a whole would benefit by reducing recidivism and improving the quality of life for victims. Victim advocacy groups could educate victims and their families and provide them with information on resources, legal remedies, and long-term assistance (Nerenberg, 2008).

Professional Trainings

As our understanding of elder abuse evolves, there is a need for sophisticated training for professionals and paraprofessionals. Examples of critical training needs in financial abuse are as follows (Nerenberg, 2008, p. 235):

- The dynamics between victims and perpetrators.
- How financial abuse is related to other forms of elder abuse.
- Strategies for investigating complex financial abuse such as abuse involving securities and annuities, living wills, and powers of attorney.
- The role of federal agencies in investigations, including the IRS, the Social Security Administration, the FBI, the U.S. Postal Service, the Secret Service, and U.S. Attorneys.
- How financial predators operate, "red flags" that signal that elders have been targeted or are chronic victims, and whom to report to.
- Legal, ethical, and practice issues associated with self-neglect.

Other areas of need include training for caregivers to assess high-risk situations, for example, previous history of family violence; training for medical professionals to distinguish abuse-related marks from age-related or accidental ones; training for advocates to attain information about service needs and available resources for the elderly; and information on how to work with crime victims with dementia (Nerenberg, 2008).

Key Terms Involving Elder Abuse

Elder abuse—such abusive behaviors toward elders as physical, sexual, financial, or material exploitation, emotional or psychological, or neglect or abandonment.

Physical abuse—inflicting, or threatening to inflict, physical pain or injury on a vulnerable elder, or depriving an elder of a basic need.

Sexual abuse—nonconsensual sexual conduct of any kind or coercing an elder to witness sexual behaviors.

Financial or material exploitation—illegal taking, misuse, or concealment of funds, property, or assets of a vulnerable elder.

Emotional or psychological abuse—inflicting mental pain, anguish, or distress on an elder person through verbal or nonverbal acts.

Neglect—refusal or failure by those responsible to provide food, shelter, healthcare, or protection for a vulnerable elder.

Self-neglect—a condition in which an elder fails to satisfy his own needs and places his own health or safety at risk.

Abandonment—desertion of a vulnerable elder by anyone who has assumed that responsibility for the care or custody of that person.

Social exchange theory—assumes that dependency in relationships contributes to elder abuse.

Activities of daily living (ADL)—Such basic self-care tasks as housekeeping, toileting, grooming, bathing, meal preparation, and money management.

Multidisciplinary team—an integrated team from different disciplines exchanges information and assesses different intervention options to achieve care goals.

Resources for Elderly Victims

A number of agencies and organizations provide resources for victims of crime.

Aging/Domestic violence resources

National Center on Elder Abuse Promising Practices Database (www.elderabusecenter.org/default.cfm?p=toolsresources.cfm). This national database includes projects that are working with domestic violence programs.

Wisconsin Coalition Against Domestic Violence, National Clearinghouse on Abuse in Later Life (www.ncall.us/docs/NCALL_Directory.pdf). This organization has compiled a directory of services specific to the elderly provided by domestic violence programs.

American Bar Association Commission on Law and Aging (www.abanet.org/aging/resourcepack.pdf). Through funding from the Office on Violence Against Women at the U.S. Department of Justice, this organization has compiled the Resource Packet on Domestic Violence and Sexual Abuse in Later Life.

Victims of financial exploitation

Internet Crime Complaint Center (IC3; https://www.ic3.gov/default.aspx). The IC3 provides the public with a mechanism to submit information to the Federal Bureau of Investigation regarding online criminal activity. Information is analyzed and disseminated for investigative and intelligence purposes to law enforcement and for public awareness. The IC3 accepts online Internet crime complaints from either the actual victim or from a third party to the complainant. There is an online step-by-step process for making a complaint.

Federal Trade Commission (FTC; https://www.identitytheft.gov/). The FTC enhances consumer protection through information sharing (with state and federal governments and international agencies) and educational tools. The agency seeks to prevent business practices that are harmful to consumers without curtailing normal business activities. There is an online step-by-step process for making a complaint.

Health and Human Services Office of the Inspector General (OIG, http://oig.hhs.gov/). The OIG hosts a hotline that addresses complaints of fraud, waste, abuse, and mismanagement in programs handled by the Department of Health and Human Services.

American Association of Retired Persons (AARP, http://www.aarp.org/money/scams-fraud/). Generally recognized as a retiree organization, the AARP's membership actually includes people age 50 and older. The AARP offers a number of informational and educational services, particularly on issues related to fraud and scams that tend to affect older adults and how individuals can protect themselves from such schemes.

Victims of sexual abuse

National Sexual Violence Resource Center (http://www.nsvrc.org/publications/taxonomy/term/16 references). The Center offers a variety of resources including Working with Older Survivors of Abuse: A Framework for Advocates.

Rape, Abuse & Incest National Network (RAINN; https://www.rainn.org/articles/elder-abuse). This network offers general information on elder abuse.

Summary

Aging brings individuals insecurity and vulnerability, especially as their health status and cognitive impairment could generate an overall increased risk of victimization. Yet, the services and interventions for elderly victims are particularly challenging. Elderly victims are reluctant to seek services or report cases because a vast majority of perpetrators are family members, especially their adult children. Even if an elderly victim has to be removed from her home, available shelters are limited and not designed to address the specific needs of elders. One promising strategy is a multidisciplinary team approach that brings diverse perspectives and provides case-by-case services. Professionals and service providers who interface with elderly victims could particularly benefit from having training about the family dynamics of elder people in their respective cultures, symptoms, and marks of specific types of abuse.

Discussion Questions

1. What are some reasons elder abuse has received less attention than child abuse and spousal abuse?
2. Why is elder abuse difficult to detect? Discuss the issues from micro and macro perspectives.
3. Should self-neglect be included as an elder abuse category? Why or why not?
4. Your elderly neighbor who is living with her son had bruises and black eyes the other day. She told you that she fell down, but you suspect elder abuse. What would you do and why?

References

Abrams, R., Lachs, M., McAvay, G., Keohane, D., & Bruce, M. (2002). Predictors of self-neglect in community-dwelling elders. *American Journal of Psychiatry, 159*(10), 1724-1730.

Acierno, R., Hernandez, M. A., Amstadter, A. B., Resnick, H. S., Steve, K., Muzzy, W., & Kilpatrick, D. G. (2010). Prevalence and correlates of emotional, physical, sexual, and financial abuse and potential neglect in the United States: The national elder mistreatment study. *American Journal of Public Health, 100*(2), 292-297.

Adams, V., Bagshaw, D., Wendt, S., & Zannettino, L. (2014). Financial abuse of older people by a family member: A difficult terrain for service providers in Australia. *Journal of Elder Abuse and Neglect, 26*(3), 270-290.

Anetzberger, G. (1998). Psychological abuse and neglect: A cross-cultural concern to older Americans. In Archstone Foundation (Ed.), *Understanding and combatting elder abuse in minority communities* (pp. 141-151). Long Beach, CA: Archstone Foundation.

Anetzberger, G. (2005). The reality of elder abuse. *Clinical Gerontologist, 28*(1), 1-25.

Bonnie, R. J., & Wallace, R. B. (2003). *Elder mistreatment: Abuse, neglect and exploitation in an aging America.* Panel to Review Risk and Prevalence of Elder Abuse and Neglect. Committee on National Statistics and Committee on Law and Justice, Division of Behavioral and Social Sciences and Education National Research Council. Washington, DC: National Academic Press.

Bowes, A., Avan, G., & Macintosh, S. B. (2012). Cultural diversity and the mistreatment of older people in Black and minority ethnic communities: Some implications for service provision. *Journal of Elder Abuse & Neglect, 24*(3), 251–274.

Brown, A. (1989). A survey on elder abuse at one Native American tribe. *Journal of Elder Abuse & Neglect, 1*(2), 17–37.

Burgess, A., & Clements, P. (2006). Information processing of sexual abuse in elders. *Journal of Forensic Nursing, 2*(3), 113.

Burgess, A., & Phillips, S. (2006). Sexual abuse, trauma and dementia in the elderly: A retrospective study of 284 cases. *Victims & Offenders, 1*(2), 193-204.

Buzawa, E., & Buzawa, C. (2003). *Domestic violence: The criminal justice response.* Thousand Oaks, CA: Sage Publications.

California Elder Justice Coalition. (2016, January). *From blueprint to benchmarks: Building a framework for elder justice.* Sacramento, CA: Author.

Chihowski, K., & Hughes, S. (2008). Clinical issues in responding to alleged elder sexual abuse. *Journal of Elder Abuse & Neglect, 20*(4), 377-400.

Choi, N. G., & Mayer, J. (2000). Elder abuse, neglect, and exploitation: Risk factors and prevention strategies. *Journal of Gerontological Social Work, 33*(2), 5–25.

Cohen, D. (2000). An update on homicide-suicide in older persons: 1995-2000. *Journal of Mental Health and Aging, 6*(3), 195-197.

Collins, K., & Presnell, S. (2006). Elder homicide: A 20-year study. *American Journal of Forensic Medicine and Pathology, 27*(2), 183-187.

Dimah, K. P., & Dimah, A. (2004). Elder abuse and neglect among rural and urban women. *Journal of Elder Abuse and Neglect, 15*(1), 75–93. doi:10.1300/J084v15n01_06

Doerner, W. G., & Lab, S. P. (2005). *Victimology.* Cincinnati, OH: Anderson Publishing Company.

Dong, X., Simon, M., & Evans, D. (2013). Elder self-neglect is associated with increased risk for elder abuse in a community-dwelling population: Findings from the Chicago Health and Aging Project. *Journal of Aging and Health, 25*(1), 80-96.

Dyer, C. B., Connolly, M. T., & McFeeley, P. (2003). The clinical and medical forensics of elder abuse and neglect. In R. J. Bonnie & R. B. Wallace (Eds.), *Elder mistreatment: Abuse, neglect, and exploitation in an aging America* (pp. 339-381). Washington, DC: National Academics Press.

Ernst, J., & Smith, C. (2011). Adult protective services clients confirmed for self-neglect: Characteristics and service use. *Journal of Elder Abuse & Neglect, 23*(4), 289-303.

Flynn, C. (2000). Why family professionals can no longer ignore violence toward animals. *Family Relations, 49*(1), 87-95.

Fulmer, T., Rodgers, R., & Pelger, A. (2014). Verbal mistreatment of the elderly. *Journal of Elder Abuse and Neglect, 26*(4), 351-364.

Gibson, S., & Greene, E. (2013). Assessing knowledge of elder financial abuse: A first step in enhancing prosecutions. *Journal of Elder Abuse and Neglect, 25*(2), 162-182.

Goergen, T. (2001). Stress, conflict, elder abuse and neglect in German nursing homes: A pilot study among professional caregivers. *Journal of Elder Abuse & Neglect, 13*(1), 1-26.

Gorbien, M. J., & Eisenstein, A. R. (2005). Elder abuse and neglect: An overview. *Clinics in Geriatric Medicine, 21*(2), 279–292.

Hansberry, M. R., Chen, E., & Gorbien, M. J. (2005). Dementia and elder abuse. *Clinics in Geriatric Medicine, 21*(2), 315–332.

Harris, S. (1996). For better or for worse: Spouse abuse grown old. *Journal of Elder Abuse & Neglect, 8*(1), 1-33.

Heisler, C. (2013). Elder abuse. In R. Davis, A. Lurigio, & S. Herman (Eds.), *Victims of crime* (pp. 161-184). Thousand Oaks, CA: Sage Publications.

Himes, C. L. (2002, June). Elderly Americans. *Population Bulletin, 56*(4), 3–40. A Publication of the Population Reference Bureau.

James, M. P. (1992, June). The elderly as victims of crime, abuse and neglect. *Trends & Issues in Crime and Criminal Justice, 37*. Canberra: Australian Institute of Criminology. Retrieved August 18, 2013, from www.aic.gov.au/documents/5/7/E/%7B57ED2491-7C7D-498F-A12C-7626D80D6339%7Dti37.pdf

James, B. D., Boyle, P. A., & Bennett, D. A. (2014). Correlates of susceptibility to scams in older adults without dementia. *Journal of Elder Abuse & Neglect, 26*, 107-122. doi:10.1080/08946566.213.821809

Jasinski, J., & Dietz, T. (2004). Domestic violence and stalking among older adults: An assessment of risk markers. *Journal of Elder Abuse & Neglect, 15*(1), 3-18.

Kemp, B., & Mosqueda, L. (2005). Elder financial abuse: An evaluation framework and supporting evidence. *Journal of the American Geriatrics Society, 53*(7), 1123-1127.

Krienert, J. L., Walsh, J. A., & Turner, M. (2009). Elderly in America: A descriptive study of elder abuse examining National Incident-Based Reporting System (NIBRS) data, 2000–2005. *Journal of Elder Abuse & Neglect, 21*(4), 325–345.

Lachs, M., & Pillemer, K. (2004). Elder abuse. *The Lancet, 364*(9441), 1263-1272.

Laumann, E., Leitsch, S., & Waite, L. (2008). Elder mistreatment in the United States: Prevalence estimates from a nationally representative study. *Journals of Gerontology Series B—Psychological Sciences and Social Sciences, 63*(4), S248-S254.

Lee, H., & Lightfoot, E. (2014). The culture-embedded social problem of elder mistreatment: A review of international literature on Asian elders. *Journal of Aggression Maltreatment & Trauma, 23*(1), 5-19.

Malphurs, J., & Cohen, D. (2001). A state-wide case-control study of spousal homicide–suicide in older persons. *Gerontologist, 41*, 177.

Marchiori, H. (2009). The elderly: The victimization processes and their victim assistance. *International Perspectives in Victimology, 4*(2), 56–62.

McClane, G., Strack, G., & Hawley, D. (2001). A review of 300 attempted strangulation cases—Part ii: Clinical evaluation of the surviving victim. *Journal of Emergency Medicine, 21*(3), 311-315.

Mihaljcic, T., & Lowndes, G. (2013). Individual and community attitudes toward financial elder abuse. *Journal of Elder Abuse and Neglect, 25*(2), 183-203.

Moskowitz, S. (2003). Golden age in the Golden State: Contemporary legal developments in elder abuse and neglect. *Loyola of Los Angeles Law Review, 36*(2), 589.

Myers, R. K. (2015, Fall). "Epidemic" of financial fraud techniques targets the elderly. *Family & Intimate Partner Violence Quarterly, 8*(2), 189-196.

National Center on Elder Abuse. (n.d.). Frequently asked questions. Washington, DC: Author. Retrieved June 27, 2016, from http://www.ncea.aoa.gov/faq/index.aspx

National Center on Elder Abuse. (1998). *The National Elder Abuse Incidence Study, Final Report.* Washington, DC: Author.

Nerenberg, L. (2008). *Elder abuse prevention: Emerging trends and promising strategies.* New York: Springer.

Norman, J. (2010, May 3). Health care law includes long-sought abuse protection for the elderly. *CQ Weekly*, 1066.

Oh, J. (2003). Assessing the social bonds of elderly neighbors: The roles of length of residence, crime victimization, and perceived disorder. *Sociological Inquiry*, *73*(4), 490–510.

Oh, J., Kim, H. S., Martins, D., & Kim, H. (2006). A study of elder abuse in Korea. *International Journal of Nursing Studies*, *43*(2), 203–214.

Ottley, S. (2009, January/February). Health as a risk factor for elder abuse. *Victimization of the Elderly and Disabled*. Civic Research Institute. Retrieved August 18, 2013, from http://www.civicresearchinstitute.com/ved.html

Patterson, M., & Malley-Morrison, K. (2006). A cognitive-ecological approach to elder abuse in five cultures: Human rights and education. *Educational Gerontology*, *32*(1), 73–82.

Payne, B. K. (2005). *Crime and elder abuse: An integrated perspective*. Springfield, IL: Charles C. Thomas.

Payne, B. K. (2010). Understanding elder sexual abuse and the criminal justice system's response: Comparisons to elder physical abuse. *Justice Quarterly*, *27*(2), 206–224.

Payne, B. K., & Cikovic, R. (1995). An empirical examination of the characteristics, consequences, and causes of elder abuse in nursing homes. *Journal of Elder Abuse & Neglect*, 7(4), 61–74.

Payne, B. K., & Gainey, R. R. (2005). *Family violence and criminal justice: A life-course approach* (2nd ed.). Cincinnati, OH: Anderson.

Pillemer, K., & Finkelhor, D. (1988). The prevalence of elder abuse: A random sample survey. *The Gerontologist*, *28*, 51–57.

Pillemer, K., & Moore, D. (1989). Abuse of patients in nursing-homes: Findings from a survey of staff. *Gerontologist*, *29*(3), 314–320.

Pillemer, K., & Suitor, J. J. (1992). *Elder abuse: Conflict in the family*. New York: Auburn House Publication.

Rabiner, D. J., Brown, D., & O'Keeffe, J. (2004). Financial exploitation of older persons: Policy issues and recommendations for addressing them. *Journal of Elder Abuse & Neglect*, *16*(1), 65–84.

Ramsey-Klawsnik, H., & Brandl, B. (2010). Sexual abuse in later life. *Family & Intimate Partner Violence Quarterly*, *3*(1), 87–96.

Ramsey-Klawsnik, H., Teaster, P., Mendiondo, M., Marcum, J., & Abner, E. (2008). Sexual predators who target elders: Findings from the first national study of sexual abuse in care facilities. *Journal of Elder Abuse & Neglect*, *20*(4), 353–376.

Roberts, A., & Willits, D. (2012). Lifestyle, routine activities, and felony-related eldercide. *Homicide Studies*, *17*(2), 184–203. doi:10.1177/1088767912438713

Schaffer, J. (1999). Older and isolated women and domestic violence project. *Journal of Elder Abuse & Neglect*, *11*(1), 59–77.

Schiamberg, L. B., Oehmke, J., Zhang, Z., Barboza, G. G., Griffore, R. J., Von Heydrich, L., Post, L. A., Weatherill, R. P., & Mastin, T. (2012). Physical abuse of older adults in nursing homes: A random sample survey of adults with and elderly family member in a nursing home. *Journal of Elder Abuse & Neglect*, *24*(1), 65–83.

Strasser, S., & Fulmer, T. (2007). The clinical presentation of elder neglect: What we know and what we can do. *Journal of the American Psychiatric Nurses Association*, *12*(6), 340–349.

U.S. Census Bureau. (2011). *Statistical brief: Sixty-five plus in the United States*. Retrieved fromhttps://www.census.gov/population/socdemo/statbriefs/agebrief.html

Vandecar-Burdin, T., & Payne, B. K. (2010). Risk factors for victimization of younger and older persons: Assessing differences in isolation, intra-individual characteristics, and health factors. *Journal of Criminal Justice*, *38*(2), 160–165.

Vierthaler, K. (2008). Best practices for working with rape crisis centers to address elder sexual abuse. *Journal of Elder Abuse & Neglect*, *20*(4), 306–322.

Wiglesworth, A., Austin, R., Corona, M., Schneider, D., Liao, S., Gibbs, L., & Mosqueda, L. (2009). Bruising as a marker of physical elder abuse. *Journal of the American Geriatrics Society*, *57*(7), 1191–1196.

Wiglesworth, A., Mosqueda, L., Mulnard, R., Liao, S., Gibbs, L., & Fitzgerald, W. (2010). Screening for abuse and neglect of people with dementia. *Journal of the American Geriatrics Society*, *58*(3), 493–500. doi:10.1111/j.1532-5415.2010.02737.x

Winterstein, T. (2012). Nurses' experiences of the encounter with elder neglect. *Journal of Nursing Scholarship*, *44*(1), 55–62.

World Health Organization (WHO). (n.d.). *Action for ageing: A toolkit for organizing innovative events on the World report on ageing and health*. Retrieved from http://www.who.int/ageing/events/world-report-2015-launch/ageing-health-events-toolkit.pdf?ua=1

14

PROVIDERS' AND LATINA IMMIGRANTS' VIEWS OF ANTI-DOMESTIC VIOLENCE SERVICES IN THE MIDWEST

Angelica S. Reina and Cecilia Menjívar

Keywords

undocumented Latinas; Latina immigrants; domestic violence; help-seeking; intersectionality

Objectives

After studying this chapter, the reader should understand:

- The challenges faced by battered undocumented Latinas when seeking help from advocacy organizations and social services.
- The problems encountered by advocates as they try to perform outreach to and serve this population.
- What is needed from formal community institutions, policymakers, and the United States Citizenship and Immigration Services (USCIS) to meet the specific needs of these women.

Introduction

> *That moment when he physically assaulted me, when he hit me, it was a surprise. . . he had always convinced me that he loved me so it was something that came from nowhere. . .. (one day) he was drinking in my house. . . and we went to bed and we turned off the light and he began punching on my face while I was sleeping. . . he destroyed my face, he almost destroyed it. I know he was sure that because I was illegal that I wouldn't call the police so . . . in the moment he was hitting me I tried to calm him down and I told him "please do not hit me". . .*

When women are battered by their loved ones and the abuse takes place within contexts of "illegality,"[1] isolation, under education, lack of support and English proficiency, and economic deprivation, challenges concerning their safety and well-being become more complex (Bonilla-Santiago, 2002). The purpose of this chapter is to analyze the experiences of undocumented Latina immigrant domestic violence (DV) survivors and members of anti-violence organizations who have worked with this population in the U.S. Midwest. We seek to examine and contribute to ongoing discussions of the challenges that battered Latina immigrants face when seeking help from advocacy agencies and social services as well as the problems and pitfalls agencies might encounter when trying to perform outreach to Latina immigrant survivors.

The chapter is structured as follows: First, we review the literature that focuses on the different challenges affecting Latina immigrant women in DV situations as they pursue protection from formal institutions, such as anti-DV agencies. Second, we present the intersectionality framework we utilize to examine the experiences of the study participants. In our examination we deploy the intersectionality framework as it allows us to highlight the combined effects of race, gender, citizenship, and DV, and how these intersections complicate and constrain the lives of undocumented Latinas who suffer DV. Third, based on interviews with 14 undocumented immigrant Latina DV survivors and four anti-violence advocates from central Iowa as well as a focus group conducted with four DV survivors, we examine the participants' accounts to illustrate interlocking systemic oppression. We lay out the factors that arose through the accounts of the Latina immigrant women in the study, as well as those of the advocates, to demonstrate how illegality and other forms of marginalization permeate the lives of undocumented battered Latinas and aggravate their victimization even after they leave their abusers. Finally, we provide the theoretical and practical implications of our study.

Background

Latinos constitute the largest ethnic minority group in the U.S. According to the 2013 U.S. Census Bureau, 54 million Latinos live in U.S., and represent the fastest growing segment of the U.S. population (U.S. Census Bureau, 2013). During the last decade, extensive research on Latino immigration has been conducted, but little effort has gone towards understanding and conceptualizing Latina immigrants' experiences living in situations of DV (Thapar-Björkert & Morgan, 2010). The little we do know focuses on the battering experiences of Latina undocumented women and how immigration policies facilitate violence from their male batterers (Salcido & Aldeman, 2004; Salcido & Menjívar 2012); the effects of Latina immigrants' participation in the workforce on conflict dynamics within their intimate partnerships (Grzywacz et al., 2009; Menjívar, 2003); the help-seeking efforts of diverse battered women living in DV shelters (Moe, 2007); the barriers preventing Latina immigrants from seeking advocacy services (Reina, Lohman, & Maldonado, 2014); and the role of social networks in the process of seeking help from partner abuse (Reina, Maldonado, & Lohman, 2013; Kyriakakis, 2014; Villalón, 2010). Few studies have focused on the perceptions of DV service providers on interventions that help Latina victims meet their needs (Eastman et al., 2007; Macy et al., 2010a; Villalón, 2010). In this chapter we attempt to fill this gap by adding the perceptions of Latina women in DV situations. Our approach presents a more holistic picture of the process of seeking and obtaining help by including the point of view of both the Latina immigrants and the service providers who attempt outreach towards them.

Definition of Domestic Violence

The Centers for Disease Control and Prevention (CDC) define domestic violence as the physical and/or sexual violence, stalking, and psychological aggression by a current or former intimate partner (CDC, 2015) that can easily escalate into high risk for major life-threatening injuries (Stark, 2007). Women from minority communities, for instance foreign-born Latinas, are believed to be at higher risk. Studies demonstrate that Latina immigrants experience higher rates of DV when compared with other non-Latina women (Field & Caetano, 2005; Klevens, 2007). In addition, Latina immigrants are less likely to report the abuse, because in some Latin American countries where immigrants originate, the use of violence against women is sometimes perceived as normal, and sanctions and laws against abusers are often non-existent or poorly enforced (Jewkes, 2002; Menjívar 2011; Drysdale Walsh & Menjívar, 2016).

From a critical, theoretical perspective, DV has been defined as the violence that arises from a patriarchal society that subordinates women, and violence is part of that subordination (Dobash & Dobash, 1997). Also, the intersections of violence and poverty are clearly evident. Violence against women, especially Latina women, becomes normalized in contexts of structural violence (e.g., low-income and deeply unequal) and symbolic violence (e.g., internalizations of gender inequalities). Violence against Latina women becomes normalized (Menjívar, 2011), an "expression of male powerfulness and dominance over women . . . rooted in male vulnerability stemming from social expectations of manhood that are unattainable because of factors such as poverty" (Jewkes, 2002, p. 1424). Symbolic and gender violence combine to shape expectations of male dominance and definitions of "good behavior" for women (Menjívar, 2011), notions that are sometimes challenged when women move to the U.S., exacerbating partner abuse among Latina immigrants (Grzywacz et al., 2009).

What do we know about the challenges Latina immigrant survivors, especially when undocumented, face when seeking out help from formal institutional services?

Challenges at the Institutional Level

While it is true that institutional responses to DV in the United States have improved in recent years, many Latina immigrants do not seek or delay seeking assistance (Klevens, 2007). There is evidence that agencies that work to combat DV and sexual assault experience challenges in providing accessible services for all survivors. This is particularly the case for agencies that serve populations with different racial, ethnic, and cultural backgrounds, sexual orientations, disabilities, and immigration statuses (Villalón, 2010). It is also the case for those seeking to provide comprehensive services to assist those with mental illnesses and substance abuse disorders (Macy et al. 2010b; Ingram et al. 2010). Agencies also lack funding to pay staff regularly and sustain shelters or new programs. Limited funds also exacerbate problems of employee burnout, recruitment, and retention (Macy et al., 2010a). In addition, the need for services available in different languages and funding to pay bilingual employees or translators is a challenge for personnel working to address DV, a situation that greatly affects service users (National Network to End Domestic Violence, 2010).

The scholarship on the perceptions of service providers addressing DV among Latinos indicates that distrust of the police prevent Latina victims from reporting the abuse (Menjívar & Bejarano 2004; Menjívar & Salcido, 2002). Law enforcement agents explain this as a victim's fear of being detained and losing her children (Lewis et al., 2005). Other barriers identified in the literature include economic dependence on the abuser, lack of support from family, and fear of deportation for their lack of documentation (Abraham, 2000; Lewis et al., 2005; Menjívar & Salcido, 2002).

At the Individual Level: Experiences with Service Outreach

Although there are institutional services providing support and legal services to Latina immigrants who experience DV, many of them do not turn to formal or public forms of support or assistance (Salcido & Adelman, 2004). Latina immigrants are the least likely among all female victims to engage in help seeking (Rizo & Macy, 2011). Sometimes they do not know about services, but other times they do not trust the authorities or the laws in place to protect them (Kyriakakis, 2014; Grossman & Lundy, 2007). Additional reasons affecting their capacity to seek help and/or escape from intimate violence include immigration status/fear of deportation, lack of English proficiency, and institutional racism and discrimination (Menjívar & Salcido, 2002; Salcido & Adelman, 2004; Villalón, 2010).

Undocumented battered women are deterred by immigration status to contact the legal system or law enforcement (Klevens, 2007; Salcido & Adelman, 2004). Furthermore, undocumented intimate partner-abused Latinas seek formal help less frequently than documented Latinas (Brabeck &

Guzman, 2009). These women are often afraid to experience their own or their partners' deportation, therefore they remain silent (Menjívar & Bejarano, 2004; Salcido & Aldeman, 2004). In one study of battered undocumented-immigrant women, researchers found that women were afraid to call the police because they thought it would lead to their own arrest or deportation. These women felt that reporting the abuse would both exacerbate men's violence as they were breaking traditional social rules, and increase law enforcement surveillance against their immigrant partners (Salcido & Aldeman, 2004). In a recent study conducted in the Midwest, undocumented Latinas reported being threatened with deportation by their partners and did not know that services or assistance for undocumented immigrants were available in their community (Silva-Martínez, 2016).

Furthermore, research shows that a lack of English language proficiency can undermine Latinas' decision of seeking help from formal avenues of services (Villalón, 2010; Menjívar & Salcido, 2002). Once they reach out to DV agencies, services in Spanish are often limited (Moe, 2007). Monolingual Spanish speakers need an interpreter, so they typically ask a family member or friend to talk and translate for them. This sometimes causes discomfort and distress for the women and makes them feel ashamed about telling their story (Silva-Martínez, 2016).

Also, the decision to seek help or use public services is influenced by victims' perceptions of racism and discrimination from institutional service providers. Latinas not only experience humiliation and frustration in their intimate relationships, but are often revictimized by police officers, legal and health services personnel, and public service providers (Silva-Martínez, 2016; Ingram et al., 2010), the very persons charged with protecting them. DV cases of Latinas are often treated as unimportant, policemen refer to Latina victims as bad mothers, and physicians stigmatize them because they are seen as using social welfare services (i.e., food stamps) (Ingram et al., 2010), even though this is often a misperception. Importantly, service providers make Latina immigrants feel like they do not have the right to get services. Additionally, there is evidence that the oppression and exclusion in Latina immigrants' daily lives that come from community members influence their understanding of help-seeking and DV itself which, in turn, leads them to stay silent (Silva-Martínez, 2016). In short, and, as we shall see, violence against Latina immigrants transcends/transgresses the private and public arenas, disproportionally affecting their ability to secure their own safety, protection, and welfare.

Social science research has provided insights into the social contexts in which violence and victimization are conceptualized (Thapar-Björkert & Morgan, 2010), but only a few studies have examined "the various ways in which race. . . gender [and other identity categories] intersect in shaping structural and political aspects of violence against [battered Latinas]" (Crenshaw, 1991, p. 1244; Villalón, 2010). This is the gap we are trying to fill in this chapter, and thus we turn to intersectionality as our theoretical framework.

Intersectionality as Theoretical Framework

The framework of intersectionality allows us to explore how the social dimensions of race, gender, and class intersect and constrain the context and experiences of minority female survivors (Crenshaw, 1991; Sokoloff & Dupont, 2005). Research has found that socioeconomic status shapes the experiences of women of color in situations of DV (Richie, 2000; Molina et al. 2009), experiences further molded by level of schooling and English language proficiency (Vidales, 2010; National Latino Alliance for the Elimination of Domestic Violence, 2003). These intersections make these women increasingly dependent on their partners. Adding another layer of disadvantage, women who are undocumented "struggle simultaneously around being 'illegal' and battered" (Salcido & Aldeman, 2004, p. 163) because, on the one hand, their husbands or partners use their immigration status as a battering strategy to exercise control over their victims (Hass, Dutton, and Orloff, 2000) and, on the other hand, because without legal documents, undocumented immigrant women cannot attain a job that would enable them to gain the economic security and independence they need in order to leave their abusers (Reina & Lohman, 2015; Salcido & Aldeman, 2004; Villalón 2010). The everyday life experiences of these women, informed by their intersecting positions of disadvantage, challenge "the erroneous assumption that all individuals are equally capable of creating safe lives" (Brabeck & Guzman, 2009, p. 819).

We follow closely Crenshaw's intersectionality postulate as she takes into account legal status in addition to other social positions. Crenshaw (1994, p. 95) states, "Economic considerations–access to employment, housing, and wealth–confirm that class structures play an important part in defining the experience of women of color vis-à-vis battering." What is more,

> race, gender, and class are implicated together because the fact of being a woman of color correlates strongly with poverty. Moreover, the disparate access to [resources], housing and jobs—that is, the phenomenon of discrimination—is reproduced through their race and gender identity.
>
> *(p. 96)*

Therefore, DV cannot be explained, understood, and addressed exclusively as a "private matter" but rather, as a social and systemic domination (Crenshaw, 1991) oppressing Latinas (as women, as Latinas, and as poor). We use the intersectionality framework to focus on the layer of legal status to uncover related factors, such as language, government assistance eligibility, and of shelters that are immigrant-specific. These intersections are crucial to capturing how Latina immigrants, in situations of legal vulnerability, understand DV and how they make sense of the resources available to them.

In the following section we describe the method we used and the data on which we rely. We then proceed with the empirical sections where we focus on factors such as legal status, language, and views about government assistance and shelters, as seen from the point of view of the women in situations of violence as well as the advocates who work with them.

Data and Methods

The data for this study come from interviews with providers in four organizations. The Domestic Violence Advocate Response (DVAR)[2] is an organization that provides assistance and education to programs that serve battered women and their children. The second organization, HELP, an agency created by DVAR, addresses specific needs of immigrant clients across Iowa. VIDA is an institution that provides culturally specific services to Latina victims of DV and sexual assault. These three organizations are located in central Iowa. We also obtained data from SAFE, a shelter that is also located in central Iowa.

Research Procedures

After obtaining approval from the university's institutional review board, the lead investigator contacted the participants for the study in 2008 through the community program coordinator of the HELP agency. The coordinator of advocate and volunteer work at VIDA helped to recruit Latina participants for the subsequent study conducted in 2010. Face-to-face interviews for both studies were scheduled for a time and location that was convenient for all participants. Some interviews with Latina participants were conducted in a private room at the service organization's facilities, while others were conducted at the participant homes. Interviews with advocates took place at the agency locations. After the interview phase in the study conducted in 2010, ten Latina participants were invited to participate in a focus group, in which four of them participated. The rest of the participants were unavailable at the time of the focus group. The focus group took place at a social service agency known by the participants.

The first author, a bilingual researcher, conducted in Spanish all the interviews and the focus group with the Latina participants. All the advocate participants were interviewed in English.

Interviews and focus group data were recorded and transcribed verbatim. Following Spradley's (1980) thesis for data analysis procedures, we analyzed the data in Spanish (the language used by participants) in order to capture significant clues and the cultural meanings of participants' responses. We translated only the quotes used in this paper. The names of participants and anti-violence agencies were kept confidential and were replaced by pseudonyms in all transcripts.

Participants

A total of eighteen women (14 Latina survivors and four advocates) were invited to participate in a two-stage study: one study with four Latinas and four advocates in 2008 and a subsequent research study with other ten Latinas in 2010. Table 14.1 provides detailed participant demographics on

Table 14.1 Demographic Characteristics of Participants

Pseudonym	*Age*	*Nationality*	*No. children*	*Education*	*Job status*	*English skills*	*Length of time in the U.S.*	*Length of time in Iowa*	*Data collected*
Maria	41	Ecuadorian	2	Technical degree[A]	Not employed	None	12 years	12 years	2010
Sonia	35	Salvadorian	2	Elementary school	Sales job	None	5 years	5 years	2010
Melba	32	Mexican	1	High school	Suite manager	None	10 years	10 years	2010
Rubi	37	Mexican	3	High school	Not employed	None	14 years	14 years	2010
Lola	25	Mexican	2	High school	Cashier	Some	8 years	8 years	2010
Lucia	44	Mexican	3	Assistant nurse	Office cleaning	None	15 years	11 years	2010
Ana	31	Mexican	2	High school	Waitress	None	11 years	10 years	2010
Isabel	34	Mexican	3	Elementary school	Hotel cleaning	None	11 years	5 years	2010
Angela	37	Mexican	5	High school	Not employed	None	10 years	10 years	2010
Lina	37	Mexican	3	High school	Sales job	Some	6 years	6 years	2010
Berta	33	Mexican	4	High school[B]	Clothing store coordinator	Some	12 years	11 years	2008
Juliana	45	Colombia	3	College[C]	Childcare	Some	2 years 6 mo.	2 years	2008
Delia	35	Honduras	3	Technical degree[D]	House cleaning	Some	15 years	13 years	2008
Ada	30	Mexican	2	Elementary school	Product packing	None	4 years	4 years	2008

Notes. A) She obtained a high school diploma with a minor in accounting. High school technical degrees in some Latin American countries allow students to pursue specialization while they obtain their high school degree. In the case of this participant, she had developed skills in accounting knowledge, analysis and interpretation of financial statements, and computer skills (e.g., Word, Excel, PowerPoint); B) This participant graduated from high school and took two semesters of college in chemistry engineering; C) She has a law degree in Colombia with a specialty in public and economic law; D) She obtained a high school diploma with a minor in commercial secretary.

Latina DV survivors. All participants were legally married or cohabited at the time of the abuse. Only one Latina remained with her partner at the time of the study. All Latinas had immigrated to Central Iowa and had sought help and used services from a DV agency.

The advocate participants were four DV advocates. These participants ranged in age from 22 to 36. Two described themselves as Latinas, the other two as White. One of the Latina advocates was in charge of providing immigration services, technical assistance to DV projects in the state, including assistance to organizations such as HELP, SAFE and VIDA, and cultural competence training to staff members and others. The other Latina advocate was in charge of the support programs to prevent sexual assault and DV, and parenting classes at day care centers at VIDA. From the same organization, a White advocate was in charge of the counseling and legal services, training with clients and everything related to DV situations. The advocate from SAFE was in charge of doing outreach for a university located in the same area through undergraduate classes and fraternities and sororities.

Data Analysis

We analyzed the data with Charmaz's (2006) qualitative research approach through the coding method. We coded transcripts line-by-line and by completed answers. Then we compared the coded data among participant responses and developed themes by common responses. Subsequently, we grouped themes into categories, including the challenges that battered undocumented Latinas faced when seeking out help from anti-violence services, the experiences of advocates when they performed outreach to battered Latinas, and the potential changes needed to better serve this population were grouped into categories. We made appropriate interpretations of these categories guided by the intersectionality framework. In the following section, we present participant quotes that illustrate each category.

Violence in the Lives of Latina Immigrant Women

The first part of this section presents key definitions of DV from the point of view of Latina immigrant participants, noting the differences of their perceptions from formal definitions of DV by mainstream scholarship and advocacy organizations. We then discuss the challenges that undocumented Latina immigrants living in Iowa faced as they tried to connect with non-profit organizations that work to address DV problems. We present how these Latinas defined and encountered DV, how they dealt with it, how they endured and escaped from it, and how they survived (Lawless, 2001). To present a rounded view, we also share information about the challenges DV agencies encountered as they attempted to outreach towards this population.

What Do Latina Immigrants Understand as Domestic Violence?

Based on their personal experiences, study participants were inclined to understand DV in ways that normalized and further entrenched partner violence. Some of the study participants associated DV only with physical abuse, while others thought it was simply part of the relationship (see also Menjívar 2016). Importantly, most of our study participants stated that they learned more expanded definitions of DV at the support groups from the DV agencies and providers. The following quotes from Juliana and Ada help to illustrate our study participants' changing understandings of what DV encompasses:

> *I'll tell you. . . in Colombia I never had to stop and think about what was violence. . .in my mind I thought that violence was physical attacks but I never believed that violence also was trying to belittle someone or try to impose one's will on them or taking advantage of them in some circumstances (Juliana).*

> *Since we were dating. . . we have problems. . . I did not know I was in a domestic violence problem but later I realized that what was going on wasn't right. . . I experienced it in Mexico. . . but didn't notice it. . . I thought that everybody has those problems (Ada).*

The first author asked Ada if she started experiencing DV in the United States, to which she responded: "*No. I experienced it in Mexico. . . but I didn't notice it. . . I thought that everybody had those problems.*" When women experience violence routinely it is often difficult to identify it (Menjívar, 2011, 2016). Compounding her problems with DV, Ada was sexually abused as a child by a family member.[3] As a result, she had problems with trust and it was not easy for her to be in a relationship or to allow any male to come close to her daughters.

Sometimes, it took a shocking event for women to realize that they were in a DV situation. For instance, Delia is a Honduran woman who was battered for about six years. As a result, she suffered from depression and at some point was hospitalized for three weeks for a physical illness and depression symptoms. At the time of the study she was still taking medicine to control her depression. The critical moment that made Delia realize the seriousness of her abusive relationship was when her partner tried to sexually abuse her younger sister and beat up one of her children (a child from a previous relationship). The following quote describes how Delia started to reflect on the meaning of DV:

> *when one is in a circle of violence one doesn't know what one is experiencing at home. . . one believes that is what one has to endure because he is like that. . . .that he is my husband and I have to live with that. . . to not be alone, to not leave my children without a father. . . and that is how things start. . . there are so many things that run in one's mind.*

Socioeconomic position or educational levels often do not offset the effects of other factors for these immigrant women. For instance, Juliana graduated as a lawyer in Colombia with a specialization in Public and Economic Law. She entered the United States on a tourist visa and came from a higher socio-economic standing. Ada finished two semesters of college in chemical engineering. Even with their higher educational levels, they experienced similar problems as women in this study who had less education. In the United States, both women experienced downward mobility, as most immigrants do, and thus could get only low-skill job opportunities. This situation placed them at a financial disadvantage and made them economically dependent on their partners.

Furthermore, the narratives of our study participants show their views of violence as a normalized phenomenon. Lucia, a Mexican woman who endured DV for five years, believed that in Mexico, fights between a couple were perceived as normal and were part of the marriage. Similarly, Lina conveyed that Latina women do not recognize the abuse, and because Latino men can "do and undo," as they wish, the abuse can be easily perceived as normal. Interestingly, they did not see their Catholic religion as influencing their decisions of leaving or staying with their partners/husbands, which is common in many Latino families:

> *at first, I did not feel like I was involved in an abusive relationship, I mean is like one's culture. . . you think is normal . . . in Mexico it is normal to have fights, that they (Latinos) can drink, is like there still machismo in Mexico . . . you feel like it (the abuse) is part of your marriage . . . I thought it was part of the marriage (Lucia).*

> *we are Catholics. . . my parents got divorced. . . so we didn't have the idea that if your husband hits you, you had to stay? No! . . . we didn't think that way. . . but I did not know what abuse was back then. . . didn't know exactly what abuse meant. . . in the movies, you can see a guy yelling at her or*

> *whatever but that's it but they stay . . . I mean how much can it (the abuse) be is what we, Latinas, don't know . . . that is what we don't recognize . . . we think is normal . . . men can come and go . . . they can do and undo . . . that's normal in quotation marks (Lina).*

The definitional question is important. According to Janet, the Latina advocate who worked for DVAR, knowing what DV is and how to detect it can help her clients understand their rights:

> *I usually don't start talking about domestic violence. I start talking about how is your relationship, how do you feel in your relationship, things that are concrete . . . I say this is domestic violence . . . I mean if you are going through those things they are considered domestic violence in this country and you do have rights.*

Laura, one of the Latina advocates, stressed the same point and mentioned that abused Latina immigrants did not know that DV was a crime in the U.S. Once Latinas learn that, they can identify and understand they are in an abusive relationship. In Laura's words:

> *We face this every day and they don't even know this is a crime so when they get here they start to realize that everything that they have been living has been abuse. They do not understand how the system works. In our countries it's not very common to get help even if they go to the police. It's not very easy for them (Latina immigrants) to get help so I think it takes time for them to start to trust in women's agency.*

Challenges Latinas Face when Seeking Institutional Help

For many Latinas in the state of Iowa, overcoming DV is often complex due to immigration status, lack of English language skills, poor financial situation, lack of government assistance and housing, and negative experiences at shelters. Following previous research (Salcido & Adelman, 2004), our observations reveal that advocates and Latina immigrant victims identified an undocumented legal status as a critical barrier that keeps them from seeking help. Both Latina immigrants and the advocates perceived the available government assistance as limited and insufficient. Noteworthy, after several years of abuse, the participants in this study tried and were successful in their efforts to connect with formal DV institutions.

Legal Status

An undocumented status was commonly mentioned as a limiting factor for the women to turn to institutional assistance and access resources. According to the study participants, their partners, whether documented or not, were constantly making threats about the women's undocumented status. Thus, the women could not report their abusive situations to law enforcement because they believed they could be deported. Juliana, one study participant, stated:

> *My ex-husband believed that because he was legal he could go anywhere and because he had his green card he could do whatever he wanted like hold me against my will. At the beginning he was successful because I wasn't aware of or have a clear idea about any of the rules here. I didn't know how the laws favor the woman and the kids . . . and I didn't even know that if I declared psychological abuse that they could help me become legal.*

The stories shared by these study participants show that U.S. citizens can also exert power over their partners/wives through their immigration status (Reina, Lohman, & Maldonado, 2014). Consider the case of Lina, a Mexican woman who was married to a White U.S. citizen who threatened to deport her. Lina's undocumented condition occluded her ability to seek out help. She explained:

> *I thought I did not have the opportunity of. . . that I wasn't going to get help because I was in a relationship with an American and he would tell me he could get me deported, that I couldn't get any type of help because I did not have papers (legal papers to live in the U.S.).*

Similarly, advocates identified legal status as a factor limiting Latina immigrant women accessing assistance from formal institutions. According to advocates, undocumented women stay in a cycle of violence because their status keeps them from accessing information about the community resources available to them. Melisa from the shelter noted:

> *An individual who is undocumented would say (to wife/partner): "if you leave, they (police) will arrest you and they are going to deport you." This is the reason for people to stay in this cycle, because they don't think there is anything out there for them.*

Laura shared a specific example of how abusers take advantage of their wives' legal status to intimidate or exercise power over them. She noted:

> *This husband went to a batterer educational class . . . then used his wife's ignorance (about how the legal system works in the U.S.) to tell her: "this officer told me that I have my rights and if you keep calling the police I'm going to deport you, I am going to tell them you are the abuser" so many of them (abused women) don't have any idea how the system works so they really trust what they (partners) say . . . so it's like you open his eyes to come back and abuse her again.*

Pam, the American advocate who worked for HELP, suggested that the legal status barrier is a factor that makes it very difficult for undocumented Latinas to even survive after they leave their partners. Though there are some legal remedies that protect undocumented women, such as the U nonimmigrant status (U visa)[4], many of these women do not qualify for public assistance. The advocate also complained about the lack of funding to support survivors. She stated:

> *many of our clients are illegal so with that there are a lot of services they cannot use . . . [from] the police department there is a lot of stuff that they cannot qualify for those services. . . sometimes they don't have a place to live, they don't have a food on the table, so we don't have the money in hand and we don't have people to donate these things to them.*

Language

Latina participants talked about having to navigate across cultural and linguistic boundaries when they tried to communicate with advocacy personnel. Because they lived in a predominantly English-speaking community, and they did not understand the language, they felt they were punished for that. Language was a barrier for accessing services, but not a barrier that kept these women from actually obtaining help. In their own words, these Latina immigrants described their struggles and how service providers responded to them. Melba and Angela talked about the lack of bilingual personnel when they called the police and when they stayed at a shelter:

> *No one spoke Spanish. . . they spoke English and I did understand a little. . . I can't speak English because it's hard for me but I tried. . . they gave me food. . . brought me diapers. . . they communicate through signs for food and everything (Melba).*

> *I stayed there for one week . . . like I said I don't speak English and I didn't know how to drive at that time . . . there was somebody speaking Spanish during the morning shifts and it was perfect but later in the afternoon and night they change staff and it was hard . . . because you cannot . . . I couldn't tell them anything . . . I couldn't go out, I mean nothing . . . I felt like I was there for nothing . . . and then he (partner) asked me to come back, and you know, I didn't have more options . . .[then] I went back to the shelter and it was all the same again . . . like there was not more options . . . it was the same thing . . . going back and forth . . . going back and forth in a year I went there 5 or 6 times. . . (Angela).*

Angela's experience at the shelter was so difficult and meaningless that she went back and forth between her abuser and the shelter several times during the same year. Angela also commented on her difficulties with the language when she reported the abuse and explained how her partner, who spoke English, was able to get away with the abuse, and even made her look like she was crazy:

> *one day my partner was throwing pillows at me and I didn't even know why so I called a police officer [one she knew spoke Spanish] and then he sent other police officers to check out what was going on . . . and I do not know how to speak English, and they did, so they talked to my partner because he speaks English . . . and my partner told them I was crazy and that he was leaving to go to work so they left . . . then the officers called the one who spoke Spanish and he told me about the shelters . . .*

Advocates also identified and addressed language barriers. Janet compared how contact and interactions with service providers differ between White and immigrant survivors. She emphasized that immigrant survivors are more likely to go back to their partners:

> *A White woman goes to get services at a shelter and everyone at the shelter speaks their language, if she goes to DHS to get the food stamps everyone at DHS will be able to communicate with her, if she needs to go to the hospital or court everybody will be able to communicate with her. This does not happen with those women who do not speak English. When you encounter so many barriers you are more likely to go back to your home because you don't have the support out there to live on your own, support your kids and live free of violence.*

Melisa talked from her extensive experience in working at the shelter and highlighted the lack of language translation in relation to law enforcement:

> *We have them (brochures in Spanish) around the community but I'm not exactly sure where. I know we have them in offices around the county attorney office, the court house, the sheriff's office. All the police officers have our information so if there is a domestic abusive situation they could contact us but a lot of times if it's within the population the police officers can't even communicate with them. It's a big barrier.*

Melisa felt that having enough bilingual employees in law enforcement services was a critical need. She also emphasized this barrier when asked about the types of DV she frequently sees:

> *I think one of the larger one for the immigrant population is financial abuse and intimidation especially if they have a language barrier with local law enforcement, their (women's) partners might say they (police) are not going to help you they only help people who speak English, and a lot of times they really restrict the knowledge of the women.*

Government Assistance and Housing

Government assistance and lack of access to housing were not barriers preventing undocumented Latina immigrants from seeking out help for DV. However, both the advocates and the women experiencing DV believed that government assistance and the lack of access to housing create obstacles in rebuilding the women's lives after they leave their partners. Both groups of participants conveyed that there was a lack of access to good quality and stable housing and a lack of public policies that benefit low-income families facing DV. When asked about the use of welfare or any type of government assistance, some of the women agreed they were receiving this kind of assistance for their U.S.-born children, yet some criticized the way the system dispenses these resources. Other participants were unable to apply for public resources for their children because they feared they could be perceived as a burden to the government and this would seriously undermine the process of stabilizing their legal status. Lucia reported the following:

> *The government should give one a place to live where one would be able to establish oneself . . . right now I am living in an apartment but I am just allowed to live here for a month . . . after that I have to look for another place . . . they (social workers) were going to give me a house and now they said no . . . I reapplied again . . . I have been accepted but in one year they will give me an apartment . . . during this year you have to look for a way . . . you have to look for where you are going to live.*

Highlighting the misinformation that circulates in immigrant communities, Delia thought that receiving financial help for her family could cause her problems once she becomes eligible for a U.S visa but she did not know why:

> *I can keep it as much as I want . . . if I want it they keep sending the money to me . . . but that does not benefit me . . . I mean it doesn't help in me trying to get my papers . . . I know that for a certain length of time it would hurt me . . . I'm not sure about the reasons.*

In contrast, Maria and Sonia were told by their lawyer not to apply for public assistance as they could be perceived as a burden for the government:

> *my lawyer told me I shouldn't (apply for cash assistance) because that was a problem for the Government . . . She told me I couldn't apply for it if I was trying to get my legal papers, because I was gonna be like a burden to the government (Maria).*
>
> *I think it would be very helpful for us to know that information. . . how that process works. . . because . . . lawyers like to frighten us . . . my lawyer told me "if you get government benefits that would play against your citizenship process". . . He told me that if I ask for help to the government they might think I was like a burden, so they could deny my petition . . . when you live out of the government you are a burden for them . . . (Sonia).*

Latina participants' narratives show that even if they reside legally in the U.S. they face additional problems. They described their inability to find a well-paid job due to their lower levels of education and the work experience needed, and when they find a job it is likely low-skilled, such as product packaging, domestic service, or retail stock service. Furthermore, efforts to improve their level of education are undermined by a lack of childcare. Access to decent housing compounds their predicament. Rubi, another Latina participant explained:

> *When you have your social security and work permit you want to find a job but they require experience but you don't have it . . . it hasn't been easy for me to find a job . . .and it's only me and my three children . . . we lived in an apartment subsidized by the government but it wasn't a good place to raise my children . . . so I rented an apartment for $565.00 . . . I got a job I didn't like . . . but you know I needed the job . . . I got my GED for 5th level because I wanted to move forward . . . I only could get a job at a factory because I don't have enough education . . .and I can't work 'cause I don't have the support for my children.*

The experiences of advocates varied. Some complained about the transition housing process for women, while others did not agree with the government's role in providing support and aid to battered women:

> *I would think of like transition housing that also seems to be a huge issue . . . like sometimes the shelters are full and even if they go to a shelter where do they go after that? . . . I mean what happens in the middle . . . a lot of times women are having to move out of a shelter finding their own place but in the shelters where they stay a lot of times there are rules and regulations . . . you have three months, you have six months, you have one year . . . well if you've had a lifetime of bad experience with DV how do you fix that in three months to where you become stable and able to raise a healthy family. . . (VIDA).*

> *There are always seem to be changes and you know there is a lot of documenting that comes with that too so while they (staff) are meeting with women I'm looking at a number so I can record that for the government because they are more worried about how many numbers versus actual . . . you know . . . the exact needs of the client . . . I mean I think that's always something that we need to keep addressing and keep working on the legislation (DVAR).*

Shelters

Some women expressed their frustration with the rules and regulations for the use of a shelter, a place that is supposed to provide safety, especially when they do not know anybody else in the U.S. The participants believed shelters should not restrict the time of stay, but rather allow women to remain as long as they need. This participant's narrative resonates with the perspectives of advocates about the importance of having a transition housing program for battered women. Lucia explained,

> *If you go to a refuge you go because you look for safety . . . so one is safe and has a place to live because . . . in my case . . . I do not have my family here I only have some friends . . . they (at shelters) allow you to bring a friend . . . you can stay there just for one month . . . so if you ask for help it is because you need to be helped . . . I think they should let you stay as long as is needed . . . that way you have enough time to look for your own place . . .*

For Sonia, the services that shelters provided were not as helpful as they could be because they lacked enough personnel who spoke Spanish. Research has shown that the lack of bilingual personnel turn non-speaking English battered women away from such services (Crenshaw, 1991). Sonia perceived this as discrimination against women from her community:

> *They (services) are very bad . . .by that time none of the employees spoke Spanish . . . well some of them did but they worked for some hours . . . they weren't there when you needed them . . . They didn't make you feel calmed or comfortable . . . when you finally get out from a problem like that you need that type of help . . . there was discrimination . . . yeah . . . there is discrimination against Hispanic women.*

Discussion and Implications for Practice

The purpose of this study was to explore the challenges that battered undocumented immigrant Latinas face when seeking out help from advocacy organizations and social services, and the problems that advocates and shelter personnel encounter as they try to perform outreach to this population. Our data analysis indicates that the experiences of undocumented Latinas in DV are shaped by the interaction of different social locations, such as gender, race, and citizenship, with sociostructural factors such as poverty, low education, and lack of English language skills. Undocumented Latina immigrants in this study were abused by their partners, were undocumented, lived in poverty and were financially dependent on their abusers, did not speak English, and most had a lower educational level. These conditions produced multilayered forms of marginalization in their lives that affected their potential for leaving their partners/husbands and seek personal well-being and safety. But even those who leave later face several socio-structural limitations: A poor financial situation; inadequate housing; low-paid jobs; and no access to public assistance, except for assistance limited to their children. This finding is consistent with previous intersectionality scholarship that women of color, undocumented Latinas in this case, experience both marginalization and discrimination through the lack of specific multicultural/multilingual public policies and services attending their needs (Crenshaw, 1991). Furthermore, limited government funding and the discriminatory and exclusionary practices among service providers (Reina & Lohman, 2015; Silva-Martínez, 2016) and law enforcement officials implicitly and explicitly permeate/restrict undocumented battered Latinas' possibility of pursuing protection, so they end up staying in or going back to abusive relationships. This finding provides an intersectional foundation for understanding, explaining, and addressing DV among undocumented battered Latinas.

The evidence we do have strongly suggests that Latina immigrant survivors are often socialized into denying, minimizing, renaming, or normalizing the violence against them (Menjívar, 2011; Perilla, 1999). While some Latina immigrants associated DV only to physical attacks, others believed it was a normal part of a relationship (see also Menjívar 2016) and did not want their children to grow up without a father; thus, they felt they had no other choice but to stay with their abusers. Importantly, this does not mean that DV among Latina immigrants should be couched as simply determined by tradition or culture. Rather, their situation should be understood within broader macrostructural and institutional forces within which the normalization of violence against women takes place and exacerbates their vulnerability. Although DV services and community organizations cannot alter broader structural conditions through their work, they can contribute to reconfigure notions about what women and men do, about the expectations of behavior that undermine and subordinate women, and about the social expectations of manhood (Jewkes, 2002) that perpetrates DV. In this way women will be equipped to identify and define DV when they see it and experience it. As our research shows, the first step in addressing this problem is to recognize instances of violence and abuse.

Battered immigrant Latinas who are undocumented tend to underutilize services and programs that formal sources of help offer, specifically advocacy agencies. Legal status is a critical barrier that keeps these women from leaving an abusive relationship as they fear for their own deportation, or even the deportation of the partner when they are financially dependent on them. In these situations, abusers tend to use the immigration status of their victims to hold them against their will and perpetrate the abuse (Salcido & Adelman 2004; Dutton, Orloff, & Hass, 2000). Because undocumented battered Latinas are often unfamiliar with the laws that can protect them in the United States, they are reluctant to report the abuse (Raj & Silverman, 2002; Reina & Lohman, 2015). Furthermore, without a social security card and a work permit, undocumented Latina survivors are unable to find paid work or to afford childcare or housing, and therefore are less likely to leave their abusers and start a new life. But when women leave abusive relationships, they also face the situation of separating their families and withstanding the socio-economic consequences of the separation (Crenshaw, 1991). These findings offer a central implication for policy and practice: Advocates, law enforcement personnel, and service provider organizations should inform (and be informed) about the rights of undocumented women victims of abuse, the laws that can protect them, and the services they are eligible for (Villalón, 2010; Reina & Lohman, 2015). Community response efforts (i.e., anti-violence organizations; criminal justice agencies) should distribute this type of information at schools, churches, supermarkets, Latino/a stores, family centers, Head Start locations, clinics, Latino radio stations, Latino newspapers and magazines, and through social media. This information should also be placed at booths/stands at Latino community parties and events.

Advocate participants stated that most battered undocumented immigrant Latinas who seek help are seldom proficient in English; when they try to report the abuse to the authorities, law enforcement personnel are not able to communicate directly with victims. While police officers are aware of the services provided by anti-violence agencies, when they interact with Latina immigrant victims they simply do not know how to help the women to connect with the agencies because they do not speak the same language. The language barrier findings have implications for the administration of services assisting Latina immigrant women who experience DV and who do not speak English. Anti-DV advocates and law enforcement personnel serving and responding to Latinos should accommodate their language needs through recruiting qualified personnel to work with this population.

Previous studies have shown that frequently, women who leave their abusers depend on the government for financial support during and after that process (Purvin, 2007). Undocumented Latinas in this study could not access such services. The road to legalization is long and arduous for many Latina immigrants (Salcido & Menjívar, 2012), if it exists at all. In the meantime, advocates and social service providers can proactively explore with their Latina service recipients ways to locate affordable childcare and assist them with educational and job-seeking plans (Kyriakakis, 2014; Reina, Lohman, & Maldonado, 2014).

Advocate participants described the lack of resources as a major barrier to provide services and programs to serve the Latino/a community. The members of anti-violence organizations complained about not having enough funding to hire and pay bilingual employees and staff members who can do outreach and provide services to the Latino population. This finding is consistent with previous studies indicating that anti-violence service providers work with limited resources and scarce funding (Macy et al., 2010a; National Network to End Domestic Violence, 2010). Although preventing and addressing DV should be a responsibility for the society as a whole, it is imperative that the government takes responsibility for creating and sustaining laws and policies to ensure the protection of all individuals living within its borders, whether legal or not, in particular the most vulnerable and most in need.

To close, we would like to acknowledge the agency that our study participants exercised—brave women who have stood up to violence, threats, and countless challenges. All of these women crossed the border, live in a foreign country, experienced DV, do not speak the English language, and are undocumented. Yet, they have learned to escape from violence, and are trying to recover from emotional wounds while at the same time seeking to transform their lives with very limited choices and resources. We also want to acknowledge the arduous work being done by anti-DV advocates in Iowa and around the nation. As they manage to work within funding constraints, advocates reach out to battered Latinas and provide them with the support they need.

Summary

Battered undocumented Latinas who attempt to seek out help from anti-violence organizations face multiple barriers that exacerbate their efforts to seek and find protection. Legal status represents a primary obstacle for these women, as batterers use it as a strategy to exert control over their victims, and because legal status prevents them from fully utilizing resources available for women in DV situations. Further, undocumented Latinas are frequently unaware of U.S. laws that protect women in DV situations. Other barriers identified were the lack of government assistance specifically for these women and access to proper housing. In addition, the lack of Spanish language proficiency among service providers and the negative experiences of undocumented battered Latina immigrants at shelters hindered their ability to cope with the aftermath of DV. Once battered Latinas escape from the abuse, they experience structural problems that make it difficult for them to achieve economic stability. These socio-economic constraints include unfavorable economic conditions, restricted access to high-skilled jobs, and little or no access to public assistance. Lastly, Latina survivors of DV are socialized into denying, minimizing, renaming, or normalizing DV. Interventions to serve these women must tackle the notions about what women and men do, so that women are well equipped to identify and define what DV is.

Discussion Questions

1. What are the challenges that battered undocumented Latinas face when seeking help from advocacy organizations and social services?
2. What are the problems that advocates encounter as they try to perform outreach to and serve this population?
3. What is needed from formal community institutions, policymakers, and the United States Citizenship and Immigration Services (USCIS) to meet the specific needs of these women?

Notes

1 The term "illegality" is used frequently in the scholarship because it refers to the condition and it specifically points to the creation of this condition by law (Menjívar & Kanstroom, 2014).
2 All names of participants and organizations were replaced by pseudonyms.
3 The experience of this participant is not isolated. It has been researched by other scholars precisely to bring attention to the sexual abuse problem, which is actually quite widespread (González-López, 2015).
4 The U visa allows qualifying undocumented battered women to stay in the U.S. as long as they cooperate with law enforcement or government officials in the investigation or prosecution of cases of abuse (U.S. Citizenship and Immigration Services, 2016).

References

Abraham, M. (2000). *Speaking the unspeakable: Marital violence among South Asians in the U.S.* New Brunswick, NJ: Rutgers University Press. (Reprinted 2002).

Bonilla-Santiago, G. (2002). Latina battered women: Barriers to service delivery and cultural considerations. In A. R. Roberts (Ed.), *Handbook of domestic violence intervention strategies: Policies, programs, and legal remedies* (pp. 464–471). New York: Oxford University Press.

Brabeck, K. M., & Guzman, M. R. (2009). Exploring Mexican-origin intimate partner abuse survivors' help-seeking within their sociocultural contexts. *Violence and Victims*, *2*, 817–832.

Centers for Disease Control and Prevention. (2015). Injury prevention and control: Division of violence prevention. Intimate partner violence: Definitions. Retrieved from http://www.cdc.gov/violenceprevention/intimatepartnerviolence/definitions.html.

Charmaz, K. (2006). *Constructing grounded theory. A practical guide through qualitative analysis*. California: Sage Publications Ltd.

Crenshaw, K. (1991). Mapping the margins: Intersectionality, identity politics, and violence against women of color. *Stanford Law Review*, *43*, 1241–1299.

Crenshaw, K. (1994). Mapping the margins: Intersectionality, identity politics, and violence against women of color. Mapping the margins: Intersectionality, identity politics, and violence against women of color. In M. Albertson Fineman & R. Mykitiuk (Eds.), *The public nature of private violence: The discovery of domestic abuse* (pp. 93–142). New York, NY: Routledge.

Dobash, R. E., & Dobash, R. (1997). *Violence against wives*. New York: Free Press.

Dutton, M. A., Orloff, L. E., & Hass, G. A. (2000). Characteristics of help-seeking behaviors, resources and service needs of battered immigrant Latinas: Legal and policy implications. *Georgetown Journal on Poverty Law & Policy*, 7, 245–305.

Drysdale Walsh, S., & Menjívar, C. (2016). "What guarantees do we have?" Legal tolls and persistent impunity for feminicide in Guatemala." *Latin American Politics and Society*. doi: 10.1177/0011392116640474

Eastman, B. J., Bunch, S. G., Williams, A. H., & Carawan, L. W. (2007). Exploring the perceptions of domestic violence service providers in rural localities. *Violence Against Women*, *13*, 700–716.

Field, C. A., & Caetano, R. (2005). Longitudinal model predicting mutual partner violence among White, Black, and Hispanic couples in the United States general population. *Violence and Victims*, *20*, 499–511.

González-López, G. (2015). *Family secrets: Stories of incest and sexual violence in Mexico*. New York: New York University Press.

Grossman, S. F., & Lundy, M. (2007). Domestic violence across race and ethnicity: Implications for social work practice and policy. *Violence Against Women*, *13*, 1029–1052.

Grzywacz, G. J., Rao., P. Gentry, A., Marín, A., & Arcury, T. A. (2009). Acculturation and conflict in Mexican immigrants' intimate partnerships: The role of women's labor force participation. *Violence Against Women*, *15*, 1194–1212.

Hass, G. A., Dutton, M. A., & Orloff, L. E. (2000). Lifetime prevalence of violence against Latina immigrants: Legal and policy implications. *Domestic Violence: Global Responses*, 7, 93–113.

Ingram, M., McClelland, D. J., Martin, J., Caballero, M. F., Mayorga, M. T., Gillespie, K. (2010). Experiences of immigrant women who self-petition under the Violence Against Women Act. *Violence Against Women*, *16*, 858–880.

Jewkes, R. (2002). Intimate partner violence: causes and prevention. *Lancet*, *359*, 1423–1429. Retrieved from http://ethicsinhealth.org/wp-content/uploads/2012/01/intimate-patner-violence-jewkes.pdf

Klevens, J. (2007). An overview of intimate partner violence among Latinos. *Violence Against Women*, *13*, 111–122.

Kyriakakis, S. (2014). Mexican immigrant women reaching out: The role of informal networks in the process of seeking help for intimate partner violence. *Violence Against Women*, *20*, 1097–1116.

Lawless, E. J. (2001). *Women escaping violence empowerment through narrative*. Columbia: MO: University of Missouri Press.

Lewis, M. J., West, B., Bautista, L., Greenberg, A. M., & Done-Perez, I. (2005). Perceptions of service providers and community members on intimate partner violence within a Latino community. *Health Education & Behavior*, *32*, 69–83.

Macy, R. J., Giattina, M. C., Johns Montijo, N., Ermentrout, D. M. (2010a). Domestic violence and sexual assault agency directors' perspectives on services that help survivors. *Violence Against Women*, *16*, 1138–1161.

Macy, R. J., Giattina, M. C., Parish, S. L., & Crosby, C. (2010b). Domestic violence and sexual assault services: Historical concerns and contemporary challenges. *Journal of Interpersonal Violence*, *25*, 3–32.

Menjívar, C. (2003). The intersection of work and gender: Central American immigrant women and employment in California. In P. Hondagneu-Sotelo (Ed.), *Gender and U.S. immigration: Contemporary trends* (pp. 101–126). Berkeley: University of California Press.

Menjívar, C. (2011). *Enduring violence: Ladina women's lives in Guatemala*. Berkeley, CA: University of California Press.

Menjívar, C. (2016). Normalizing suffering, robadas, and marital unions among ladinas in Eastern Guatemala. In K. Yllö, & G. Torres (Ed.), *Marital rape: Consent, marriage and social change in global context* (pp. 75–85). Oxford: Oxford University Press.

Menjívar, C., & Salcido, O. (2002). Immigrant women and domestic violence: Common experiences in different countries. *Gender & Society*, *16*, 898–920.

Menjívar, C., & Bejarano, B. (2004). Latino immigrants' perceptions of crime and of police authorities: A case study from the Phoenix metropolitan area. *Ethnic and Racial Studies*, *27*, 120–148.

Menjívar, C., & Kanstroom, D. (2014). *Constructing immigrant "illegality": Critiques, experiences, and responses*. New York, NY: Cambridge University Press.

Moe, A. M. (2007). Silenced voices and structured survival: Battered women's help. *Violence Against Women*, *13*, 676–699.

Molina, O., Lawrence, S. A., Azhar-Miller, A., & Rivera, M. (2009). Divorcing abused Latina immigrant women's experiences with domestic violence support groups. *Journal of Divorce & Remarriage*, *50*, 459–471.

National Latino Alliance for the Elimination of Domestic Violence. (2003). *Developing linguistically and culturally responsive materials for Latina survivors of domestic violence*. Washington, DC: Office on Violence Against Women, Office of Justice Programs, U.S. Department of Justice.

National Network to End Domestic Violence. (2010). *Domestic violence counts 2009: A 24 hour census of domestic violence shelters and services*. Washington, DC: Author.

Perilla, J. L. (1999). Domestic violence as a human right issue: The case of immigrant Latinos. *Hispanic Journal of Behavioral Science, 21*, 107–133.

Purvin, D. M. (2007). At the crossroads and in the crosshairs: Social welfare policy and low-income women's vulnerability to domestic violence. *Social Problems, 54*, 188–210.

Raj, A., & Silverman, J. (2002). Violence against immigrant women: The roles of culture, context, and legal immigrant status on intimate partner violence. *Violence Against Women, 8*, 367–398.

Reina, A. S., & Lohman, B. J. (2015). Barriers preventing Latina immigrants from seeking advocacy services for domestic violence victims: A qualitative analysis. *Journal of Family Violence, 30*, 479–488.

Reina, A. S., Maldonado, M. M, & Lohman, B. J. (2013). Undocumented Latina networks and responses to domestic violence in a new immigrant gateway: Toward a place-specific analysis. *Violence Against Women, 19*, 1472–1497.

Reina, A. S., Lohman, B. J., & Maldonado, M. M. (2014). "He said they'd deport me": Factors influencing domestic violence help-seeking practices among Latina immigrants. *Journal of Interpersonal Violence, 29*, 593–615.

Richie, B. (2000). A Black feminist reflection on the antiviolence movement. *Signs, 25*, 1133–1137.

Rizo, C. F., & Macy, R. J. (2011). Help seeking and barriers of Hispanic partner violence survivors: A systematic review of the literature. *Aggression and Violent Behavior 16*, 250–264.

Salcido, O., & Aldeman, M. (2004). "He has me tied with the blessed and damned papers": Undocumented-immigrant battered women in Phoenix, Arizona. *Human Organization, 63*, 162–172.

Salcido, O., & Menjívar, C. (2012). Gendered paths to legal citizenship: The case of Latin American immigrants in Phoenix. *Law & Society Review 46*, 335–368.

Silva-Martínez, E. (2016). "El silencio": Conceptualizations of Latina immigrant survivors of intimate partner violence in the Midwest of the United States. *Violence Against Women, 22*, 523–544.

Sokoloff, N. J., & Dupont, I. (2005). Domestic violence at the intersections of race, class, and gender: Challenges and contributions to understanding violence against marginalized women in diverse communities. *Violence Against Women, 11*, 38–64.

Spradley, J. (1980). *Participant observation*. New York, NY: Holt, Rinehart, & Winston.

Stark, E. (2007). *Coercive control: How men entrap women in personal life*. New York: Oxford University Press.

Thapar-Björkert, S., & Morgan, K. J. (2010). "But sometimes I think they put themselves in the situation": Exploring blame and responsibility in interpersonal violence. *Violence Against Women, 16*, 32–59.

U.S. Census Bureau. (2013). 2013 Population estimates. Retrieved December 5, 2015, from http://factfinder2.census.gov/faces/tableservices/jsf/pages/productview.xhtml?pid=PEP_2013_PEPASR6H&prodType=table

U.S. Citizenship and Immigration Services (2016). Victims of Criminal Activity: U Nonimmigrant Status. Retrieved May 13, 2016, from https://www.uscis.gov/humanitarian/victims-human-trafficking-other-crimes/victims-criminal-activity-u-nonimmigrant-status/victims-criminal-activity-u-nonimmigrant-status

Vidales, G. T. (2010). Arrested justice: The multifaceted plight of immigrant Latinas who faced domestic violence. *Journal of Family Violence, 25*, 533–544.

Villalón, R. (2010). Violence against Latina immigrants: Citizenship, inequality, and community. New York, NY: New York University Press.

15

VICTIM IMPACT STATEMENTS

Understanding and Improving Their Use

Chadley James

Keywords

victim impact statements; victims' rights; victim participation; criminal justice system

Objectives

After studying this chapter, the reader should be able to:

- Discuss the application of victim impact statements.
- Explain the reasons for and against using victim impact statements.
- Identify the differences between victim satisfaction and recovery.
- Identify possible solutions to improve the use of victim impact statements.

Introduction

The old adage of victims being the "forgotten actors" in the criminal justice system no longer applies. Today, victims play an important role in the criminal justice process and are afforded various opportunities to participate within the system. The "rights" victims are afforded include but are not limited to, being treated with dignity and respect, receiving information pertaining to their case, protection from the accused, and participation at various stages in the criminal justice process. This has moved the system to being more victim orientated; one that acknowledges victims and attempts to reduce the impact the victimization has had on their lives (Dussich, 2014; Cassell, 1999; 2009).

Victim participation in the criminal justice system may involve meeting with the prosecutor before a case is dismissed or a plea agreement is entered, presenting a victim impact statement at sentencing hearings, or discussing concerns about the release of an offender with a parole board (Cassell, 2009; Englebrecht & Chavez, 2014; Johnson & Morgan, 2008). Whether victim participation in criminal justice proceedings is in the best interest of and/or meets the needs of victims has been the subject of much debate. Arguments have been made to stress the voice and "therapeutic" value it provides to victims (Cassell, 1999; Chalmers, Duff & Leverick, 2007; Fivush, 2005; Krause, 2004; Roberts & Erez, 2004). While others have expressed concern that the criminal justice system is not built nor capable of meeting the needs of victims, and may lead to secondary victimization (Achilles & Stutzman-Amstutz, 2006; Sanders, Hoyle, Morgan & Cape, 2001; Lens, Pemberton, Brans, Braeken, Bogaerts & Lahlah, 2015).

Irrespective of the arguments posited, victim participation in the criminal justice system is here to stay. Arguably, the most common form of participation is the victim impact statement (VIS). VISs are written or oral statements made on behalf of the victim or by the victim at the sentencing phase, at plea-bargaining hearings, at parole hearings, and at some bail hearings to express how the crime impacted them psychologically, physically, and financially (Erez, 2004; Clark, 1994). This chapter will address the issues that surround VISs. It will provide a discussion on the intent of victim impact statements, and the arguments both for and against its continued use in courts. Lastly, the chapter will address the affect of VISs on victims.

Victim Impact Statements

The first victim impact statement to be presented in the U.S. was in Fresno, California, in 1976 (Johnson & Morgan, 2008). VISs were the brainchild of James Rowland, who at the time was the chief probation officer in Fresno County. Rowland's argument for VISs grew from watching convicted offenders present themselves in a more favorable light during the sentencing phase, while the victim and their families had to watch and remain in silence (Alexander & Lord, 1994). This idea for change in how the victim interacted with and participated in the criminal justice system spread. This was at the same time when the victims' rights movement in the 1970s and 80s was evolving. Victim advocates argued that the criminal justice system took greater care of the rights of the offender and ignored those of the victim. These sentiments along with other shortcomings within the criminal justice system were detailed in the President's Task Force on Crime Victims, in 1982. The report acknowledged the disparities in the treatment options and rights awarded to offenders and not to victims; and put forward solutions for them to be countered (Dussich, 2015; Johnson & Morgan, 2008). Importantly, the report "acknowledged [that victims' need to be treated equally] and with dignity, [along with] reminding judges, juries, and prosecutors that behind the 'state' is a real person with an interest in how the case is resolved" (Kelly & Erez, 1997, p. 236). Today, victims have the opportunity to present VISs in all 50 states and at varying stages of the criminal justice process (Cassell, 1999; Kelly & Erez, 1997). The scale to which the criminal justice system makes use of victim impact statements today, marks a shift to want to improve the lives of those who deal with the reality of criminal victimization. However, the arguments for the use of VISs have not been accepted by all in the criminal justice system and by the public.

Reasons for Having Victim Impact Statements

The primary reasons for incorporating VISs into the criminal justice system are to provide a balanced picture of both offender and victim when determining the most appropriate sentence for the offender (Alexander & Lord, 1994); and, increase compensation and restitution[1] orders payable to victims (Johnson & Morgan, 2008). In conjunction with these arguments, VISs provide an opportunity for victims to inform court officials of the harm they have suffered and, that they have a vested interest in the outcome of the case (Moriarty, 2005). This, too, applies to the surviving family of victims who are able to contextualize the life of the victim to the court and the suffering experienced as a result of their loss. Providing a VIS is further argued to aid in bringing back a sense of control to the victim's life (Kay, 2006), and allow him or her to make better sense of what happened (Kauffman, 2006). This form of empowerment offered to the victim and assistance with the harmful consequences of victimization is believed to foster positive attitudes about the criminal justice system (Englebrecht & Chavez, 2014; Erez, 1994).

However, the inclusion of VISs during the sentencing phase has sparked much debate and research. Allowing such statements has been argued to make sentencing decisions more accurate when victims express the harm they've suffered (Erez, 1990; Erez & Rogers, 1999). To test the effect of these statements, research has been conducted on their use in specific outcomes of the judicial process. The results, however, do not provide clear evidence to support the argument that VISs make sentencing more accurate. This is evidenced with studies demonstrating that sentences were more punitive with the use of VISs (Myers, Lynn, & Arbuthnot, 2002; Myers, Roop, Kalnen, & Kehn, 2013), while few studies found that such a contribution by the victim had little to no impact on the accuracy of sentencing (Eisenberg, Garvey, & Wells, 2003; Erez & Rogers, 1999; Erez & Tontodonato, 1990). Studies using mock juries have also found conflicting evidence to support the use of VISs during sentencing. What these studies found was that VISs lead jurors to concentrate on the victim's character more, i.e., that the victim was a contributing community member, and/or a fun-loving person. This led the jurors to show more compassion for the victim and their families, and ultimately make a harsher sentencing decision (Myers *et al.*, 2002). This was also the case when mock jurors were presented with more emotional statements highlighting the psychological trauma suffered, compared with statements that had little to no psychological trauma depicted (Nadler & Rose, 2003).

Despite the evidence used to support the use of VISs being less than clear, Victims' Rights Amendments have been made to two-thirds of the states in the U.S. constitutions. Moreover, 49 of the 50 states have gone as far as to enact specific laws that allow VISs to be used at the sentencing phase of criminal trials (The National Center for Victims of Crime, 2012; Johnson & Morgan, 2008), supporting the statement made earlier, that victim participation in the CJS is here to stay.

Reasons against Having Victim Impact Statements

Irrespective of the legal advocacy victim impact statements have received, their use continues to be the subject of debate. The most noted reason against the use of VISs is their potential influence on making sentencing decisions more punitive. Over the years much research has been conducted to evaluate this argument. The growing body of literature and evidence to suggest that the inclusion of VISs at the sentencing phase does increase sentencing severity (Myers *et al.*, 2013; Myers & Arbuthnot, 1999; Paternoster & Deise, 2011), seems to outweigh the results and political interest of those researchers and legal commentators who argue that the statements have little effect on sentencing outcomes (Acker, 1992; Karp & Warshaw, 2006; Rosebury, 2011).

The political interest in the use of VISs is another area that contributes to the debate against their use. Proponents of this argument point out that by using the courtroom to pay tribute to loved ones or detailing the impact of a victimization plays to public interest by prosecutors, elicits emotionally charged decisions by jurors, and may negatively affect victims perceptions of the criminal justice system (Englebrecht & Chavez, 2014; Kirchhoff, 2005). Victim impact statements are without question emotionally filled statements. Victims are encouraged to create and share narratives of their loved ones and provide detailed descriptions of the impact of their victimization. This generates sympathy from jurors toward the victim and contempt for the offender (Englebrecht & Chavez, 2014; Johnson & Morgan, 2008). However, the process by which the VIS is created and intended to help bring back a sense of control to the victims' life and help them to better understand what happened (Krause, 2004) – is also questioned. This is because the content of the statement is often limited or constrained. Victim impact statements are highly regulated by the court, and designed to fit the goals of the justice process (Englebrecht, 2012). This is done so that court officials can avoid the use of threatening language or comments made to the offender by the victim (but does not eliminate dehumanizing language when speaking about the offender), and or derogatory statements made about the criminal justice system. It is not surprising that the content of statements are controlled and vetted, and only those that align with the systems goals and endorse it are voiced. This is not forgetting that the system wants to be seen to be improving the lives of those who have been criminally victimized, and providing justice to victims (Roberts & Erez, 2004). But the degree to which officials limit and constrain what is included in the statement may negatively affect victims' perceptions of the system, as victims are not allowed to express what they truly feel. Moreover, only providing strong statements that depict a picture of good versus evil, serves as a strong justification for harsher punishment and helps reinforce the goals of the criminal justice system (Englebrecht & Chavez, 2014). This then leaves the question, what is the victimological yield of such statements to victims' recovery?

Effects of VISs on Victims

In addition to the argument that allowing victims to detail the impact of their victimization balances treatment options and rights awarded to offenders and not to victims (Dussich, 2015; Johnson & Morgan, 2008), VISs are supposed to have "therapeutic" benefits and contribute to the overall recovery of victims (Cassell, 1999; Chalmers *et al.*, 2007; Lens *et al.*, 2015). Just as the use of VISs has been debated, so has the argument for their effectiveness in assisting with victims' recovery. Researchers have posited that VISs do work to assist recovery, specifically for those who take the time to give them (Chalmers *et al.*, 2007). Whereas others have argued that they can have the opposite effect, leading to secondary victimization and hampering victims' recovery (Sanders *et al.*, 2001). Adding to this debate in facilitating recovery are the limitations of language. According to Lens *et al.* (2015, p. 19), using the word "satisfaction (or a similar construct)" as an outcome measure can be misleading, as satisfaction and its antonym cannot be used to mean the same thing as therapeutic effects. This is similar with both those for and against the use of VISs extending the use of satisfaction and/or dissatisfaction to other effects. Again, Lens *et al.* (2015), argue that not meeting the expectations of victims' may indeed lead to dissatisfaction, but it is not the same as secondary victimization. This is because secondary victimization adversely affects victims' well-being (Condry, 2010; Lens *et al.*, 2015).

Victim Impact Statements and Recovery

The consequences of victimization have been extensively researched and documented. Its effects can be both short and/or long term, with each victim reacting differently to different victimizations (Kirchhoff, 2005; Verdun-Jones & Rossiter, 2010). However, Bonanno (2004) writes that there are four main paths for mental health recovery following traumatic events. These range from mild, moderate, to high symptoms of distress and functional abilities to feelings of no distress and impairment in functional abilities. According to Lens, Pemberton, and Bogaerts (2013), victims experiencing higher levels of emotional distress after victimization were those more likely to deliver a VIS. The same authors write that those victims had persistent mental health problems and high levels of anger, anxiety and stress leading up to their court appearance, whereas the victims who did not deliver a VIS were comparatively free of emotional distress (Lens *et al.*, 2013). Research into emotional recovery argues that the delivery of one statement, where a victim expresses their feelings and emotions has not provided conclusive evidence that doing so reduces symptoms of severe emotional distress or aids in their recovery (Kennedy-Moore & Watson, 1999; Van Emmerik, Kamphuis, Hulsbosch, & Emmelkamp, 2002). Moreover, the social sharing of emotions from a traumatic event has been argued to not have any direct effect on recovery, particularly in decreasing the emotions of anger (Rimé, Kanyangara, Yzerbyt, & Paez, 2011). Additionally, criminal justice proceedings are notoriously long-winded. It can take many months or even years before the victim and/or his or her family can deliver the VIS. Going through the process to create and deliver a VIS a considerable time after the victimization may counter steps already taken to recover. The potential for re-victimization is shown to be a relevant consideration, when victims are asked to retell and relive their victimization experience (Englebrecht & Chavez, 2014; Moriarty, 2005). Then, the ability to further facilitate recovery is diminished when it is recalled that often victims are not allowed to express what they truly feel in VISs, as they are screened and controlled by CJS officials.

Irrespective of there being little to suggest that VISs facilitate recovery, this does not suggest that the use of VISs should be done away with. As mentioned above, current policy dictates that they will continue to be used. Instead, a rethinking of how their use can better facilitate recovery is needed. Lens *et al.* (2015) argue that approaches to using VISs should be conditional and differential. This is because often those who choose to deliver a VIS differ from those who choose not to, more often than not, by their emotional distress. Therefore, greater care needs to be given to the expectations of victims' who deliver these statements. For example: that by detailing the impact of the victimization in court and to the offender may not be the "therapeutic" experience victims believe it to be and that further counseling may be needed; and that sentences cannot exceed the sentencing guidelines for the criminal offense. The importance to and advocacy of information to victims and their recovery and satisfaction has been a key outcome of victimological scholarship (Groenhuijsen, 2009). Providing clearer information to victims about what they can and cannot include in a VIS and explaining why certain material may be deemed inadmissible is key (Englebrecht & Chavez, 2014). Better training for victim advocates to guide victims through the process of making a VIS is just as important. It is, too, vital that victim advocates identify those victims who may need additional support before and after the delivery of a VIS, and establish collaborative networks that are ready to provide the support and care needed to help victims. The criminal justice system is argued to be an overburdened system already (Johnson & Morgan, 2008), and one that views crime as an offence against the state not the individual. However, if such effort has been expended to include the victim within the system and to recognize and meet the needs of those adversely affected, surely more can be done to ensure that what is being done will aid in their recovery.

The right to participate in court and give a VIS did not come easily. The fact that victims have a greater role to play in the criminal justice system needs to be embraced and it is, but it must be done in a way that is balanced (which remains the challenge).

Conclusion

Victim participation is and has been a key move and feature of the criminal justice system to being more victim orientated. The entrenchment of victim participation in the system has been made clear with the majority of states enacting specific laws that encourage the use of victim impact statements, most often, at the sentencing phase of criminal trials (The National Center for Victims of Crime, 2012; Johnson & Morgan, 2008). The reasons set forth for the use of such statements are that they have a positive impact on the victim and help them to regain a sense of control over their lives. That it helps to foster a positive perception of the criminal justice system and its willingness to take the victim seriously, balancing the rights offered to offenders with those offered to victims. Lastly, that it helps the "jurors to see the humanity of the case" (Johnson & Morgan, 2008, p. 128).

Conversely, reasons posited against the use of the victim impact statements are that such statements lead to more punitive sentencing decisions, which are influenced by emotionally charged statements.

Often, the inclusion of these statements prolongs an already drawn out process. This is further complicated when, often, victims realize that they do not have full control over what is allowed to be included in the statement, as it does not meet the goals of the criminal justice system. Then, by giving such a statement it may not be the therapeutic experience victims are led to believe it will be and does not necessarily lead to recovery.

Whether or not victim impact statements will be welcomed by all, their inclusion in the CJS is here to stay. Their purpose is to facilitate in recovery and increase satisfaction with the system, but the evidence to suggest that this is what is being achieved is inconclusive and, in fact, suggests that a rethinking of their use in needed. Potential solutions to this rethinking are better training and education of victim advocates and court officials who work with victims, along with more information provided to the victim regarding the process and potential outcomes of delivering such a statement to manage their expectations. Doing this may help to better elicit the victimological yield of victim impact statements.

Summary

The old adage of victims being the forgotten actors in the criminal justice system (CJS) seems to no longer apply. Today, victims' rights ensure the participation of victims at various stages of the criminal justice process. The most notable form of participation is the creation and delivery of a victim impact statement at the sentencing phase of a criminal trial; however, the use of victim impact statements has ignited a debate as to who actually benefits from these statements: the victim? Or the CJS? The emotionally charged statements arguably lead to more punitive sentencing decisions, and have shown little in the way of victim satisfaction with the criminal justice system and recovery from the trauma experienced. Irrespective of the debates that surround victim impact statements their inclusion in the CJS is here to stay. Despite inconclusive evidence to suggest that victim impact statements achieve what they set out to achieve, a rethinking of their use is needed. Potential solutions are better training and education of victim advocates and court officials who work with victims, along with more information provided to the victim regarding the process and potential outcomes of delivering such a statement to manage their expectations. Doing this may help to better elicit the victimological yield of these statements.

Discussion Questions

1. What are the purposes of a victim impact statement?
2. How much weight do judges assign to victim impact statements?
3. Identify the differences between victim satisfaction and recovery.
4. Identify possible solutions to improve the use of victim impact statements.

Note

1 There is an important distinction between compensation and restitution. Compensation is financial assistance by the state to victims of crime. Every state has a crime victim compensation program that can provide substantial financial assistance to crime victims and their families. Restitution, on the other hand, is payment by an offender to the victim for the harm caused by the offender's actions (Kirchhoff, 2005; National Association of Crime Victim Compensation Boards (NACVCB), 2007).

References

Achilles, M. & Stutzman-Amstutz, L. (2006). Responding to the needs of victims: What was promised, what has been delivered. In D. Sullivan & L. Tifft (Eds.), *The handbook of restorative justice: A global perspective* (pp. 211–220). London: Routledge.

Acker, J. (1992). Social sciences and the criminal law: Victims of crime-plight vs. rights. *Criminal Law Review*, 28, 64–77.

Alexander, E. K. & Lord, J. H. (1994). Impact statements: A victim's right to speak, a nation's responsibility to listen. American Prosecutors Research Institute. Retrieved on 28 December, 2016, from: https://www.ncjrs.gov/ovc_archives/reports/impact/welcome.html

Bonanno, G. A. (2004). Loss, trauma and human resilience: Have we underestimated the human capacity to thrive after extremely aversive effects? *American Psychologist*, 5, 20–28.

Cassell, P. (1999). Barbarians at the gates? A reply to the critics of the victims' rights amendment. *Utah Law Review*, 179(2), 479–544.

Cassell, P. G. (2009). In defense of victim impact statements. *Ohio State Journal of Criminal Law*, 6, 611–648.

Chalmers, J., Duff, P. and Leverick, F. (2007). Victim impact statements: Can work, do work (for those who bother to make them). *Criminal Law Review*, May, 360–379.

Clark, C. (1994). Crime victims' rights. *CQ Researcher*, 627–643.

Condry, R. (2010). Secondary victims and secondary victimization. In S. G. Shoham, P. Knepper, and M. Kett (Eds.), *International handbook of victimology* (pp. 219–250). Florida: CRC Press.

Dussich, J. (2015). The evolution of international victimology and its current status in the world today. *Revista de Victimologia / Journal of Victimology*, 1 (1), 1–42.

Eisenberg, T., Garvey, S. P. and Wells, M. T. (2003). Symposium: Victims and the death penalty: Inside and outside of the courtroom: Victim characteristics and victim impact evidence in South Carolina capital cases. *Cornell Law Review*, 88, 306–342.

Englebrecht, C. M. (2012). "Where do I stand?" Exploring the rules regulating victim participation in the criminal justice system. *Victims & Offenders*, 7, 161–184.

Englebrecht, C. M. & Chavez, J. M. (2014). Whose statement is it? An examination of victim impact statements delivered in court. *Victims and Offenders: An International Journal of Evidence-Based Research, Policy, and Practice*, 9, 386–412.

Erez, E. (1990). Victim participation in sentencing: Rhetoric and reality. *Journal of Criminal Justice*, 18, 19–31.

Erez, E. (1994). Victim participation in sentencing: And the debate goes on. . . *International Review of Victimology*, 3, 17–32.

Erez, E. (2004). Integrating restorative justice principles in adversarial proceedings through victim impact statements. In E. Cape (Ed.), *Reconcilable rights? Analysing the tension between victims and defendants*. London: Legal Action Group.

Erez, E. & Rogers, L. (1999). Victim impact statements and sentencing outcomes and processes: The perspectives of legal professionals. *British Journal of Criminology*, 39, 216–239.

Erez, E. and Tontodonato, P. (1990). The effect of victim participation in sentencing and satisfaction with justice. *Justice Quarterly*, 9 (3), 393–415.

Fivush, R. (2005). Reconciling trauma and the self. In A. B. Brown & K. M. Poremski (Eds.), *Roads to reconciliation: Conflict and dialogue in the twenty-first century* (pp. 89–106). New York: M. E. Sharpe.

Groenhuijsen, M. (2009). The current status of the 2006 convention. In J. P. J. Dussich & K. G. Mundy (Eds.), *Raising the global standards for victims: The proposed convention on justice for victims of crime and abuse of power*. Tokyo: Seibundo Publishing Company Co. Ltd, pp. 1–9.

Johnson, I. M. & Morgan, E. F. (2008). Victim impact statements: Fairness to defendants? In L. J. Moriarty (Ed.), *Controversies in victimology* (pp. 115–131). New Jersey: Anderson Publishing.

Karp, D. and Warshaw, J. (2006). Their day in court: The role of murder victims' families in capital juror decision making. In J. Acker & D. Karp (Eds.), *Wounds that do not bind: Victim-based perspectives on the death penalty* (pp. 275–296). North Carolina: Carolina Academic Press.

Kauffman, J. (2006). Restoration of the assumptive world as an act of justice. In D. Sullivan and L. Tifft (Eds.), *The handbook of restorative justice: A global perspective* (pp. 221–229). London: Routledge.

Kay, J. (2006). Murder victims' families for reconciliation: Story-telling for healing, as witness, and in public policy. In D. Sullivan and L. Tifft (Eds.), *Handbook of restorative justice: A global perspective* (pp. 230–245). New York: Routledge.

Kelly, D. P. & Erez, E. (1997). Victim participation in the criminal justice system. In R. C. Davis, A. J. Lurigio, and W. G. Skogan (Eds.), *Victims of crime* (pp. 231–244). Los Angeles: SAGE.

Kennedy-Moore, E. and Watson, J. C. (1999). *Expressing emotion: Myths, realities, and therapeutic strategies*. New York: Guilford.

Kirchhoff, G. F. (2005). *What is victimology?* Tokyo: Seibundo Publishing Co., Ltd.

Krause, T. (2004). Murder, mourning and the ideal of reconciliation. In A. B. Brown & K. M. Poremski (Eds.), *Roads to reconciliation: Conflict and dialogue in the twenty-first century* (pp. 53–68). New York: M. E. Sharpe.

Lens, K. E., Pemberton, A., and Bogaerts, S. (2013). Heterogeneity in victim participation: A new perspective on delivering a victim impact statement, *European Journal of Criminology*, 10, 479–495.

Lens, K. E., Pemberton, A., Brans, K., Braeken, J., Bogaerts, S. & Lahlah, E. (2015). Delivering a victim impact statement: Emotionally effective or counter-productive? *European Journal of Criminology*, 12 (1), 17–34.

Moriarty, L. (2005). Victim participation at parole hearings: Balancing victim, offender, and public interest. *Criminology & Public Policy*, 4, 385–390.

Myers, B. and Arbuthnot, J. (1999). The effects of victim impact information on the verdicts and sentence recommendations of mock jurors. *Journal of Offender Rehabilitation*, 29, 95–112.

Myers, B., Lynn, S., & Arbuthnot, J. (2002). Victim impact testimony and juror judgments: The effects of harm information and witness demeanor. *Journal of Applied Social Psychology*, 32, 2393–2412.

Myers, B., Roop, A., Kalnen, D., & Kehn, A. (2013). Victim impact statements and crime heinousness: A test of the saturation hypothesis. *Psychology, Crime & Law*, 19, 129–143.

Nadler, J. and Rose, M. R. (2003). Symposium: Victims and the death penalty: Inside and outside of the courtroom: Victim impact testimony and the psychology of punishment. *Cornell Law Review*, 88, 419–450.

National Association of Crime Victim Compensation Boards (2007). *Crime victim compensation: Resources for recovery*. Alexandria, VA.

The National Center for Victims of Crime, (2012). *Victim Impact Statements*. Retrieved on December 10, 2015, From: http://www.victimsofcrime.org/help-for-crime-victims/get-help-bulletins-for-crime-victims/victim-impact-statements

Paternoster, R. and Deise, J. (2011). A heavy thumb on the scale: The effect of victim impact evidence on capital decision making. *Criminology*, 49, 129–161.

Rimé, B., Kanyangara, P., Yzerbyt, V., and Paez, D. (2011). The impact of Gacaca tribunals in Rwanda: Psychosocial effects of participation in a truth and reconciliation process after a genocide. *European Journal of Social Psychology*, 41, 695–706.

Roberts, J. V. & Erez, E. (2004). Communication in sentencing: Exploring the expressive function of victim impact statements. *International Review of Victimology*, 10, 223–244.

Rosebury, B. (2011). The political logic of victim impact statements. *Criminal Justice Ethics*, 30 (1), 39–67.

Sanders, A., Hoyle, C., Morgan, R., & Cape, E. (2001). Victim impact statements: Don't work, can't work. *The Criminal Law Review*, 6, 447–458.

Van Emmerik, A. P., Kamphuis, J. H., Hulsbosch, A. M., and Emmelkamp, P. M. G. (2002). Single session debriefing after psychological trauma: A meta-analysis. *The Lancet*, 360, 766–771.

Verdun-Jones, and Rossiter (2010). The psychological impact of victimization: Mental health outcomes and psychological, legal, and restorative interventions. In S. G. Shoham, P. Knepper, and M. Kett (Eds.), *International handbook of victimology* (pp. 611–638). Florida: CRC Press.

16

VICTIMS' NEEDS AND RESTORATIVE JUSTICE

Andrew S. Gladfelter and R. Barry Ruback

Keywords

restitution; financial compensation; procedural justice; informational justice; interpersonal justice; restorative justice; community justice

Objectives

After studying this chapter, the reader should understand:

- The tangible losses that crime victims suffer.
- The intangible costs of crime.
- The impact of victimization on families, friends, and communities.
- Restitution to victims.
- Victim compensation and victim assistance.
- Historical and cultural background of restorative justice.
- Effectiveness of restorative justice.
- Criticisms of restorative justice.

Introduction

Even though crime rates have generally declined since 1993, in both absolute and relative terms, a large number of people in the United States are touched by crime. In 2013, the prevalence was 1.1 percent for violent crime and 8.9 percent for property crime (Lauritsen & Rezey, 2013), meaning that annually roughly 3.5 million Americans are victims of at least one violent crime and 11 million households are victims of at least one property crime. The incidence of crime (the number of crimes per 1,000) is higher, with a violent victimization rate of 19.3 per 1,000 persons and a property victimization rate of 125.4 per 1,000 households.

The risk of criminal victimization is not the same for all people, in that victimization tends to be concentrated in only a subset of the population. Characteristics such as lifestyle choices and behavioral patterns (Hindelang et al., 1978; Jennings et al., 2012), age, gender, marital status, and race (Truman & Langton, 2014), spatial proximity to prior victims (Bernasco, 2008), and social class (Harrell et al., 2014; Xie et al., 2012) are correlated with victimization. And individuals who are victimized once have a greater risk of being victimized again. One classic study reported that 59 percent of personal crimes and 41 percent of property crimes were experienced by 1 percent and 2 percent of people, respectively (Pease, 1998). That is, victimization disproportionately affects certain types of people who live in certain types of places.

Because a large number of individuals are victims of crime, the overall costs are quite high. Some estimates even suggest that costs to victims exceed the costs of criminal justice system administration (Cohen, 2005, p. 41). And, because many costs-of-crime estimates are based only on counts of known crime reported to police, the "true" costs to victims may be even greater (Welsh & Farrington, 2015).

Given these extensive and costly impacts of crime, it is important to consider whether and how society meets the varied needs of victims. In this chapter, we discuss a wide range of victims' needs, the role of the offender, state, and community in meeting those needs, and several key methods through which such needs can be met. We focus on restorative justice interventions, in particular, because of their ability to bring victims, offenders, and communities together to repair the harm caused by criminal offending. We emphasize that—particularly in the United States—current policies aimed at meeting the needs of victims are only modestly effective at doing so and that we are unlikely to be able to fully meet victims' needs moving forward.

Victims' Needs and the Costs of Crime

It is easiest to consider the needs of victims in light of the costs of crime to victims, or the ways in which victims are deprived of certain economic, social, or emotional resources (Tobolowsky et al., 2010). Such costs include tangible costs (e.g., financial loss, medical bills), intangible costs (e.g., pain and suffering, psychological trauma), and indirect costs (e.g., to employers and insurance companies), costs that total more than $450 billion (Cohen, 2005). The most easily estimated costs of crime are those associated with tangible needs, because such costs involve direct replacement or compensation. Tangible needs include the recompense of any form of monetary loss, including damages to property, medical expenses, and lost wages due to incapacitation or hospitalization. About 24 percent of tangible costs involve property losses (Miller et al., 1996). Not surprisingly, crimes involving high-value property like cars or homes, such as motor vehicle theft, alcohol- and drug-related vehicular crashes, and arson, are the most costly. Additionally, victims of identity theft suffer estimated losses of $17.3 billion annually (Langton & Planty, 2010). Lost wages due to time off from work are another cost to victims. According to Cohen (2005), 16 days, 14 days, and 12.5 days of work are lost for the average rape, assault, and robbery, respectively.

For many victims, tangible costs represent only a small fraction of all victim-incurred costs of crime (e.g., Cohen, 2005). Intangible costs, such as psychological trauma or pain and suffering, are long term and may require extensive therapy or treatment (Norris & Kaniasty, 1994). Longitudinal studies of children and youth show that anxiety, depression, loneliness, and psychosomatic symptoms (e.g., headaches, loss of appetite) are modestly but consistently elevated following criminal victimizations, and these effects can persist for several years (Reijintjes et al., 2010). Another meta-analysis across 16 domains of psychological distress in 50 studies also reported higher levels of distress following violent victimization (Weaver & Clum, 1995).

Additionally, like victims of trauma generally (Lowe et al., 2015), victims of crime have higher rates of post-traumatic stress disorder and depression than non-victims (McCart et al., 2010). The effect is especially pronounced for repeat victims (Kimerling et al., 2007). Poly-victimization—or being a victim of multiple types of crime—is especially associated with poor mental health status and declines in self-esteem (Finkelhor et al., 2007; Turner et al., 2015). However, despite this high prevalence of mental health concerns, less than a fifth of victims use mental health resources following victimization (McCart et al., 2010).

Victimization may also contribute to other risky behaviors, such as alcohol and drug use and involvement in offending (Kort-Butler, 2010). Analyses suggest these behaviors in turn increase the risk for subsequent victimization (Jennings et al., 2012; Ruback et al., 2014a), presumably by increasing exposure to risky situations. For these individuals who may require repeated interventions (e.g., mental health treatment, drug and alcohol programming, potential criminal sanctioning), the costs of crime are especially profound.

Finally, victims may express a need for fairness or justice (Tobolowsky et al., 2010). This need includes fair treatment by the criminal justice system, satisfaction with the handling of the case and interactions with the sanctioning process, and protection from wrongdoing at the hands of the state (Bazemore & Walgrave, 1999). Research suggests that victims who perceive a sense of control over the criminal justice process report greater satisfaction (Fisher, 2015; Hotaling & Buzawa, 2003).

Impact on Third Parties

In addition to the direct victims of crime, both tangible and intangible costs may be incurred by other parties, including families, friends, communities, and even the broader society (Cohen, 2005). For instance, peers or relatives may need to care for injured victims, leading to a loss in productivity. If a victim is killed as a result of crime, other parties will often have to pay for funeral expenses and will likely experience a loss in companionship. Insurance companies and employers have to pay for losses (e.g., health and auto insurance, employee training and replacement). Friends, relatives and neighbors may feel inclined to purchase equipment such as alarms, locks, cameras, weapons, or other protective devices in an attempt to reduce their own perceived risks of criminal victimization.

Research suggests that indirect victimization (e.g., victimization of a relative, peer, or neighbor) increases the risk for direct victimization (for conceptual overview, see Farrell, 2015). The contagion, or spread, of crime is best evidenced by the "boost hypothesis" for burglary (Townsley et al., 2003): when a particular structure is targeted for a burglary, that structure is likely to be burglarized again (Lantz & Ruback, in press), and other structures within close proximity are also more likely to be burglarized in the following weeks. Other research has supported the direct-indirect victimization links across a variety of crime types: shootings (Papachristos et al., 2015; Ratcliffe & Rengert, 2008); assaults, burglaries, and robberies (Grubesic & Mack, 2008); and arson (Grubb & Nobles, 2016). Thus, another potential need is the desire to protect oneself and others from subsequent victimization.

History of the Victims' Rights Movement

For most criminal offenses, a crime occurs only when (1) an offender and (2) a victim converge in (3) the same place at the same time (http://www.popcenter.org/about/?p=triangle). However, the importance of victims in the "crime triangle" went largely ignored until the 1980s. In 1982, the President's Task Force on Victims of Crime (Herrington et al., 1982) argued that the government has a compelling interest in, and responsibility for, assisting victims. For instance, the Task Force recommended that victims be financially compensated for the harms suffered as a result of crime and that victims be allowed to provide statements about the impact of victimization in sentencing decisions. Two years later, the Attorney General's Task Force on Family Violence (Hart et al., 1984), recognizing that family violence often was more complex in both causes and consequences than violent victimization at the hands of strangers, similarly presented a set of guidelines for addressing the needs of domestic violence victims. The overarching goal of these recommendations was better treatment of victims under the assumption that better treatment would lead to greater satisfaction, greater cooperation with authorities, and, ultimately, greater prosecution and lower crime rates (Hudson, 1984).

The guidelines could be considered a sweeping success. By 1998, every state established a victim compensation fund and had some form of victims' rights legislation. Additionally, over 10,000 victim assistance agencies had been established nationwide (Office for Victims of Crime, 1998). However, the Office for Victims of Crime (OVC, 1998) noted that victims were still primarily passive participants in the criminal justice process. Looking toward the future, the OVC presented over 250 recommendations to improve the treatment of victims and their participation in criminal justice processes. The first step in this process, however, is to acknowledge the many and varied needs of crime victims.

Role of the State in Meeting Victims' Needs

Meeting victims' needs is an important goal of the justice system. Victims report greater satisfaction with the criminal justice process when they believe that their needs have been met by the system. In turn, satisfaction leads to greater participation in the criminal justice process and a greater willingness to cooperate (Hudson, 1984). Additionally, victims who believe they were treated fairly by both the criminal justice process and agents of the criminal justice system indicate a greater willingness to report future victimization to the police (Ruback et al., 2008). Consequently, Langton (2011) found, in an analysis of data from the National Crime Victimization Survey (NCVS), that victims of violent crime who received support from some form of agency were more likely to file a complaint about the crime.

In the 34 years since the President's Task Force published its report, states and the federal government have sought to improve the treatment of victims. Since 1996, restitution, or monetary compensation for harm caused by the crime, has been mandatory in nearly all federal cases (Dickman, 2009). Thirty-two states have adopted constitutional amendments concerning the rights of victims, and 20 states now give victims a constitutional right to the receipt of restitution (Haynes et al., 2015). Thus, at least in theory, the increased adoption of these provisions means that victims' needs are being met with greater frequency.

Despite the improvements in victims' rights over the past three decades, the criminal justice system generally does a poor job at meeting the needs of victims. In this section, we review the primary forms of assistance afforded to victims of crime by the state and why those forms of assistance are generally ineffective. We then turn to alternative forms of assistance delivered through community-based resources, including restorative justice practices, and examine how community resources could fulfill the needs left unmet by the state.

Forms of State Aid

Three primary forms of victim resources are provided through the state: restitution; victim compensation funds; and victim assistance. Restitution involves a court-ordered direct repayment, by the offender to the victim, for any tangible losses (e.g., property, medical bills) *directly resulting* from the crime (NCVC, 2002; Ruback & Bergstrom, 2006). Additionally, "restitution addresses victims' emotional needs by legitimizing, in an official and public manner, that what happened to the victim was wrong and should be rectified" (Haynes et al., 2015, p. 452).

However, restitution is generally ineffective at meeting the financial needs of victims. Ruback and Shaffer (2005) examined the imposition of court-ordered restitution in Pennsylvania, which is a state that legally mandates restitution for *eligible cases*. Eligible cases include any case where a) a quantifiable harm was suffered by b) an identifiable victim, including an individual, business, or insurance agency. For instance, a commercial burglary would be eligible due to property losses (e.g., merchandise, broken windows), but a drug possession—where there is no clear victim—should not be. Despite the legal mandate, restitution was ordered in only about two-thirds of eligible cases (Ruback & Shaffer, 2005).

The national average is much lower: only around 18 percent of all cases include a restitution order (Rosenmerkel et al., 2009). Even in cases where restitution is ordered the full amount may not be paid, because offenders are responsible for making payments and offenders are generally poor, incarcerated, and/or unemployed. In one study, less than half of victims said the restitution they received fully covered their losses (Davis et al., 1992). Indeed, total collections in Vermont are less than one quarter of that imposed (National Center for Victims of Crime, 2011). In one study in Pennsylvania, no restitution was paid in 48 percent of the cases, there was partial payment in 28 percent of the cases, and there was full payment in only 24 percent of the cases (Ruback et al., 2008). One experiment induced offenders to pay more restitution by providing them with information about the amount of restitution still owed (Ruback et al., 2014b), but even so most offenders did not pay the total amount.

An additional concern is the lack of standardization across the states for the implementation of restitution (Haynes et al., 2015). Unpaid restitution at the time of release from supervision automatically becomes a civil judgment—an additional, legally binding liability—on the offender in 14 states. In the remaining states, unpaid restitution remains unpaid. In 6 states, judges *cannot* consider the ability of the offender to pay any ordered restitution—effectively meaning that the needs of victims trump the needs of offenders—whereas 23 states expressly permit the consideration of ability to pay. Because of this consideration, these 23 states may impose less restitution than would cover the costs to the victim.

In the absence of restitution, victims can apply for assistance through a victim compensation fund (National Center for Victims of Crime, 2003). Every state maintains a crime victim compensation program, each of which is funded directly by convicted offenders. For instance, for each case in Pennsylvania, the first $60 paid in court costs and fees goes to a state victim compensation fund. Additionally, a federal fund, which is financed by offenders convicted of federal offenses, provides approximately $360 million in compensation to state programs annually (Office for Victims of Crime, n.d.). It is unclear how many victims apply for and receive state-sponsored forms of compensation, though one source suggests that nearly $500 million is paid annually to over 200,000 victims across the United States (National Association of Crime Victim Compensation Boards, n.d.).

Despite their goals of helping victims, compensation programs have several restrictions that limit how much benefit victims actually receive. Compensation funds typically cover only medical expenses, lost wages, counseling, and other expenses suffered as a result of violent victimization. Not all victims are eligible to receive compensation through a state fund; some states restrict compensation to victims of crime who suffered physical injury, and property crime victims are universally excluded. Furthermore, even if a victim qualifies for compensation, every state imposes some limit on the amount of money that can be disbursed for each victimization claim. According to the National Center for Victims of Crime (2003), the state limits range from $10,000 to $100,000 per occurrence. Reimbursement may take several months, and the amount of supporting documentation required to submit a claim may be seen as a burden to some victims. Finally, compensation programs are a measure of "last resort" and provide financial aid only after all other sources (e.g., medical insurance) have been exhausted (National Association of Crime Victim Compensation Boards, n.d.).

Forms of Community Aid

Given the modest ability of traditional forms of government aid to meet the needs of victims, communities frequently provide several support-based resources that may supplement state-sponsored financial resources to aid victims following a crime. The range of goals, structure, target clients, and funding sources among these organizations are too numerous to discuss in detail here. Instead, we provide one example of an organization that has been successfully helping victims since 1975. The Pennsylvania Coalition Against Rape (PCAR), a state-level advocacy organization, works with local rape crisis centers to ensure access in all counties to quality services (e.g., crisis counseling, court advocacy) for victims and their families. Importantly, although PCAR receives funds from state and federal grants, it also receives funding from private and public foundations and donations from individuals and corporations, including insurance companies, healthcare organizations, attorneys, and the National Football League (http://www.pcar.org).

Role of Restorative Justice

Restorative justice represents a shift in the goals of sanctioning from retribution to reintegration, that is, from punishing and "banishing" offenders to reincorporating them into society as productive members of the group (McCold, 2000; Zehr, 1990). Generally, this process entails acknowledging and repairing the harm—literally, restoring the victim—after the crime: "Crime is defined by the harm it has caused to victims, and the primary function of the reaction against it is not to punish, nor even to rehabilitate, but to repair or compensate for the harm caused by the crime" (Bazemore & Walgrave, 1999: 49). Under the restorative model, all parties (offenders, victims, and the community) come together to address the harm caused by the crime.

According to Bazemore and Umbreit (1995), restorative justice differs from a traditional retributive model in several key ways that have implications for victims. Under a retribution model, crime is a violation against the state, and the victim's primary role is to provide evidence of the harm done to the state. Further, under the retribution model, offenders are labeled, alienated, and physically segregated from mainstream society in jails and prisons.

In contrast to this model, under a restorative approach, crime is viewed as an act against a person and the community rather than against the state and, consequently, crime control is a goal of the community rather than the criminal justice system. Therefore, the ultimate goal is reconciliation between victim and offender. Rather than solely seeking punishment, a restorative system seeks to repair the harm caused by the offense. It follows that victims take a more central role in the criminal justice response as opposed to being peripheral actors; victims are active participants in face-to-face interactions with the offender, and a greater emphasis is placed on meeting both victims' and offenders' needs.

While relatively new to Western justice systems, restorative justice has been a common practice among indigenous peoples for centuries (Bazemore & Walgrave, 1999; Yazzie & Zion, 1996). In such societies—where the success of the group is dependent upon the contribution of all members—stigmatizing punishment, such as exile from the group, would decrease the welfare of the group as a whole and would thus be reserved for only the most heinous offenses. Instead of using stigmatizing punishment, the goal of restorative justice in these societies is, on the one hand, to acknowledge that an offense occurred, that it caused harm, and that those sorts of actions will not be tolerated while, on the other hand, simultaneously acknowledging that the offender was and remains a valuable member of the group. Braithwaite (1989; 1993) noted that this two-prong process, which he labeled *reintegrative shaming*, is an extremely effective form of social control.

Historically, as societies centralized social control functions under state authority (Black, 1976), restorative practices were dismantled (Weitekamp, 1999). Adversarial systems of jurisprudence, which relegated dispute resolution to courtrooms rather than informal community-based processes, replaced many of the indigenous restorative practices (Bazemore & Walgrave, 1999; Yazzie & Zion, 1996). However, restorative systems are still found in indigenous cultures around the globe, including the Maori of New Zealand and Native American and aboriginal Canadian tribes (Zehr, 2002).

In light of the apparent failures of an era of mandatory sentencing, mass incarceration, and other tough-on-crime policies (Kelly, 2015; Lynch & Sabol, 1997), scholars have argued for an "outcome-focused approach" to criminal sanctioning (Johnstone & Van Ness, 2007). Acknowledging that punishment and restoration are linked when attempting to repair the harm caused by the crime, the outcome-focused approach blends restorative and retributive principles. For instance, punishment is necessary (Daly, 2002; Duff, 2003), especially when offenders refuse to acknowledge and repair the harm and there is no other recourse to restore the victim (Zernova & Wright, 2007).

Ultimately, the goals of a restorative or blended approach to justice relate to meeting the needs of victims, needs that, under a retributive model of justice, are rarely met. Five goals were described by Zehr (2002): (1) to provide information about the legal process; (2) to discuss the victimization experience and its impact, especially in the presence of the offender when possible; (3) to empower victims of crime by providing them a greater role in the justice process; (4) to repair any harm caused by the crime; and (5) to punish offenders if doing so makes them aware of responsibilities to victims.

Programmatic implementations of restorative justice principles are generally tailored toward meeting some or all of the above goals. For instance, restitution and other victim compensation programs provide information about the ability of victims to recuperate losses (the first goal) and directly repair the harm by providing financial aid (the fourth goal). Victim impact statements, victim–offender mediation, restorative group conferences, and other forms of group-based interventions are intended to meet the second, third, and fifth goals.

Effectiveness of Restorative Programming

Given the ambitious goals of a restorative approach to justice, do implementations of restorative principles meet those goals and, if so, how effectively? Before considering the empirical evidence, it is important to note two serious limitations of existing restorative justice programs. First, most restorative justice programs are voluntary. Therefore, it is likely that selection bias exists in terms of who participates, and thus the sample of participants may differ in fundamental ways from nonparticipants. That is, participants—for instance, victims willing to meet offenders face-to-face and vice versa—are by definition willing to make amends whereas nonparticipants presumably would be less likely to do so.

Second, most programs evaluate effects on the offender, particularly recidivism. Reflecting broader trends in the criminological literature, analyses of the effects of restorative programming on victim outcomes are limited in scope. That said, reduced recidivism may indirectly benefit victims because lower rates of offending entail lower rates of future victimization. However, problems with the definition of recidivism limit the generalizability of findings to other contexts. Not surprisingly, wide recidivism nets (e.g., self-reported offending; arrest) suggest that restorative programs are ineffective at reducing recidivism, whereas narrow nets (e.g., new conviction) demonstrate that restorative programs are a resounding success with vast reductions in recidivism (Bergseth & Bouffard, 2007).

Definitional issues notwithstanding, restorative programs have mild to moderate reductions in recidivism, on average. One meta-analysis of 32 studies found a 7 percent reduction in new arrests compared with probation (Latimer et al., 2005). While an average effect size of 7 percent seems small, two points are worth considering. First, individual studies reported up to a 39 percent reduction in rearrest, suggesting that some programs are highly effective. Second, if the results generalize to a broader population of offenders, a 7 percent reduction—which could mean several hundred thousand arrests prevented nationally—no longer seems modest. Importantly, restorative programs are less effective for serious or chronic offenders who are incapable of or unwilling to show remorse and take responsibility for the harm that they caused to the victim; more severe sanctions are necessary in these cases (Rodriguez, 2007).

Larger effect sizes tend to be found in more recent studies with rigorous methodological designs (Bradshaw & Roseborough, 2005). Additionally, some programs appear to be more effective than others. For instance, Sherman and colleagues (2015) found a modest but cost-effective reduction in recidivism for restorative conferencing. Victim–offender mediation programs entailed a 34 percent reduction in rearrests and family group conferencing programs reported an 11 percent reduction on average across 23 studies (Bradshaw & Roseborough, 2005).

Studies also suggest that restitution payment, while not a traditional "hands on" form of restorative justice programming, is associated with reduced recidivism for both juveniles (Haynes et al., 2014) and adults (Heinz et al., 1976; Outlaw & Ruback, 1999; Farrington & Welsh, 2005). Restitution instills a sense of responsibility to the victim, and payment provides a sense of accomplishment for offenders. Accordingly, restitution may reduce reoffending by providing some form of moral and behavioral incentives.

In terms of impacts of restorative programming on victims, only two outcomes have been subjected to empirical study. First, as discussed previously, restitution—the financial recompense for any harm suffered—is generally ineffective due to unstandardized imposition, low collection rates, and the fundamental problem that most offenders are poor and cannot afford to make payments. Second, research finds that, among both juveniles and adults, victims (and offenders) who participate in restorative programs, compared with those who participate in traditional court processes, tend to be more satisfied with the sanctioning process (Hayes, 2005; Latimer et al., 2005; Strang et al., 2006; Sherman et al., 2005). Research supports the idea that, more than financial compensation for any harm suffered, victims want an apology from the offender. Victims are most satisfied when an apology is coupled with monetary reimbursement (Okimoto & Tyler, 2007), which is presumably the ultimate goal of restorative justice: for offenders to acknowledge, take responsibility for, and repair the harm that directly resulted from their actions.

Unresolved Issues in Restorative Justice

Victims of crime suffer greatly, but their needs are generally not met by society. Victim needs include both tangible costs, such as medical expenses, lost wages, funeral expenses, and property damage or loss, and intangible costs, such as pain and suffering, fear, and psychological distress. In response to high rates of victimization in the 1980s and 1990s, states and communities developed several resources for meeting the needs of victims, such as victim compensation funds and restitution laws. But generally these interventions do not fully repair the harm victims suffer as a result of crime.

An additional method of meeting victims' needs is provided by restorative justice. Under a restorative justice paradigm, all parties who have been affected by crime—including the victim, the offender, and the community—work together to undo the harm caused by the offense. There are three aspects to restorative justice: (1) the offender being sincerely sorry for the harm caused by the crime, (2) the offender performing some action to help restore the victim to the status he or she was in before the crime, and (3) the victim accepting the offender's apology and restorative actions. Although complete restoration is the goal, that goal is usually unrealistic because offenders do not have the resources to completely provide the financial restitution needed to compensate the victim for any incurred costs. That being the case, under current systems victims must typically be content with, at best, partial restitution.

Scholars have criticized both the victim-centered and restorative paradigms of justice administration on multiple grounds. In the remainder of this chapter, we highlight some of the primary criticisms of both approaches and highlight future directions.

Criticisms of a Victim-centered Approach

That victims bear the brunt of harm as a result of crime, that this harm includes extensive tangible and intangible costs, and that restorative justice is one potentially effective method of repairing the harm is only one view. Scholars have criticized the costs of crime literature and the restorative justice literature on both theoretical and pragmatic grounds. For example, Tonry (2015) raised three criticisms of a narrow focus on the costs of crime literature. First, valuations of the costs of crime to victims ignore the costs of crime to offenders and their dependents. Punishment also "victimizes" offenders—and society more generally—through lost wages, legal expenses, social welfare costs, relationship dissolution, and the effects of incarceration on the children of prisoners.

Second, victim cost estimates are inflated by including intangible costs of crime, such as pain and suffering. Using these estimates, Tonry (2015: 660) argued, "almost any imaginable policy could be justified" as cost effective, because the estimated intangible costs are exponentially higher than the administration of the entire criminal justice system. Additionally, the methodologies used in victim cost studies are inherently flawed. For instance, jury awards are held against property owners of hotels, malls, and other locations where the crime occurred—people with money—rather than the actual offenders, because offenders cannot afford to pay for intangible "pain and suffering" costs.

Third, the victim costs literature ignores social justice. Offenders subjected to the payment of restitution and other forms of victim compensation are disadvantaged, poor minorities. Tonry pointed to the historical trend that high estimates of victim costs were used to justify newer, harsher legislation, such as truth in sentencing and mandatory sentencing laws. Accordingly, states were required to abide by this legislation in order to receive federal funds, which led to racial and ethnic disparities in punishment. Beckett and Harris (2011; also Harris et al., 2010) additionally argued that economic sanctions, such as restitution, further disadvantage offenders and perpetuate inequality. Rather than replacing other forms of sanctions, as Beckett and Harris argued should be the case, restitution is today generally an additional punishment and burden.

Criticisms of the Restorative Justice Movement

Restorative justice programs have been implemented and assessed in Canada, Europe, Australia, and New Zealand, and they have become increasingly popular in these countries. In contrast, with a few exceptions (e.g., the juvenile justice system), retributive justice remains the most popular paradigm for handling offenders in the United States, and there have been few evaluations of restorative justice programs. For six very pragmatic reasons, it is unlikely that restorative justice will become widely popular in the U.S.

First, American culture has historically been incompatible with a restorative paradigm. In particular, as Beale (2003) highlighted, three facets of American culture fundamentally conflict with the goals of restorative justice: (1) the market-driven media, which support punitive responses to crime; (2) a political system that rewards candidates who appear "tough on crime" because of the perception that harsh sanctions reduce crime rates; and (3) recent sentencing changes (i.e., tough on crime policies) that are incompatible with restorative justice goals.

Second, restorative justice may not be widely adopted because its goals do not have high priority. As Karp and Frank (2016) noted, one of the current priorities of policymakers is reform to reduce prison overcrowding. However, the reduction of mass incarceration and prison overcrowding is not a goal of the restorative justice movement. Restorative justice interventions are instead typically reserved for juveniles and low-level offenders, the types of individuals for whom incarceration is not a likely form of punishment (Wood and Suzuki, 2016). Therefore, restorative justice may not be adopted simply because its goals are not central to American priorities.

Third, restorative justice programs are fundamentally voluntary. If either the victim or offender refuses to engage in restorative programs, the goals of restorative justice are undermined. Even in the UK and Australia, which have pushed for restorative interventions, takeup rates were modest for several programs in one systematic review (Strang et al., 2013). Another review of 25 programs in the US, UK, Australia, and New Zealand noted that offender participation was voluntary in 23 programs and victim participation was voluntary in all 25 programs (Roche, 2003). As Strang and colleagues (2013) noted, the types of cases where both victims and offenders consent to restorative conferencing probably do not generalize to all forms of criminal cases. For instance, it is likely that participants in restorative justice programs were the most open to change or reconciliation in the first place and, for offenders, the least likely to recidivate in the future. Some victims may view participation as an unnecessary burden and may feel "re-victimized" if pressured to meet an offender face-to-face or participate in other conference-style interventions (Hoyle & Rosenblatt, 2016; Roche, 2003).

Fourth, one of the key aspects of the restorative justice movement is that justice is restored not just by compensating victims for the harm done to them but by inducing offenders to acknowledge their guilt and apologize to victims and to the community. Both critics and proponents of restorative justice have noted that it is not clear whether offenders are genuinely apologetic and truly accept accountability for their actions or, for example, are simply grateful for the opportunity to be diverted from incarceration (see e.g., Jennings et al., 2008; Roche, 2003).

Fifth, restorative justice principles have been co-opted by the criminal justice system, leading to "program goals such as case processing, growth, and efficiency being given priority over the needs of victims and offenders" (Wood & Suzuki, 2016, p. 155) That is, the criminal justice system seeks to process cases as rapidly and efficiently as possible, both of which are goals that conflict with the case-specific approach grounded in restorative justice. In other words, advocates of restorative justice have to some extent undermined their position by employing metrics that are incompatible with the underlying philosophy of restorative justice.

Finally, because restorative justice is generally only vaguely and broadly defined, it is difficult to see how policymakers could be convinced to widely adopt the practice through a substantial expenditure of public funds (Wood & Suzuki, 2016). Operational clarity and consistency are critical for empirical evaluations of the effectiveness of policy changes assessed in terms of monetary costs and benefits. Because the victim- and community-centered outcomes of restorative justice programs are not central to traditional criminal justice and are difficult to operationalize, policymakers might be particularly skeptical of changes that are only loosely defined and that cannot be rigorously tested.

Concluding Remarks

Despite criticisms, the restorative justice paradigm has become dominant in juvenile justice systems across the United States (see e.g., Akers et al., 2008; Jennings et al., 2008; McCold, 2008). To the extent that restorative programming increases victim satisfaction and permits forgiveness of the offender, that is, restores victims to their status prior to the crime, such programs could be considered successful. However, evaluations of these programs rarely consider the impact of restorative justice sanctions on the victims of crime. Future research must evaluate the impact of restorative programming on victims relative to traditional forms of retributive justice in addition to the effects on offender-related outcomes.

Future work will need to address ways in which the needs of victims might be better met, particularly through a restorative justice framework. Evidence suggests that restorative justice programs increase victim satisfaction and may reduce offender recidivism (Latimer et al., 2005). But if the overwhelming majority of victims refuse to participate in restorative programs (e.g., Hoyle & Rosenblatt, 2016), and if the majority of restitution to victims goes unpaid, it is difficult to argue that restorative interventions meet the needs of victims any better than traditional court processes.

Discussion Questions

1. Should the criminal justice system be primarily focused on the offender, as it is now, or should the victim be the focus?
2. How should the costs of crime to victims, to their friends and families, to communities, and to society in general be computed? How difficult is it to calculate intangible losses?
3. A single victimization can lead to further victimizations. What can victims, their friends, and their families do to reduce the likelihood of a re-victimization? Are there any special actions that police can take to prevent these re-victimizations?
4. In most cases, victims do not receive enough money to cover their losses due to the crime. Does society have an obligation to help all victims? Only poor victims? Should victim blameworthiness be a factor that is considered?
5. Restorative justice is not the traditional approach to criminal justice in the United States. Is this likely to change in coming years?

References

Akers, R. L., Lane, J., & Lanza-Kaduce, L. (2008). Faith-based mentoring and restorative justice: Overlapping theoretical, empirical, and philosophical background. In H. V. Miller (Ed.), *Restorative justice: From theory to practice* (pp. 139–165). Bingley, UK: Emerald Group Publishing Limited.

Bazemore, G., & Umbreit, M. (1995). Rethinking the sanctioning function in juvenile court: Retributive or restorative responses to youth crime. *Crime & Delinquency, 41*(3), 296–316.

Bazemore, G., & Walgrave, L. (1999). *Restorative juvenile justice: Repairing the harm of youth crime.* Monsey, NY: Criminal Justice Press.

Beale, S. S. (2003). Still tough on crime-prospects for restorative justice in the United States. *Utah Law Review,* 413–437.

Beckett, K., & Harris, A. (2011). On cash and conviction. *Criminology & Public Policy, 10*(3), 509–537.

Bergseth, K. J., & Bouffard, J. A. (2007). The long-term impact of restorative justice programming for juvenile offenders. *Journal of Criminal Justice, 35*(4), 433–451.

Bernasco, W. (2008). Them again? Same-offender involvement in repeat and near repeat burglaries. *European Journal of Criminology, 5,* 411–431.

Black, D. (1976). *The behavior of law.* New York: Academic Press.

Bradshaw, W., & Roseborough, D. (2005). Restorative justice dialogue: The impact of mediation and conferencing on juvenile recidivism. *Fed. Probation, 69,* 15–21.

Braithwaite, J. (1989). *Crime, shame and reintegration.* Cambridge, England: Cambridge University Press.

Braithwaite, J. (1993). Shame and modernity. *British Journal of Criminology, 33*(1), 1–18.

Cohen, M. A. (2005). *The costs of crime and justice.* New York, NY: Routledge.

Daly, K. (2002). Restorative justice The real story. *Punishment & Society, 4*(1), 55–79.

Davis, R. C., Smith, B., & Hillenbrand, S. (1992). Restitution: The victim's viewpoint. *Justice System Journal, 15*(3), 746–758.

Dickman, M. (2009). Should crime pay? A critical assessment of the Mandatory Victims Restitution Act of 1996. *California Law Review, 97,* 1687–1718.

Duff, A. (2003). Restoration and retribution. In von Hirsch, A., Roberts, J. V., Bottoms, A. E., Roach, K., & Schiff, M. (Eds.), *Restorative justice and criminal justice: Competing or reconcilable paradigms.* London: Bloomsbury Publishing, pp. 43–60.

Farrell, G. (2015). Crime concentration theory. *Crime Prevention & Community Safety, 17*(4), 233–248.

Farrington, D. P., & Welsh, B. C. (2005). Randomized experiments in criminology: What have we learned in the last two decades? *Journal of Experimental Criminology, 1*(1), 9–38.

Finkelhor, D., Ormrod, R. K., & Turner, H. A. (2007). Poly-victimization: A neglected component in child victimization. *Child Abuse & Neglect, 31*(1), 7–26.

Fisher, C. (2015). *What matters: An analysis of victim satisfaction with the criminal justice system in a procedural justice framework* (Unpublished doctoral dissertation). University of Maryland, College Park.

Grubb, J. A., & Nobles, M. R. (2016). A spatiotemporal analysis of arson. *Journal of Research in Crime and Delinquency, 53*(1), 66–92.

Grubesic, T. H., & Mack, E. A. (2008). Spatio-temporal interaction of urban crime. *Journal of Quantitative Criminology, 24*(3), 285–306.

Harrell, E., Langton, L., Berzofsky, M., Couzens, L., & Smiley-McDonald, H. (2014). Household poverty and nonfatal violent victimization, 2008–2012. *Bureau of Justice Statistics, November*. NCJ 248384 available at https://www.bjs.gov/content/pub/pdf/hpnvv0812.pdf

Harris, A., Evans, H., & Beckett, K. (2010). Drawing blood from stones: Legal debt and social inequality in the contemporary United States. *American Journal of Sociology, 115*(6), 1753–1799.

Hart, W. L., Ashcroft, J., Burgess, A., Flanagan, N., Meese, U., Milton, C., Narramore, C., Ortega, R., & Seward. (1984). *Attorney General's task force on family violence. Final report*. Washington, DC: Author. https://babel.hathitrust.org/cgi/pt?id=mdp.39015001605800;view=1up;seq=3

Hayes, H. (2005). Assessing reoffending in restorative justice conferences. *Australian & New Zealand Journal of Criminology, 38*(1), 77–101.

Haynes, S. H., Cares, A., & Ruback, R. B. (2014). Juvenile economic sanctions: An analysis of their imposition, payment, and effect on recidivism. *Criminology & Public Policy, 13*, 31–60.

Haynes, S. H., Cares, A. C., & Ruback, R. B. (2015). Reducing the harm of criminal victimization: the role of restitution. *Violence and Victims, 30*(3), 450–469.

Heinz, J., Galaway, B., & Hudson, J. (1976). Restitution or parole: A follow-up study of adult offenders. *The Social Service Review*, 148–156.

Herrington, L. H., Bobo, G., Carrington, F., Damos, J. P., Dolan, D. L., Eikenberry, K. O., Miller, R. J., Robertson, P., & Samenow, S. E. (1982). *President's task force on victims of crime. Final report*. Washington, DC: Author. https://ojp.gov/ovc/publications/presdntstskforcrprt/87299.pdf

Hindelang, M. J., Gottfredson, M.R. and Garafalo, J. (1978). *Victims of personal crime: An empirical foundation for a theory of personal victimization*. Cambridge, MA: Ballinger.

Hotaling, G. T., & Buzawa, E. S. (2003). *Victim satisfaction with criminal justice case processing in a model court setting*. National Institute of Justice, Office of Justice Programs, U.S. Department of Justice.

Hoyle, C., & Rosenblatt, F. F. (2016). Looking back to the future: Threats to the success of restorative justice in the United Kingdom. *Victims & Offenders, 11*(1), 30–49.

Hudson, P. S. (1984). The crime victim and the criminal justice system: Time for a change. *Pepperdine Law Review, 11*, 23–62.

Jennings, W. G., Gover, A. R., & Hitchcock, D. M. (2008). Localizing restorative justice: An in-depth look at a Denver public school program. In H. V. Miller (Ed.), *Restorative justice: From theory to practice* (pp. 167–187). Bingley, UK: Emerald Group Publishing Limited.

Jennings, W. G., Piquero, A. R., & Reingle, J. M. (2012). On the overlap between victimization and offending: A review of the literature. *Aggression and Violent Behavior, 17*(1), 16–26.

Johnstone, G., & Van Ness, D. W. (2007). *Handbook of restorative justice*. Portland, OR: Taylor & Francis.

Karp, D. R., & Frank, O. (2016). Anxiously awaiting the future of restorative justice in the United States. *Victims & Offenders, 11*(1), 50–70.

Kelly, W. R. (2015). *Criminal justice at the crossroads: Transforming crime and punishment*. New York, NY: Columbia University Press.

Kimerling, R., Alvarez, J., Pavao, J., Kaminski, A., & Baumrind, N. (2007). Epidemiology and consequences of women's revictimization. *Women's Health Issues, 17*(2), 101–106.

Kort-Butler, L. A. (2010). Experienced and vicarious victimization: Do social support and self-esteem prevent delinquent responses? *Journal of Criminal Justice, 38*(4), 496–505.

Langton, L. (2011). *Use of victim services agencies by victims of serious violent crime, 1993–2009*. Washington, DC: Bureau of Justice Statistics.

Langton, L., & Planty, M. (2010). *Victims of identity theft, 2008*. Washington, DC: U.S. Department of Justice, Bureau of Justice Statistics.

Lantz, B., & Ruback, R. B. (in press). A networked boost: Burglary co-offending and repeat victimization using a network approach. *Crime and Delinquency*. doi:10.1177/0011128715597695. Published online at http://journals.sagepub.com/doi/pdf/10.1177/0011128715597695

Latimer, J., Dowden, C., & Muise, D. (2005). The effectiveness of restorative justice practices: A meta-analysis. *The Prison Journal, 85*(2), 127–144.

Lauritsen, J. L., & Rezey, M. L. (2013). *Measuring the prevalence of crime with the National Victimization Survey*. Washington, DC: US Department of Justice, Bureau of Justice Statistics.

Lowe, S.R., Sampson, L., Gruebner, O., & Galea, S. (2015). Psychological resilience after Hurricane Sandy: The influence of individual- and community-level factors on mental health after a large-scale natural disaster. *PLOSone*, doi:10.1371/journal.pone.0125761.

Lynch, J. P., & Sabol, W. J. (1997). *Did getting tough on crime pay?* Program on Law and Behavior, State Policy Center, the Urban Institute.

McCart, M. R., Smith, D. W., & Sawyer, G. K. (2010). Help seeking among victims of crime: A review of the empirical literature. *Journal of Traumatic Stress, 23*(2), 198–206.

McCold, P. (2000). Toward a holistic vision of restorative juvenile justice: A reply to the Maximalist Model. *Contemporary Justice Review, 3*(4), 357–414.

McCold, P. (2008). Evaluation of a restorative milieu: Restorative practices in context. In H. V. Miller (Ed.), *Restorative justice: From theory to practice* (pp. 99–137). Bingley, UK: Emerald Group Publishing Limited.

Miller, T. R., Cohen, M. A., & Wiersema, B. (1996). Victim costs and consequences: A new look. NCJRS 155282. Washington, DC: National Institute of Justice. Available at https://www.ncjrs.gov/pdffiles/victcost.pdf

National Association of Crime Victim Compensation Boards (nd). Crime victim compensation: An overview. Retrieved June 23, 2016 from http://www.nacvcb.org/index.asp?bid=14

National Center for Victims of Crime (2002). *Ordering restitution to the crime victim.* Washington, DC: U.S. Department of Justice.

National Center for Victims of Crime (2003). Crime victim compensation. Retrieved May 4, 2016 from https://victimsofcrime.org/help-for-crime-victims/get-help-bulletins-for-crime-victims/crime-victim-compensation.

National Center for Victims of Crime (2011). *Making restitution real: Five case studies on improving restitution collection.* Washington, DC: U.S. Department of Justice.

Norris, F. H., & Kaniasty, K. (1994). Psychological distress following criminal victimization in the general population: Cross-sectional, longitudinal, and prospective analyses. *Journal of Consulting and Clinical Psychology, 62*(1), 111–123.

Office for Victims of Crime (n.d.). Crime victims fund. Retrieved May 4, 2016 from http://ojp.gov/ovc/pubs/crimevictimsfundfs/intro.html.

Office for Victims of Crime (1998). *New directions from the field: Victims rights and services for the 21st century.* Washington, DC: U.S. Department of Justice. https://www.ncjrs.gov/ovc_archives/directions/welcome.html

Okimoto, T. G., & Tyler, T. R. (2007). Is compensation enough? Relational concerns in responding to unintended equity. *Group Processes and Intergroup Relations, 10*(3), 399–420.

Outlaw, M. C., & Ruback, R. B. (1999). Predictors and outcomes of victim restitution orders. *Justice Quarterly, 16*(4), 847–869.

Papachristos, A. V., Wildeman, C., & Roberto, E. (2015). Tragic, but not random: The social contagion of nonfatal gunshot injuries. *Social Science & Medicine, 125*, 139–150.

Pease, K. (1998). *Repeat victimisation: Taking stock.* Crime Prevention and Detection Series Paper 90. London: Home Office.

Ratcliffe, J. H., & Rengert, G. F. (2008). Near-repeat patterns in Philadelphia shootings. *Security Journal, 21*(1), 58–76.

Reijintjes, A., Kamphuis, J. H., Prinzie, P., & Telch, M. J. (2010). Peer victimization and internalizing problems in children: A meta-analysis of longitudinal studies. *Child Abuse & Neglect, 34*(4), 244–252.

Roche, D. (2003). *Accountability in restorative justice.* New York: Oxford University Press.

Rodriguez, N. (2007). Restorative justice at work: Examining the impact of restorative justice resolutions on juvenile recidivism. *Crime & Delinquency, 53*(3), 355–379.

Rosenmerkel, S., Durose, M., & Farole, D. (2009). *Felony sentences in state courts, 2006: Statistical tables.* Washington, DC: U.S. Department of Justice, Bureau of Justice Statistics.

Ruback, R. B., & Bergstrom, M. H. (2006). Economic sanctions in criminal justice: Purposes, effects, and implications. *Criminal Justice and Behavior, 33*(2), 242–273.

Ruback, R. B., Cares, A. C., & Hoskins, S. N. (2008). Crime victims' perceptions of restitution: The importance of payment and understanding. *Violence and Victims, 23*(6), 697–710.

Ruback, R. B., Clark, V. A., & Warner, C. (2014a). Why are crime victims at risk of being victimized again? Substance use, depression, and offending as mediators of the victimization-revictimization link. *Journal of Interpersonal Violence, 29*, 157–185.

Ruback, R. B., Gladfelter, A. S., & Lantz, B. (2014b). Paying restitution: Experimental analysis of the effects of information and rationale. *Criminology & Public Policy, 13*(3), 405–436.

Ruback, R. B., & Shaffer, J. N. (2005). The role of victim-related factors in victim restitution: A multi-method analysis of restitution in Pennsylvania. *Law and Human Behavior, 29*(6), 657–681.

Sherman, L. W., Strang, H., Angel, C., Woods, D., Barnes, G. C., Bennett, S., & Inkpen, N. (2005). Effects of face-to-face restorative justice on victims of crime in four randomized, controlled trials. *Journal of Experimental Criminology, 1*(3), 367–395.

Sherman, L. W., Strang, H., Mayo-Wilson, E., Woods, D. J., & Ariel, B. (2015). Are restorative justice conferences effective in reducing repeat offending? Findings from a Campbell systematic review. *Journal of Quantitative Criminology*, *31*(1), 1–24.

Strang, H., Sherman, L., Angel, C. M., Woods, D. J., Bennett, S., Newbury-Birch, D., & Inkpen, N. (2006). Victim evaluations of face-to-face restorative justice conferences: A quasi-experimental analysis. *Journal of Social Issues*, *62*(2), 281–306.

Strang, H., Sherman, L. W., Mayo-Wilson, E., Woods, D., & Ariel, B. (2013). Restorative justice conferencing (RJC) using face-to-face meetings of offenders and victims: Effects on offender recidivism and victim satisfaction. A systematic review. *Campbell Systematic Reviews*, 12. doi: 10.4073/csr.2013.12

Tobolowsky, P. M., Gaboury, M. T., Jackson, A. L., & Blackburn, A. G. (2010). *Crime victim rights and remedies* (2nd ed.). Durham, NC: Carolina Academic Press.

Tonry, M. (2015). The fog around cost-of-crime studies may finally be clearing. *Criminology & Public Policy*, *14*(4), 653–671.

Townsley, M., Homel, R., & Chaseling, J. (2003). Infectious burglaries. A test of the near repeat hypothesis. *British Journal of Criminology*, *43*(3), 615–633.

Truman, J. L., & Langton, L. (2014). *Criminal Victimization, 2014*. NCJ Bulletin 248973. Bureau of Justice Statistics.

Turner, H. A., Shattuck, A., Finkelhor, D., & Hamby, S. (2015). Effects of poly-victimization on adolescent social support, self-concept, and psychological distress. *Journal of Interpersonal Violence, June 1* (online), 1–26.

Weaver, T. L., & Clum, G. A. (1995). Psychological distress associated with interpersonal violence: A meta-analysis. *Clinical Psychology Review*, *15*(2), 115–140.

Weitekamp, E. G. M. (1999). The history of restorative justice. In G. Bazemore & L. Walgrave (Eds.). *Restorative juvenile justice: Repairing the harm of youth crime* (pp. 75–102). Monsey, NY: Criminal Justice Press.

Welsh, B. C., & Farrington, D. P. (2015). Monetary value of early developmental crime prevention and its policy significance. *Criminology & Public Policy*, *14*(4), 673–680.

Wood, W. R., & Suzuki, M. (2016). Four challenges in the future of restorative justice. *Victims & Offenders*, *11*(1), 149–172.

Xie, M., Heimer, K., & Lauritsen, J. L. (2012). Violence against women in U.S. metropolitan areas: Changes in women's work status and work. *Criminology*, 50, 105–143.

Yazzie, R., & Zion, J. W. (1996). Navajo restorative justice: The law of equality and justice. In B. Galaway & J. Hudson (Eds.), *Restorative justice: International perspectives*. Monsey, NY: Criminal Justice Press, pp. 157–173.

Zehr, H. (1990). *Changing lenses: A new focus for crime and justice*. Scottsdale, PA: Herald Press.

Zehr, H. (2002). Journey to belonging. In E. G. M. Weitekamp & H-J. Kerner (Eds.), *Restorative justice: Theoretical foundations*. New York: Routledge, pp. 21–31.

Zernova, M., & Wright, M. (2007). Alternative visions of restorative justice. In G. Johnstone & D. W. Van Ness (Eds.), *Handbook of restorative justice*. Portland, OR: Willan Publishing and Taylor & Francis.

17

HELPING SEXUAL ASSAULT VICTIMS

Suzanne Overstreet, Susan McNeeley, Kathryn Elvey, and Whitney Gass

Keywords

sexual victimization; rape crisis centers; Sexual Assault Nurse Examiner (SANE); victim compensation; male sexual assault victims; university campus

Objectives

After studying this chapter, the reader should understand:

- The medical and financial consequences of sexual victimization.
- The types of services available to victims of sexual assault.
- The ways in which the criminal justice system connects victims with resources.
- The role of rape crisis centers in helping sexual assault victims.
- The services that are offered to varying populations, such as college students and males.

Introduction

Sexual assault is a serious social problem affecting millions in the United States each year. According to the Uniform Crime Reports, over 116,000 rapes were reported to the police in 2014 (Federal Bureau of Investigation, 2015). According to the National Violence Against Women Survey, one in six women and one in 33 men have been raped at some point during their life (Tjaden & Thoennes, 1998). While arrests and convictions of offenders can provide a sense of closure to victims and their families, there are other ways in which the criminal justice system and other agencies can assist victims. Victims of sexual assault have a range of medical, psychological, and financial concerns that must be addressed after the crime takes place.

This chapter begins by outlining several areas in which sexual assault victims require assistance. In particular, we discuss the medical, psychological, and economic needs of victims; the systems that currently exist to provide support, such as the criminal justice system and rape crisis centers; and recommendations for improving services. We then address a particular arena in which sexual victimization has received a great deal of attention—the university. Rather than focusing on reducing victimization on college campuses, we examine the needs of college students who have been victimized and consider the ways in which universities can provide aid to victims. Finally, a majority of the efforts on helping sexual assault victims has taken on a feminist viewpoint, and therefore resources for victims tend to focus on female issues. As a result, less is known about how to help men who have experienced sexual assault. We discuss some consequences of victimization that are unique to men and the implications of these consequences for service providers.

Needs of Sexual Assault Victims

Victims of sexual assault experience mental, emotional, and physical trauma as a result of their victimization. Many sources provide services for sexual assault victims, but victims do not often take advantage of available services. Victims of sexual assault do not seek out resources for help for a variety of reasons including embarrassment, shame, fear, ignorance, or lack of awareness regarding available services (Fisher et al., 2000; Fisher et al., 2003). Victims may experience embarrassment because sex is a very private matter—having sex, whether it is consensual or non-consensual, could be embarrassing if anyone were made aware of the incident. Sexual assault victims may feel ashamed because of the social situation or the location of where the assault took place, or they may feel ashamed of consensual sexual relationships from the past and therefore feel a sense of personal responsibility based on their sexual history.

Fear is an emotion felt by many sexual assault victims. They are often fearful of their perpetrator's potential reprisal, as sexual assault perpetrators often threaten to re-victimize victims or to harm the victims' families and loved ones if they alert authorities or speak to anyone regarding the victimization. Sexual assault has only recently been acknowledged as a problem that should be taken seriously. Because sexual assault has not been seriously recognized in the past, many victims are unaware that there are services available to them. Next, we discuss in detail the services needed by victims, as well as different avenues for services that are available through the criminal justice system, medical professionals, and university offices and personnel.

Medical Needs

Victims of sexual assault are likely to experience physical injuries or mental health issues. For example, victims often suffer from depression, anxiety, or posttraumatic stress disorder; abuse alcohol and drugs; and contemplate suicide (see Daigle, 2012; Kehner, 2004). Therefore, medical attention is crucial for these victims. In addition, the role of medical personnel is vital for these cases because proper procedure must be followed for the purpose of evidence collection.

Sexual Assault Nurse Examiners (SANE) are the medical personnel who examine sexual assault victims. They receive specialized education in the medical, forensic, and legal treatment of sexual assault victims (see Bimber, 2014). Some programs are coordinated by law enforcement or rape crisis centers rather than hospitals (see Campbell et al., 2006). The SANE documents information about the victim, including the victim's history, details of the sexual assault, and the findings from the forensic examination. The SANE also collects and maintains custody of forensic evidence, interprets findings, and provides expert witness testimony to the judicial system (Bimber, 2014).

The medical examination process for sexual assault victims begins with the initial contact. During this time, it is important that medical personnel immediately assess the victim's need for care concerning life-threatening or serious injuries and inform the victim of the steps in the exam process. At this time, medical personnel should also quickly respond to requests for victim assistance, such as safe housing or counseling (U.S. Department of Justice, 2013). The initial contact is then followed by the triage and intake. It is crucial that medical personnel consider sexual assault patients a priority and perform a thorough medical assessment in a timely manner. Medical personnel should also determine and respond to the safety concerns of the victim. Victim advocates should be contacted as well (Cole & Logan, 2008).

The next step in the examination process is documentation, the medical forensic history, and photography. Gathering the medical forensic history of the victim is important. Information concerning the suspect, the date and time of the sexual assault, post-assault activities, and the description of the sexual assault is necessary during the exam process. Performing an exam on the victim and collecting evidence such as clothing, hairs, and debris are also necessary steps taken during the examination process (U.S. Department of Justice, 2013).

Sexual assault evidence collection kits are used by SANE to collect evidence during a sexual assault case. These kits may vary by jurisdiction in the types of samples collected, techniques and materials used for collection, and the vocabulary used to describe evidence (Bimber, 2014). Despite these varying differences, all kits must meet or exceed minimum guidelines for content. Sexual assault evidence collection kits must include a kit container. Evidence collected during the process of a sexual assault case is placed into the container once the items are dried, packaged, labeled, and sealed (Campbell et al., 2006). The kits must include a checklist or instruction sheet that assists examiners in collecting evidence, as well as forms that guide evidence collection and analysis. Finally, sexual assault evidence collection kits should contain materials for collecting and preserving evidence. Forms of evidence that may be collected and preserved during the process of a forensic examination include the victim's clothing and undergarments; foreign materials on the victim's body including blood, fibers, and loose hairs; vaginal or cervical swabs; penile swabs; anal or perianal swabs; oral swabs; body swabs; and saliva samples or buccal swabs for DNA analysis and comparison (U.S. Department of Justice, 2013).

The final steps in the examination process are testing the victim for sexually transmitted diseases, pregnancy, and whether they have drugs or alcohol in their system, as well as providing emergency contraception and access to crisis intervention counseling, when necessary. A discharge and follow up with the victim is required. Victims are also encouraged to testify in court.

Financial Needs

Another potential problem for victims of sexual assault is the financial burden that arises due to the crime (see Miller, Cohen, & Wiersema, 1996; Elvey & Clutter, 2014). Most notably, there are costs associated with medical and mental health care provided to sexual assault victims. There are also financial costs due to decreased productivity. Victims may have to miss work due to injury or illness caused by the incident, visits to receive health care, or participation in stages of the criminal justice process. The cost of expenses accumulated by victims of rape has been estimated at over $5,000 (Miller et al., 1996).

All states must pay for the forensic medical exam, regardless of whether the victim reported the sexual assault to law enforcement (U.S. Department of Justice, 2013). The Violence Against Women Act (VAWA) and the STOP Violence Against Women Formula Grant Program provide funds to pay for the medical forensic exam, but require states to meet certain standards in order to be eligible to receive these funds. Funds are provided to all states, territories, and the District of Columbia under the STOP Program. All facilities must be certified each year that they have complied with VAWA requirements (Campbell, 2008). In order for states to receive STOP Program funds to pay for medical exams, the states cannot require victims of sexual assault to seek reimbursement from their insurance companies, and a trained examiner for victims of sexual assault must perform the medical exam. Jurisdictions that require victims to submit the charges of the medical exam to their insurance carrier may also require victims to pay a deductible or copayment for the exam. Victims must be notified of the jurisdictional policies regarding payment for medical care and the forensic exam related to the sexual assault (U.S. Department of Justice, 2013).

Medical services that are unrelated to evidence collection are not covered by STOP Program funds. Therefore, medical treatments for injuries or sexually transmitted diseases are often not provided as part of a rape exam. Victims may not seek out medical assistance, counseling, or other services because doing so is unaffordable or because the victim cannot afford to miss a day's wages. Victim reparation funds are available in many states and application can be made to help with expenses such as medical and prescription expenses, mental health counseling, loss of earnings or support, and child or dependent care (U.S. Department of Justice, 2013). Victims who are eligible to apply for monies from reparation funds are innocent victims of violent crimes who suffer physical and/or emotional harm.

Reparation funds are available as a result of the Victims of Crime Act of 1984 (VOCA), which created the Crime Victims Fund. This fund is supported through monies paid by convicted offenders and is offered to states by the federal government. Offenders may be required to contribute to this fund as part of their sentence, a sentence handed down by the courts. While an offender is on trial, the courts will freeze their financial accounts so that the money cannot be spent or relocated, ensuring that the victim will be financially compensated (Office for Victims of Crime, n.d.). The amount of funding that a victim can apply for as well as the amount of time the victim has to file for such compensation varies widely on a state-by-state basis (for a review of states' rules regarding victim compensation, see Solimine & Elvey, 2015). For example, the maximum amount that a victim can receive from Alabama is $15,000 and the victim has one year from the time of conviction of the offender to apply for compensation. In contrast, Ohio has no time limit on when a victim may file for compensation and there is a maximum $50,000 limit.

An offender's sentence can also involve direct payment to the victim, which is known as restitution (see Daigle, 2012). Victims can be paid to cover the cost of medical care, mental health treatment, lost wages, or property that was stolen or damaged. Restitution is limited to expenses that are documented and therefore does not include damages for pain and suffering. Victims are also able to seek repayment for victimization, including damages, through civil litigation. However, as many offenders are indigent, their inability to pay restitution to the victim or fines that contribute to the Crime Victims Fund may impact the victims' ability to receive help with the economic burdens of victimization.

Sources of Assistance for Sexual Assault Victims

Criminal Justice System

Involving the police after a crime has occurred should be one of the first actions taken, second only to necessary immediate medical attention. Police departments can provide transportation to medical appointments if personal transportation is not available to the victim. Police officers can also assist by listening to the victim, offering consolation when needed, and staying with the victim until a family member, friend, or significant other arrives.

Police departments are also important providers of education about other services that are available to sexual assault victims in their city, state, or region. They provide information about medical care which is either necessary for prosecution of sexual assault perpetrators or simply beneficial for the victim: a rape kit for the purposes of evidence collection; administration of Plan B to prevent unwanted pregnancy as a result of the sexual assault; and testing for HIV, AIDS, and other sexually transmitted diseases. The police not only provide information about outlets for physical care but also about outlets for mental and emotional care. Police departments are often familiar with local mental health professionals who can counsel with and even assess a sexual assault victim's trauma and need for services. These professionals can offer suggestions to victims to help them successfully cope with their victimization and move forward with their lives.

Victim/witness assistance programs educate victims about their rights and the resources that are available to them (see Daigle, 2012). These programs are also designed to encourage victim participation in the criminal justice process, as the victim must act as a witness in order for prosecution against the offender to be successful. While these programs are not always associated with the criminal justice system, victim/witness coordinators are often housed within prosecutors' offices or police departments. In addition to providing information about services available to victims, victim/witness coordinators are able to keep victims updated about the status of the case and make sure that they are informed about scheduled hearings.

Rape Crisis Service Programs

Rape crisis centers are community-based organizations that help victims of rape, sexual abuse, and sexual violence. These programs aim to improve societal response to rape, provide support and services to victims, and to help reduce the incidence of rape, victimization, and sexual violence (Woody & Beldin, 2012). These programs offer free services to all victims of sexual assault. The programs provide 24/7 hotline counseling, information, and referral. In many cases, victims are not able to access services for treatment. This is often the case for victims living in remote and rural areas. Videoconferencing technology has made it possible for rural residents to access specialized treatment services available to them (Hassija & Gray, 2011). Rape crisis programs also assist victims during the court process and during hospital emergency room visits. Nationwide outreach programs include the joyful heart foundation and the V-Day organization. The mission of these programs is to heal, educate, and empower survivors of sexual assault through healing, education, and advocacy (Joyful Heart Foundation, 2016).

Rape crisis service programs were first introduced in the 1970s. When these programs were initially established, they represented a feminist response to society's violence against women, the lack of societal resources to assist rape victims, and the tendency to place blame on the victim (Decker & Naugle, 2009). In the past, victims of rape and sexual assault were not taken seriously. There were also minimal resources available to victims. In recent years, victim advocates and rape crisis programs have helped to change the landscape for rape and sexual assault victims. While issues still exist, conditions have drastically improved in recent decades.

The primary treatment methods offered today to victims of rape and sexual assault are crisis intervention, advocacy, and counseling. Crisis intervention involves emergency assistance either face-to-face or through a telephone hotline. These interventions have broadened in recent years and now draw on numerous theoretical approaches and models, such as the equilibrium, cognitive, developmental, and ecological models (Woody & Beldin, 2012). Advocacy consists of providing victims with crisis information, support and referral, assisting a victim throughout the court process, and helping a victim navigate the numerous providers to meet needs in an appropriate time frame (Sharma & Cheatham, 1986). Counseling services are often performed by licensed personnel to provide therapy, psychotherapy, and psychological treatment to victims. These counseling services draw on theories and research on human behavior, mental health disorders, and treatment models to provide victims with a well-rounded treatment program. More recently, mental health providers have focused on the range, severity, and predictors of symptoms. They have also focused on the need for specialized treatment (Woody & Beldin, 2012).

Rape crisis personnel often apply these methods in a professional, but informal manner. These personnel must encompass cultural competency, listening skills, and a wide range of assessment skills and intervention strategies. Building a trusting relationship with the victim is vital for rape crisis personnel, given that they are tasked with providing support, expanding client options, offering guidance and protection, and promoting mobilization for the victim (Woody & Beldin, 2012).

Unfortunately, many barriers still exist today in regard to working with sexual assault victims. Victim advocates have addressed concerns related to limited resources, environmental factors, in some circumstances a lack of professionalism, and racism. Another major barrier is advocates often burnout quickly as a result of low wages combined with job responsibilities. The most noticeable and important barrier to working with sexual assault victims is secondary victimization by the criminal justice system and medical or mental health systems (Ullman & Townsend, 2007).

University Resources for Sexual Assault Victims

Because college and university campuses serve a population that is primarily in the 18–24 age range—the age range when individuals are most likely to be victimized—it is important that sexual assault victimization services be made available. However, universities did not always provide prevention and intervention measures to their students. It was not until the passage of the *Jeanne Clery Disclosure of Campus Security Policy and Campus Crime Statistics Act* (1998; hereinafter Clery Act) that universities were required to provide resources for victims of sexual assault on their campuses. The Clery Act, which was signed into law in the early 1990s by President H. W. Bush, required all institutions of higher education that received federal student aid under Title IV of the *Higher Education Act of 1965* to adhere to the reporting and program requirements articulated in the Clery Act. The Clery Act has several key requirements, including, but not limited to:

- Provide an annual security report, which discloses the type and amount of crime on and around campus.
- Timely warnings and information disclosure regarding ongoing threats to the health and safety of the campus community
- Requires that institutions outline and describe their policies regarding sexual assault prevention and procedures following the disclosure of an assault. The policies must include a clear statement regarding the rights for both the accused and accuser.

(Clery Act, 1998)

In conjunction with the Clery Act, the *Federal Campus Sexual Assault Victims' Bill of Rights* (hereinafter Victims' Bill of Rights), which was signed into law in 1992, guarantees the following:

- Survivors shall be notified of their options to notify law enforcement.
- Accuser and accused must have the same opportunity to have others present.
- Both parties shall be informed of the outcome of any disciplinary proceeding.
- Survivors shall be notified of counseling services.
- Survivors shall be notified of options for changing academic and living situations.

Above and beyond the Clery Act, universities must also comply with Title IX regulations. Title IX "promotes equal opportunity by providing that no person may be subjected to discrimination on the basis of sex under any educational program or activity receiving federal financial assistance" (U.S. Department of Education, 2015). Thus, students who are victims of sexual assault must be allowed to continue their education unhindered as outlined by Title IX. Furthermore, universities must provide Title IX coordinators that ensure schools are responding to and reporting complaints in compliance with the law (Lhamon, 2014). Both Title IX and the Clery Act intersect under the law and together comprise the majority of rules and regulations that schools must comply with once a sexual assault has been reported (Intersection of Title IX and the Clery Act, n.d.).

However, despite all of these measures, the language of the Clery Act and Title IX is in some places vague, allowing for a great deal of variation on the part of the university. For example, the services that schools are required to provide are not outlined in the Clery Act; therefore, each university provides services at its own discretion and typically on a case-by-case basis (Lhamon, 2014). Given the vague nature of the Clery Act and Title IX, the Department of Education has issued several documents clarifying laws and regulations, as well as recommendations for education and prevention programs. For example, the U.S. Department of Education, Office for Civil Rights issued a "Dear Colleague" Letter (Ali, 2011) that lists several specific measures, beyond those specified in the Victims' Bill of Rights, that universities may provide for victims of sexual assault. These include:

- Providing an effective escort to ensure that the complainant can move safely between classes and activities;
- Providing comprehensive, holistic victim services including medical, counseling and academic support services, such as tutoring;
- Arranging for the complainant to have extra time to complete or re-take a class or withdraw from a class without an academic or financial penalty; and
- Reviewing any disciplinary actions taken against the complainant to see if there is a causal connection between the sexual violence and the misconduct that may have resulted in the complainant being disciplined.

(Lhamon, 2014, p. 35; Ali, 2011, pp. 16–17)

Moreover, the U.S. Department of Education has also recommended wider measures in order to help prevent sexual assault on campuses, such as developing and disseminating material on sexual violence to students and offering bystander intervention training and programs (Lhamon, 2014).

College students have additional issues to consider after experiencing sexual assault. Therefore, universities may also offer interim housing, counseling, and legal services to students whose cases are currently going through investigation and hearing procedures at the university. However, universities are not required to offer these services to alleged victims and may do so on a case-by-case basis (Lhamon, 2014, pp. 32–33).

In addition to the above-outlined services, many college campuses provide more services than the minimum federal mandate. For instance, the University of Wisconsin at Madison has a Crisis Support and Counseling service for victims. This resource makes students aware of the services at their disposal. Some of these services include the Rape Crisis Center for the county, Sexual Assault Nurse Examiner Program, and the National Sexual Assault/RAINN Hotline (University of Wisconsin-Madison, n.d.). Bowling Green State University provides on-campus victims' advocates through the SAAFE Center that are available 24 hours per day, 7 days per week. These advocates are trained to be emotionally supportive and provide information and referrals when needed for medical or legal services (Bowling Green State University, n.d.).

Beyond federal law and programs provided through universities there are also national victim assistance academies (NVAA) whose goal it is to help develop, promote, educate, and train professionals on best practices when dealing with victims of sexual assault. For example, the Office for Victims of Crime Training and Technical Assistance Center and the National Organization for Victim Assistance offer NVAA trainings throughout the year to interested parties. These programs are also offered by many universities.

Helping Male Sexual Assault Victims

While sexual assaults against men are rarely reported to the police, community surveys show that these crimes are not as rare as official data would suggest. Estimates of the rate of sexual assault victimization among men range from 3–16 percent (for a review of the literature on sexual assault against men, see Davies, 2002). Most of these assaults are perpetrated by women, usually within a dating context. While these cases usually involve psychological coercion, physical force is used in about a quarter of cases. Research suggests that sexual assault victimization is somewhat more common among gay or bisexual men than among heterosexual men (e.g., Krahe et al., 2000). Because these assaults also commonly occur within a dating context, gay and bisexual men are more often sexually assaulted by other men than by women. While most offenders are dating partners, sexual violence against men can also be a form of anti-gay hate crime.

Resources for sexual assault victims should consider the unique needs of male victims in order to provide the best assistance. The first step in providing effective services to male victims is to increase awareness among service providers about male sexual assault victims. Centers of service such as rape crisis centers should attempt to expand their services to provide care to male victims as well. Undoubtedly, further research must be conducted to better understand the experiences of men who experience victimization. In addition, because reporting to police and medical services is lower among men (see Davies, 2002), we should attempt to reduce stigma associated with sexual victimization so that men who have been victimized feel comfortable seeking help.

Based on the existing literature on male victims, we have several recommendations for providing medical and psychological assistance to men who have become victims of sexual assault. First, male sexual assault victims who seek medical services are more likely than female victims to have serious physical injuries (Frazier, 1993). Medical providers should be aware of the increased injuries among male victims. In addition, SANE should be trained on collecting forensic evidence during an examination of a male patient.

The psychological consequences of sexual assault among male victims can include questioning of one's identity (see Davies, 2002). The experience may cause male victims to feel less masculine, as men are generally considered more sexually dominant in our society while women are believed to be sexually passive. Sexual assault of heterosexual men that is perpetrated by other men can also lead victims to question their sexual orientation. Gay or bisexual men sometimes experience internalized homophobia after an attack because they may attribute the victimization to their sexual identity; this can, in turn, negatively affect self-worth. In order to effectively provide treatment to male sexual assault victims, counselors should keep in mind the implications of victimization for feelings of masculinity, uncertainty regarding sexual orientation, and self-worth. In addition, therapists should consider the possibility that the crime may be a hate crime, and adjust the therapeutic approach accordingly.

Summary

Sexual victimization is a serious social concern affecting millions of people per year. As has been discussed in this chapter, there are serious medical, psychological, and economic consequences of sexual assault. Therefore, services have been made available to victims through local, state, and federal governments. Still, many requirements must be met in order for victims to be eligible for assistance, leaving many victims without aid. The process that victims must go through in order to receive compensation can be complicated, causing further difficulty during an emotional time in their lives. Lawmakers and service providers should consider revising the requirements and processes in order to better serve a larger number of victims.

In addition to the resources commonly available to sexual assault victims, federal law has mandated that universities provide certain responses after a sexual assault is reported. These laws are often unclear, creating confusion about how to deal with sexual assault and creating variation across universities—and even across cases—in the kind of resources that are available. In addition, college students often have unique needs regarding housing, scheduling, and academic assistance following a sexual assault. Universities are not required to address many of the problems faced by victims of sexual assault on campus and usually do so on a case-by-case basis. We suggest that the university responses be more standardized nationwide, allowing college students to receive appropriate assistance regardless of where they are enrolled.

Finally, because the stereotypical victim of sexual assault is female, most of the conversation around helping victims has focused on women. However, the number of men affected by sexual assault per year is not negligible. Males are less likely to report sexual assault, making it difficult to connect them with resources that are available to address their needs. In addition, males are affected differently by sexual assault than their female counterparts, which means that their needs after an assault are different. Increased awareness about male victims of sexual assault will both improve resources available to male victims and encourage medical and criminal reporting among males—allowing them to access these services.

Discussion Questions

1. What role does the local, state, and federal government play in offering services to victims of sexual assault?
2. What are the steps taken by Sexual Assault Nurse Examiners during the medical examination process?
3. What is the role of rape crisis centers in helping victims of sexual assault?
4. What are the different services offered to victims of sexual assault? Do you believe there should be other services offered beyond those discussed here? If so, what?
5. Do you think the police and/or prosecutor should be responsible for connecting victims with resources? Why or why not?
6. What are universities required to provide to victims of sexual assault? Are universities currently providing adequate services to victims? Why, or why not?
7. What are the unique issues associated with helping male victims of sexual assault? How should programs change in order to better help men who have been sexually assaulted?

References

Ali, R. (2011). Dear colleague letter. U.S. Department of Education: Office for Civil Rights, Office of the Assistant Secretary. Retrieved from https://www.whitehouse.gov/sites/ default/files/dear_colleague_sexual_violence.pdf.

Bimber, T. (2014). The medical/legal aspects of sexual assault nurse examiner (SANE) programs in emergency departments. *Journal of Legal Nurse Consulting*, 25, 32–35.

Bowling Green State University Department of Recreation and Wellness. (n.d.). Resources for assistance. Retrieved from http://www.bgsu.edu/recwell/wellness-connection/sexual-assault-awareness/resources-for-assistance.html.

Campbell, R. (2008). The psychological impact of rape victims' experiences with the legal, medical, and mental health systems. *American Psychologist*, 63, 702–717.

Campbell, R., Townsend, S. M., Long, S. M., Kinnison, K. E., Pulley, E. M., Adames, B. S., & Wasco, S. M. (2006). Responding to sexual assault victims' medical and emotional needs: A national study of the services provided by SANE programs. *Research in Nursing & Health*, 29, 384–398.

Cole, J., & Logan, T. K. (2008). Negotiating the challenges of multidisciplinary responses to sexual assault victims: Sexual assault nurse examiner and victim advocacy programs. *Research in Nursing & Health*, 31, 76–85.

Daigle, L. (2012). *Victimology: A text/reader*. Thousand Oaks, CA: Sage.

Davies, M. (2002). Male sexual assault victims: A selective review of the literature and implications for support services. *Aggression and Violent Behavior*, 7, 203–214.

Decker, S. E., & Naugle, A. E. (2009). Immediate intervention for sexual assault: A review with recommendations and implications for practitioners. *Journal of Aggression, Maltreatment & Trauma*, 18, 419–441.

Elvey, K., & Clutter, J. (2014). Costs of crime: Issues in measurement. In Jay Albanese (Ed.), *Encyclopedia of Criminology and Criminal Justice*. New York: Wiley-Blackwell, pp.1–5.

Federal Bureau of Investigation. (2015). Retrieved February 12, 2016 from http://www.fbi.gov.

Federal Campus Sexual Assault Victims' Bill of Rights. (1992). Public Law: 102–325, Section 486(c).
Fisher, B., Cullen, F., & Turner, M. (2000). *The sexual victimization of college women*. Washington, DC: National Institute of Justice and Bureau of Justice Statistics.
Fisher, B., Daigle, L., Cullen, F., & Turner, M. (2003). *Reporting sexual victimization to the police and others: Results from a national-level study of college women*. Thousand Oaks, CA: Sage.
Frazier, P. A. (1993). A comparative study of male and female rape victims seen at a hospital-based rape crisis program. *Journal of Interpersonal Violence*, 8, 64–76.
Hassija, C., & Gray, M. J. (2011). The effectiveness and feasibility of videoconferencing technology to provide evidence-based treatment to rural domestic violence and sexual assault populations. *Telemed J E Health*, 17, 309–315.
Intersection of Title IX and the Clery Act. (n.d.). Retrieved from https://notalone.gov/assets/ ferpa-clery-chart.pdf.
Jeanne Clery Disclosure of Campus Security Policy and Campus Crime Statistics Act. (1998). 20 U.S.C. § 1092 [f].
Joyful Heart Foundation. (2016, May). Retrieved from www.joyfulheartfoundation.org.
Kehner, G. (2004). *Date rape drugs*. New York, NY: Chelsea House Publishers.
Krahe, B., Schutsche, S., Fritsche, I., & Waizenhofer, E. (2000). The prevalence of sexual aggression and victimisation in homosexual men. *Journal of Sex Research*, 37, 142–150.
Lhamon, C. E. (2014). Questions and answers on title IX and sexual violence. U.S. Department of Education: Office for Civil Rights, Office of the Assistant Secretary. Retrieved from http://www2.ed.gov/about/offices/list/ocr/docs/qa-201404-title-ix.pdf
Miller, T. R., Cohen, M. A., & Wiersema, B. (1996). *Victim costs and consequences: A new look*. Washington, DC: United States National Institute of Justice.
Office for Victims of Crime. (n.d.). Crime Victims' Fund. Retrieved from http://www.ovc.gov/ about/victimsfund.html.
Sharma, A., & Cheatham, H. E. (1986). A women's center support group for sexual assault victims. *Journal of Counseling and Development*, 64, 525–527.
Solimine, M. E. & Elvey, K. (2015). Federalism, federal courts, and victims' rights: Reviewing the Victims' Rights Amendment. *Catholic University Law Review*, 64(4), 909–948.
Tjaden, P., & Thoennes, N. (1998). *Prevalence, incidence, and consequences of violence against women: Findings from the National Violence Against Women Survey*. Washington, DC: National Institute of Justice and Centers for Disease Control and Prevention.
Ullman, S. E., & Townsend, S. M. (2007). Barriers to working with sexual assault survivors. *Violence Against Women*, 13, 412–443.
University of Wisconsin-Madison University Health Services. (n.d.). Help following a sexual assault. Retrieved from http://uhs.wisc.edu/emergencies/sexual-assault/.
U.S. Department of Education: Office for Civil Rights. Title IX and sex discrimination. (April, 2015). Retrieved from http://www2.ed.gov/about/offices/list/ocr/docs/tix_dis.html.
U.S. Department of Justice. A national protocol for sexual assault medical forensic examinations adult/adolescents second edition. (2013, April). Retrieved from https://www.ncjrs.gov/pdffiles1/ovw/241903.pdf.
Woody, J. D., & Beldin, K. L. (2012). The mental health focus in rape crisis services: Tensions and recommendations. *Violence and Victims*, 27, 95–108.

18

VICTIM WITNESSES IN INVESTIGATIVE INTERVIEWS AND COURT PROCESSES

Jacqueline M. Wheatcroft

Keywords

investigative interview; victim; witness; court; cross-examination

Objectives

After studying this chapter, the reader should understand:

- The context of the investigative interview and in-court examination in the production of evidence for the victim witness.
- The leading issues affecting witnesses in investigative interviews and in the courtroom.
- Why these issues are important in criminal justice.
- New directions.

Introduction

Witnesses are pivotal to any criminal justice system (Wheatcroft, 2016a). In 2015 in England and Wales (and Northern Ireland; NI) the Ministry of Justice published the Code of Practice for Victims of Crime, which was presented to Parliament pursuant to section 33 of the Domestic Violence, Crime and Victims Act, 2004. The document details the key entitlements for victims of crime, who is required to provide the services, and who may receive them. The entitlements apply to police investigation through to trial and in complaints, and represent a more comprehensive consideration of victims of crime than has previously been observed. There is a growing appetite for procedural change in criminal justice systems where the evidence base supports such an amendment be made and this chapter will outline some developments which have taken place in the UK jurisdiction, where the applications of new insights have been applied, and where potential modifications are being considered. It will discuss the current position of victim witnesses (as vulnerable witnesses) in the UK in, a) investigative interviews, and b) in procedures and examination in the courtroom.

Context of Investigative Interviews

Victims and witnesses are a fundamental component of the criminal justice system in that they provide the information, intelligence and evidence to investigators that enables offenders to be brought to justice (ACPO, 2005). There are, however, differences between the terms victims and witnesses, which are differentiated in *Black's Law Dictionary* (2004). A victim is defined as one who is harmed by a crime, tort or other wrong, whereas the witness is defined as one, who sees, knows or vouches for something. Also, one who gives testimony under oath or affirmation, in person, by oral or written deposition or by affidavit. A witness must be legally competent. In our consideration of the victim witness in this context it is important to recognize that despite the differences all victims are potential witnesses.

In the maximization of the accuracy of information interviews represent a key strategy employed by investigators in the overall process of investigation. In 1982, Wagstaff informed the police how they might best help witnesses to remember accurate and useful information in an investigation. Despite the many years devoted to field research, evidence suggests that witnesses remain vulnerable to the various ways they are questioned about events (Fisher, 1995; Wheatcroft, 2016c) and across contexts (Wheatcroft & Woods, 2010). In the United Kingdom (UK) in 2011 it was announced that the National Policing Improvement Agency would be wound down and its functions transferred to other organizations; the Home Office, the Serious Organized Crime Agency and the newly established College of Policing (Pinel, 2012). It is against this backdrop that police officers receive training in how to conduct PEACE model interviews. PEACE represents the interview stages of Planning and Preparation, Engage and Explain, Account, Closure and Evaluation; elements that map directly onto procedures used across international contexts and investigative domains (Wheatcroft, Wagstaff & Russell, 2013).

Within this recognized framework [and levels 1–4 of Professionalising Investigative Practice (PIP; see College of Policing [2016] for details)] the methods of interviews have been scrutinized. What follows is a summary of some of the findings of the literature and what research informs of their usefulness.

One significant development in the context of investigative interviews is the enhanced cognitive method (ECI; Fisher, Brennan & McCauley, 2002; Geiselman, Fisher, MacKinnon, & Holland, 1986), which has over the years been compared with other memory enhancement methods (Wheatcroft *et al.*, 2013). The main elements are "report everything" (RE), "context reinstatement" (CR), "change perspective" (CP), "change order" (CO), and "build rapport" (BR). Evidence suggests that, if used appropriately, the procedure does not necessarily disrupt confidence-accuracy relationships (Dornburg & McDaniel 2006; Wright & Holliday, 2007). However, more recently, the investigative interviewing literature has looked broadly toward the development of a toolbox approach (Wheatcroft *et al.*, 2013) incorporating potentially useful aspects, such as the Sketch Reinstatement of Context procedure (Dando, Wilcock, Milne & Henry, 2009) and Self-Administered Interview (SAI; Gabbert, Hope & Fisher, 2009). While the toolbox approach offers benefits, one study has suggested that CR alone yields as much information as the complete ECI (Milne, 1997). This, amongst other work, demonstrates the superior usefulness of CR (Hammond, Wagstaff & Cole, 2006; Milne & Bull, 2002). CP and CO, however, are rarely used (Clifford & George, 1996; Wheatcroft *et al.*, 2013). Moreover, in practice, because of time and complexity issues police investigators are known to not adhere to the procedures (Dando, Wilcock & Milne, 2009; Wheatcroft *et al.*, 2013).

Whilst the ECI may have, at one time, been recommended, limitations are clearly evident. For example, young children's free reports can be restricted and leave the interviewer little information upon which to base follow-up questions (Davies *et al.*, 1995). Transcripts illustrate that children are still questioned repeatedly, assertively and with suggestion such that they may be misled (Taylor, 2004) as compared with adults, particularly at the latter end of the judicial process (Wheatcroft, 2016c). The importance of child evidence comes to the fore when jurists may hold misconceptions about witnesses' credibility or where stereotypical beliefs of the witness exist (Quas, Thompson & Clarke-Stewart, 2005). Despite the fact that young children are capable of accurate autobiographical recall (Fivush & Shukat, 1995), memory improves from 3 years to the age of 12 (Aldridge, 1999), the strength of children's memories is good if asked neutral, direct/simple questions (Gordon, Baker-Ward & Ornstein, 2001), and lasting memories for salient events can be evident from a very young age (Howe, 2000), difficulties for children remain. Yet, herein lays a contradiction. On the one hand, children are classified as vulnerable, yet research suggests their memories are fairly robust in certain circumstances. It is recognized that the process hinders those who are vulnerable in giving their best. For example, witness testimony can be influenced by question type, both in police interviews and in court (Wheatcroft, Wagstaff & Kebbell, 2004; Wheatcroft, Caruso & Krumrey-Quinn, 2015) and it is therefore likely that any effects will be enhanced when those with specific difficulties give evidence. To illustrate, while persons with learning difficulties (LDs) generally provide less information they appear to give relevant details. Still, on a cautionary note, there is a wide range of intellectual disability that falls under the general LD term, varying in nature and severity; thus, it is not entirely useful to categorize individuals with a LD, nor indeed examine the literature in broad terms (see Advocates Training Council, 2011). Even young children then can report accurate free recall information if interviewed in an age appropriate manner, and if that interview includes appropriate questioning (Wheatcroft *et al.*, 2015).

In 2011, the UK released a revised version of Achieving Best Evidence in Criminal Proceedings: which provides guidance on interviewing victims and witnesses, and guidance on using special measures (ABE 2011, originally drafted in 2002 as *Guidance for Vulnerable or Intimidated Witnesses, Including Children*). Of course, adult female rape complainants are, too, considered vulnerable within this framework; though the rhetoric for female rape complainants continues to be myth-laden with consequent echoes of revictimization (Wheatcroft *et al.*, 2009; Jordan, 2004; Kelly, 2010). One key element of the interaction between victim and/or vulnerable witnesses and investigator or judicial agent is that of trust and belief, and it is these elements that are particularly salient for victim witnesses. As the literature is large and diverse the chapter here will draw upon sexual assault victims as an example to illustrate the importance of communication and rapport.

In 2014, Wheatcroft and Walklate discussed the concept of belief and trust in the context of false allegations in sexual crime. The extent of false allegations made by children has been suggested to be *circa* 1 percent (Jones & McGraw, 1987), and Kelly (2010) similarly notes that false allegations are no higher for rape where adults are concerned than for other crimes (see also Gilmore & Pittman, 1993). The same is the case for children. Yet in both child sexual abuse and adult cases of rape/sexual assault the practitioner role in the investigation of crime is not only core (ACPO, 2005), it is crucial in the contribution made to the value of the information provided by complainants, witnesses, and victims of crime (Wheatcroft & Walklate, 2014).

In approaching interactions with children, research indicates advantages of rapport (Wheatcroft & Walklate, 2014). For example, Collins and Eaton (2013) have recognized the necessity of rapport in highlighting that interpersonal styles show improvements in children's communication during interviews. This is a position supported by psychological evidence (Warren, *et al.*, 1996; Patterson, 2011). It is therefore important to recognize that the interaction between investigator and victim witnesses can strengthen or weaken an investigation and thereby impact on whether a case is prosecuted or not. For example, police investigators have tended to dominate interviews of rape complainants (Kebbell & Westera, 2011), which has been shown to be a factor relevant to the potential to retract a statement (Hopkins, Walklate & Wheatcroft, 2015). Other factors include the interview atmosphere, which can facilitate or hinder trust (Saywitz & Camparo, 1998) and authoritative style, which can be equally intimidating, affecting reliability by increasing compliance (Leichtman & Ceci, 1995). In a study on the impact of interviews on rape survivor's reduction of hierarchy accomplished through mutual dialogue resulted in greater levels of comfort and disclosure (Campbell *et al.* 2010). A technique of rapport (i.e., commencement or maintenance of a trusting relationship perhaps through discussion of neutral topics, process, and/or interpersonal approach to the victim) can be an especially effective tool to encourage truthful disclosure (Wheatcroft & Walklate, 2014). In addition, most individuals have limited knowledge of the legal system, which can contribute to heightened anxiety during investigative interviews. On this basis, Wheatcroft and Walklate (2014) proposed *interactional belief* as the method of initial interaction in interviews and communications with victim witnesses. The authors state that "in order to move this process from one that is rooted in disbelief to one rooted in belief it is important to appreciate the truth generating process as a holistic one in which there are competing perspectives and interests" (p. 7). For instance, for the rape complainant there exist three potential interfaced perspectives that are relevant to understanding how "what happened" might be made sense of: the experiential, the practice, and the legal. What this means is that in the case of police officers, they may have a tendency to seek an explanation for the allegation and how it might be invalidated, rather than take the allegation to be the basis of what did happen. What is important here is to recognize that the interview context is complex and the interactions that take place are multi-layered and multifaceted and convey messages to the victim. Clearly, without some measure of trust and belief the process of police interview can be burdensome and add to the stresses and strains already experienced—and being experienced by the victim. A number of agencies who work with victims are aware of the importance of belief in the reports of victims of crime (e.g., Crime Survivors; Victim Support).

In addition, evidence shows that high levels of anxiety and stress hinder cognitive function, divert attention, and reduces motivation; all vital for accurate memory retrieval (ABE, 2011). The phenomenon of flashbulb memories highlights the impact that emotion has on memory (Brown & Kulik, 1977), in which people report they can remember shocking emotional events vividly, with almost detailed perceptual clarity. Although laboratory studies have found anxiety can enhance memory, for both central and peripheral details (Ginet & Verkampt, 2007), a large body of the literature tends to confirm that it has damaging effects. Waring, Payne, Schacter and Kensinger (2010) found anxiety results in an automatic mood-congruent attentional bias towards threatening information, probably serving as an evolutionary response mechanism for survival (Öhman & Mineka, 2001). The consequence is a trade-off in memory in which memory enhancement for negative arousing stimuli is at the expense of neutral peripheral information (Kensinger, Garoff-Eaton & Schacter, 2006). Valentine and Mesout (2009) argue laboratory studies undermine the detrimental effects of anxiety on memory performance because of the difficulty in replicating the experience of real eyewitness anxiety. Results of their naturalistic study showed that 75 percent of participants who were below the median state anxiety score correctly identified the culprit. However, substantial impairments were found with those who scored above the median, with only 17 percent correctly identifying the culprit, as well as reporting significantly fewer correct descriptors overall. The varying results can be explained by Deffenbacher's (1994) catastrophe model of anxiety on memory performance, and the experimental differences in level of anxiety inducement. Deffenbacher (1994) termed lower anxiety conditions as having an arousal-mode of attention control. This refers to physiological responses, including slightly increased heart rate, blood pressure and skin conductance, allowing for alertness and responsiveness to the environment, orienting attention to the most informative aspects of the scene. Conversely, high anxiety conditions are termed as having an activation mode of attention control. Deffenbacher (1994) expands on the notion of the "worry" component associated with anxiety, in that it results in a preoccupation of internal sensations and interfering negative thoughts about task performance (Clarke & Wells, 1995). The processing efficiency theory states that the attention to worry results in reduced cognitive resources available to allocate to the task at hand (Eysenck & Calvo, 1992). This response, along with a conscious perception of increased physiological activation, once the optimal point is passed, leads to a catastrophic drop in performance.

Research also shows even the mere presence of another individual is arousing enough to potentially impair memory performance (Wagstaff *et al.*, 2008). Kebbell, Hatton and Johnson (2004) also explain how the task that interviewers employ further affects performance. They propose cued recall can place increased demands on social-cognitive processing compared with free recall for anxious individuals. Performance may be impaired because rather than having mental capacity to choose whatever they find easiest to recall from memory, as in free recall, witnesses may feel the demands of the task change to satisfying the interviewer in cued recall; increasing arousal levels of stress and uncertainty. Therefore, although anxious individuals may compensate by allocating further resources to the task, there is only limited capacity available (Macleod & Matthews, 2004), which can result in anxious individuals potentially exhibiting poorer cued recall performance. Interestingly, research shows anxious arousal and negative effect largely consume right hemisphere resources (Davidson, 1992). This could explain why Ready, Bothwell and Brigham (1997) found, when anxiety was induced, that CR was an ineffective technique for producing accurate factual memory in response to cued recall questions. Perhaps the experimental conditions (i.e., inducing high anxious arousal right hemisphere processing) did not allow for beneficial executive left hemisphere processing. On balance, the research suggests some mixed findings in respect of CR and cued recall on memory performance in certain circumstances.

As noted earlier, because the ECI is a complex procedure, which requires substantial training to learn and a long time to conduct. Many trained officers can end up avoiding the use of recommended procedures (Dando, Wilcock, & Milne, 2009) or favour some components as more useful than others irrespective of what the literature tells us about their effectiveness (Wheatcroft, Wagstaff, & Russell, 2013). In light of these limitations, and as part of the toolbox approach, the Liverpool Interview Protocol (LIP) has been developed (Wagstaff & Wheatcroft, 2012) by re-examining useful components (i.e., relaxation, context reinstatement [with report everything], and eye-closure, with a view to presenting them in a brief, easily understood format that is easy to learn and apply (Wheatcroft & Wagstaff, 2014). The LIP is thus a memory facilitation tool that is currently used across a range of investigatory departments (e.g., police investigators, governments and in critical contexts worldwide). As a result, LIP has been positively received by investigators and researchers in terms of its ease of use and documented ability to enhance memory whilst reducing error rates (Wheatcroft & Wagstaff, 2014).

The success of such techniques lie in the cognitive effects of the processes applied; context reinstatement increases the likelihood of other memory details being cued, focused meditation calmly instructs witnesses to focus on breathing rhythms, which reduces distraction and optimizes frontal and temporal processing (Wagstaff, Brunas-Wagstaff, Cole, & Wheatcroft, 2004; Wagstaff *et al.*, 2008), whilst the option to close ones eyes, if one feels comfortable to do so, reduces visual interference and enhances visualization (see Wagstaff, 1982; Wagstaff, *et al.*, 2004; and more recently, Perfect, *et al.*, 2008; Vredeveldt, Hitch, & Baddeley, 2011). The cognitive effects seem clear. Neuropsychological research explains that the process of relaxing the witness in particular reduces cognitive load and demands anxiety may place on executive and prefrontal lobe areas (Wagstaff, *et al.*, 2008), freeing systems for attentional tasks.

Advances have been made in methods of obtaining best information using investigative interviews. As the evidence can be mixed as to what is the most effective procedure, the toolbox approach holds most promise in this domain. LIP seems intuitively helpful for use with victim witnesses as they are likely to experience anxiety as a result of observing, being a victim of crime, and/or being asked to recall events via a standard interview procedure. It is also recognized that witnessing a crime can be psychologically and physically traumatic (Shepherd, Mortimer, Turner & Watson, 1999), that police interviews are unpleasant experiences involving probing tasks (Malone, Hoffman, & Bocchino, 2007) and testifying in court can be retraumatizing (Wheatcroft, Wagstaff & Moran, 2009).

Given that witnesses, in particular victim witnesses, continue to remain vulnerable in court, this chapter will turn its attention to the leading issues and steps taken in consideration of those issues that affect victim witnesses in court.

Victim Witnesses and Court Processes

The Leading Issues Affecting Victim Witnesses

One key aspect of justice is the right of the defendant to confront the witness (Dennis, 2010), usually through means of a confrontation (i.e., challenge). The role of challenge is considered a central and defining feature of adversarial criminal trials (Lusty, 2002) and fundamental to the concept of fairness. In fact, Lord Bingham described "a long established principle of the common law that the defendant in a criminal trial should be confronted by his accusers" (Davis, 2008, p. 5). Further, the case of *Saidi v France* (1994) illustrates that the European Court of Human Rights has sometimes referred to a "lack of confrontation" as ground for a trial to have been unfair (Dennis, 2010).

The right to a public trial and the principle of orality, as opposed to private depositions, assist in ensuring and improving the accuracy of testimony. In discussing the heart of the Anglo-American system Friedman (2004) notes that transparency ensures "the witness's testimony is not the product of torture or milder forms of coercion and intimidation" (p. 15) and that confidence in the administration of criminal justice is maintained. Lord Hewart CJ notably commented "that justice should not only be done, but should manifestly be seen to be done" (*R v Sussex Justices*, 1924). In the modern day, however, that very transparency can impact on other parts of the judicial process and some argue, for example, that problems associated with the rise of social media have gone too far and thereby provided potential for conflict. To illustrate, concerns have been raised in the England and Wales (and NI) jurisdiction around juror access to the Internet during trials to assess material (e.g., a defendant's past history). Lord Chief Justice, Lord Judge was reported to have noted that "the jury system may not survive if it is undermined by social networking sites" (BBC News, 2010). Furthermore, according to preliminary research led by Thomas (2013), almost a quarter of jurors (23 percent) are unclear about the rules surrounding Internet use during a trial; thus, conditions for juror contempt were growing. Tensions can be seen to be rising between the principles of fairness and transparency and the ability of the modern system to maintain these aspects of justice. Legitimacy of verdicts could also be called into question as the quality of a verdict is such that the state is entitled to call for its acceptance and respect, as an authoritative adjudication (Dennis, 2010).

Never before has the justice system been under so much scrutiny and pressure to consider the impact of procedures on those who are victims and, by definition, vulnerable (Wheatcroft *et al.*, 2009). Where the cross-examination of witnesses is concerned this is of note and some concern. The term confrontation conjures up images and meanings that surround terms such as, hostility, war, battle, fight, and so on. Dennis (2010) notes "puzzling features" (p. 256) of this fundamental right, as whilst "there is acceptance on the right there is less consensus about its scope" (p. 256). The claim to fair treatment is not unique to the defendant, either; it applies to all—defendants, victims and witnesses alike. However, the foundation of challenge remains but, subject to numerous limitations and exceptions, is a "shrinking right" (Dennis, 2010). The concept of the right and its long and unquestioned application together with the appetite for procedural change has informed the range of special measures (i.e., processes and procedures to assist participants to give of their best evidence in court) available to vulnerable and intimidated witnesses, which now sit in stark opposition to that right (Dennis, 2010).

As a backdrop, in 1998 the Home Office introduced the "Speaking up for Justice Initiative" (summarized in Burton, Evans, & Sanders, 2006). The initiative attempted to make the criminal justice system more victim-centered with emphasis on facilitating the gaining and giving of evidence through safeguarding witnesses at all stages of proceedings (e.g., Achieving Best Evidence and use of Special Measures). It discussed more effective evidence collection through ABE interview procedures and video recorded evidence in chief, which would be played in court. There is protection for witnesses at court such as, live TV links which means the witness could provide evidence from a room separate to the courtroom, provision of screens or curtains which could be placed around the witness box to prevent the witness confronting the defendant, and clearing the gallery. There is also provision of social support through specially trained interviewers, pretrial and trial support; and the moderation of adversarial conventions (court dress, use of intermediaries and video cross-examination). Such special measures were introduced under the Youth Justice and Criminal Evidence Act (YJCEA, 1999), forming part of measures used to assist vulnerable and intimidated witnesses. Importantly, the report and researchers have recognized that being a witness in proceedings can be a stressful affair (Ewin, 2016).

In order to trigger a measure or for the individual concerned to be able to access the support it is first necessary to determine whether that individual is classified as vulnerable. In England and Wales (and NI) vulnerable witnesses are those who are under 18 years of age at the time of the hearing of the application for special measures; those with mental disorder; significant impairment of intelligence and social functioning; a physical disability or a physical disorder. Further, if the quality of evidence is likely to be reduced because of fear of intimidation or distress in relation to giving evidence, then the vulnerable and victim witness will be eligible for special measures to assist them in giving the best evidence possible.

Importantly, at what point vulnerability would be assessed and by whom has been raised by the Scottish Evidence and Procedure Review: Next Steps (2016) report. Whilst the age or the nature of offense is often clear, the report notes the capacity of police officers, as first responders or in interview, to reliably identify vulnerability may be problematic. Neither the police themselves are experts nor is the process of assessment a straightforward one. Thus, identification of vulnerability will be a more difficult task where the needs of the witness may not be immediately apparent or requires some professional expertise in recognizing those needs and how best to provide for them (for example, with a witness who has a mild learning disability or one who is on the autistic spectrum, respectively). Importantly, implications exist for those individuals to be enabled to participate in interviews and in the subsequent court proceedings where any vulnerability is missed. One key issue here is in the consideration of how the police can access appropriate information.

In 2016, in the England and Wales (and NI) jurisdiction, special measures have grown to include a major significant change; the attention given to communication through the use of aids and intermediaries (Plotnikoff & Woolfson, 2014). Registered intermediaries are available to vulnerable and/or intimidated witnesses to help victims, witnesses and defendants who find it difficult to understand questions and give answers. The intermediary assists the individual to communicate answers during a police interview or when giving evidence at court. Communication aids may also be used to assist in that process (e.g., symbol books and alphabet aids). The concept of the registered intermediary is a new, active role, which has been reported to have a number of merits. In a series of interviews performed with judges, advocates and intermediaries in England and Wales the findings have shown there is little to fear from the intermediary system (Henderson, 2015b). Nevertheless, whilst improvement and support for witnesses is ongoing, victim witnesses continue to suffer impediments in process when coming to court to give evidence.

As alluded to earlier, one significant part of giving evidence in court is the challenge process of cross-examination. Lawyers have controlled interactions with witnesses in the courtroom since the 1700s (Wheatcroft, 2016b), but, of course, the mechanism of cross-examination is designed to break down dubious testimony and if it does then it is to be applauded. However, as early as 1907, research has demonstrated witness reliability drops when witnesses answer questions applied during cross-examination (Munsterberg, 1907; see also Wheatcroft *et al.*, 2015 for a detailed review of the current position). Research has also shown that lay witnesses (Wheatcroft, Wagstaff, & Kebbell, 2004), and experts (Gudjonsson, 1996; 2008) are vulnerable to cross-examination procedures. It is reasonable, therefore, to say that those classified as vulnerable are especially susceptible to the process of cross-examination. For example, research interviews conducted with rape victim witnesses found one theme emergent from the data was court re-victimization (Wheatcroft, Wagstaff, & Moran, 2009). Sally (anonymized) reflected on her courtroom experience and gave a brief account. She notes:

> I had to sit in front of the man who raped me and tell loads of strangers what he did to me. They exhibited my underwear, talked about my body, and called me a liar. They showed intimate pictures of my body, you know injuries and stuff, and I felt violated all over again. The defence just seemed to want to break me. They raped me again. I felt so ashamed. I was on trial, not him. I went there as a liar to try and prove what I was saying was the truth. I had to account for every aspect of my life.
>
> *(Sally, 247–253)*

Further, a girl aged nine who faced aggressive cross-examination says she has never recovered (The Independent, 2015). She describes her experience of being cross-examined over video link below:

> They took me to a tiny room with a TV screen. It wasn't like a front room it was very cold and blank. There was a lady I hadn't met before and one I'd met once. I didn't really know who they were. When I started to get upset, I was allowed to sit outside the room for five minutes and sit in a corridor on some chairs. The women comforted me, but not really.

Frances Andrade, a talented violinist, took her own life after being called a liar and a fantasist in court by the barrister (The Guardian, 2013). It was reported the overdose was a way of the witness coping with the trial. Such cases illustrate the in-court process as very stressful for witnesses and highlight the need for the development and maintenance of *effective* support to assist witnesses in the giving of their best evidence (Wheatcroft, 2016b).

Despite the amendments to procedure and rule it remains that witnesses still find the cross-examination process arduous and stressful. In 2005, it was recognized by the English courts that witnesses in court face a difficult task and that such parties to court could be familiarized to the process. The method, endorsed in *R v Momodou* (2005), aimed to demystify the process and through practical guidance assist witnesses to give their best evidence in legal proceedings with the result that they are less likely to be confused, misled or unduly influenced by the process of cross-examination (Wheatcroft & Ellison, 2012). The advice is essentially confined to directing witnesses to speak slowly, to ask for questions to be repeated if they are not understood and not to guess if they do not know the answer to a question. Witness services do offer varying pre-trial support and advice to lay witnesses but this does not extend to preparation for the process of testifying. As Riding (1999) notes, witness services take the view that volunteers should not make any attempt to talk to witnesses even in general terms about how they might conduct themselves in the witness box or what they might expect from cross-examination—for fear of allegations of witness coaching (Ellison & Wheatcroft, 2010).

At that time, little research had empirically considered the effects of preparing witnesses for cross-examination. In order to explore the utility of witness familiarization Wheatcroft and Woods (2010) conducted an initial study focused upon short familiarization statements and leading question style effects upon witness accuracy and confidence. The findings revealed that directive leading questioning styles, as used in cross-examination (e.g., "He didn't touch you did he?") had clear detrimental effects upon witness accuracy. Nevertheless, if question examples were provided prior to questioning this would help witnesses apply higher levels of confidence to their accurate responses. A further, more ecologically valid, study was carried out to assess familiarization to complex and simple cross-examination questioning strategies. One group of community participants received preparation whilst another group received no preparation. Initial analysis showed that those who received familiarization gave more accurate responses, made fewer errors, and were enabled to seek clarifications from the cross examining lawyer. Further analysis revealed that familiarization to certain question types found increased accuracy and reduced errors to multiple-parts, and reduced errors made in response to negatives, and some complex vocabulary. The process did not, however, assist in increasing the amount of information given by the witness, confidence to interrupt the lawyer, or ask the lawyer to repeat the question (Wheatcroft & Ellison, 2012).

The findings, nevertheless, lend initial support to those who assert that witness preparation is essential for the improvement of witness evidence in court. However, as familiarization is in its infancy and complex reflection on the permissibility of directive leading questions during cross-examination in court could well be warranted (Wheatcroft & Woods, 2010). Moreover, Scotland's most senior judge, Lord Justice Clerk, Lord Carloway, has warned judges must step in to protect complaining witnesses from "protracted or vexatious questioning" from counsel who insult alleged rape victims during cross-examination (Herald Scotland, 2015). The comment in part was made as an advocate had begun cross-examination with the opening line; "You are a wicked, deceitful, malicious, vindictive, liar?" (see *R v Begg*, 2015). For examples of convoluted questions used in actual criminal trials see Fielding (2006) who illustrates how a defendant with acknowledged learning difficulties was asked "you can't be certain that you think it was not possible that you filled in the first side of the form?" (p. 178).

It could be argued that tinkering with the process to assist witnesses in abilities to cope with cross-examination techniques would be alleviated more readily by dealing with the root of the difficulty: the question types and forms themselves. A recently published paper outlines in detail the empirical research that strongly suggests justice systems should develop best practices for elicitation of accurate evidence and not leave it to witnesses to combat any adversarial system's shortcomings. Given this is particularly acute for vulnerable and victim witnesses the authors put that the question form shown to create the primary mischief in meeting trial goals is that which is directive; its prohibition in cross-examination is proposed (Wheatcroft, Caruso, & Krumrey-Quinn, 2015). The work also draws attention to the idea that there is no right to put a case to a witness in child cases. In the beginning of this section of the chapter the right to challenge was noted as the central and defining feature of adversarial criminal trials (Lusty, 2002). The concept is now tested as a number of cases in England and Wales have supported the idea that children, in particular, require additional support (see *R v Dixon*, 2013 and *R v Lubemba*, 2014). Indeed, the debate has gone further. Empirical research on robust adult witnesses suggests consideration may need to be given to extending reforms of cross-examination . . . beyond vulnerable witnesses (Henderson, 2015a), and that leading questions may not even be a suitable and proper means of challenging robust adult witness accounts (Wheatcroft, Wagstaff & Kebbell, 2004; Cooper *et al.*, 2015).

Importance of Issues and New Directives

In respect of investigative interviews, Kebbell *et al.*, (1996) asked how often eyewitnesses provide the major leads in investigations, 36 percent stated "always/almost always" and 51 percent responded "usually." It is critical for justice that when victim witnesses are interviewed that the most accurate information is enabled. Getting the information right as soon after the event as possible is a leading and significant issue that underpins criminal justice. Methods of investigation, and in particular those of interviews, are paramount in the production of the most accurate reports available. Rationalization through austerity cuts is likely to play a significant role in the development of future pressures on investigative authorities worldwide and will necessarily impact on the quality of procedure and effective support. The tool-belt approach and shorter but effective protocols, such as the LIP, are likely to be in greater demand over the coming years.

It has been recognized that support is important for some when being interviewed by investigators. The use of intermediaries in police interviews and in court has showed promise. However, it is essential to ensure that any joint investigative interview is consistently of a high standard, and follows a methodology that produces the best possible outcome in terms both of the witness' experience and the quality of the evidence elicited (Scottish Evidence & Procedure Review: Next Steps, 2016). There are issues to address in respect of join investigative interviews. For example, the appropriateness of investigators in the assessment of vulnerability (age, mental capacity and so on) and the welfare of victim witnesses (including emotional health). Similar issues align themselves to the court process. In addition, the prevention of further offenses taking place, such as intimidation, is also important. The balance between the right to challenge and the right of the victim witness to speak honestly and openly without fear of the investigative process or re-victimization by the court is a critical one as this may impact on the outcome of the trial should their testimony be less accurate as a result.

There has also been considerable interest shown, for example, in the Norwegian Barnehus model in terms of the environment in which vulnerable witnesses provide evidence, in particular, child witnesses. The concept of a purpose-built multi-agency centre that provides a "wraparound" service seems highly attractive. In the words of one English commentator there is a strong argument for:

> the establishment of Young Witness Advocacy Centres, where children and young people between 4 and 18 years and their families would have a wraparound support pathway from identification of the crime to the post-trial period. Specialist key workers would operate from a single child-centred hub, alongside multi-agency professionals including the CPS, police, social care, intermediaries and therapists, coordinating individual support plans. The Centres would be equipped with the technology for pre-trial cross-examination, and trial testimony through remote live link. The notable success of the one-stop Norwegian Children's Houses in reducing secondary traumatisation for children makes a powerful case for its translation into the English CJS. Other aspects of the Norwegian system, such as forensic medical examination suites and on-going family therapy, should be considered.
>
> *(Hoyano, 2015, p. 9)*

Specialist centres with multi-disciplinary teams seem a more efficient way of engagement with and management of some of these issues.

Summary Conclusion

The Honourable Justice Green recently said that "how the courts treat those who are exposed and weak is a barometer of our moral worth as a society" (p. xiii; 2016). As such, serious reconsideration of how justice systems treat vulnerable (and victim) witnesses in the criminal justice process has been one which has been talked about in the England and Wales (and NI) jurisdiction since around 1988. New approaches to obtaining information from interviews and special measures for those classed vulnerable have been introduced and found to be helpful. However, more needs to be done both in the investigative interview approach and to processes in court to assist the aim of investigation and trial. Some of these are to rethink the ways in which we obtain information, the environment, and how a society positions itself when speaking with and questioning victims and witnesses in the legal process in order that they may provide the most accurate information, intelligence and evidence possible. Only then will adversarial justice systems around the world enable the aim of the investigation and trial procedure to be met; the search for truth is fulfilled.

Discussion Activities

1. Discuss issues relevant to victim witnesses in police interviews.
2. Consider the impact of court process on victim witnesses.
3. Evaluate victim witnesses with reference to interview and cross-examination questioning.
4. Assess the relevance and usefulness of special measures for vulnerable witnesses.

References

Achieving Best Evidence in Criminal Proceedings (2011). *Guidance on interviewing victims and witnesses, and guidance on using special measures*. London: Home Office.

Advocates Training Council (2011). *Raising the bar: The handling of vulnerable witnesses, victims and defendants in court*. ATC: London.

Aldridge, N. C. (1999). Enhancing children's memory through cognitive interviewing: An assessment technique for social work practice. *Child & Adolescent Social Work Journal, 16*(2), 101–126.

Association of Chief Police Officers (2005). *Management of volume crime*. Bramshill: National Centre for Policing Excellence.

BBC News (2010). *Facebook juror sentenced to eight months for contempt*. See http://www.bbc.co.uk/news/uk-13792080

Black's Law Dictionary (2004, 8th Edn), B.A. Garner (Ed.), St. Paul, MN: West Group.

Brown, R., & Kulik, J. (1977). Flashbulb memories. *Cognition, 5*, 73–99.

Burton, M., Evans, R., & Sanders, A. (2006). *An evaluation of the use of special measures for vulnerable and intimidated witnesses*. London: Home Office Research Findings, 270.

Campbell, R., Adams, A. E., Wasco, S. M., Ahrens, C. E., & Sefl, T. (2010). What has it been like for you to talk with me today? The impact of participating in interview research on rape survivors. *Violence Against Women, 16*(1), 60–83. http://dx.doi.org/10.1177/1077801209353576

Clark, D., & Wells, A. (1995). A cognitive model of social phobia. In R. Heimberg, M. Liebowitz, D. Hope, & F. Schneier. (Eds.), *Social phobia, diagnosis, assessment and treatment*, (pp. 69–93). New York: Guilford Press.

Clifford, B. R., & George, R. (1996). A field evaluation of training in three methods of witness/victim investigative interviewing. *Psychology, Crime and Law, 2*, 231–248.

College of Policing (2016). Accessed 25 June 2016, see www.college.police.uk/What-wedo/Learning/Curriculum/Investigation/Pages/default.aspx.

Collins, K., & Eaton, A. (2013). Communicative scaffolding in the rapport phase of child investigative interviews. *Paper presented to the 6th Annual Conference of the International Investigative Interviewing Research Group, Maastricht University, The Netherlands, 3–5 July 2013.*

Cooper, P., Backen, P., & Marchant, R. (2015). Getting to grips with ground rules hearings: A checklist for judges, advocates and intermediaries to promote the fair treatment of vulnerable people in court. *Criminal Law Review, 6*, 417–432.

Crime Survivors. See http://www.crimesurvivors.org/page/ accessed 21 May 2016.

Dando, C., Wilcock, R., & Milne, R. (2009). The cognitive interview: novice police officers' witness/victim interviewing practices. *Psychology, Crime & Law, 15*(8), 679–696. http://dx.doi.org/10.1080/10683160802203963

Dando, C., Wilcock, R., Milne, R., & Henry, L. (2009). A modified cognitive interview procedure for frontline police investigators. *Applied Cognitive Psychology, 23*, 698–716. http://dx.doi.org/10.1002/acp.1501

Davidson, R. (1992). Anterior cerebral asymmetry and the nature of emotion. *Brain & Cognition, 10*, 125–151. PMID: 1389117.

Davies, G. M., Wilson, C., Mitchell, R., & Milsom, J. (1995). *Videotaping children's evidence: An evaluation*. London: HMSO.

Davis, I. (2008). UKHL 36; [2008] 3 All E.R. 461.

Deffenbacher, K. (1994). Effects of arousal on everyday memory. *Human Performance*, 7, 141–161.

Dennis, I. (2010). The right to confront witnesses: Meanings, myths and human rights. *Criminal Law Review*, *4*, 255–274.

Domestic Violence, Crime and Victims Act 2004 (c 28; see UK Legislation at http://www.legislation.gov.uk/ukpga/2004/28).

Dornburg, C. C., & McDaniel, M. A. (2006). The cognitive interview enhances long-term free recall of older adults. *Psychology and Aging*, *21*(1), 196–200. http://dx.doi.org/10.1037/0882-7974.21.1.196

Ellison, L. E., & Wheatcroft, J. M. (2010). Could you ask me that in a different way please? Exploring the impact of courtroom questioning and witness familiarisation on adult witness accuracy. *Criminal Law Review*, *11*, 823–839.

Ewin, R. (2016). The vulnerable and intimidated witness: A study of the special measure practitioner. *Journal of Applied Psychology & Social Science*, *2*(1), 12–40.

Eysenck, M., & Calvo, M. (1992). Anxiety and performance: The processing efficiency theory. *Cognition & Emotion*, *6*, 409–434. http://dx.doi.org/10.1080/02699939208409696

Fielding, N. (2006). *Courting violence*. Oxford: Oxford University Press.

Fisher, R. P. (1995). Interviewing victims and witnesses of crime. *Psychology, Public Policy and Law*, *1*, 732–764. http://dx.doi.org/10.1037/1076-8971.1.4.732

Fisher, R. P., Brennan, K. H., & McCauley, M. R. (2002). The cognitive interview method to enhance witness recall. In M. L. Eisen, J. A. Quas, & G. S. Goodman (Eds.), *Memory and suggestibility in the forensic interview* (pp. 265–285). New Jersey: Lawrence Erlbaum.

Fivush, R., & Shukat, J. (1995). Content consistency and coherence of early autobiographical recall. In M. S. Zaragosa and G. C. N. Hall (Eds.), *Memory and testimony in the child witness* (pp. 5–23). Thousand Oaks: Sage.

Friedman, R. (2004). Face to face: Rediscovering the right to confront prosecution witnesses. *International Journal of Evidence & Proof*, *8*, 1–30. http://dx.doi.org/10.1350/ijep.8.1.1.36509

Gabbert, F., Hope, L., & Fisher, R. P. (2009). Protecting eyewitness evidence: Examining the efficacy of a self-administered interview tool. *Law & Human Behavior*, *33*, 298–307. http://dx.doi.org/10.1007/s10979-008-9146-8

Geiselman, R. E., Fisher, R. P., MacKinnon, D. P., & Holland, H. L. (1986). Enhancement of eyewitness memory with the cognitive interview. *American Journal of Psychology*, *99*, 385–401.

Gilmore, K. & Pittman, L. (1993). To Report or Not To Report: A Study of Victim/Survivors of Sexual Assault and Their Experience of Making an Initial Report to the Police. Melbourne: Centre Against Sexual Assault (CASA House) and Royal Women's Hospital.

Ginet, M., & Verkampt, F. (2007). The cognitive interview: Is its benefit affected by the level of witness emotion? *Memory*, *15*, 450–464. http://dx.doi.org/10.1080/09658210601092670

Gordon, B. N., Baker-Ward, L., & Ornstein, P. A. (2001). Children's testimony: A review of research on memory for past experiences. *Clinical, Child and Family Psychology Review*, *4*(2), 157–181. PMID: 11771794.

Green, The Hon. Justice (2016). Introduction. In P. Cooper & L. Hunting (Eds.), *Addressing vulnerability in justice systems*. London: Wildy, Simmonds & Hill Publishing.

The Guardian (2013). Frances Andrade killed herself after being accused of lying, says husband. See https://www.theguardian.com/uk/2013/feb/10/frances-andrade-killed-herself-lying, accessed 21st May 2016.

Gudjonsson, G. H. (1996). Psychological evidence in court: Results from the 1995 survey. *The Psychologist*, *52*, 213–217.

Gudjonsson, G. H. (2008). Psychologists as expert witnesses: The 2007 BPS Survey. *Forensic Update*, *92*, 23–29.

Hammond, L., Wagstaff, G. F., & Cole, J. (2006). Facilitating eyewitness memory in adults and children with context reinstatement and focused meditation. *Journal of Investigative Psychology and Offender Profiling*, *3*, 117–130. http://dx.doi.org/10.1002/jip.47

Henderson, E. (2015a). Bigger fish to fry: Should the reform of cross-examination be expanded beyond vulnerable witnesses? *The International Journal of Evidence & Proof*, *19*(2), *83–99*. http://dx.doi.org/10.1177/1365712714568072

Henderson, E. (2015b). A very valuable tool: judges, advocates and intermediaries discuss the intermediary system in England and Wales. *International Journal of Evidence & Proof*, *19*(3), 154–171. http://dx.doi.org/10.1177/1365712715580535

Herald Scotland (2015). *Judge calls stop to prolonged questioning of rape victims in court after woman called 'malicious, vindictive liar*. See http://www.heraldscotland.com/news/13582843 accessed 15 May 2016.

Hopkins, A., Walklate, S. & Wheatcroft, J. M. (2015). Indicative influences of retraction in domestic violence. *Paper presented to the European Conference on Domestic Violence, Queens University, Belfast, Ireland, 6–9 September 2015.*

Howe, M. L. (2000). *The fate of early memories: Developmental science and the retention of traumatic memories.* Washington DC: American Psychological Society

Hoyano, L. (2015). Reforming the adversarial trial for vulnerable witnesses and defendants. *Criminal Law Review, 2*, 107–129.

The Independent (2015). See http://www.independent.co.uk/news/uk/crime/court-is-just-astraumatic-girl-who-faced-aggressive-crossexamination-aged-nine-says-she-has-neverrecovered-8631662.html, accessed 29th May 2016.

Jones, D., & McGraw, E. M. (1987). Reliable and fictitious accounts of sexual abuse to children. *Journal of Interpersonal Violence*, 7(4), 532–542.

Jordan, J. (2004). *The word of a woman: Police, rape and belief.* London: Palgrave. http://dx.doi.org/10.1057/9780230511057

Kebbell, M., Hatton, C., & Johnson, S. (2004). Witnesses and intellectual disabilities in court: What questions are asked and what influence do they have? *Legal and Criminological Psychology, 9*, 23–25.

Kebbell, M. R., Milne, R., & Wagstaff, G. F. (1996). Enhancing the practicality of the cognitive interview in forensic situations. *Psycoloquy*, 7(16); witness memory. Available from: http://www.cogsci.ecs.soton.ac.uk/cgi/psyc/newpsy?article=7.16&submit=View+Article

Kebbell, M. R., & Westera, N. J. (2011). Promoting pre-recorded complainant evidence in rape trials: Psychological and practice perspectives. *Criminal Law Journal, 35*, 376–385.

Kelly, L. (2010). The (in)credible words of women: False allegations in European rape research. *Violence Against Women, 16*(12), 1345–1355. http://dx.doi.org/10.1177/1077801210387748

Kensinger, E. A., Garoff-Eaton, R. J., & Schacter, D. L. (2006). Memory for specific visual details can be enhanced by negative arousing content. *Journal of Memory & Language, 54*, 99–112. http://dx.doi.org/10.1016 /j.jml.2005.05.005

Leichtman, M. D., & Ceci, S. J. (1995). The effects of stereotypes and suggestion on preschoolers' reports. *Developmental Psychology, 31*, 568–578. http://dx.doi.org/10.1037/0012-1649.31.4.568

Lusty, D. (2002). Anonymous accusers: An historical and comparative analysis of secret witnesses in criminal trials. *Sydney Law Review, 24*, 361–426.

MacLeod, C., & Matthews, A. (2004). Selective memory effects in anxiety disorders: An overview of research findings and their implications. In D. Reisberg & P. Hertel, (Eds.), *Memory & emotion* (pp. 155–185). New York: Oxford University Press.

Malone, D., Hoffman, P., & Bocchino, A. (2007). *The effective deposition.* Chicago: National Institute for Trial Advocacy.

Milne, R. (1997). *Application and analysis of the cognitive interview.* Doctoral Dissertation. University of Portsmouth

Milne, R., & Bull, R. (2002). Back to basics: A componential analysis of the original cognitive interview mnemonics with three age groups. *Applied Cognitive Psychology, 16*, 743–753. http://dx.doi.org/10.1002/acp.825

Ministry of Justice (2015). *Code of Practice for Victims of Crime.* Williams Lea Group: HMSO.

Munsterberg, H. (1907). *On the witness stand.* New York: Doubleday, Page & Company.

Öhman, A., & Mineka, S. (2001). Fear, phobias and preparedness: Toward an evolved module of fear and fear learning. *Psychological Review, 108*, 483–522. PMID: 11488376.

Patterson, D. (2011). The impact of detectives' questioning techniques on rape victims disclosure. *Violence Against Women, 17*(11), 1349–73. http://dx.doi.org/10.1177/1077801211434725

Perfect, T., Wagstaff, G., Moore, D., Andrews, B., Cleveland, V., Newcombe, S., Brisbane, K. A. & Brown, L. (2008). How can we help witnesses to remember more? It's an (eyes) open and shut case. *Law and Human Behaviour, 55*, 486–496. http://dx.doi.org/10.1007/s10979-007-9109-5

Pinel, J. (2012). NPIA moves towards closedown. *National Policing Improvement Agency*, accessed 10 February 2013.

Plotnikoff, J. & Woolfson, R. (2014). *Making the Most of working with an intermediary: toolkit.* Lexicon Ltd: Preston.

Quas, J. A., Thompson, W. C. & Clarke-Stewart, A. (2005). Do jurors "know" what isn't so about child witnesses? *Law & Human Behaviour, 29*(4), 425–456.

R v Begg [2015] HCJAC 69.

R v Dixon [2013] EWCA Crim 465.

R v Lubemba [2014] EWCA Crim 2064; (2015) 1 Cr. App. R. 12.

R v Momodou [2005] EWCA Crim 177; (2005) 1 W.L.R. 3442.

R v Sussex Justices, Ex parte McCarthy [1924] 1 KB 256, [1923] All ER Rep 233.

Ready, D., Bothwell, R., & Brigham, J. (1997). The effects of hypnosis, context reinstatement and anxiety on eyewitness memory. *International Journal of Clinical & Experimental Hypnosis, 45*, 55–67.

Riding, A. (1999). The Crown Court witness service: Little help in the witness box. *Howard* Journal, *38*(4), 411–420. http://dx.doi.org/10.1111/1468-2311.00144

Saidi v France [1994] 17 E.H.R.R. 251 ECtHR at [44].

Saywitz, K., & Camparo, L. (1998). Interviewing child witnesses: A developmental perspective. *Child Abuse & Neglect, 22*(8), 825–843. http://dx.doi.org/10.1016/S0145-2134(98)00054-4

Scottish Evidence & Procedure Review (2016). *Next steps*. Scottish Courts and Tribunals Services, 26 February.

Shepherd, E., Mortimer, A., Turner, V., & Watson, J. (1999). Spaced cognitive interviewing: Facilitating therapeutic and forensic narration of trauma memories. *Psychology, Crime & Law, 5*, 117–143.

Taylor, C. (2004). *Court licensed abuse, patriarchal lore and the legal response to intrafamilial sexual abuse of children.* New York: Peter Lang.

Thomas, C. (2013). See http://www.ucl.ac.uk/news/news-articles/0513/150513-jury-profect-internetuse-cheryl-thomas#sthash.Docu2eUx.dpuf

Valentine, T., & Mesout, J. (2009). Eyewitness identification under stress in the London Dungeon. *Applied Cognitive Psychology, 23*, 151–161. http://dx.doi.org/10.1002/acp.1463

Victim Support. See https://www.victimsupport.org.uk/ accessed 21 May 2016.

Vredeveldt, A., Hitch, G. J., & Baddeley, A. D. (2011). Eye closure helps memory by reducing cognitive load and enhancing visualisation. *Memory & Cognition, 39*(7), 1253–63. http://dx.doi.org/10.3758/s13421-011-0098-8

Wagstaff, G. F. (1982). Helping a witness remember: A project in forensic psychology. *Police Research Bulletin, 38*, 56–58.

Wagstaff, G. F., & Wheatcroft, J. M. (2012). *The Liverpool interview protocol: Manual*. Liverpool, UK: University of Liverpool.

Wagstaff, G., Brunas-Wagstaff, J., Cole, J., Knaptop, L., Winterbottom, J., Crean, V., & Wheatcroft, J. (2004). Facilitating memory with hypnosis, focused meditation, and eye closure. *The International Journal of Clinical and Experimental Hypnosis, 52*, 434–455. http://dx.doi.org/10.1080/00207140490889062

Wagstaff, G., Brunas-Wagstaff, J., Cole, J., & Wheatcroft, J. (2004). New directions in forensic hypnosis: facilitating memory with a focused meditation technique. *Contemporary Hypnosis, 21*(1), 14–27. http://dx.doi.org/10.1002/ch.284

Wagstaff, G., Wheatcroft, J., Cole, J., Brunas-Wagstaff, J., Blackmore, V., & Pilkington, A., (2008). Some cognitive and neuropsychological aspects of social inhibition and facilitation. *European Journal of Cognitive Psychology, 20*, 828–846. http://dx.doi.org/10.1080/09541440701469749

Waring, J., Payne, J., Schacter, D., & Kensinger, E. (2010). Impact of individual differences upon emotion-induced memory trade-offs. *Cognition and Emotion, 24*, 150–167. http://dx.doi.org/10.1080/02699930802618918

Warren, A. R., Woodall, C. E., Hunt, J. S., & Perry, N. W. (1996). It sounds good in theory, but . . . .: Do investigative interviewers follow guidelines based on memory research? *Child Maltreatment, 1*, 231–245. http://dx.doi.org/10.1177/1077559596001003006

Wheatcroft, J. M. (2016a). Judicial processes. Invited chapter, in G. Davies, & A. Beech (Eds.), *Forensic psychology: Crime, justice, law, interventions, 3rd Edn*. Chichester: John Wiley & Sons.

Wheatcroft, J. M. (2016b). Avoiding miscarriages of justice. Invited chapter, in P. Cooper & L. Hunting (Eds.), *Addressing vulnerability in justice systems*. London: Wildy, Simmonds & Hill Publishing.

Wheatcroft, J. M. (2016c). The realities of addressing vulnerabilities in the courts: Constraint or best practice. *Invited paper presented to the Faculty of Advocates International Conference on Vulnerable Witnesses, Parliament House, Edinburgh, Scotland, 17–18 June, 2016.*

Wheatcroft, J. M., Caruso, D., & Krumrey-Quinn, J. (2015). Rethinking leading: The directive, non-directive divide. *Criminal Law Review, 5*, 340–346.

Wheatcroft, J. M., & Ellison, L. E. (2012) Evidence in court: Witness preparation and crossexamination style effects on adult witness accuracy. *Behavioral Sciences & the Law, 30*, 821–840. http://dx.doi.org/10.1002/bsl.2031

Wheatcroft, J. M., & Wagstaff, G. F. (2014). An example of a solution-focused academic practitioner co-operation: How the iIIRG facilitated the development of the Liverpool Interview Protocol. *Investigative Interviewing: Research and Practice (II-RP), 6*(1), 42–50. http://www.iiirg.org/journal/volume-6-issue-1/

Wheatcroft, J. M., Wagstaff, G. F., & Kebbell, M. R. (2004). The influence of courtroom questioning style on actual and perceived eyewitness confidence and accuracy. *Legal & Criminological Psychology*, 9, 83–101. http://dx.doi.org/10.1348/135532504322776870
Wheatcroft, J. M., Wagstaff, G. F., & Moran, A. (2009). Re-victimising the victim? How rape victims experience the UK legal system. *Victims and Offenders* 4(3), 265–284. http://dx.doi.org/10.1080/15564880903048529
Wheatcroft, J. M., Wagstaff, G. F., & Russell, K. (2013). Specialist police interviewer perceptions of the enhanced cognitive interview: Usefulness, confidence and witness reliability. *Police Practice and Research: An International Journal, 15*(6), 505–518. http://dx.doi.org/10.1080/15614263.2013.819616
Wheatcroft, J. M., & Walklate, S. (2014). Thinking differently about "false allegations" in cases of rape: The search for truth. *International Journal of Criminology & Sociology, 3*, 239–248. http://dx.doi.org/10.6000/1929-4409.2014.03.20
Wheatcroft, J. M., & Woods, S. (2010). Effectiveness of witness preparation and crossexamination non-directive leading and directive leading question styles on witness accuracy and confidence. *International Journal of Evidence & Proof, 14*(3), 189–207. http://dx.doi.org/10.1350/ijep.2010.14.3.353
Wright, A. M., & Holliday, R. E. (2007). Enhancing the recall of young, young-old and old-old adults with cognitive interviews. *Applied Cognitive Psychology, 21*, 19–43. http://dx.doi.org/10.1002/acp.1260
Youth Justice and Criminal Evidence Act (1999).

PART IV

Victim Service Organizations

In this concluding section of the handbook, Part IV, various victimology and victim service organizations are discussed. Chapter 19, written by the prominent victimologist and friend John Dussich, discusses one of the most important organizations involving victimology and victim services, the World Society of Victimology (WSV). Professor Dussich also has served as the President of the WSV. In Chapter 20, editor Cliff Roberson discusses other prominent organizations devoted to victims' rights. The concluding chapter, Chapter 21, does not fit comfortably in any of the four sections of the handbook, but because of its importance it is set as the last chapter in the handbook. Too often, in dealing with victims we tend to forget that victims need help in dealing with the media. Chapter 20 on victims and the media provides guidance in this important process.

19

HISTORY OF THE WORLD SOCIETY OF VICTIMOLOGY

John P. J. Dussich

history. . . is not a burden on the memory but an illumination of the soul.

Lord Acton

Keywords

advocacy; convention; declaration; international; newsletter; proceedings; research; rights; society; symposia; victimology

Objectives

After studying this chapter, the reader should understand:

- What the World Society of Victimology is.
- How and why the World Society of Victimology was created.
- Who the main persons were that helped launch the WSV.
- How the WSV influenced victims' rights in the world.
- Which nations and organizations were the primary collaborators with the WSV.
- How the WSV influenced the development of the discipline of victimology.

Introduction

It is my honor to write this article about the history of such a significant organization as the World Society of Victimology (WSV). Not only am I very pleased to have been asked to chronicle this unique organization, but it also permits me to share an important part of my professional life with the WSV simply because I had the privilege of being present during all the International Symposia and many of the other related WSV events (especially the Executive Committee meetings and the Post-Graduate Courses). My intent with this article is to: explain how this Society came into being, identify the key persons that influenced it, provide insights into the WSV as a sub-culture, mention the major resources it offers, and describe how this Society affected public policy, victim rights and victim services around the world. It was Beniamin Mendelsohn, a Romanian defense attorney, who about six decades ago, in his early victimological writings, recommended the creation of "an international journal, victim clinics, university courses and an international society with periodic symposia"

(Dussich 2012, p. 15). Thus, by forming an international society the legacy of Mendelsohn's work was significantly acted upon by the WSV to help reduce human suffering and significantly improve victim justice the world over. The amount of information spanning almost four decades of the Society's existence is enormous. My challenge here is to also prioritize, summarize and, above all, balance objectivity and subjectivity within the limits of one article. Finally, I am aware that the value of my text will ultimately be in the eye of the reader: a broad audience of scholars, students, practitioners and the general public who would like to have a coherent overview of an organization that has been dynamic, has grown in response to the times and continues to spread its message of humanity by understanding and recommending changes for this part of the human experience.

Conceptual Precursors—1536 to 1947

The first use of the word "victim" in English was taken from the Latin word *victima* in 1497, which was applied to animals killed as religious sacrifices (Drapkin, 1980; Oxford Dictionary, 1983 as cited in Wemmers, 2009). The first time this word was applied to a human was in Latin in 1536 to characterize the sacrificial Jesus in the *magnum opus* by the French theologian John Calvin titled *Institutio Christianae Religionis* as representing the foundation of the Protestant faith used throughout Europe in the middle sixteenth century (Dussich, 2015). The first published record of the English word "victim" used to refer to a human person was in 1736 "as an honorary name for Jesus Christ, the Crucified, in a translation of the *New Testament*. Christ was called the *expiatory victim*: the person who through his victimhood redeemed mankind" (van Dijk, 2008, p. 17).

Through the ages using the word victim for humans who were injured, tortured or killed gradually became commonplace. The word "victimology" emerged from two roots: the first from the original Latin *victima* (a religious sacrifice), which evolved into the English word, "victim"; and, from the Greek *logos* (a science), which evolved into the English suffix "logy." Victimology means the study of victims. As such, victimology was first coined by Beniamin Mendelsohn when he was applying the rules of science to better understand victims and wrote about his work in his seminal lecture, "New Bio-Psycho-Social Horizons: Victimology" to the Romanian Psychiatric Society in 1947.

In the aftermath of two World Wars and the horrific holocaust the United Nations came into being on October 24, 1945 because of the persistent statesmanship of Franklin Delano Roosevelt who hoped to create an international process that would provide opportunities for nations to resolve their disagreements and thereby avoid future wars (Kaplan, 2010; Dussich, 2015; United Nations, n.d.).

Significant Organizational Forerunners—1947 to 1979

In 1955 in Geneva, Switzerland, the First UN Congress on the Prevention of Crime and the Treatment of Offenders was launched and became an important organization because its Fourth International Congress in Madrid, Spain of 1970 gave rise to the key discussions which recommended the launching of a victimology symposium which three years later took place in 1973 in Jerusalem hosted by Israel Drapkin (Marchiori, 2001). This event "provided scholars, practitioners, researchers and students with the first international forum to focus on victimology" (WSV, n.d.). As a sequel to this unique event a special workshop/seminar was organized by Emilio Viano in Bellagio, Italy, two years later called the International Study Institute on Victimology. This special two-week long gathering of about 50 of the top victimologists of that time were brought together from July 1–12, 1975 and given the opportunity to discuss at great length and depth most of the key concepts that had just been presented at the 1973 symposium in Israel. Some of the key persons who attended this institute, became friends and later became notable victimologists: Beniamin Mendelsohn, Israel

Drapkin, Stephen Schafer, Ezzat Fattah, Robert Towel, Nwokocha Npa, Murray Straus, Hazel Genn, Leonard Bickman, Jan Fiselier, Sandra Borges, David Friedman and others. Some of these would become involved in the World Society of Victimology: Koichi Miyazawa, Hidemichi Morosawa, John Dussich, Gerd Kirchhoff, Irvin Waller, Kurt Weis, and Stanley Johnston. This event took place in Bellagio, Italy, and was instrumental in creating consensus on many aspects of this newly launched discipline: definitions, future symposia, the direction of victims' rights, the relationship of victimology to criminology, the nature of victim services, possibilities for research, the need for legislation at the national and international levels, and ultimately and perhaps most important was the establishment of long lasting professional friendships. The product of that event was condensed into an anthology of articles by the participants and served as a valuable resource to the timely advancement of victimology at that unique point in time (Viano, 1976). This group of victimologists also supported the idea of having symposia every three years; and, in 1976, one of the Bellagio notables, Stephan Schafer, organized the Second Symposium on Victimology and, although he passed away just prior to its realization, his colleagues and students fulfilled his wish to host the symposium in Boston. Like the 1973 symposium this was also a successful event, which attracted many scholars and practitioners (especially in the USA), supported the idea of having an international organization and supported the idea of the triennial symposia. A German scholar Hans Joachim Schneider took the initiative in 1979, from 2–8 September, and hosted the Third Symposium on Victimology. This was held under the auspices of the United Nations and the Council of Europe with the cooperation of the International Society of Criminology and with financial support from the German government, the state of North Rhine-Wesfalia and a number of German business supporters. About 400 persons were in attendance coming from 37 countries (Schneider, 1982). Additionally, on 8 September 1979, with the support of most of the symposium participants, Schneider was able to launch the World Society of Victimology at the symposium's closing ceremony (Dussich, 2015). The Founding Executive Committee was made up of Hans Schneider as President, Koichi Miyazawa as Vice President, John P. J. Dussich as Secretary General, Sarah Ben David as Treasurer, and Irvin Waller, and Zvonimir Paul Šeparović as members at large. The first Executive Committee meeting was full of optimism and new ideas, one of which was to establish a Society journal. It was decided that within the three year cycle the terms of office for the Executive Committee members also would last for three years; however, the duration of membership on the EC was to be six years thereby enhancing its continuity. The WSV became a member-driven organization, led by an Executive Committee that met every year and hosted the triennial symposia. The proceedings of this symposium were edited by Hans Schneider and it established a precedent, which became key publications of each WSV symposia starting with the Fourth Symposium held in Japan in 1982 and continuing to the present (see Appendix IV for a listing of WSV symposia selected proceedings' publications).

Early Organizational Successes: Precocious Endeavors—1979 to 1985

The three key persons of the organization during its infancy were: the President—H. Schneider, the Secretary General—J. Dussich, and the newsletter editor—G. Kirchhoff, all living in Germany at that time and all within driving distance of each other, especially from 1980 to 1983. During those formative years, numerous meetings between these three victimologists greatly facilitated the coordination needed to establish the World Society of Victimology. Like all new organizations, the WSV had to transition from concept, to structure, to recognition, to operations. The circle logo with the letters WSV inside was created by John Dussich; Hildegard Schneider took on the onerous task of bookkeeping, Gerd Kirchhoff started the "WSV Newsletter" (which lasted for 12 years and he was later joined by co-editor Claudia Kirchhoff), brochures were printed and annual EC meetings were established. Armed with these basic resources the Society soon began to look and behave like a professional international organization. It was ready to carry the victimology banner and facilitate the growth of a new discipline in support of its ideals. The WSV was registered with the Court's Corporation Register in Mönchengladbach, Niederrhein, Germany, as a not-for profit organization (see Appendix II for the first page of the WSV's *Basic Statutes of Incorporation*). The WSV then became officially affiliated with the Social Council of the United Nations (ECOSOC) and with the Council of Europe. Membership was open to all persons (and national/regional societies/associations and corporations as collective memberships) who had "concern for victims, especially victim assistance practitioners, social scientists, social workers, physicians, lawyers, civil servants, volunteers, university professors and students" (see: www.worldsocietyofvictimology.org/welcome). Many of the national victimology societies used the WSV as a model in terms of its objectives, not for profit status and nonpolitical activities. The WSV often played a mentoring role with these national societies. Some of the early affiliated national victimology societies were from: Argentina, Australia, Bosnia, Brazil, Croatia, El Salvador, Greece, India, Ireland, Japan, Mexico, and Serbia. In addition to these societies, there were a handful of other affiliated organizations as well, mostly concerned with victim assistance. Today, there are 27 affiliated organizations posted on the WSV website.

The original purposes of the WSV were:

> to advance victimological research and practices in the entire world, to encourage interdisciplinary and comparative work and research in this field, and, to advance cooperation of international, national, regional and local agencies and work groups who are concerned with the problems of victims in the entire world.
>
> *(Dussich, 2001, p 1)*

The WSV was a Society of members who were given the opportunity to nominate and elect an Executive Committee of 12 persons who then selected 3 additional persons from developing countries that were not (or were poorly) represented by the 12 elected EC members. Standing committees were formed to address: membership, public relations and symposia, mostly made up of EC members. There was also the General Membership, the body of persons who became official members; and then there was the Membership Assembly, the gathering of members who came to the Symposia at a specific place and time to discuss issues of concern to the organization and to give direction and guidance to its Executive Committee. With an organization in place, decisions were made to promote this new discipline and to create ways to ultimately improve the wellbeing of victims the world over. Three years later, in 1982, the proceedings of the Third Symposium was published by Hans Schneider under the title: the *Victim in International Perspective* (see Appendix IV for the complete list of subsequent symposia and selected proceedings' publications).

The Fourth Symposium was held from August 29 to September 4, 1982, in Tokyo (for the first half of the week) and in Kyoto (for the second half of the week) with Koichi Miyazawa serving as a model host. The teamwork of the Japanese, the uniqueness of two venues, the food, the entertainment, the quality of the presentations and the organizational smoothness was something very special to experience. The Executive Committee was enlarged with H. Schneider as President, K. Miyazawa as Vice President, J. Dussich as Secretary General, S. Ben David as Treasurer, and the Members at Large were: Z. Šeparović, J. Freeman, L. Lamborn, R. Whitrod, I. Waller, with G. Kirchhoff as the newsletter editor. At this symposium for the first time the WSV presented two awards: "The Hans von Hentig Award" to Israel Drapkin; "The Certificate of Appreciation" to Beniamin Mendelsohn. The Executive Committee was now meeting once per year and, for the sake of stability, it re-elected Hans Schneider for another three-year term as President (see Appendix I for the list of Presidents and the years they served).

During the year 1983, in Mönchengladbach, Germany, Gerd Kirchhoff and his wife Claudia (early WSV Newsletter editors) were hosting two WSV victimologist friends at his home, Zvonimir

Paul Šeparović and Paul Friday. From this meeting came the idea to launch a postgraduate victimology course at the University of Zagreb's Inter University Centre in the city of Dubrovnik, Croatia, in coordination with the WSV in the following year 1984 (Šeparović, 2009). In the "1980s Dubrovnik was the world center of the victimology movement, the *World Society of Victimology (WSV)* held here its EC annual meetings in connection with the IUC courses" (Šeparović, 2009, p 11). An annual tradition was born that has continued to this day. The basic concept of the two-week WSV affiliated postgraduate course was also adopted by John Dussich in Asia mostly hosted by the Tokiwa International Victimology Institute with some slight modifications: the focus was on general victims and with the main objective of providing basic victimological understanding for students who mostly had not had prior victimology lectures and less on professors' making academic presentations. Two Asian postgraduate courses have also been held in Indonesia and one in India. In addition to the Asian-based courses, two similar courses were regularly held in Central American (mostly in El Salvador and Guatemala) and another for South America (with two in Colombia and one in Venezuela). In the last few years, these WSV affiliated Asian, Central American and South American courses have not been held. More recently, another WSV postgraduate course was begun in South Africa by Robert Peacock and has been held annually. In all of these courses there was a clear affiliation with the WSV and most of the lecturers were WSV members and local non WSV lecturers of the host country. Postgraduate courses have also been attached to each of the WSV International Symposia; however, at the recent symposia, the course length has been reduced to only one week due to the added burden to the symposia hosts and the lecturers who would have to arrive at the symposia venue many days prior and cover their own expenses. These entire postgraduate courses have operated on the non-profit principle so as to break-even, thus, allowing low fees to the students to just cover the administrative expenses. All the professors lecture as volunteers and cover their own expenses. The WSV exercises a loose mentorship relationship with these courses as they all carry the WSV banner in cooperation with a local host university.

Often, in the early years critical WSV decisions about the next President or the location of the next WSV symposium were made at the postgraduate courses held in Dubrovnik (Waller, 2009). The dream of a United Nations declaration for victims was also conceived there; mostly led by WSV EC members Irvin Waller and LeRoy Lamborn. These declaration discussions helped motivate Zvonimir Paul Šeparović to mold the content of the Fifth Symposium, which he would host in Zagreb, Croatia, the next year, in 1985. This included the scheduling of the symposium to precede the 7th UN Congress on Crime Prevention and Criminal Justice to take place at the Millefiori Hall, in Milan, Italy, only a few hours' drive from Zagreb. These preparations of the WSV community in collaboration with other sympathetic organizations eventually led to the adoption of the *UN Declaration of Basic Principles of Justice for Victims of Crime and Abuse of Power* at the UN Headquarters in New York on November 29, 1985 (Kirchhoff, 2009).

WSV Enters Its Adolescence—1985 to 1996

The jubilation that followed the adoption of the UN Declaration was immediate and far reaching. All forms of communication were used to let the members of the World Society of Victimology know of this great success on behalf of victims and mostly because of the team efforts of many WSV Executive Committee members and other non-WSV members who participated from other organizations including advocates at the United Nations UNODC (United Nations Office on Drugs and Crime). Although there were numerous members of the WSV involved in the key discussions, prior to and during the UN debates, at the center was always Irvin Waller and LeRoy Lamborn. They were the WSV's leaders in this unique process. They were seen as significantly responsible for having launched the WSV's credibility as the dominant world advocate organization for victims; thanks to them, the WSV took center stage in the international fora for victimology, victim assistance and victims' rights. This backdrop of world leadership not only filled its members (and a number of other non-WSV members and organizations as well) with great pride, it also suddenly created a serious sense of responsibility, of mission, of necessity to maintain this new-found status. The discussions became oriented around the theme, of "wanting to seize the moment" and finding ways to institutionalize the very ideals that had been voiced, especially by the early (pre-1973) passionate pioneers of victimology: Mendelsohn, Drapkin, Fattah, Schafer, Schneider, Miyazawa, Nagel and Ellenberger. The conversations began to focus on "getting the word out to all scholars," to all nations and to all people. The Executive Committee revised discussions started at the Third Symposium's first EC meeting about establishing a journal for the Society, even though Emilio Viano had already started his very respectable *Victimology an International Journal* in 1976 just three years earlier. The sentiment was, there was room for another voice, another perspective. In spite of having just been elected to the EC in 1982 and being somewhat of a newcomer, John Freeman stepped forward and volunteered his services to the WSV and this new mission. His zeal was obvious and he began to plan this new academic venture with great persistence (Kirchhoff, 2000). He was convinced he could enlist the assistance of other like-mined scholars and practitioners. After founding the *International Review of Victimology*, with APA Publishers from England in 1989, he became a co-editor with Leslie Sebba. However, a few years later, due to ill health, he retired as co-editor and was replaced by David Miers; and Joanna Shapland became the Associate Editor. In spite of its WSV origins, the journal eventually became editorially independent from the WSV, yet, it has maintained its association with the World Society of Victimology until the present.

Idealistic Aspirations and Barriers to Change—1996 to 2015

It would be a serious omission not to mention the many other important aspects of the WSV that have not yet been mentioned and that are important parts of its totality. These would include: the WSV membership, both individual and organizational, which maintain their links to the spirit and life of WSV activities; the *WSV Newsletter* which, in 1997, morphed into its current form called *The Victimologist* (first managing editor: Jo-Anne Wemmers, editors: Elmar Weitekamp and Paul Omaji) and continued to serve the membership with current events and commentary on the ever-changing face of victimology until the last issue May–July 2012; the triennial awards and honors, which reflect the WSV's esteem and respect for those who have made significant and lasting contributions to the field of victimology: the Hans von Hentig Award, the Beniamin Mendelsohn Young Scholar Award, Certificate of Appreciation and the Honorary Membership (see Appendix III for the recipients' list).

At the 10th International Symposium in the year 2000, in addition to a successful event, the newly elected President was Gerd F. Kirchhoff. While he was in office he brought to fruition the WSV Victimology Bibliography (WSVBib) with roughly 1800 victimological references. These references were made available to all WSV members. This database was maintained at the University of Mönchengladbach Library and its maintenance was paid for by the World Society of Victimology and directed by Professor Kirchhoff (2001a). Also a product of this symposium was the appointing of Irvin Waller to be the first official liaison person to the UN based on his successful experiences with the Declaration in 1985 (Kirchhoff, 2001b, p. 4); this work he did until 2008 when John Dussich was appointed the Chair of the newly formed WSV UN Liaison Committee (his tenure lasted until 2015, followed by Janice Joseph to the present time).

Also, in 2003, for the 11th Symposium held in Stellenbosch, South Africa, a student paper competition was initiated and thereafter this competition became part of each symposium. The student paper selected for special recognition of the first-place winner was "Balancing Approach: The use of apology in Japanese society" written by Yoshiko Takahashi a Japanese student studying at the University of North Carolina (Dussich, 2003, p. 6). This special student-focused competition continues to the present.

For a handful of nations the initial response to the *UN Declaration of Basic Principles of Justice for Victims of Crime and Abuse of Power* was generally positive; however, this was not the case for all; not even for most. Between 1986 and 1996 a series of implementation recommendations were made; yet, the results were still incomplete among both the developing world and the first world and even among the affluent countries (Groenhuijsen, 2009). In recognition that many nations were not adopting the UN Declaration's basic principles of justice on behalf of victims, the UN Commission on Crime and Prevention and Criminal Justice decided to take action at its 5th Session. So, in May 1996, the UN Commission adopted a formal resolution to publish a manual(s) that would explain and encourage nations to fully implement the UN Declaration. This intent produced two manuals: a *Handbook on Justice for Victims* aimed primarily at victim services; and, a short *Guide for Policymakers* to help nations with the development of policies, programs and support to facilitate implementing victim services across the globe. The expertise for the writing of these two books existed largely among the members of The World Society of Victimology, about 20 of its members who offered their services as volunteers, and, some experts who were not WSV members, principally from the United States and The Netherlands. The funding of these two manuals was provided by the UN Office for Victims of Crime, US Department of Justice (UNODC, 1999). In 1999, these two manuals were published and made available to all the nations of the world. The publications did prove to be of assistance to many countries and a variety of organizations, especially those that helped the WSV to promote the enactment of the UN Declaration; however, most nations did not avail themselves of these resources and avoided adoption of the significant changes called for in the Declaration. Subsequently, in an attempt to measure the extent of the UN Declaration's adoption in Europe, the International Victimology Institute Tilburg (INTERVICT, 2009) in the Netherlands, conducted a 22 country study. Even though Europe generally has higher victim rights standards than other parts of the world, the findings were disappointing. Thus, under the leadership of Marc Groenhuijsen, the then director of INTERVICT, a collaborative meeting was held at INTERVICT, with the World Society of Victimology, the Tokiwa International Victimology Institute (TIVI) from Japan and with INTERVICT serving as host. The objective was to find a remedy by creating a stronger UN instrument at the next higher level: a convention. This meeting took place in December 2005 in order to create a draft *Convention on Justice and Support for Victims of Crime and Abuse of Power* so as to move forward with the implementation of the *UN Declaration*'s fundamental recommendations (Groenhuijsen and Letschert, 2012). Over the course of the next four years, four more drafts were produced. In a further attempt to move forward and to find a way to realize the full adoption of the UN draft Convention at the United Nations, under the leadership of John Dussich TIVI hosted a special symposium in Mito, Japan, in February 2008, mostly made up of senior victimologists from the WSV (who were also members of INTERVICT and TIVI). The intent of this working symposium was to improve the 4th draft of the Convention and to develop new strategies for its adoption. The target of these strategies was to "enhance the chances of having the draft Convention adopted at the 12th Crime Congress of the UN to be held in Salvador, Brazil in Spring, 2010" (Dussich, 2009, p. i). Based on the conclusions of this "working symposium," a proceeding's book was published by TIVI and immediately distributed in mid-2009. Using the details of this "working symposium" a 5th draft Convention was completed by Sam Garkawe, Marc Groenhuijsen and John Dussich in early December 2009. The following year this new draft was brought to the mid-April 2010, Salvador, Brazil, UN's 12th Crime Congress where the WSV came prepared with its 13-member UN Liaison Committee and distributed the new draft UN Convention to most member nations, engaged many representatives from member nations, and held meetings with officials and staff of the UN Commission with other NGOs. These WSV activities were able to realize some positive results: greater awareness of the new draft UN Convention by the member nations, which permitted its distribution to all member nations in attendance at the Crime Congress in Salvador, and the inclusion of numerous UN Convention principles included in the final Crime Congress' statement called the "Salvador Declaration." The WSV's UN Liaison team was also successful in obtaining 21 signatures on a petition from member states, other NGOs and individuals present at the Salvador Crime Congress in support of the Resolution to adopt the Convention at the General Assembly as soon as possible. However, and unfortunately, the WSV was not successful in formally introducing the draft UN Convention for adoption in the upcoming UN Commission meeting in the following year. In spite of this long and intense process the ultimate WSV's objective to have the UN Convention brought to the General Assembly was not realized (O'Connell, 2012).

Over the course of the next five years the WSV's UN Liaison Committee decided to focus on five new strategies:

1. To lend the WSV's support for any and all UN proposals that involved victims, especially those dealing with human trafficking and femicide.
2. To promote the WSV Mission with more intensity.
3. To start much earlier in the UN five-year cycle by being active at the Four Regional Preparatory meetings in advance of the 2015 13th Crime Congress to be held in Doha, Qatar.
4. To find ways to integrate our objectives into the Crime Congress' theme: "Integrating crime prevention and criminal justice into the wider United Nations agenda to address social and economic challenges and to promote the rule of law at the national and international levels, and public participation" (https://www.moi.gov.qa/UNCCPCJDoha/English/Profile.html).
5. To use the draft UN Convention as a major reference document as often as was appropriate to assure the UN community that it is still the WSV's intent to one day realize its full adoption by the UN General Assembly.

The result of these strategies prior to and during the next Crime Congress in Doha, Qatar was an improvement over the prior Congress. The World Society of Victimology was able to better asserted itself, had greater visibility, was involved in more Congress events, established new alliances, secured more support from member nations and was more often deferred to on multiple victim matters during the 13th Crime Congress. The WSV has established itself in the international arena as the leading non-governmental organization advocating for victims. From the extensive work that WSV members started in 1985 with the UN Declaration, this activity has evolved into an established accredited process of advocacy and consulting. Specific members who, by virtue of their expertise and stature, have earned the privilege to become accredited by the WSV President to represent the Society at various events, especially those involved with the United Nations and the Council of Europe and in conjunction with other international organizations (WSV, n.d.).

Our Contemporary Victimological Dialectic: Stagnation or Stability—2015 to Present

From the time when victims were beginning to be studied in a scientific way, about eight decades have passed. A new discipline has been born, has grown and is maturing with each symposium, emerging new dedicated organizations have appeared addressing new types of victims, institutes have been founded and fostered needed research, laws have been created to protect victims' rights, special services have been strengthened with new techniques and higher standards aimed at helping more victims to recover sooner, international legal instruments have been crafted that espouse basic principles to be applied within and across all countries; however, and unfortunately, a large percentage of nations are still ignoring most of these noble principles with impunity. The World Society of Victimology, since 1985, has been promoting the implementation of these rights with information, conferences, regional courses, and dispatching experts using a wide variety of methods which have been tried, mostly in vain. In spite of these shortcomings, since the launching of the *UN Declaration of Basic Principles of Justice for Victims of Crime and Abuse of Power* in 1985, the WSV continues to provide international leadership with expertise, inspiration, and offerings of assistance to encourage all member nations to adopt the basic principles of the 1985 UN Declaration and its current successor, the draft Convention.

Summary

Among the significant challenges currently facing the World Society of Victimology is bringing about the universal institutionalization of victim participation and legal standing in criminal justice and social welfare systems across the globe.

Although victim participation is implied in the texts of the *UN Declaration of Basic Principles of Justice for Victims of Crime and Abuse of Power*, and the proposed WSV draft *UN Convention on Justice and Support for Victims of Crime and Abuse of Power*, today the actual phrase, "victim participation" is not present in either of these instruments and measures to enforce it are also not mentioned. On a positive note, currently there are new discussions in a number of countries in support of the legal standing of victims to enhance their participation throughout government proceedings that are related to their victimization (Dussich & Hestermann, 2016). The World Society of Victimology continues to be at the forefront of these discussions.

As the twenty-first century unfolds. the World Society of Victimology will likely continue to support the three major international instruments focused on victims' rights: *UN Declaration for Basic Principles of Justice for Victims of Crime and Abuse of Power*, its upgraded version, the WSV *draft UN Convention on Justice and Support for Victims of Crime and Abuse of Power*, and the much broader *Basic Principles and Guidelines on the Right to a Remedy and Reparation for Victims of Gross Violations of International Human Rights Law and Serious Violations of International Humanitarian Law*. This support will likely be manifested in offering its resources to assist in the measurement of implementation, educate member nations that are not yet in compliance, use these instruments as key references in their future writings, seminars, symposia, courses, and publications; and, continue to seek strategies to bring the draft UN Convention to the UN General Assembly for adoption. In addition, the World Society of Victimology will likely be on the vanguard of victimology to engage newer relevant topics such as: preventing human trafficking and femicide victimization and serving its victims, including compelling language directly focused on the legal standing of victims especially their active participation in the criminal justice and welfare systems, adding consideration for victims of identity theft, cybercrimes, terrorism, hate crimes, traffic accidents, wars, disasters and civil disorders. Finally, the WSV will likely demonstrate its concern for newer conditions of traditional victims, such as those who have disabilities, are immigrants, refugees, have PTSD, and are members of the LGBTQ community.

With the above expanded challenges will come the need for a stronger Society of dedicated members and leaders. Unfortunately, over the past 15 years the membership level has dropped significantly: in 2001 there were 460 members (Dussich, 2001); however, as of April 2016 the WSV membership was at 326 (WSV website directory). The countries with the most members in 2001 were: the USA—73, Canada—28, Japan—22, Mexico—18, and Australia—18, Germany—14, and the Netherlands—14; in 2016 it was: the USA—10, Germany—9, the Netherlands—9, India with 8, Canada—7, and Australia—7. With a handful of countries with 5 or fewer members, the bulk of the 196 countries in the world have no WSV members. Never in the history of the world has there been more information, manpower, services and funds available for victims. The resources to make significant changes exist; however, they must be managed by competent leadership at all government and organizational levels. The masthead on the WSV homepage reads:

> *The purpose of the WSV is to advance victimological research and practices around the world; to encourage interdisciplinary and comparative work and research in this field, and to advance cooperation between international, national, regional and local agencies and other groups who are concerned with the problems of victims.*

An organization that wants to have this type of significant influence in the world, must have an adequate number of members to volunteer their time, influence and energy to take on these enormous challenges. As the only international victim-focused non-profit organization in existence, the WSV must alter its course if it wants to continue to contribute its expertise, manpower and time to adequately address the plight of victim and in so doing improve the human condition worldwide.

> *A small body of determined spirits fired by an unquenchable faith in their mission can alter the course of history.*
>
> *Mahatma Gandhi*

References

Drapkin, I. (1980) El derecho de las victimas, *Anuario de Derecho Penal y Ciencias Penales*. Madrid.

Dussich, J. P. J. (ed.) (2001) WSV *Membership Directory*, Mito: World Society of Victimology Publishing, p. 1.

Dussich, J. P. J. (2003) Winners of the WSV Student Paper Competition 2003, *The Victimologist*, Vol. 7, No. 3, 6.

Dussich, J. P. J. (2009) Preface, in J. P. J. Dussich and K. G. Mundy (eds.) *Raising the Global Standards for Victims: The Proposed Convention on Justice for Victims of Crime and Abuse of Power*, Tokyo, Japan: Seibundo Publishing Co., Ltd, pp. i–ii.

Dussich, J. P. J. (2012) Opening Address of the 13th International Symposium on Victimology (Excerpts) by the President of the World Society of Victimology, in H. Morosawa, J. P. J. Dussich and G. F. Kirchhoff (eds.) *Victimology and Human Security: New Horizons*. Nijmegen, The Netherlands: Wolf Legal Publishers, pp. 15–19.

Dussich, J. P. J. (2015) The Evolution of International Victimology and its Current Status in the World Today, *Revista de Victimología / Journal of Victimology*, Vol. 1, 37–81. Online ISSN 2385-779X, www.revistadevictimologia.com | www.journalofvictimology.com, DOI 10.12827-RVJV-1-02.

Dussich, J. P. J. and Hestermann, T. (2016) A Comparison of Three Countries: Victim Participation in the United States, Japan and Germany, *Scientific Journal of Tokiwa University Graduate School*, No. 3, March, 1–12.

Groenhuijsen, M. (2009) Current Status of the Convention on Justice for Victims of Crime and Abuse of Power, in J. P. J. Dussich and K. G. Mundy (Eds.) *Raising the Global Standards for Victims: The Proposed Convention on Justice for Victims of Crime and Abuse of Power*, Tokyo, Japan: Seibundo Publishing Co., Ltd, pp. 7–20.

Groenhuijsen, M. & Letchert, R. (2012) Preface to the third (revised) edition, in M. Groenhuijsen, & R. Letschert (Eds.) *Compilation of International Victims' Rights Instruments*, Third (revised) Edition. Nijmegen, The Netherlands: Wolf Legal Publishers, pp. 1–3.

INTERVICT, (2009) *The Victimologist: Newsletter of the World Society of Victimology*, Vol. 12, No. 3, July–September.

Kaplan, M. (2010) FDR and the United Nations: An Enduring Legacy, *Citizens for Global Solutions*, Retrieved on June 9, 2016 from: http://globalsolutions.org/blog/2010/04/FDR-and-United-Nations-Enduring-Legacy#.V1nBKmf2aCo.

Kirchhoff, G. F. (2000) Memorial for John Charles Freeman, in P. C. Friday and G. F. Kirchhoff (Eds.) *Victimology at the Transition, From the 20th to the 21st Century*. Aachen, Germany: Shaker Verlag GmBH in cooperation with the World Society of Victimology Publishing.

Kirchhoff, G. F. (2001a) Victimological Websites, *The Victimologist*, Vol. 5, No. 1, March, 3.

Kirchhoff, G. F. (2001b) Letter from the President, *The Victimologist*, Vol. 5, No. 1, March, 4.

Kirchhoff, G. F. (2009) The Functions of UN Instruments and the Path Towards Success, in J. P. J. Dussich and K. G. Mundy (Eds.) *Raising the Global Standards for Victims: The Proposed Convention on Justice for Victims of Crime and Abuse of Power*. Tokyo: Seibundo Publishing Co., Ltd, pp. 50–63.

Marchiori, H. (2001) *The Victim of Crime*. Córdoba, Argentina: Marcos Lerner Editora Córdoba.

Mendelsohn, B. (1947) New Bio-psychosocial Horizons: Victimology, Lecture to the Romanian Psychiatric Society, Coltzea State Hospital, Bucharest, Romania.

O'Connell, M. (2012) United Nations Economic and Social Council—Quadrennial Reports—Non-Governmental Organizations, *The Victimologist, Newsletter of the World Society of Victimology*, Vol. 14, No. 1, Jan–May, 5–7.
O'Connell, M. (2016) Email message with author June 17. 2016.
Schneider, H. J. (1982) Acknowledgements of the editor. *The Victim in International Perspective*. Berlin: Walter de Gruyter, p. v.
Šeparović, Z. P. (2009) 25 Years of Victimology in Dubrovnik, in Z. P. Šeparović (ed.) *25 Years of Victimology in Dubrovnik*, Zagreb. Croatia: Croatian Society of Victimology, p. 10.
United Nations (n.d.) *History of the United Nations*, Retrieved on June 2, 2016 from http://www.un.org/en/sections/history/history-united-nations/.
UNODC (1999) *Handbook on Justice for Victims*. New York: Centre for International Crime Prevention.
Van Dijk, J. J. M. (2008) In the Shadow of Christ? On the use of the word "victim" for those affected by crime. *Criminal Justice Ethics*, Vol. 27, No. 1, 17.
Viano, E. (1976) *Victims and Society*. Washington, DC: Visage Press Inc.
Waller, I. (2009) Post Graduate Course on Victimology, in Z. P. Šeparović (Ed.) *25 Years of Victimology in Dubrovnik*. Zagreb, Croatia: Croatian Society of Victimology.
Wemmers, J.-A. (2009) A Short History of Victimology, in O. Hagemann, P. Schäfer and S. Schmidt (Eds.) *Victimology, Victim Assistance and Criminal Justice*. WAZ – Druck, p. 33.
WSV (n.d.) World Society of Victimology website, *History and overview*, retrieved on June 6, 2016 at: http://www.worldsocietyofvictimology.org/about-us/history-and-overview/.

Appendix I WSV Presidents

1979–1982	Hans Joachim Schneider, Germany
1982–1985	Hans Joachim Schneider, Germany
1985–1988	Zvonimir Paul Šeparović, Croatia
1988–1991	Koichi Miyazawa, Japan
1991–1994	Chris Sumner, Australia
1994–1997	Irvin Waller, Canada
1997–2000	Jan J. M. van Dijk, The Netherlands
2000–2003	Gerd Ferdinand Kirchhoff, Germany
2003–2006	Marlene A. Young, The United States of America
2006–2009	John P. J. Dussich, The United States of America
2009–2012	Marc Groenhuijsen, The Netherlands
2012–2015	Marc Groenhuijsen, The Netherlands
2015–2018	Marc Groenhuijsen, The Netherlands

Website: http://www.worldsocietyofvictimology.org/

Appendix II Basic Statute of Incorporation (first page)

World Society of Victimology, founded 1979

Registered with the Court's Corporation Register in Münster, Westfalia, Germany, Document # 3040/1992 of WSV Notar Dr. Clauss in 41065 Mönchengladbach, Kaiserstraße 22, FRG; (corresponding to Court Document 2709/1994)

§ 1 Name, Office and Legal Form

1. The Society takes the name World Society of Victimology e. V.
2. The Society is listed as a legally competent organization in the register of the office of the court in Mönchengladbach, Niederrhein, Germany.
3. The office of the Society is Mönchengladbach. Office relocations can be made by the Executive Committee. The primary determinant in location should be its accessibility to the largest number of Executive Committee members.
4. The business year will be the calendar year.
5. The business language will be in English.

§ 2 Purpose and Task of the Society

1. The Society exclusively and directly follows the common and scientific aims according to the chapters on tax privilege aims of the German Tax Law.
2. Purpose of the Society:

   a) To advance victimological research and practices in the entire world.
   b) To encourage interdisciplinary and comparative work and research in this field; and, to advance cooperation of international, national, regional and local agencies and work groups who are concerned with the problems of victims in the entire world. The purpose of the Basic Statute of Incorporation is realized especially:
   c) by providing an International Symposium for Victimology ordinarily every three years that will serve as a forum for international scholars, practitioners, and students,
   d) periodic seminars, workshops and institutes;
   e) a variety of publications;
   f) cooperation between victimologists throughout the world so as to initiate and maintain an active exchange of ideas.

3. The World Society of Victimology may give or take financial supports, scholarships, or grants.

§ 3 Unselfishness

1. The Society is active in altruistic endeavors.
2. In the first place it does not pursue profitable purposes. It may not give benefits which are unknown to the purpose of the corporation, not favors which are not equitable.
3. Resources of the Society may only be used in accordance with the Basic Statute of Incorporation: The members may not receive dividends nor other profits from Society sources. By dissolving the Society or by abolition of its purpose, the capital of the Society will go to the International Red Cross whose main office is in Geneva and who will use the capital directly and only for charitable purposes.

Appendix III List of Award and Honors Recipients

Hans von Hentig Award recipients:

- Israel Drapkin, Israel (1982)
- Marlene Young, USA (1985)
- Marvin Wolfgang, USA (1988)
- Beniamin Mendelsohn, Israel (1991)
- Irene Melup, USA (1994)

- Luis Rodrìguez Manzanera, Mexico (1997)
- Zvonimir Paul Šeparović, Croatia (2000)
- Jan van Dijk, Netherlands (2003)
- Hans Joachim Schneider, Germany (2006)
- Ezzat A. Fattah, Germany (2009)
- Emilio Viano, USA (2012)
- Dame Helen Reeves, United Kingdom (2015)

Beniamin Mendelsohn Young Scholar Award recipients:

- Rianne M. Letschert, Netherlands (2009)
- Chie Maekoya, Japan (2012)
- Chadley James, South Africa (2015)

Certification of Appreciation recipients:

- Beniamin Mendelsohn, Israel (1982)
- John P. J. Dussich, USA (1985)
- Chris Sumner, Australia (1987)
- Irene Melup, USA (1988)
- Heber Vargas, Brazil (1991)
- Hilda Marchiori, Argentina (1991)
- Elias Neuman, Argentina (1994)
- V. R. Krishna Iyer, India (1994)
- Ray Whitrod (1994)
- Hidemichi Morosawa, Japan (1997)
- Wesley G. Skogan, USA (2000)
- Marc Groenhuijsen, Netherlands (2003)
- John Stein (2007)
- Sarah Ben David (2009)
- Andrew Karmen (2012)
- Jo-AnneWemmers (2015)

Honorary Membership recipients:

- Willem Hendrik Nagel, Netherlands (year not available)
- Henri Ellenberger, Canada (year not available)
- Beniamin Mendelson, Israel (year not available)
- Israel Drapkin, Israel (year not available)
- Elias Neuman, Argentina
- Hans-Joachim Schneider, Germany (2006)
- Hilda Marchiori, Argentina (2009)
- Koichi Miazawa, Japan (2009)
- Irvin Waller, Canada (2015)

Appendix IV List of WSV Hosted Events

- 4th Symposium; 1982 August 29–Sep 4, Tokyo/Kyoto, Japan, ***Victimology in Comparative Perspective***, Tokyo, Japan: Seibundo Publishing Co. Ltd., K. Miyazawa and M. Ohya (eds.) (1986).
- 5th Symposium; 1985 Aug 18–23, ***Victimology: International Action and Study of Victims*** vols. I & II, Zagreb, Croatia, Yugoslavia: "Zagreb," Samobor, Z. P. Šeparović (ed.) (1988).

- 6th Symposium; 1988 Aug 29–Sep 2, Jerusalem, Israel, ***International Faces of Victimology***, Mönchengladbach, Germany: WSV Publishing, S. Ben David & G. F. Kirchhoff (eds.) (1992).
- 7th Symposium; 1991 Aug 25–31–Rio de Janeiro, Brazil, ***International Debates of Victimology***, Mönchengladbach, Germany: WSV Publishing, G. F. Kirchhoff, E. Kosovski, & H.-J. Schneider (1994).
- 8th Symposium; 1994 Aug 21–26, Adelaide, Australia, ***International Victimology: Selected Papers from the 8th International Symposium***, Canberra, Australia: Australian Institute of Criminology, C. Sumner, M. Israel, M. O'Connell & R. Sarre (eds.) (1995).
- 9th Symposium; 1997 Aug 25–29, Amsterdam, The Netherlands, ***Caring for Crime victims: Selected Papers of the 9th International Symposium***, Monsey, USA: Criminal Justice Press/ Willow Tree Press, J. J. M. van Dijk, R. G. M. van Kaam & J.A. Wemmers (eds.) (1999).
- 10th Symposium; 2000 Aug 6–11, Canada, ***Victimology at the Transition from the 20th to the 21st Century***, Mönchengladbach, Germany: WSV Publishing, P. C. Friday & G. F. Kirchhoff (eds.) (2000).
- 11th Symposium; 2003 July 13–18, Stellenbosch, South Africa, papers planned for WSV website publication.
- 12th Symposium; 2006 Aug, Orlando, USA, ***Victimology in a Multi-disciplinary Key: Recent Advances in Victimology***, Nijmegan, The Netherlands: Wolf Legal Publishers, F. W. Winkel, P. C. Friday, G. F. Kirchhoff and R. M. Letschert (eds.) (2012).
- 13th Symposium; 2009 Aug 23–28, Mito, Japan, ***Victimology and Human Security: New Horizons***, Nijmegan, The Netherlands: Wolf Legal Publishers, H. Morosawa, J. P. J. Dussich, G. F. Kirchhoff (eds.) (2012).
- 14th Symposium; 2012 May 20–24, The Hague, The Netherlands, ***Justice for Victims; Perspectives on rights, transition and reconciliation***, London, England: Routledge; Taylor and Francis Group, I. Vanfraechen, A. Pemberton and F. M. Ndohinda (eds.) with I. Aertsen, V. Jammers, S. Leferink, R. Letschert and S. Parmentier (2014).
- 15th Symposium; 2015 Jul 5–8, Perth, Australia, papers are "published online and the key-note presentations are available as videos on the AIC Criminology TV channel via YouTube" (O'Connell, 2016).

20

VICTIMOLOGY AND VICTIMS' SERVICE ORGANIZATIONS

Cliff Roberson

Keywords

American Society of Victimology; NOVA; MADD; OVC; ACJS; ASC; VALOR

Objectives

After reading this chapter, the reader should understand and be able to discuss the following objectives and issues:

- Understand and explain the goals and missions of the selected victims' service providers.
- Understand the need for a national survey on victims' service providers.
- Explain why the American Society of Victimology has not flourished as has the World Society.

Introduction

In this chapter, we will take a look at the leading victimology and victims' organizations in the United States.

American Society of Victimology

The American Society of Victimology (ASV) was founded in 2003 by a group of interested professors and victims' service professionals during a meeting at a community college in Kansas City, Missouri. The stated purposes of ASV were to sponsor events that encourage participation in providing victims' services between practitioners, educators, and researchers. The stated mission of the American Society of Victimology is to advance the discipline of victimology by promoting evidence based practice and by providing leadership in research and education.[1]

Officers of ASV

The bylaws of ASV states that the principal office of the ASV would be in the City of McLean, Virginia. The business and affairs of the ASV are managed by a president and Board of Directors. The members of the board of directors serve three-year terms with one-third elected each year and should include colleges and universities with training programs in Victimology or victim services, survivors of crime and their advocates and victim service providers. The president and vice-president are to be elected biannually.

Events Sponsored by ASV

From 2003 until 2010, the ASV sponsored a series of symposiums and colloquiums. The First American Symposium on Victimology held by the ASV was in January 2003 in Kansas City, Kansas. The first speaker was John Dussich (who contributed the chapter in the handbook on the World Society of Victimology). Professor Dussich discussed the evolution of victimology and victim services. The next speaker was Professor Steven Walker, California State University, Fresno. Professor Walker discussed the development of academic programs in the field and the circumstances involving the first use of a victim impact statement by James Rowland who at the time was the Chief Probation Office in Fresno County, California.

The ASV in February 2010 held a half-day colloquium at the beginning of the Academy of Criminal Justice Sciences (ACJS) annual meeting in San Diego, California. The colloquium was followed by an awards reception and a joint reception with the newly formed ACJS Victimology Section. The colloquium was entitled "The Changing Politics of Victim Rights and Services: International, National, State, and Local Perspectives." That was apparently the last official meeting of the ASV.

Demise of the ASV

The joint meeting between the ASV and the ACJS in February 2010 probably marked the end of the ASV. It has not been active since that date and the new victims' sections in ACJS and in the American Society of Criminology have taken over those functions that had previously been served by the ASV. Unfortunately, there is still a need for the ASV, but informal talks with the past leaders of ASV indicate that for all practical purposes the organization is dead.

Academy of Criminal Justice Sciences

ACJS was founded in 1963 as an international association established with the goal to foster professional association in the field of criminal justice. ACJS promotes criminal justice education, research, and policy analysis within the discipline of criminal justice for both educators and practitioners. The Victimology Section is one of the newest sections and was not founded until February 2009. The email address for the section is acjs.victimology@gmail.com.[2]

Victimology Section

The stated mission of the Victimology Section of ACJS is to facilitate and encourage research and theory development related to victimology; encourage appropriate and effective teaching techniques and practices for victimology-related courses; encourage organization of and participation in conference sessions related to victimology; and serve as a resource network for and encourage interaction among academic, research, practitioner, and policy-making sectors in order to further knowledge of victimology.

Activities of Section

At every annual meeting of ACJS since the earlier mentioned meeting in 2009 at San Diego, the Section has had meetings and frequently followed by an ice cream social that was open to all ACJS members. For example, at the 2016 ACJS Annual Meeting, the Section directed their advertising of their general meeting to all ACJC members who are interested in crime victimization. The advertising flyer solicited persons who study crime victimization, or crime victims and their interactions with and treatment by the criminal justice system and to individuals who were concerned with the quality of crime victims' services.

American Society of Criminology

The American Society of Criminology (ASC) started out as the National Association of College Police Training Officials in 1941 at the home of August Vollmer in Berkeley, California. Approximately 15 years later it was renamed to its present name.[3]

Division of Victimology (DOV)

Similar to the ACJS section of Victimology, the ASC section was only founded in 2012 and is one of the newest divisions of the ASC. As of 2016, the section had over 140 members from seven different countries. The section holds panels and presentations on victimology subjects. For example, in the fall of 2016, in New Orleans, a program was presented on the History of Victimology, Victimological Research, and Victim Services. The program discussed the almost 100-year history of victimology and its evolution to the present day.

The division has several annual awards including the Larry J. Siegel Graduate Fellowship for Victimology Studies (given by the Darald and Julie Libby Foundation), which is designed to recognize an exceptional graduate student in the field of victimology.

As of 2016, the division leaders were working on establishing a new victimology journal for DOV members (ASC) and in conjunction with the Section on Victimology members (ACJS).

Mission Statement of the ASC Division of Victimology

The stated mission as published on its website is summarized as follows: To promote the professional growth and development of its members through scholarship, pedagogy, and practices associated with the field of Victimology. The Division of Victimology strives to ensure that its members will:

1. Contribute to the evolution of the Victimology discipline by supporting and disseminating cutting edge research.
2. Develop and share pedagogical resources.
3. Support professional enhancement workshops and activities.
4. Embrace the development of evidence-informed programs and services.
5. Advance victims' rights.
6. Encourage the advancement of the intersection of scholarship and practices.

National Organization for Victim Assistance

The National Organization for Victim Assistance (NOVA) was the first national victim assistance organization founded in the United States. It was founded in 1976 by Professor John Dussich and is a private, non-profit charitable organization.[4] The stated values of NOVA include:

- Compassion: NOVA is concerned about and responds to the plight of people and one another.
- Accountability and collaboration: NOVA stresses excellence and justice in the cause and honors their commitments. It also stresses teamwork at every level.
- Passion: NOVA states that it is driven by the hope that what it does makes a difference.

Oral History of the Crime Victim Assistance Field

For an extensive history on the crime victim assistance field, visit the NOVA website (http://www.trynova.org/about-us/overview/) or the University of Akron website (http://vroh.uakron.edu/about.php). Akron University was selected as the host university for the development of an oral history of the crime victim assistance field. The Oral History Project was started by the Office for Victims of Crime within the U.S. Department of Justice in 2002 and the co-sponsors of the project were Justice Solutions, the National Organization for Victim Assistance, the National Association of VOCA Assistance Administrators and the National Association of Crime Victim Compensation Boards. A grant to provide the funds for the project was sponsored by the Office for Victims of Crime, Office of Justice Programs, U.S. Department of Justice.

According to NOVA's website, previously noted, the Oral History of the Crime Victim Assistance Field Video and Audio Archive is the world's only archive of its kind and serves as the crime victim assistance field's primary repository of historically significant documents and oral history video and audio files. These histories record not only the factual development of the movement, but also the driving energy and passion evident in the works of the pioneers.

The archives have three components:

- An online video archive;
- An on-site video archive; and
- An on-site collection of historical documents.

Crime Victim Advocacy

One of NOVA's main activities is to assist individuals and organizations in crime victim advocacy. NOVA contends that every victim of crime is entitled to victim advocacy.

According to NOVA's website, advocates, both professional and volunteer, will work to affirm victims' rights and to provide information and services to victims of crime.

Their advocacy units are organized locally. And the starting point is a victim advocate in the jurisdiction of the crime. Because of the many jurisdictions in our nation, it is not possible to list all the agencies providing victim advocacy and assistance. To search, use keywords "Victim Assistance (County) (State)." If a victim is not able to determine contact information for a local victim advocate, it is possible that there is a state directory of advocacy programs. Their contact number for more information is 800-TRY-NOVA.

Victims' Rights

NOVA's website notes that the majority of states have some expression of crime victims' rights in their constitutions or state laws. According to NOVA, some of the most commonly affirmed victims' rights include:

- The right to protection from intimidation and harm.
- The right to be informed concerning the criminal justice process.
- The right to reparations.
- The right to preservation of property and employment.
- The right to due process in criminal court proceedings.
- The right to be treated with dignity and compassion.
- The right to counsel.

The website for NOVA notes that the rights may differ from state to state and that an individual may call 800-TRY-NOVA for more specific information.

Victims' Assistance Legal Organization

The Victims' Assistance Legal Organization (VALOR) was founded in 1979 by Frank G. Carrington. Many individuals consider Carrington as the father of the crime victims' rights movement. He was very active in victims' rights and played a significant role in the development and passage of the Campus Security Act of 1990. VALOR was originally named the Crime Victims' Legal Advocacy Institute. It was renamed to its present name in 1981.

VALOR works to advance victims' rights through public policy efforts on the federal, state, and local levels. Through the promotion of education and awareness about the rights and needs of crime victims, the organization works to improve services for victims to assist in their emotional, financial, and physical recovery. VALOR accomplishes its mission through support from private and corporate foundations, government grants, and individual contributions. VALOR's contact information is:[5]

Victims' Assistance Legal Organization
8180 Greensboro Drive, Suite 1070
McLean, Virginia 22102-3860

National Victim Assistance Academy

In 1995, the Office for Victims of Crime at the U.S. Department of Justice awarded a grant to the VALOR to plan and produce the annual National Victim Assistance Academy (NVAA). VALOR developed an intensive 40-hour Academy training program that was conducted annually at several universities across the nation. VALOR also managed a project team of victim advocates and victim service providers. Academics wrote and later revised the National Victim Assistance Academy Text, an 800-page comprehensive review of crime victim legal and service issues that is the principal teaching text for the five-day training. For information about the NVAA go to http://www.nvaa.org.

Ethics in Victim Services

In 1999, with the assistance and support of the Office for Victims of Crime, VALOR helped develop a program to create ethical standards of conduct for professionals in victims' services. The Office for Victims of Crime also created the National Victim Assistance Standards Consortium (NVASC). NVASC's goal was to create a model for competency and ethical standards of conduct for the field of victim assistance. To do this, the Consortium researched existing standards in similar professions, polled the field of victim assistance, and utilized the expertise and experience of a representative and diverse core of victim assistance professionals. NBASC under the leadership of Dana De Hart created a document that set forth ethical standards for victims' assistance providers. *Ethics in Victim Services* is available for purchase through the VALOR website.

U.S. Office for Victims of Crime

The Office for Victims of Crime (OVC) was established in the Office of Justice Programs, U.S. Department of Justice.[6] The OVC was established by a federal statute, 42 USC 10605: Establishment of Office for Victims of Crime. It was established in 1988 through an amendment to the Victims of Crime Act (VOCA) of 1984, OVC is charged by Congress with administering the Crime Victims

Fund (the Fund). Through OVC, the Fund supports a broad array of programs and services that focus on helping victims in the immediate aftermath of crime and continuing to support them as they rebuild their lives. Millions of dollars are invested annually in victim compensation and assistance in every U.S. state and territory, as well as for training, technical assistance, and other capacity-building programs designed to enhance service providers' ability to support victims of crime in communities across the Nation.[7]

The OVC website is a valuable source of information on victims' service rights and assistance. For example, under help for crime victims the site has a web page on domestic terrorism and mass violence, provides list of local victim service organizations, and state contract information on state victims' services organizations. As noted earlier, the OVC was the supporter of the victim assistance academies and many other programs designed to train victims' service providers. Professionals can learn more about OVC by examining the new video series that provides information about OVC and is available on their website.

Crime Victimization Glossary

One of the most used groups of information provided by the website is the crime victimization glossary. For example, it lists the types of victim/victimization, which are important to understand. The types of victimization are listed as follows:

Adult molested as child. Adult aged 18 or older who was sexually abused as a child (see child sexual abuse definition below).

Adult sexual assault. Sexual offense—including rape, incest, fondling, exhibitionism, or pornography—of an adult aged 18 or older.

Aggravated assault. Unlawful, intentional causing of serious bodily injury with or without a deadly weapon, or unlawful, intentional attempting or threatening of serious bodily injury or death with a deadly or dangerous weapon.

Arson. Any willful or malicious burning or attempt to burn, with or without intent to defraud, a dwelling, house, public building, motor vehicle or aircraft, or personal property of another.

Assault. An unlawful attack by one person on another, with or without a weapon, that inflicts, or attempts or threatens to inflict, physical injury.

Child. A person under the age of 18 or as otherwise defined by state law.

Child physical abuse. Nonaccidental injury to a child by a parent or other adult that may include severe beatings, burns, strangulation, or human bites.

Child sexual abuse. Sexual offense (see definition below) against a child by a parent or other adult.

Domestic violence. Violent acts involving a current or former spouse or domestic partner.

DUI/DWI crash. Accident involving one or more motor vehicles in which at least one driver was under the influence of alcohol and/or drugs (DUI) or was legally intoxicated (DWI) at the time of the crash.

Elder abuse. Abuse perpetrated by a caretaker on an elderly individual who depends on others for support and assistance.

Fraud. A deliberate deception perpetrated for unlawful or unfair gain.

Gang violence. Criminal acts committed by a group of three or more individuals who regularly engage in criminal activity and identify themselves with a common name or sign.

Human trafficking. Sex trafficking in which a commercial sex act is induced by force, fraud, or coercion, or in which the person induced to perform such act has not attained 18 years of age; or the recruitment, harboring, transportation, provision, or obtaining of a person for labor or services, through the use of force, fraud, or coercion, for the purpose of subjection to involuntary servitude, peonage, debt bondage, or slavery.

Identity theft. A crime in which an imposter obtains key pieces of personal information, such as Social Security or driver's license numbers, to impersonate someone else.

Robbery. Taking or attempting to take anything of value from the care, custody, or control of a person or persons by force or threat of force or violence.

Sexual offense. Forcible rape, attempted rape, statutory rape, sexual harassment, prostitution, or other unlawful sexual contact and other unlawful behavior intended to result in sexual gratification or profit from sexual activity.

Stalking. Any unwanted contact between two people that directly or indirectly communicates a threat or places the victim in fear.

Survivor of homicide victim. Family member or loved one of a murder victim.

Terrorism. Use of violence or intimidation to coerce a government or civilian population to further political or social objectives.

Victims with disabilities. Victims of crime who have a physical or mental disability.

White-collar crime. Nonviolent crime for financial gain committed by means of deception by persons with special technical and professional knowledge of business or government.

The OCV website glossary also provides an extensive list of victims' services provided by OVC and a list of civil remedies.

Crime Victims' Notification Systems

Another feature of the OVC website is a list of the crime victims' notification systems. The website notes that the right to notification is supported by each state, the U.S. Department of Justice through the Victim Notification System (VNS), and the Immigration and Customs Enforcement's (ICE) Victim Notification Program (VNP).

While the system by which victim notification is performed in each state may vary, if you are seeking information about an offender that has been incarcerated, the best place to start to ensure you receive victim notification is your state's department of corrections.

Victims of federal crimes are able to obtain information about events pertaining to the criminal case and/or any defendants in the case through VNS, a cooperative effort between the Federal Bureau of Investigation, the United States Postal Inspection Service, the United States Attorneys' offices, and the Federal Bureau of Prisons. Launched in 2001 as a pilot program with funding support from OVC, it became fully operational in 2002 under the development and oversight of the Executive Office for United States Attorneys. This free, computer-based system provides important information to victims of federal crimes. This information is also available in English and Spanish on the Internet and through a toll-free telephone number (1-866-365-4968).

VNP is another type of notification system and is a service of U.S. Immigration and Customs Enforcement Homeland Security Investigations, U.S. Department of Homeland Security. Once a person that has entered the United States illegally has been convicted of a crime and served their prison sentence, he/she is transferred to ICE for deportation proceedings. The VNP provides information to eligible victims and witnesses about the offender's release and/or deportation activities. Eligible victims and witnesses can register to receive notifications by completing a Victim Request for Notification of Criminal Alien Status form found on the VNP website.

National Survey of Victim Service Providers

Bureau of Justice Statistics' (BJS) has established a project designed to provide information on victims' services providers.[8] As noted in the National Survey of Victim Service Providers (NSVSP) website, the national survey is a project aimed at closing the information gap in the public's understanding of victimization, namely the range of services available for and provided to different types of crime victims. NSVSP officials noted that for more than two decades, programs such as the Office for Victims of Crime (OVC) and the Office on Violence Against Women (OVW) have been working to enhance our nation's capacity to assist crime victims and promote justice through the delivery of support services to victims of crime. However, relatively little research has been done to demonstrate the coverage and effectiveness of this service infrastructure or to identify areas in which victims are still in need of services.

The National Crime Victimization Survey (NCVS) conducted research and collected statistics from crime victims since 1972. While the NCVS has a great deal of information on victims and the crimes they experience, these efforts have limitations in terms of answering questions about what is and is not being done to provide support and services to victims, as well as what support programs are and are not effective. According to the project, the victim service field lacks complete and reliable information about the range of services being provided to crime victims every day across the country, how many crime victims are being served each year, and how many victims are seeking unavailable services. Similarly, with a few exceptions, limited information exists about the organizations and agencies that comprise the victim service field, including how they are funded and the organizational resources required to provide certain services.

In justifying the survey, the project directors contend that there are no baseline measures about the current services provided or the organizations that provide them, and there is no way to measure progress in terms of the number and range of victims served by these organizations or the effectiveness of services provided. The lack of a clear understanding about how current victim service funding is being used limits the ability of the field to work more effectively in providing assistance to crime victims, to seek future funding, or to identify underserved populations. BJS recognizes the limits of the NCVS to fully address issues related to victims' receipt of services, and therefore, with collaboration and funding from OVC, developed the National Survey of Victim Service Providers (NSVSP). On June 26, 2012, BJS issued a solicitation for the 2012 NSVSP, requesting applications to respond to this interest in developing a statistical system about services provided to crime victims.

The RAND Corporation, working in collaboration with the National Opinion Research Center (NORC) and the National Center for Victims of Crime (NCVC), awarded the cooperative agreement. The awardees are working to carry out the NSVSP's two primary objectives:

- To design a data collection that will produce reliable statistics about both the crime victims served and the victim-serving providers, and
- To implement the design to obtain national and subnational data to generate a specified set of statistics.

The NSVSP aims to produce estimates, such as the number of victims served by victim service providers, the types and duration of services provided, the cost of providing services, the number of victims for whom services could not be provided, the types of organizations providing services, the funding sources for victim service providers, the number and characteristics of staff in victim service organizations, and the policies and practices of these organizations as they relate to the provision of services to crime victims.

Mothers Against Drunk Drivers

Mothers Against Drunk Drivers (MADD) was incorporated in September 1980 with the mission of aiding victims of crime that were caused by individuals driving under the influence of drugs or alcohol. MADD chapters currently operate in all 50 states and the District of Columbia. In 2015, MADD revised its mission statement to: "The mission of Mothers Against Drunk Driving is to end drunk driving, help fight drugged driving, support the victims of these violent crimes and prevent underage drinking."[9]

While MADD is concerned primarily with preventing DWI/DUI crimes, it has provided valuable services for victims of those crimes. For example, for several years when editor Cliff Roberson was a professor of criminology at California State University, Fresno, he worked with the local MADD chapters and developed victim impact statements to ensure that the victims of those crimes were represented when the offender was being prosecuted for DWI/DUI offenses. And in one case, he filed a complaint with the State Bar of California because the trial court judge rendered a relative light sentence to the son of the trial judge's friend in a DWI case.

United Kingdom Victim Support

The Victim Support organization is an independent charity for victims and witnesses of crime in the United Kingdom. The organization provides free and confidential help to victims of crime, their family, friends, and anyone else affected. Victim Support provides information, emotional support, and practical help. You don't have to report a crime to the police to get help and support at any time from Victim Support. The Victim Support line number in the UK is: 0845-303-0900. The websites for Victim Support are: In England and Wales: http://www.victimsupport.org.uk/. In London: http://www.vslondon.org/. In Scotland: http://www.victimsupportsco.org.uk/.[10]

Victim Services in Canada

As of 2016, there were over 900 programs or organizations providing services to victims of crime in Canada. Most of these programs were police or community based. Victim service providers in Canada serve many, and in some cases, multiple locations. As noted in the Victim Services in Canada website, a victim service located in a higher density area may also serve surrounding lower population density areas or reserves, or vice versa. In 2009/2010, 68 percent of victim service providers reported that they served areas that had a minimum population concentration of 1,000. Another 58 percent reported serving areas that included small towns, villages, and other populated places of less 1,000 people. In addition, 29 percent reported serving reserves (with 4 percent located on a reserve).[11] For more information on victim services in Canada see the Victim Services Directory located at http://www.justice.gc.ca/eng/cj-jp/victims-victimes/vsd-rsv/index.html.

Discussion Questions

1. NOVA has contributed significantly to the development of victims' services. What are some of its chief contributions?
2. Why was a survey of victims' service providers developed by the BJS?

3. What steps should we take to improve victims' services?
4. List the objectives of the leading victims' service providers.
5. Explain the growth of victims' service providers organizations in the past 40 years.

Notes

1 Information obtained from personal knowledge and from the ASV website at http://www.american-society-victimology.us/. Accessed on August 29, 2016.
2 Information obtained from ACJS website http://www.acjs.org/. Accessed on August 29, 2016.
3 Information for this section obtained from ASC website http://asc41.com/. Accessed on August 29, 2016.
4 National Organization for Victim Assistance at http://www.trynova.org/. Accessed on August 29, 2016.
5 VALOR website at http://www.valor-national.org/. Accessed on August 29, 2016.
6 OVC website at http://www.ovc.gov/awareness/index.html. Accessed on August 29, 2016.
7 Office of Justice Programs website at http://ojp.gov/ovc/about/index.html. Accessed on August 29, 2016.
8 The Help for Crime Victims' website at http://www.ovc.gov/help/index.html. Accessed on August 31, 2016.
9 MADD website http://www.madd.org/about-us/mission/. Accessed on August 31, 2016.
10 Victim Support website at http://photos.state.gov/libraries/unitedkingdom/164203/cons-acs/victims_of_crime2.pdf. Accessed on August 31, 2016.
11 Victim Services in Canada website at http://www.statcan.gc.ca/pub/85-002-x/2012001/article/11626-eng.htm. Accessed on August 31, 2016.

21
VICTIMS AND THE MEDIA

Annette Van de Merwe

Keywords

crime victims' right to privacy; media interviews; victim protection; broadcast trial; media attention; in camera proceedings; victims' consent

Objectives

After studying this chapter, the reader should understand:

- The tension between the principle of open courts, freedom of speech and crime victims' right to privacy.
- Victims' choices in dealing with the media, such as allowing interviews or the publication of images and making use of media experts.
- The benefits and disadvantages of media involvement.
- The role service providers can play in assisting victims and the media to ascertain sensitive and respectful news coverage of the crime.
- The effect that a broadcast trial may have on victims.

Introduction

Crime statistics and consequent crime victimization differ throughout jurisdictions,[1] as well as within populations.[2] However, once a victim of crime, in particular a violent or a high profile crime,[3] such a person (and his or her close family) may become the centre of media attention.[4] Victims are mostly ill-prepared for this exercise[5] and often suffer from the effect of being exposed to the public eye[6] and, at times, aggressive and/or unethical reporting by journalists.[7] This chapter examines competing interests at play in the media coverage of crime victims, general issues that might arise for victims in dealing with the media, the positive and negative side of talking to the media, the role of service providers in guiding victims in this regard, and concludes with a brief case study of the broadcast murder trial of Oscar Pistorius, the Paralympic gold medal athlete, and its effect on the victims.

Public interest, the principle of open courts, freedom of speech and privacy of victims

The safety and well-being of all citizens are concerns for the community as a whole. Thus, any threat or attack in this regard is of great importance and, as demanded by public interest, journalists have a duty to report on such matters. Incidents of attacks, assaults, murder and kidnapping, as well as the way in which such matters are handled by the police and the justice system, normally fall into the category of information being in the public interest.[8] Media reaction often leads to positive outcomes, such as being instrumental in identifying and apprehending offenders, contributing to law reform and disclosing abuses within the criminal justice system.[9] On the other hand, media reaction may sometimes be intrusive and victims in general, but particularly vulnerable victims and those in cases that attract a lot of media attention, may need protection and support in dealing with the media.

At supra-national level guidelines for best practices exist with regards to victims in general,[10] as well as child victims in particular.[11] These instruments follow a rights-based approach and those relevant to victims and the media include the rights to dignity and compassion,[12] and to protection of privacy.[13] The manner in which countries (and states) have formulated corresponding domestic laws and guidelines complying with these standards, as well as the extent of its implementation, vary to a great extent.[14] Victims' right to protection of their privacy, inter alia, recognizes the fact that secondary victimization may not only result within the context of criminal justice procedure, but also from other sources, such as the press. Victims may suffer negative reactions from the way the media portrays them and consequently develop psychological complaints.[15] This has been a particular complaint from co-victims of homicide[16] and victims of sexual violence.[17]

There are a number of measures that provide protection from publicity for victims that would allow a restriction on the publication of their details. It should, however, be understood that these measures challenge the principle of publicity that generally governs the criminal trial. Amongst other things, this principle requires that trials should be open to public and it is meant to "ensure a fair trial for the accused and inspire public confidence in the administration of justice."[18] An exception to this rule, in the form of *in camera* proceedings, is possible for protecting the privacy of victims involved in criminal proceedings. When the court orders that proceedings be held *in camera* it implies that the criminal proceedings (or part thereof) are held behind closed doors, without the public or the press being present. The identity of victims and/or details divulged during their testimony are thus prevented from being published. This may apply in case of only certain crimes and/or if the victim so requests or where publicity may cause "social or cultural disgrace, or stigmatization for the victim."[19] *In camera* proceedings are regulated either by a statutory obligation or where the court exercises its discretion in making a non-publication order.[20]

A survey of European countries in this regard reveals that the reasons for courts using their discretionary power to order *in camera* proceedings differ between countries and may rely on any of the following reasons:[21] the protection of the private life of parties, following a request of parties involved, the minor age of the victim or the minor age of the offender, the mental disabilities of the victim, the protection of the persons involved,[22] the vulnerability of certain witnesses,[23] the sort of offence committed ("crimes against morals and sexual inviolability"); "sexual offences" and "terrorism offences," the necessity to protect a professional or commercial secret, reasons of public order and national security or the fact that the victim or witness is subject to non-disclosure of identity. Relying purely on the court's discretion for protection of victims' privacy is viewed as the weakest form thereof. The highest form of protection, on the other hand, is to make hearings *in camera* obligatory if the victim so requests.[24]

The abovementioned survey further highlights that instances where courts are obliged to close a hearing often refer to *victims' characteristics*. Examples are cases involving victims of sexual offenses[25] and young victims.[26] The largest group of obligatory exceptions to the principle of publicity is related to *types of offences*. Examples of offences that warrant a closed session are: sexual offences,[27] honor crimes, libel or slander and cases related to private life. Closed hearings can also relate to the *type of information* that may be disclosed in the case.

It is not clear from the study above whether the protection of a child's identity extends beyond him or her reaching the age of majority. It is submitted that this protection should not then cease, as it will result in the child being labeled as a victim for ever and will destroy the child's chances of living a normal adult life.

In camera orders may be adapted to the circumstances. It is possible that only the public is excluded from the hearing but the media allowed, subject to the proviso that the name of the victim who testifies as a witness, or any details that might offer clues as to that, not be disclosed. A witness can even testify masked or under a pseudonym or testify behind one-way glass.[28] In the event of the media being barred from the proceedings, a summary of the victim's testimony may be provided to them.

In addition to *in camera* proceedings, another measure to prevent the violation of victims' privacy is an independent order prohibiting the press from revealing the identity of a victim. This measure of merely restricting press coverage is, in comparison to the protection afforded through legislation or *in camera* proceedings, perceived to be a much weaker safeguard for protecting a victim's identity. Nonetheless, such restriction is sometimes also regulated internally by the press itself in the form of a journalistic code of ethics.

Linked to the principle of publicity mentioned above, is the fundamental principle of freedom of expression, and, in the context of this chapter, press freedom in particular. Together, these principles amount to the right to open justice, which entitles the media to gain access to, to observe and to report on the administration of justice and the right to have access to papers and written arguments that are an integral part to court proceedings. The open justice principle is, however, not absolute and may be limited by legislation or common law when fair trial rights, dignity, privacy or the rights of the child or other vulnerable groups are implicated. The interests of justice may dictate that certain information be prohibited from publication. In each case the court will have to weigh the competing rights or interests carefully, with the view to ensuring that the limitation it places on open justice is properly tailored and proportionate to the end it seeks to attain.[29]

Journalists who publish information prohibited by legislation or subject to a non-publication order, would be in contempt of court. They may be fined on conviction and, in addition, be liable for compensation to the victim.[30] In addition, a complaint may be lodged at the office of the Press Ombudsman or Council, which might result in a public apology from the guilty media house.[31]

Notwithstanding, one of the findings of the European study above indicates that all Member States viewed victims' privacy as being insufficiently protected from the media. Recommendations to improve the situation address the issue of victims' consent, which should always be obtained for print images of the victim, and publication of intrusive personal details about the crime or about the victim or their family, such as the "victims' last words." Apart from infringing victims' privacy, the concern is that intrusive media coverage is also likely to deter other victims from reporting a crime and engage with the criminal justice authorities, which will have a negative impact on the criminal justice system as a whole.[32]

General Issues That Might Arise in Dealing with the Media

Though journalists may regard it as their job and duty to report on incidents of crime victimization, direct victims or their family members who are contacted by the press are under no obligation to talk to them and have the right to decide whether or not to divulge any details to the media. An important issue is thus whether they should give the media an interview. Relatives of a deceased person are, while they are at their most vulnerable and emotional immediately after the incident, often approached in this regard. The press has been accused of sometimes thriving on the discomfort and pain experienced by victims and their relatives and of subordinating the right to privately grief to the "public's right to know."[33] In the event of refusing an interview, there is no need to provide an explanation. When granting an interview, victims should be aware that they are, particularly in the immediate aftermath of the crime, not well-placed to make logical or objective observations about victimhood or possible trial outcomes/ punishment, but, in the event of talking to the media, must rather simply offer their own experience.[34] Asking journalists to provide questions beforehand allows victims to consider them before making any comment or deciding to do an interview.[35] Victims may also obtain a copy of the interview. Journalists may further be requested not to report any part of it or re-record some parts. A correction must also be demanded when inaccurate information has been published.[36]

It would appear that victims would always benefit from seeking advice/ support from and/or liaising with media experts from the police and prosecution. This will prevent statements being misrepresented or having a possible negative impact on the investigation. When approached, police media experts should assist victims and their families in effectively managing the media.[37] This may be useful as early as at the crime scene since victims may be in a state of distress. On occasion, when the victim's cooperation is necessary in an appeal to the public for information to further the investigation and/or make an arrest, a joint media conference may be conducted by the police and crime victim(s).[38] During the trial, victims should refrain from giving interviews to the media. Not only may it have fair trial implications but in jurisdictions where the jury system is in place it may unjustly influence the jury members. In deciding whether a victim impact statement should be made, victims should be aware that it forms part of the public records of courts. The media has access to these court files and may thus report on the contents of, inter alia, the victim's impact statement.

Notwithstanding what decision the family members take about granting an interview after the loss of a loved one, the media would need a photo of the deceased for their stories. Relatives should consider providing good pictures otherwise the media will turn to social network sites to locate photos and they will have no control over what photo is published.[39] Unlike the prohibition that is generally in place protecting the identity of children, both as victims and witnesses, an exception often occurs in the case of a deceased child. The immediate guardian who had custody of that child can give permission for the media to name and perhaps show an image of the child. Such a decision should be carefully considered and discussed with the siblings and other close friends. The relevant newsroom can, however, at any time be notified that the permission to publish the name or image of the deceased child is withdrawn.[40]

Another issue related to a victim's interaction with the media is the question whether payment should be considered for interviews. It is entirely at the discretion of the victim. Any agreement, including the amount of money to be paid, is confidential. Victims will be bound by the conditions of the contract they entered into. Further, being filmed at various stages and places of the process of investigation and trial may be a case of concern to victims. It might be difficult for victims to avoid since the media is allowed to do that as long as is it is in a public space such as when the crime scene is in a public area, the police station, court building and movements to and from one's house from the public road.[41] Sexual assault victims should not be photographed without their permission, and as highlighted above, neither child victims nor witnesses may be photographed.

Despite the fact that some journalists might develop a close relationship with victims and maintain long-term contact with them, victims are alluded to the fact that they should not be confused with friends or a support person. Records of private conversations are most certainly kept for future use.[42]

The Negative and Positive Side of Talking to the Media

When becoming a victim of crime it is most likely the person's first encounter with the new media. Research indicates an overwhelming negative implication for victims and that the media is often responsible for further victimization of crime victims by "enhancing their feelings of violation, disorientation and loss of control."[43] The media is also faulted for interviewing victims at inappropriate times, taking insensitive photographs, searching for negative details about victims, including delving into their past. In addition, journalists are often driven by commercial concerns aimed at getting big stories with little consideration for victims. Victims can find themselves transformed into public property, at times being blamed themselves for contributing to their victimization and even harassed by members of the community. Participation in talk shows with the public freely offering subjective views gives rise to particular concern.[44] Such treatment can be devastating to victims and their families, exacerbating and prolonging their trauma and seriously impacting their attempts to re-establish their lives.[45]

Once the media reports on an interview it becomes part of the archive of the particular newspaper, radio station or television network. Information about victims thus becomes part of the public domain and could be used at any time in future as research material for new stories.[46] Sharing on social media allows anyone access to that information and might be used without adhering to standards of professional journalists.[47]

Despite possible risks involved in media interaction there are several benefits. Research highlights the following: it may be of public interest and inform members of the public; it may raise awareness of the particular crime and may present re-occurrence of similar events; victims can assist the media in getting the story right by providing the correct details; co-operation can be provided to the police in finding the perpetrator; when a person has lost his or her life due to a criminal act, remembering that person in the media is a way of paying tribute;[48] victims have the opportunity to tell their personal and full story and by facilitating this, it does not only validate victims but also humanizes crime and the impact on individuals.[49] Victims and co-victims who choose to sell their stories to the press may gain financial benefit from their ordeals.

Role of Service Providers

The above mentioned negative consequences suffered by crime victims resulting from media exposure clearly illustrate that there is a need to facilitate sensitive and respectful news media coverage of crime victims. Victim service providers can play an important role in this regard. Seymore and Bucqueroux[50] highlight a number of key concerns where advice and intervention could be helpful to crime victims facing the media. Victims should be advised that they might experience fluctuating emotional responses to the trauma of victimization which, in turn, will influence their contact with the media. In order to help them face their trauma and recover from it, victims should be referred to support services such as counseling and support groups. Notwithstanding victims' unexpected loss and trauma being a personal and private matter, matters regarding the media should be put into perspective. Victims must understand "why the media want to speak to them; the benefits of talking to reporters or issuing a public statement; and measures victims can take to increase their sense of control and confidence in interviews."[51] Victim service providers can also make a victim's wishes for privacy known and, upon request from the victim, provide helpful information to the media in lieu of a personal interview.[52]

Service providers should intervene and interact with the media in some matters of concern to victims. Firstly, the dynamic of attaching blame or shame to victimisation as rationale for why crime only happens to other people should be explained. Accurate and sensible coverage can educate the public and thereby reduce victim blaming. Secondly, confidentiality is critical to some victims' personal safety. Publishing information revealing their identities and addresses could put them at risk and service providers should alert the media and assist victims to tell their stories without violating their confidentiality or personal safety. Other areas where service providers could intervene relate to alerting journalists about the effect on victims when they use words that either glamorize offenders (victims are marginalized) or refer to the "alleged victim" (they feel degraded);[53] addressing the media's attempts to interview victims at inappropriate times (at funerals or hospitals); confronting aggressive of intrusive reporters; conveying victims and survivors' preferences and feelings; preparing a written statement for the media containing correct facts about the case and the victim; addressing inaccurate reporting; and lastly assisting victims to report any misconduct on the media's side.[54]

As highlighted above, the media might pose particular difficulties for rape and sexual assault victims since they fear that others might learn about their experience. Media houses often have policies in place to protect confidentiality, and national and/or state legislation might prohibit publication of the identity of these victims. These crimes are further generally recognized as being unique in nature but often misunderstood. Through interaction with the media, service providers can contribute to alert them about the mental health consequences for victims, their fears, such as retaliation from the alleged offender or being stigmatized and blamed.[55]

Service providers can assist victims who agree to media interviews on a practical level by helping them to plan the outline, setting the venue and time, arranging for a support person, choosing a particular reporter, setting ground rules and taping the interview themselves.[56]

Turning to social media may have a positive outcome when using it as a tool to increase awareness of victims' issues and promoting victim service work, but it may hold some dangers when victims themselves use it. Their personal information is for ever in the public domain, opinion (and not necessarily the truth) is prevalent on these platforms, others may react in a harmful way, and victims, as well as service providers, can easily be misquoted or misrepresented.[57]

Case Study: Homicide, Victims and Broadcast Trials—Remembering Reeva Steenkamp

State v Oscar Pistorius

The use of cameras in the courtroom, for broadcasting proceedings on television networks or to live stream proceedings, presents a conflict between competing interests. On the one hand are interests in a public trial (open justice) and promoting freedom of the press. On the other are, not only the offender's right to a fair trial, but also the victim's interest—in either having his or her privacy protected or in having the matter heard publicly in the broadest sense via broadcast.[58] It thus goes further than merely being concerned about the possible influence of cameras on the willingness of victims to testify, or if they testify, whether the quality of justice would be affected.[59] Unlike the position in the United States where most state courts may use their discretion to allow television cameras on a regular basis,[60] the first time a criminal trial was broadcast in South African history was in 2014 after Reeva Steenkamp lost her life on Valentine's Day 2013. Oscar Pistorius, with whom she had been in a short relationship at the time, was charged with her murder. With Pistorius being a celebrity Olympian and Paralympic athlete, the matter immediately attracted huge local and international media attention. Applications were brought by the media for permission to broadcast the entire criminal proceedings through audio, audio-visual and photographic means. All the applicants relied on the high public profile of the accused as the basis for the argument that it was in the public interest for the trial to be broadcast by the media.[61]

On the other hand, Pistorius contended that the live broadcasting of his criminal trial would infringe his right to a fair trial. His view was that the mere knowledge of the presence of audio visual equipment, especially cameras, would inhibit him as an individual as well as his witnesses when they gave evidence. He also asserted that his Counsel might also be inhibited in the questioning of witnesses and the presentation of his case. He was further of the view that covering his trial, as was sought by the applicants, would enable witnesses still to testify to fabricate and adapt their evidence based on their knowledge of what other witnesses had testified.[62]

The media's application was successful and the Judge President ordered, also providing detailed guidelines about the practical side, that the entire trial could be broadcast in audio form, and that much of the trial could also be televised.[63] While the majority of witnesses refused to be televised, live televised testimony was broadcast of all the state's police and expert witnesses. The only exception was the state pathologist, Professor Gert Saayman, who objected to the live broadcast of his evidence on the basis that it would harm the dignity of the deceased and her family. The court banned the publication of any of the images of Reeva presented,[64] but permitted, with the parties' consent, a delayed broadcast of a summary of his evidence, for example via tweeting by journalists sitting in court. In his cross-examination of the accused (who also opted not to be televised), the state prosecutor fiercely dealt with the issue of his "staged" public apology, his lack of taking full responsibility for his actions and also used graphic visual material depicting the deceased after the fatal incident. Pistorius was found guilty of culpable homicide and effectively sent to prison for one year.[65] But the state successfully appealed his conviction on a question of law and it was changed to one of murder (for shooting into the small bathroom using Black Talon bullets, believing it was an intruder behind the door) and referred back to the trial judge to impose a new sentence.[66] A new sentencing hearing took place and a sentence of six years was imposed.[67]

The arguments in the media application above focused on fair trial rights of the accused and the state, without asking questions about victims' issues or the effect on the family of Reeva. This case study briefly examines the way the media, in addition to the actual broadcast trial, handled the matter and highlights the diverse outcomes of Reeva's portrayal in the end.

A pop-up channel, Carte Blanche Channel 199, ran for 49 days spanning the duration of the trial. Apart from broadcasting all court proceedings live (and having re-runs during the night), interviews were broadcast with teachers and friends who shared their memories about both Reeva and Pistorius, video footage was shown of both (separate and as a couple), commentary was provided throughout by journalists, lawyers and psychologists and in the evening different panel-discussions were scheduled consisting of legal minds on the one hand and editors of leading newspapers on the other hand.

Unlike in most other cases, video footage of the victim was available as she was following a modeling career and had, prior to the incident, participated in a TV series. The initial swimsuit images were discontinued very quickly to be replaced by recurring images such as Reeva swimming with dolphins, being on a boat in the tropics, being at a ballet class and also at a Lady Gaga concert in an ice-blue dress. One TV presenter remarked on occasion that the last was her favorite image. As a result, albeit unintentionally, Reeva became almost like a pin-up or a familiar face from a billboard advertisement.

The above perception was, however, rectified during the family impact statement given by Reeva's cousin, Kim Martin, who opted to testify audio during sentencing.[68] In representing the family, she took the oath and paid tribute to Reeva by sharing her personal memories about them growing up and the strong family ties they had as a small family. She described her as an exceptionally caring person and how she had been loved and valued within the family. In addition, her parents had lost her much needed financial support. In response to questions from the prosecutor she indicated that the family had not accepted the apology of Pistorius at the beginning of his testimony as sincere, and that although they had not been revengeful, they thought imprisonment to be the appropriate punishment to the crime.

Though an impact statement is a much debated contribution in criminal trials,[69] it certainly had significant value in this matter. It completed the picture of a life lost through the commission of a crime. In contrast to the glamorized images on TV and in other media, Reeva became a "real" person within a family set-up, whose death continued to be mourned. The editors' forum described Martin's statement as a "harrowing narrative" and made some public concessions about their shortcomings during coverage of the trial. They voiced that they should have done more to give a balanced coverage of the crime and its victims. More specifically, that they should have acknowledged Reeva as a person.[70]

The impact of the televised trial on the immediate family was far reaching. They had to deal with several issues under the glaring eye of the court cameras—grieving, attempting to start the healing process, and questions of apology and forgiveness.[71] The money they had taken from Pistorius in secrecy, as well as their dire financial state at the time of Reeva's death, were exposed in a public forum. Yet, the family had support throughout the trial from the ANC Women's League (financially and emotionally),[72] as well as from a senior advocate appointed as their representative (inter alia, to deal with the local media on their behalf and deal with the defense). During sentencing the judge reached out to the family by acknowledging their pain and expressed the hope that the judgment would bring some closure and that the family would be able to move on with their lives.

As far as Reeva's mother, June Steenkamp, is concerned she took up her daughter's cause to establish safe houses for abused women and children. During the trial she published a book about her experience of the murder and court proceedings, travelled overseas on invitation and addressed audiences. She and Reeva's father gave exclusive international interviews and the family is suspected to have gained substantially therefrom. She almost became a celebrity figure herself. Though the state, at the time of writing had indicated that they will appeal the outcome of the re-sentencing, the Steenkamp family simply expressed their gratitude that justice took its course and announced their intention to disappear from the public eye.

Summary

Though media coverage of crimes and its victims may lead to positive outcomes, it is often seen as intrusive and may be the cause of further victimization and hindering their attempts to re-establish their lives. In aiming to protect victims' privacy and identity, an exception to the principle of open justice is allowed in the form of *in camera* hearings. Proceedings (or part thereof) are held behind closed doors and no details of the victim and/or his or her testimony may be published. Other court orders or journalistic codes of ethics may attain the same aim, but are perceived to offer weaker protection to victims in this regard. Though journalists are fulfilling their duty, as demanded by public interest, in reporting on crime that threatens the safety and well-being of citizens, victims always have a choice in consenting to interviews and publication of images. Media experts and service providers can play a significant role in guiding victims and assisting the media to ascertain sensitive and respectful news coverage of the crime. In the case of a broadcast homicide trial, when glamorous footage is available, the deceased's image can easily become superficial. A family impact statement may be of great value to rectify this and emphasize the loss of a real person and the destruction of the family.

Discussion Questions

1. Explain what is meant by an *in camera* hearing, the rationale behind it and when this procedure is applicable.
2. Discuss whether a child victim's protection of his or her identity should extend beyond the age of majority.
3. In your opinion, should cameras be allowed in court rooms? Motivate your answer.

4. Should, in your view, victims receive payment for interviews?
5. Outline the role that service providers can play in assisting victims' interaction with the media.
6. State both the positive and negative side of media involvement after becoming a crime victim.

Notes

1 UNODC (2015).
2 Davies et al. (2010:72).
3 Cook et al. (1999:72) accuse the media of over-representing violent offenses and understating property offenses, thereby presenting a false picture of the general distribution of crime. See also, Davies et al. (2010:107–8).
4 The media today take on a multitude of forms such as print (newspapers and magazines), radio, broadcast and online news websites.
5 New York City Alliance against Sexual Assault (1997); VCCAV (1994:24); Cook et al. (1999:72), citing Grabosky & Wilson (1989:112–20, 130).
6 Rentschler (2011:96) refers to the "second wounds" inflicted by engaging with the media, when the media's treatment of the victim causes additional harm to the victim and his or her loved ones.
7 Organizations such as the Media Monitoring Africa Trust (at www.mediamonitoringafrica.org) promote, inter alia, an ethical media culture and act as a watch dog in this regard. See also, United Nations (1985) promoting the observance of codes of conduct and ethical norms towards crime victims, as well as training in this regrad (clauses 4 (f) and 5 (a)).
8 Davies et al. (2010:108); Victims Services (2016:5).
9 Cook et al. (1999:72).
10 United Nations (1985). See also, European Union (1985) and (2006).
11 United Nations' Economic and Social Council (2005).
12 United Nations Declaration Annex clause 4.
13 United Nations Declaration Annex clause 6(d). The right to privacy may be protected as a common law right, a constitutional guarantee and/or via national legislation.
14 See, for example, Project Victims in Europe (2009:78–85, 92–3) for a comparison of the approach in different European countries on the right to protection (article 8 of the European Union Framework), of which the relevant part reads as follows:
"Each Member State shall ensure a suitable level of protection for victims and, where appropriate, their families or persons in a similar position, particularly as regards . . . protection of their privacy, where the competent authorities consider that there is . . . firm evidence of serious intent to intrude upon their privacy.
To that end, and without prejudice to paragraph 4, each Member State shall guarantee that it is possible to adopt, if necessary, as part of the court proceedings, appropriate measures to protect the privacy and photographic image of victims and their families or persons in a similar fashion."
15 Project Victims in Europe (2009:79), citing Maercker & Mehr (2006), points out that it is one of the most important contributing factors in developing psychological problems after crime victimization.
16 Project Victims in Europe (2009:79) citing Spungen (1997) and Rock (1998).
17 Project Victims in Europe (2009:79) citing Temkin (2002).
18 Project Victims in Europe (2009:80) citing Brienen and Hoegen (2003) 21. See also, Cameron (2003:4) where she highlights that the Supreme Court of Canada has made it clear that access to the courts and their proceedings enables public criticism of the justice system and encourages public participation in one of Canada's democratic institutions. She argues that by excluding the public from court proceedings or by banning the publication of information about the trial process undercuts one of the "core" values that is protected by s.2(b) of the *Charter's* guarantee of expressive freedom.
19 Project Victims in Europe (2009). For a study on the Canadian development of the open court principle and its possible limitation on the basis of victim privacy, see Cameron (2003:40–54). Chapter four provides an analysis of the position in the United States of America.
20 Cameron (2003:57) states that victim anonymity is protected by s.486(3) of the Canadian Criminal Code, as an exception to openness, which is justifiable because of the link between victim identification and under reporting in sexual offences. In addition, but only in circumstances where the evidence supports the order, s.486(1) permits a judge to close part or all of a proceedings.
21 Project Victims in Europe (2009:80–81).

22 See *S v Pastoors* 1986 (4)SA 222 (W) at 224B-G for a summary of how South African courts should approach an application for a closed court in the matter where there is a reasonable possibility that harm might result to a victim who testifies. If such an application is granted, his or her identity may not be revealed.
23 Such as in the UK.
24 Project Victims in Europe (2009:129).
25 See Kruger and Hiemstra (2016) for a discussion of a similar provision in South Africa where victims of sexual offences may apply for a closed court in terms of s.153 (in camera provisions) of the Criminal Procedure Act 51 of 1977. See also s.154, which deals with the prohibition of any information provided during closed trials (ss(1), and, in particular, any details of sexual offense victims (ss(3)). If the media publishes information in contravention of this section it amounts to a punishable offense (ss(5).
26 In South Africa the name of a witness under 18 may not be mentioned and particulars from which his or her identity can be inferred may not be published by the media (s.154(3) of the Criminal Procedure Act 51 of 1977). Child witnesses in South Africa are also protected from indirect disclosure of their identity (*Prinsloo and Another v Bramley Children's Home and others* 2005(2) SACR 2 (T) at 5b–c, 7e–f). However, if such publication may be to the advantage of a particular person, the court can allow so much publication as it deems fair and equitable.
27 See Beloof et al. (2010:132–146) for a discussion of the debate and position in the U.S. on protecting the identity of sexual assault victims, with particular reference to the example of legislation in Florida, namely the Crime Victims Protection Act, codified at Fla. Stat. 92.56 (at 145) that restricts disclosure of the identity of the victims of sexual assault.
28 *S v Nzama* 1997SACR 542 (D) at 544c–545b.
29 *Independent Newspapers (Pty Ltd v Minister for Intelligence Services: In re Masetlha v President of the Republic of South Africa* 2008 (5) SA 31 (CC) [45].
30 See, for example, s.154(5)-(6) of the Criminal Procedure Act 51 of 1977 for a South African perspective.
31 Note in this regard the apology of the *Daily Voice* to Zephany Nurse for defying a court order, prohibiting the media from publishing anything that might reveal her identity – Nurse, who had been kidnapped as a baby, and only discovered when she was 17, appeared in a newspaper photo with her biological family, with her face being blurred (2016:4).
32 Project Victims in Europe (2009:143–144).
33 Cook et al. (1999), note 3 above.
34 Davis & Snyman (2005:166).
35 Victims Services (2016:16).
36 New York City Alliance against Sexual Assault (1997) argued two decades ago that victims should have rights when dealing with the media.
37 Victims Services (2016:13).
38 Victims Services (2016:15).
39 Victims Services (2016:12).
40 Victims Services (2016:20) with reference to the position in NSW Australia (s.11 of the Children (Criminal Proceedings) Act 1987).
41 Victims Services (2016:22).
42 Victims Services (2016:6).
43 Cook et al. (1999:73)
44 Davis & Snyman (2005:163).
45 Cook et al. (1999:73–74); Canadian Resource Centre for Victims of Crime (2016:1).
46 Victim Services (2016:13).
47 Canadian Resource Centre for Victims of Crime (2016:3).
48 Victims Services (2016:10-11).
49 Seymore & Bucqueroux (2009:18)
50 Seymore & Bucqueroux (2009:22–24).
51 Seymore & Bucqueroux (2009:22).
52 Ibid.
53 Seymore & Bucqueroux (2009:26).
54 Complaints can be made directly to the news directors of a particular organization or to the national press council. See, for example, Victim Services (2016:27) where relevant contact details are provided aimed at empowering victims in dealing with the media.
55 Seymore & Bucqueroux (2009:26). Note that nowadays several publications exist that are aimed at educating journalists on how to approach reporting about crime victims, such as Bucqueroux & Seymore (2009).
56 Seymore & Bucqueroux (2009:50–53).

57 Canadian Resource Centre for Victims of Crime (2016:3).
58 Beloof et al. (2010:169); Seymore & Bucqueroux (2009:38).
59 Compare Supreme Court of Queensland (2015:4) where the study, in line with the application in this case study, focused merely on these concerns related to victims.
60 Ibid. Schmalleger (1997:333) points out in this earlier edition that the longstanding role of the press in reporting criminal proceedings is often overlooked as they do not have an official role, yet they are present at any given trial, more so when a celebrity is involved or where the case attracts public interest. See Supreme Court of Queensland (2015:18–21) for a brief overview of the position regarding cameras in courtrooms in other jurisdictions such as Australia, New Zealand, Scotland and Canada.
61 *Multichoice (Pty) Ltd and others v National Prosecuting Authority and another, In re: S v Pistorius and another related matter* [2014] 2 All SA 446 (GP) para [4]–[10].
62 Para [12].
63 See para [30] for a detailed approach to the technical specifications regarding the placement of cameras and arrangements aimed at as little as possible disturbance.
64 The father of Reeva, Barry Steenkamp, made an unusual request during his testimony at the re-sentencing of Pistorius, namely, that four photographs be made available to the public in order for a full appreciation of what had been done to his daughter. It should be noted that some of the media refused to publish the pictures showing Reeva's fatal injuries, e.g., the television channel ANN7.
65 The sentence imposed was in terms of s 276(1)(i) of the Criminal Procedure Act 1977, which is a term of imprisonment (maximum 5 years) from which an accused may be released by the commissioner on correctional supervision. The current directive is that one sixth of such a sentence must be served before release is considered.
66 *Director of Public Prosecutions, Gauteng v Pistorius* (96/2015) [2015] ZASCA 204 (3 December 2015). Despite the court's finding regarding the circumstances of the murder, the theme of intimate partner violence still featured on radio talk shows and in the social media. A confusing second narrative along the lines of the original state case thus continued to exist in the media and public arena.
67 *S v Oscar Leonard Carl Pistorius* (Case no CC 113/2013) HCGD (6 July 2016).
68 It was interesting that during the re-sentencing of Pistorius, Martin was called back by the state and opted to be televised. One can speculate about the reason for her decision but it is likely that she felt more comfortable (and empowered) the second time around.
69 See van der Merwe (2006) 'A critical evaluation of victim impact statements in child sexual abuse cases.' *De Jure* 422 for an analysis of the international critique on impact statements.
70 Carte Blanche, Channel 199 (October 15, 2014). Hopefully in response to this insight, shortly after the finalization of the sentencing in the court a quo, Carte Blanche broadcast a program about the life and family of another murder victim, Jayde Panayatou (on July 26, 2015).
71 Reeva's mother, June Steenkamp, shared in an international press interview, that she had forgiven Pistorius, as her religion required that from her (Gover, 2014).
72 The State alleged that the case was one of intimate femicide and that motivated them to support the Steenkamps. Though this version was rejected by the court they continued to attend the trial and showed their staunch support until the end.

References

Beloof, D. E., Casssel, P. G. & Twist, S. J. (2010) *Victims in criminal procedure*. Durham, NC: Carolina Academic Press.

Bucqueroux B. and Seymour A. (2009) *A Guide for Journalists Who Report on Crime and Crime Victims*, Justice Solutions NPO at http://www.mediacrimevictimguide.html (accessed 13 January 2017).

Cameron, J. (2003) *Victim privacy and the open court principle*. Report prepared for the Department of Justice Canada, at http://www.justice.gc.ca/eng/rp-pr/cj-jp/victim/rr03_vic1/index.html (accessed 11 August 2016).

Canadian Resource Centre for Victims of Crime (2016) *Victims and the media* at https://crcvc.ca/publications/media-guide/victims-and-media/ (accessed 24 June 2016).

Cook, B., David, F. & Grant, A. (1999) *Victims' needs, victims' rights: Policies and programs for victims of crime in Australia*. Australian Institute of Criminology, Research Paper, Policy Series No. 19.

Daily Voice 'Apology to Zephany' May 5, 2016.

Davies, M., Croall, H. & Tyrer, J. (2010) *Criminal Justice*. Englewood Cliffs, NJ: Prentice Hall.

Davis, L. & Snyman, R. (2005) *Victimology in South Africa*. Hatfield, South Africa: Van Schaik Publishers.

European Union (1985) *Recommendation 11, Position of the Victim in the European Union Framework of Criminal Law and Procedure*, June 28, 1985.

European Union (2006) *Framework Decision, Recommendation (2006) 8, Assistance to Crime Victims*, June 14, 2006.

Gover, D. (2014) June Steenkamp "has forgiven" Oscar Pistorious for killing daughter Reeva. *International Business Times* (July 7, 2014) at http://www.ibtimes.co.uk/june-steenkamp-has-forgiven-oscar-pistorious-killing-daughter-reeva-1455638 (accessed 13 August 2016).

Kruger, A. & Hiemstra, V. G. (2016) *South African criminal procedure*. Durban, South Africa: Lexis-Nexis.

New York City Alliance against Sexual Assault (1997) *Factsheets: Crime victims' rights in the news media* at http://www.svfreenyc.org/survivors_factsheet_42.html (accessed 27 June 2016).

Project Victims in Europe (2009) *Implementation of the EU Framework Decision on the standing of victims in criminal proceedings of the member states in the European Union*. Publisher in Lisboa, Portugal as a special project for the European Commission-Directorate-General Justice, Freedom and Security.

Rentschler, C. A. (2011) *Second wounds: Victims' rights and the media in the US*. Durham, NC: Duke University Press.

Schmalleger, F (1997) *Criminal justice today: An introductory text for the 21st Century*, 4th ed. Englewood Cliffs, NJ: Prentice Hall.

Seymore, A. & Bucqueroux, B. (2009) *A news media guide for victim service providers*. Justice Solutions, NPO at http://victimprovidersmediaguide.com/ (accessed 4 July 2016).

Supreme Court of Queensland (2015) *Electronic publication of court proceedings*. Issue Paper (June 2015).

United Nations *Declaration of Basic principles of Justice for Victims of Crime and Abuse of Power* (1985) (GA Res. 40/34 of November 29, 1985).

United Nations' Economic and Social Council (2005) *Guidelines on Justice in Matters involving Child Victims and Witnesses of Crime*. Resolution 2005/20 at http://www.unhcr.org/refworld/docid/468922c92.html (accessed April 30, 2009).

UNODC (2015) *Crime and criminal justice statistics* at https://www.unodc.org/unodc/data-and-analysis/statistics/crime.html (accessed August 14, 2016).

Van der Merwe, A., 'A critical evaluation of the use of victim impact statements in child sexual abuse cases', 2 *De Jure* 422 (2006), 391–406.

Victims Services (2016) *A guide to the media for victims of crime*. State of New South Wales: *Victims Services*, NSW Department of Justice, Parramatta, Aus.

Victorian Community Council against Violence (VCCAV) (1994) *Victims of crime: Inquiry into services* (Research Report).

CONTRIBUTORS

Elena Azaola is an Emeritus Professor at the Center for Advanced Studies and Research in Social Anthropology located in Mexico City. She received a Ph.D. in Anthropology from the same center and did postgraduate study at Columbia University on deviant behavior. She is also a psychoanalyst. Dr. Azaola is presently one of five Mexico citizens who are members of the National Security Agency. The National Security Agency advises the president and state governors in Mexico on matters involving criminal justice. In addition, she was an advisor with the National Commission of Human Rights and a Council Member at the Federal District Commission of Human Rights. She coordinated the European Commission project for street children in Mexico (1997–1999). She has published more than 125 journal articles and numerous books on human behavior, crime, and human rights. Her research on the commercial sexual exploitation of children was sponsored by the United Nations Children's Fund. She co-coordinated a National Report on Violence sponsored by the World Health Organization. She was the board chair of the Institute for Security and Democracy, which created the first center for police accreditation in Mexico and won the MacArthur Foundation Award for Creative and Effective Institutions.

Nana A. Serwaa Adjekum-Boateng is an Industrial Psychologist. She obtained an M.A. in Industrial Psychology from the University of Charles de Gaulle, Lille 3, France, and is currently teaching at an adjunct faculty at the University of Minnesota Crookston. Her main research interests include psychological risks at work: stress and burnout, social climate, satisfaction at work, and quantitative research. She is currently developing a manuscript that investigates the predictors of stress and burnout among medical doctors in a nonwestern society.

Francis D. Boateng is an Assistant Professor of Criminal Justice and Criminology in the department of legal studies at the University of Mississippi. He received his Ph.D. in criminal justice and criminology from Washington State University. His main research interests include comparative criminal justice, comparative policing, police legitimacy, international security, sexual assault, quantitative research, crime, law, and justice. His most recent publications have appeared or are forthcoming in *International Criminal Justice Review*, *Journal of the Institute of Justice and International Studies*, *Victims and Offenders: An International Journal of Evidence-based Research, Policy, and Practice*, *International Review of Victimology*, *Police Practice and Research: An International Journal*, *International Journal of Offender Therapy and Comparative Criminology*, *Police Journal: Theory, Practice, and Principles*, *International Journal of Police Science and Management*, and *Journal of Ethnicity in Criminal Justice*.

Tusty ten Bensel, Ph.D., is an Assistant Professor at the Criminal Justice Department at the University of Arkansas at Little Rock. Her research interests include international and domestic sexual violence, victimization, neighborhood and re-entry. Tusty has published numerous articles in peer-reviewed journals such as *Criminology, Journal of Youth & Society, International Criminal Justice Review, International Journal of Offender Therapy and Comparative Criminology*, and *Violence & Gender*.

Kris Christmann is a Research Fellow at the Applied Criminology Centre (ACC) at the University of Huddersfield. His main research interests include the study of radicalisation; counter-terrorism; and hate crime. He has researched racially and religiously motivated crime, especially offenders' motivations in such offending and the dynamics of hate crime reporting. Other research areas have included examining the effectiveness of offender programmes within the criminal justice system aimed at preventing hate crime or programmes looking to thwart religious and political violence.

Shelly Clevenger is an Assistant Professor of criminal justice at Illinois State University. Her areas of research include sexual offenses, sexual victimization and victimology. She has published works on topics such as sexual offending, victims' rights and victims' families.

John P. J. Dussich has degrees in Clinical Psychology (B.S.), Corrections and Criminology (M.S.), and Criminology and Sociology (Ph.D.) from Florida State University. For 44 years he has worked mostly in victimology and victim services. He created and founded the National Organization for Victim Assistance (NOVA), which he launched in Fresno, CA, in 1976. He served as first Executive Director for four years. He has been active in the World Society of Victimology (WSV) serving as founding Secretary General (1979–85): first for two terms then another 3-year term (2000–03); he is its immediate past President (2006–09). He recently finished 11 years teaching criminology, victimology and victim services in Japan where he was director of the Tokiwa International Victimology Institute and editor-in-chief of its journal: *International Perspectives in Victimology*. He is a Professor *Emeritus* from California State University, Fresno's Department of Criminology, where he taught: victimology, victim services, criminology, criminal justice, family violence, elder abuse, international victim services and coordinated victim service internships. As a trained crisis responder he has logged hundreds of hours volunteering in numerous disasters around the world. He has published 17 books, 130 articles and made 245 presentations. His most recent work has been at the United Nations in Vienna as the Chair of the WSV's Liaison Committee on behalf of victims' rights. On April 12, 2016 he received the Ronald Reagan Public Policy Award during National Crime Victims' Rights Week from the U.S. Attorney General.

Kathryn Elvey is an Assistant Professor of Criminal Justice at Plymouth State University. Her research interests include victimology, social justice issues, and crime prevention. She earned a Ph.D. in Criminal Justice from University of Cincinnati.

Whitney Gass is an Assistant Professor of Criminal Justice in the Behavioral and Social Science Department at Southern Arkansas University. She is pursuing a Ph.D. in Criminal Justice at the University of Arkansas at Little Rock. Her research interests include college campus crime and victimization. Whitney has published in *Human Services Today, Professional Issues in Criminal Justice*, and *Crime, Punishment and the Law*.

Andrew S. Gladfelter is an Assistant Professor of Sociology at William Paterson University. He received a B.S. in Criminal Justice and M.S. in Administration of Justice from Shippensburg

University of Pennsylvania and a Ph.D. in Criminology from the Pennsylvania State University. Gladfelter has conducted research on victimization, restorative justice, and the spatial distribution of crime, which has been supported by the National Science Foundation, the Pennsylvania Commission on Crime and Delinquency, and the Center for Rural Pennsylvania. Most recently, his dissertation examined the relationship between residential mobility and victimization. He has published articles and reports on a range of victimization-related topics, including the payment of restitution, the effectiveness of Pennsylvania's balanced and restorative justice programs, the characteristics and correlates of hate crime victimization, and the importance of neighborhood context in the study of crime.

Angela R. Gover, Ph.D., is a professor of Criminology and Criminal Justice at the School of Public Affairs at the University of Colorado Denver. Dr. Gover conducts research in the areas of crime victimization, gender and crime, and intimate partner violence. Dr. Gover regularly publishes in journals such as *Violence and Victims*, *Journal of Interpersonal Violence*, and *Violence Against Women*.

Chadley James is an Assistant Professor in the Department of Criminology at California State University, Fresno. He received his Ph.D. from the Graduate School of Victimology at Tokiwa University (Japan), where he was a recipient of the Monbukagakusho Scholarship (MEXT) for doctoral students from the Japanese Ministry of Education, Culture, Sports, Science, and Technology. In addition, he has a master's degree in Clinical Criminology from the University of Leicester (United Kingdom), where he was the recipient of the Open Scholarship Award for International Students. He has published in international journals and textbooks and has presented papers at international conferences, courses, and seminars in Africa, Asia, Europe, the Middle East, and the United States. He is the organizing co-director of a two-week Graduate Course in Victimology, Victim Assistance, and Criminal Justice held every year in Dubrovnik, Croatia, at the Inter-University Center, a co-director of the African Graduate Course on Victimology and Victim Assistance, and the assistant editor for the *International Perspectives in Victimology Journal*. In 2015, the World Society of Victimology (WSV) awarded Dr. James the Beniamin Mendelsohn Young Victimologist Award, and he is an elected Executive Committee member of the WSV.

Jennifer Katz, Ph.D., is Professor of Psychology at the SUNY College at Geneseo in upstate New York. She received her doctorate in Clinical Psychology at the University of Georgia after completing her pre-doctoral internship at the Medical University of South Carolina. Dr. Katz regularly teaches courses in Bystander Intervention, Clinical Psychology, Human Sexual Behavior and Psychology of Women. Her program of research focuses on gender, sexuality, and the sociocultural and interpersonal contexts of individual well-being. She has particular interests in a) understanding and preventing sexual assault, physical assault, and stalking among young adults, b) investigating predictors of responsive bystander behavior to promote safe communities, and c) research and practice promoting individual women's reproductive and sexual autonomy and well-being.

Catherine D. Marcum, Ph.D., is an Associate Professor of criminal justice and Criminal Justice Curriculum Coordinator at Appalachian State University. She graduated from Indiana University of Pennsylvania in 2008 with her Ph.D. in Criminology. Her areas of expertise are cybercrime, correctional issues, and sexual victimization.

Susan McNeeley is a Senior Research Analyst with the Minnesota Department of Corrections. She holds a Ph.D. in Criminal Justice from the University of Cincinnati and was a Postdoctoral Scholar at Pennsylvania State University. In addition to corrections, her research examines contextual influences on offending, victimization, fear of crime, and attitudes toward police. Her work has been published in *British Journal of Criminology, Crime and Delinquency, Deviant Behavior, European Journal of Criminology, Journal of Contemporary Criminal Justice, Journal of Crime and Justice, Juvenile and Family Court Journal, Victims and Offenders, Violence and Victims*, and *American Journal of Criminal Justice*.

Cecilia Menjívar is Foundation Distinguished Professor in Sociology at the University of Kansas. Her research falls in two areas: on immigration from Central America to the United States and on violence in Latin America. With respect to the first, she has researched the effects of immigration laws, at the federal, state and local levels, on different aspects of immigrants' lives, such as family dynamics, the workplace and schools, family separations, educational aspirations, religious participation, and citizenship and belonging. With respect to the second, she has focused on technologies of state terror, political violence, and gender, symbolic and structural violence. Both areas allow her to examine the workings of state power on the everyday lives of individuals. Menjívar's publications include, *Fragmented Ties: Salvadoran Immigrant Networks in America* (University of California Press, 2000) and *Enduring Violence: Latina Women's Everyday Lives in Guatemala* (University of California Press, 2011), and *Immigrant Families*, co-authored with Leisy Abrego and Leah Smalzbauer (Polity, 2016). In addition, she has published several edited collections. Her work has also appeared in *Social Problems, Gender & Society, American Journal of Sociology, Social Justice, International Migration Review, Journal of Ethnic and Migration Studies, Ethnic and Racial Studies*, and *Sociology of Religion*, among other journals. She has been recognized with several awards for her scholarship. Most recently, she was the recipient of a John Simon Guggenheim Fellowship. She has just finished her term as Vice-President of the American Sociological Association.

Jed Metzger, Ph.D., LCSW, is an Associate Professor of Social Work at Nazareth College. He holds a Bachelor of Arts in Psychology from Emory University, a Masters of Social Work from New York University and a Ph.D. in Clinical Social Work from New York University. He co-founded a not-for-profit 501 c3 organization whose mission is to end murder and offer needed support to the family and friends of homicide victims. He has additional professional and scholarship interests in working with children, youth and families involved in the child welfare and children's mental health systems, international contexts including trafficking, needs of children of deployed soldiers and efforts aimed at decreasing homelessness and poverty.

Jordana N. Navarro is an Assistant Professor of Criminal Justice in the Department of Criminal Justice at The Citadel. Her research interests include cyber-victimization and domestic violence. Her current research focuses on the prevalence and underreporting of domestic violence on college campuses.

Susanne Overstreet is a doctoral student in Criminal Justice at the University of Arkansas at Little Rock. She is currently in her third year and is working on her dissertation. She earned her master's degree in Criminal Justice from the University of Cincinnati. Her research interests include juvenile justice and delinquency, victimization, and policy evaluation. One major focus of her research is on sexual victimization.

Maria J. Patterson is an undergraduate student at Mount Holyoke College pursuing a B.A. in Gender Studies with a minor in English. Her future plans include obtaining a Ph.D. in Gender Studies and teaching at university level. When Maria is not studying, she enjoys reading intersectional feminist literature, working with horses and hiking in the Berkshires.

Bethany A. Poff is a two-time graduate of Appalachian State University with a bachelor's degree in psychology and a master's in Public Administration. She has worked under and with Dr. Catherine

Marcum of Appalachian State as a graduate assistant and has co-authored articles on cybercrimes, cyberbullying, victimization, and the Justice Reinvestment Initiative.

Dana L. Radatz, Ph.D., is an Assistant Professor in the Department of Criminology and Criminal Justice at Niagara University. Her primary research interests include batterer intervention programs, evidence-based practices, female offenders, and victimization. Her research has appeared in *Trauma, Violence, & Abuse*, the *Journal of Interpersonal Violence*, and the *American Journal of Community Psychology*.

Angelica S. Reina, M.S., Ph.D., is an Assistant Professor, Child Development GKFF Endowed Chair for Hispanic Outreach at Tulsa Community College. Her research interests focus on four areas impacting the Latino communities living in the U.S.: 1) the experiences of battered undocumented Latinas with institutional anti-violence services, 2) the physical and mental health among Latina mothers, 3) Latina youth schooling experience, and 4) the development of resilience in the face of life dramatic situations. Her recent work illustrates resilience as an agentive socio-cultural practice and identifies the nature of the tools/artifacts, contexts, and tasks that Latina immigrants actively use to work towards practicing, therefore, achieving resiliency. Her research work has been deeply guided by critical, feminist, and transnational perspectives and informed by socio-structural contexts and culture.

Hillary Rich attended SUNY Geneseo where she completed her psychology honors thesis on intimate partner violence and stalking victimization. She is currently a research coordinator at the University of Rochester's Women's Health Practice responsible for biomedical and psychological studies with a particular focus on family planning research. Her research interests include intimate partner violence, psychology and law, and reproductive rights. She will receive her J.D. from Cornell Law School.

R. Barry Ruback is a Professor of Criminology and Sociology at The Pennsylvania State University. He received a B.A. from Yale University, a J.D. from the University of Texas, and a Ph.D. in Social Psychology from the University of Pittsburgh. He is a member of the State Bar Associations of Texas and Georgia and has been a Visiting Fellow at the National Institute of Justice and a Judicial Fellow of the Supreme Court of the United States, assigned to the U.S. Sentencing Commission. He is a consultant to the Pennsylvania Commission on Sentencing and conducts research examining the predictors and effects of sentencing decisions. His most recent work with the Commission has focused on developing risk assessment instruments to be used at sentencing and on how to best communicate risk information to judges, attorneys, and probation officers. Professor Ruback has had four fellowships to India and South Asia (Fulbright, Fulbright-Hays, Indo-U.S. Subcommission, Fulbright South Asia Regional), where he conducted research on topics in environmental psychology, primarily crowding. Since 1998, Professor Ruback has conducted research on the imposition, payment, and effect of economic sanctions. This research, which has been published in academic journals and law reviews, was supported by the National Institute of Justice, the National Science Foundation, the Pennsylvania Commission on Crime and Delinquency, and the Pennsylvania Commission on Sentencing.

Yoshiko Takahashi, an Associate Professor of criminology, began her career at California State University, Fresno, in the fall of 2008. She has an M.S. in criminal justice and a Ph.D. in public policy with a justice concentration from the University of North Carolina at Charlotte. Her teaching specialties include, but are not limited to, victimology, research methods, and comparative systems of criminal justice. Along with teaching both undergraduate and graduate courses, she coordinates the Victimology Option program and oversees the Victim Services Certificate program at the same institution. Her current research focuses on domestic violence and gender inequality issues among the Hmong community in the United States, while serving on the Board of Directors of the Central California Asian Pacific Women (CCAPW). Born and raised in Japan, she maintains a close relationship with Asian countries; she was appointed as a member of the Board of International Advisors of the Tokiwa International Victimology Institute (TIVI) in Japan in 2014 and elected to the Executive Committee of the World Society of Victimology for a six-year term in 2015.

Maren Trochmann is a Ph.D. student and research assistant at the School of Public Affairs at the University of Colorado Denver. Her research interests include examining citizens' interactions with federal and local government and the intersections of race, class, gender, and public policy. Maren is currently employed with the U.S. Department of Housing and Urban Development and is contributing to Dr. Gover's research on the statewide study examining domestic violence offender treatment.

Annette Van der Merwe is a Professor in the Department of Criminal Law and Procedure in the School of Law at the University of Limpopo, South Africa. She holds the degrees B. Proc. (UP), LL.B. (Unisa), LL.M. (UP) and Ph.D. (Rhodes), and in addition served the required period of pupillage for admission to the bar and subsequently passed the bar examination at the Pretoria Bar. After following an initial career of public prosecutor for a few years, she entered academia. She completed her doctoral thesis during 2005, titled "Aspects of the Sentencing Process in Child Sexual Abuse Cases." Over the years she has been involved (mainly nationally but on some occasions also in Namibia and Zambia) with practical legal training of prosecutors and magistrates with regard to issues pertaining to the prosecution and adjudication of child sexual abuse cases. She has taught several modules within the criminal justice sphere such as Criminal Procedure, Evidence, Children in Criminal Justice, and different LL.M. modules/topics (relating to Behavioral Science in the Sentencing Phase, Victim Impact Statements and Sentencing). Her main areas of research interest are victims in criminal procedure, the sentencing phase, restorative justice and therapeutic jurisprudence.

David P. Weiss is Associate Professor of criminal justice and director of the Crocker Center for Civic Engagement at Fitchburg State University, located in Fitchburg, MA, where he currently teaches Victimology. He received his doctorate in political science, with an emphasis on crime policy, from Claremont Graduate University, Claremont, CA, in 2006. The author worked with victims of crime as a probation officer both for the San Diego County Probation Department and the Commonwealth of Virginia, and served as a visiting fellow to the Office for Victims of Crime, U.S. Department of Justice, in Washington, DC, from 2002 to 2004. Dr. Weiss has conducted and published prior process evaluation research on the implementation of community policing across the country, as well as on police executive leadership in the twenty-first century. Weiss and his partner divide their time between work in Massachusetts and their farm in Virginia, and can be reached at dweiss@fitchburgstate.edu.

Jacqueline M. Wheatcroft is a Chartered and Practitioner Psychologist (Forensic Specialism). She leads the Witness Research Group in the Institute of Psychology, Health & Society at the University of Liverpool in the U.K. She is Co-Chair of the British Psychological Society Division of Forensic Psychology Training Committee. Her interests are broadly in the enhancement of information, intelligence and evidence with a focus on process, procedure and questioning techniques to increase accuracy and appropriate confidence in those information forms. She upholds interdisciplinarity and her latest works have contributed to Lord Carloway's Procedure and Evidence Review—Next

Steps, in Scotland. The "rethinking leading" paper, published in Criminal Law Review, breaks new ground when cross-examination techniques are under scrutiny as never before. Her work has contributed widely to, pioneering work on witness familiarisation to cross-examination, legal and law enforcement agencies, the Witnesses Charter, the Advocacy Training Council-Gateway, and the American Society of Trial Consultants. Jacqueline is also known nationally and internationally for her development of the Liverpool Interview Protocol (LIP; with Wagstaff); adopted by law enforcement agencies in Canada, used in the U.K. in interviews and post-incident management protocols, and by the United Nations and experts in investigations. Jacqueline's vision is that all witnesses and interviewees can be supported to give their best evidence, in investigations, interviews and judicial settings worldwide.

Kevin Wong is currently Associate Director of the Policy Research and Evaluation Unit (PERU) at Manchester Metropolitan University and a former Director of the Hallam Centre for Community Justice (HCCJ) at Sheffield Hallam University. His main research interests include: offender management; rehabilitation and resettlement services; justice reinvestment; payment by results; and criminal justice system re-design. He has also researched hate crime, in particular: decision making and contributory factors to hate crime reporting; and the design and delivery of hate crime reporting and support services. Along with Kris Christmann and colleagues at the University of Huddersfield, he is developing tools to: enable more accurate estimating of unreported hate crime; and to assess the effectiveness of hate crime reporting centres. Kevin was previously an Assistant Director at Nacro, the principal crime reduction charity in the U.K. where, among other services, he set up a racial harassment prevention project in north west England.

Heather Zaykowski is an Assistant Professor of Sociology at the University of Massachusetts Boston. Professor Zaykowski earned her Ph.D. in Criminology at the University of Delaware. Her research interests include victimization, victim help-seeking, youth violence, and the victim-offender overlap.

INDEX